SOLDIER OF COURAGE, SOLDIER OF COMPASSION

THE STORY OF CAPTAIN BENNETT L. MUNGER COMPANY C, 44TH NEW YORK STATE INFANTRY

EDITED BY: BRIAN STUART KESTERSON

COVER ART BY: DALE GALLON - 2002 - "WHAT ARE YOUR ORDERS?"
HTTP://WWW.GALLON.COM

COVER DESIGN: BRIAN STUART KESTERSON

Copyright © 2017 Brian Stuart Kesterson.

Night Hawk Press
Washington, West Virginia

front cover image credit
"What Are Your Orders" by Dale Gallon www.gallon.com

All rights reserved. No part of this book may be reproduced, stored, or transmitted by any means—whether auditory, graphic, mechanical, or electronic—without written permission of the author, except in the case of brief excerpts used in critical articles and reviews. Unauthorized reproduction of any part of this work is illegal and is punishable by law.

ISBN: 978-0-9635-8024-8 (sc)
ISBN: 978-1-4834-6958-4 (e)

Because of the dynamic nature of the Internet, any web addresses or links contained in this book may have changed since publication and may no longer be valid. The views expressed in this work are solely those of the author and do not necessarily reflect the views of the publisher, and the publisher hereby disclaims any responsibility for them.

Any people depicted in stock imagery provided by Thinkstock are models,
and such images are being used for illustrative purposes only.
Certain stock imagery © Thinkstock.

Lulu Publishing Services rev. date: 6/2/2017

TABLE OF CONTENTS

ACKNOWLEDGEMENTS ... 4

INTRODUCTION- THE DISCOVERY ... 5

SOME FAMILY HISTORY ... 9

THE DIARY OF CAPTAIN BENNETT L. MUNGER ... 19

THE 1865 DIARY OF CAPTAIN BENNETT MUNGER – CO. C. 44TH NY. VOL. INF ... 93

THE LETTERS OF CAPTAIN BENNETT L. MUNGER ... 139

SERENDIPITY! A MYSTERY SOLVED AND A CHAPTER ADDED! - THE MISSING LETTERS FOUND! ... 212

SOLDIER OF COMPASSION ... 340

CONFEDERATE TESTIMONIALS ... 368

THE CLOSING STORY OF CAPT. BENNETT L. MUNGER ... 376

THE UNUSUAL STORY OF CAPTAIN BENNETT L. MUNGER'S PERSONAL EFFECTS RECOVERED IN THE 21ST CENTURY ... 378

DOCUMENTS PERTAINING TO CAPTAIN MUNGER'S SERVICE ... 386

A CLOSING WORD TO THE READER ... 416

ABOUT THE AUTHOR ... 418

BIBLIOGRAPHY ... 421

ACKNOWLEDGEMENTS

It is with my heartfelt thanks that I would like to acknowledge the contributions made by the following people who helped in some way in the process of this publication. Without their assistance, this publication would not have been possible.

John Haddox, Saint Marys, West Virginia; Shawn Darra, Merietta, Ohio; Bill Acree - Pigeon Forge, Tennessee; Gail Wiechmann - Wood Library, Canandaigua, New York; Joanie Hand, Penn Yan Public Library, Penn Yan, New York; Donna L. Setler, New Port, Ohio; Dale Gallon, Gettysburg, Pennsylvania; Shelly Case, West Chester, Pa.; Laurie Preston, McGraw-Page Library at Randolph-Macon College, Ashland, Va.; Rachel Dworkin, Booth Library at the Chemung County Historical Society, Elmira, New York; Jenny McElroy, Minnesota Historical Society, St. Paul, Minnesota

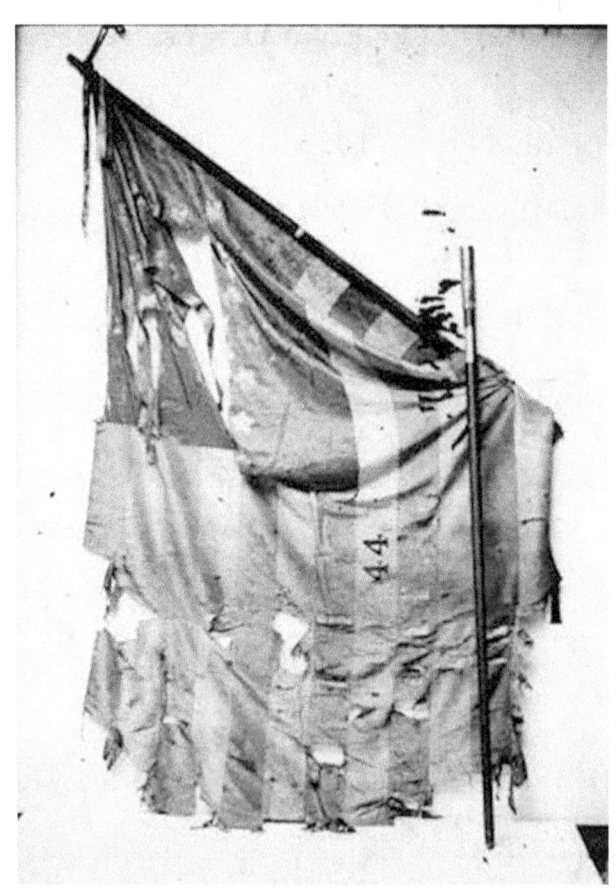

FLAG OF THE 44TH N.Y.S. INF.

PRINT FROM MATHEW BRADY STUDIO NEW YORK

INTRODUCTION- THE DISCOVERY

As with any book, there is always a back story that in some ways is just as important as the main story itself. In early 2009, I was wrapping up my book, "West Virginia National Guard 1898-1919" for Arcadia Publishing in their "Images of America" series, when I was contacted by Marietta, Ohio businessman, Shawn Darrah. Shawn had been given my name by St. Marys, West Virginia native and Civil War re-enactor and historian, John Haddox. Shawn informed me that this was concerning a Civil War diary and a grouping of Civil War letters that had once belonged to a New York officer (Captain Bennett Munger of the 44th New York Volunteer Infantry). Shawn explained to me that the letters had been recovered from an old building in downtown Marietta, Ohio that had formerly been a business a few years before in the late 1980's. The building was full of old magazines and other ephemera as well as the type of garden variety junk that one would find when cleaning out an old building. Shawn had sold off part of the magazines that he had acquired, but held on to Munger's letters and the diary. Several years passed and Shawn eventually contacted Mr. Haddox asking him if there was anyone in the area who would be interested in the letters and the diary. Mr. Haddox gave Shawn my contact information and Shawn promptly connected with me and explained what he had. I informed him that I was more interested in West Virginia and Ohio units from our area that had served in the Civil War but, that I would be glad to look at the letters.

Upon meeting with Shawn, I did not go through the collection systematically, but only glanced at one or two of the letters, and then looked at several pages in the diary superficially. I realized that the body of this work was important even though I had not given much thought to who Bennett Munger may have been or what the 44th New York had done in the Civil War. Or at least I thought that. Yet, something in the back of my mind kept nagging at me that I should know the story of both in some way, but I could not put my finger on it at that time. The excitement of finding such a large grouping of letters and a diary was all that I could focus on at the time. Shawn told me what he wanted for the collection and after some negotiation I agreed to his asking price. I went home thinking that I had broken one of my own cardinal rules of never buying anything that did not directly deal with my direct interest in Civil War research. I drove home knowing that I had a lot of research to do, and I also hoped that I had made the right decision in purchasing the collection without reading over all of the material first.

As soon as I got home I started doing research on the unit. It was then that I realized that I had visited the monument of the 44th New York Infantry at Gettysburg, Pennsylvania on Little Round Top as a young boy in 1972! I had also visited the monument many times after, on repeated trips to Gettysburg, over the past forty-four years with family members and reenacting friends. I had often read the inscriptions on the bronze tablets and climbed the narrow, stone steps to the monument observation deck, thinking to myself, "This is a neat monument! I wonder who these men were?" Even as a young boy and later as an adult, I thought to myself after reading the names of the men from Company C, 44th New York Infantry, "Captain Bennett Munger, what an unusual last name." Unfortunately, my curiosity was never piqued enough to look at this on a more in-depth basis. Sure, I knew about the story of the 20th Mane, but I only superficially gave a passing thought about the other regiments that also occupied the crest of Little Round Top. As a small boy, I had been regaled about my relatives who had served at Gettysburg in the 17th Virginia Cavalry and the 3rd West Virginia Cavalry. My mind was fixated on the grand cavalry clashes and charges of East Cavalry Field, and the surrounding Gettysburg countryside. After all, I am a cavalryman at heart. As for Bennett Munger's name, I had come across his name several months before while watching a History Channel documentary dealing with Confederate POWs housed in Yankee prison camps of the North. With these two mysteries solved, I set out on my quest to transcribe Munger's letters and diary and to understand his firsthand accounts with as much material from other sources as I could read.

I have often wondered how Munger's letters and diary ended up in an old, vacant building in downtown Marietta, Ohio being so far away from his home near Pen Yan, New York. This is a mystery that may never be solved, but it is more important that the letters and diary came to my attention and their eventual rescue, preservation and publication occurred.

The most unfortunate part of this story lies in the fact that Captain Munger's diary and letters are incomplete. His diary starts on December 1, 1862 and the last entry is dated May 12, 1863. Unfortunately, his letters start on March 21, 1863 and end on December 14, 1864. The story of the organization of the regiment and a number of major battles in the early war are missing. The later battles that the regiment engaged in for the year of 1864 until the mustering out of the regiment are also missing. It would be interesting to know what Captain Munger thought about these battles and his eventual appointment as chief inspector of Elmira Prison, and what he said to his wife about the affair, if anything. Nothing but speculation and conjecture can be concluded about these points unless Captain Munger's other letters and diaries come to light, if ever.

NOTE: See page 212, "Serendipity! A Mystery Solved and a Chapter Added!" This section gives full details on where Captain Munger's other letters & diaries were discovered in early 2016.)

With President Lincoln's second call for 300,000 troops that occurred on August 4, 1861 the men of Yates County, New York organized the best that they could. Unfortunately, a number of issues arose on filling the quota of the companies being raised. Captain Bennett L. Munger and several other offices who were trying to raise men for the 148th New York Infantry soon found that their companies were either improperly formed with inadequate numbers of enlisted men per company or the later fact that the regiment had been filled with an excess of two extra weak companies that were dropped from the organization. Captain Munger's Company M fell in this latter category. The question was where to put these men? Negotiations between Captain Munger, Lt. James and Lt. Kelly had brought the company to the minimum required strength. After the 148th New York Infantry departed for the front and left Camp Swift at Geneva, N.Y. Captain Munger and his officers contacted Major E. B. Knox of the 44th New York Infantry, known as "Ellsworth's Avengers and the People's Ellsworth Regiment". (This regiment had been raised in response to the death of Col. Elmer Ephraim Ellsworth of Saratoga Springs, New York after he had crossed the Potomac River from Washington to Alexandria, with other federal troops and rushed into the Marshall House hotel to tear down a Confederate flag that was flying from a pole on its rooftop. As Ellsworth came down the staircase with the captured prize, James Jackson the proprietor fired a shotgun striking Ellsworth in the chest, killing him instantly.)

Major Knox traveled from Albany to Geneva in the hopes that Munger and his officers would become part of the 44th. The negotiations went well and Munger and his company were mustered into the U.S. service at Albany, New York for a period of 3 years' service by 1st Lt. Alfred Foot, 14th U.S. Infantry, on October 3, 1861. The company left Albany on October 9th to join the regiment in Virginia. This company saw hard service from the start and as time went on the two weak companies that had joined the 44th, were worn down and depleted by battle and sickness totaling no more than 290 men. By September of 1864 the regiment was a shadow of its former self and was reorganized into the 44th N.Y. Battalion. By this time, Captain Munger had been placed on detached service at Elmira, New York as inspector of the prison for Confederate prisoners of war. The 44th would go on to fight in one more battle at Poplar Springs Virginia on September 30, 1864. By October the 44th would be transferred and absorbed by the 140th and the 146th New York Infantry. The men who continued to serve in these units were eventually transferred to the 5th Veteran N.Y. Infantry on June 5, 1865 and then discharged. As for Captain Bennett L. Munger, he would serve at Elmira until the end of the war even though he suffered a serious wounding that will be explained elsewhere in this publication.

This small publication is not intended as a regimental history of the 44th New York Infantry. It at best serves as a lasting memorial to the courage, dedication, and devotion of the American soldier to ease the suffering of his fellow man. For those interested in doing research into the regiment there are several minor regimental histories that were written after the war by the veterans themselves. There are also numerous accounts in period newspapers of the day, as well as books detailing the deeds of "Ellsworth's Avengers" at various battles. A number of manuscripts housed at the New York State Archives and the New York State Military Museum and Veterans Research Center, NYS Division of Military and Naval Affairs also bear witness to the service of the men in this regiment. My sole purpose in publishing this material was to save it from total obscurity and loss. With that said, I hope the reader enjoys the letters of Captain Bennett L. Munger Company C, 44th New York Infantry also known as "Ellsworth Avengers".

The following is a list prepared by the National Park Service listing the engagements that the 44th New York Infantry participated in during its time of service:

44th Regiment, New York Infantry

Overview:
Organized at Albany, N. Y., and mustered in August 30, 1861. Moved to Washington, D. C., October 21, 1861. Attached to Butterfield's Brigade, Fitz-John Porter's Division, Army of the Potomac, to March, 1862. Butterfield's 3rd Brigade, Porter's 1st Division, 3rd Army Corps, Army of the Potomac, to May, 1862. 3rd Brigade, 1st Division, 5th Army Corps, to October, 1864.

Service:
Duty in the Defenses of Washington, D. C., till March, 1862. Advance on Manassas, Va., March 1-15. Moved to the Peninsula, Va., March 22-24. Reconnaissance to Big Bethel March 30. Warwick Road April 5. Siege of Yorktown April 5-May 4. Reconnaissance up the Pamunkey May 10. New Bridge May 24. Battle of Hanover Court House May 27. Operations near Hanover Court House May 27-29. Seven days before Richmond June 25-July 1. Battles of Mechanicsville June 26. Gaines' Mill June 27. White Oak Swamp and Turkey Bend June 30. Malvern Hill July 1. At Harrison's Landing till August 16. Movement to Fortress Monroe, thence to Centreville August 16-28. Pope's Campaign in Northern Virginia August 28-September 2. Battle of Bull Run August 30. Maryland Campaign September 6-22. Battle of Antietam September 16-17. Shepherdstown September 19. At Sharpsburg, Md., till October 30. Movement to Falmouth, Va., October 30-November 19. Battle of Fredericksburg, Va., December 12-15. Expedition to Richards and Ellis Fords, Rappahannock River, December 29-30. "Mud March" January 20-24, 1863. At Falmouth till April 27. Chancellorsville Campaign April 27-May 6. Battle of Chancellorsville May 1-5. Aldie June 17. Middleburg and Upperville June 21. Battle of Gettysburg, Pa., July 1-4. Pursuit of Lee July 5-24. Duty at Warrenton, Beverly Ford and Culpeper till October. Bristoe Campaign

October 9-22. Advance to line of the Rappahannock November 7-8. Rappahannock Station November 7. Mine Run Campaign November 26-December 2. At Beverly Ford till May, 1864. Campaign from the Rapidan to the James May 3-June 15. Battles of the Wilderness May 5-7; Laurel Hill May 5; Spottsylvania May 8-12; Spottsylvania Court House May 12-21. Assault on the Salient May 12. North Anna River May 23-26. Jericho Ford May 23. On line of the Pamunkey May 26-28. Totopotomoy May 28-31. Cold Harbor June 1-12. Bethesda Church June 1-3. Before Petersburg June 16-18. Siege of Petersburg June 16 to October 11, 1864. Six Mile House, Weldon Railroad, August 18-21. Poplar Springs Church, Peeble's Farm, September 29-October 2. Mustered out October 11, 1864. Recruits transferred to 140th and 146th Regiments New York Infantry.

Regiment lost during service 4 Officers and 178 Enlisted men killed and mortally wounded and 2 Officers and 145 Enlisted men by disease. Total 329.

THE CAMP OF 44TH INFANTRY NEAR ALEXANDRIA, VIRGINIA – THIS PHOTOGRAPH WAS TAKEN IN 1864 BY MATHEW BRADY. THE ARCH LISTS THE MAJOR BATTLES THAT THE REGIMENT PARTICIPATED IN TO THAT DATE. (LIBRARY OF CONGRESS)

SOME FAMILY HISTORY

Bennett Lyman Munger was born on October 25, 1817 at Agawam, Massachusetts and died October 27, 1877. His parents were Gaius (Born: April 5, 1781) and Abigail (Hutton) Munger (Born: July 16, 1783 and Died: December 1, 1868). They are both buried in the Woodlawn Cemetery at Canandaigua in Ontario County, New York. In the "*History of Ontario Co., New York, with Illustrations Descriptive of its Scenery, Palatial Residences, Public Buildings, Fine Blocks, and Important Manufactories, from Original Sketches by Artists of the Highest Ability*", published in 1876, Bennett Munger is listed as being the teacher for School District No. 13, for the winter months of 1837-1838. Unfortunately, little if any information about his teaching career still exists, except for several notes of testimony from the inspectors of the common school of Clarendon in November of 1835 and again in letters of testimony for the common school at Canandaigua from 1836 – 1846. An account from a Confederate soldier at Elmira Prison also stated that Captain Bennett Munger had been his teacher and had taught him at Summerfield, near Selma, Alabama before this war began. The years that Captain Munger taught in the South cannot be substantiated at present. With any luck, other researches may find this information out to add one more piece to the puzzle. Munger's sister, Abigail had taught the short summer term of 1837 for the sum of sixteen dollars and fifty-three cents

In the Marriages and Deaths from the "*Ontario County Messenger*" Published in Canandaigua, Ontario County, NewYork on September 22, 1841 there is a listing stating the following information concerning the duel marriage ceremony of Bennett L. Munger and his sister, Abigail Munger:

"MARRIED - In this village, this morning, by the Rev. Mr. Webb, Mr. Abram Hills to Miss Abigail Munger, all of the former place. At the same place, by the same, Mr. Bennet Munger to Miss Mary Wilcox, both of this village." Bennett and Mary would only have one child, a daughter; Ida who would later became Mrs. Edson Case of Canandaigua and later Niagara Falls, New York.

In the Marriages and Deaths from *Ontario County Messenger* published at Canandaigua, Ontario County, New York; Gaius Munger (the father of Captain Bennett L. Munger) is listed as having died in the village of Canandaigua on July 31, 1858 at the residence of his son-in-law, Mr. Abram Hills, after an illness of three weeks. Gaius Munger was 78th year of his age at the time of his death.

In the Yates County, NY 1860 Census Bennett Munger is listed as living in the town of Milo. He and his brother Lyman are also listed in an 1861 Yates County official court document as being innkeepers. During the 19th century, anyone who kept an inn or tavern where liquor was served was required to file a bond with the County Clerk, attesting that the landlord was of good character and had the support of a number of freeholders in his town. Yates County has retained these bonds, known as innkeepers' recognizances, for the years 1823-1830 and 1855-1865. A few other documents relating to the excise laws were filed with them during the latter period. In his obituary, it is also stated that Bennett Munger ran his own business, being a house and sign painter, this being prior to the war.

According to Captain Munger's official military records he was mustered out of the service by Special Order No. 406 from H.Q. at Elmira as his term of service had expired. Munger would continue to wrap up his obligations at Elmira for the month of January and then proceed on a business venture with his brothers & nephew in the oil industry.

Julia Latham Munger was a sister of Captain Munger. She was born 1/16/1826 in West Springfield, Massachusetts and died 7/15/1908 in Los Angeles, CA. There are a number of accounts in his letters and in his diary, that he mentions receiving letters from her or in turn sending letters to her.

Abigail Munger was a sister of Captain Bennett L. Munger. She was married to Abram Hills. She is listed as a teacher prior to her marriage to Mr. Hills. There are a number of accounts in Captain Munger's letters and in his diary, that he mentions receiving letters from her or in turn sending letters to her.

Lyman Munger (1811 - 1906) was a brother of Captain Bennett L. Munger. He was a merchant and real-estate speculator in Penn Yan (1841-1856) and a dealer in drugs and medicines up to 1864 – His wife was Martha S. Munger (1811 - 1902) and they were the parents of Orett Lyman Munger who also served as an officer in Company C, G & K, 44th New York Infantry with his uncle, Captain Bennett L. Munger. In the *Yates County Chronicle* of November 14, 1861 an article appeared stating that a petition at Lyman Munger's store at 24 Main Street in Penn Yan was being circulated and signed "asking Congress to grant freedom to the Slaves and pay for those owned by loyal masters. It is already largely signed. Let those who believe in it step in and sign and let the petition be as large as possible." Lyman Munger had become an admirer of the noted orator and abolitionist speaker; Frederick Douglass after Douglass had made a public appearance and had spoken to the citizens of Penn Yan on the evils of Slavery at the Wesleyan Church in November of 1861.

In the June 27, 1919 issue of the *Penn Yan Democrat* we have the following biographical information on Lyman Munger and his family. The article notes that the information originally appeared in the Yates County Chronicle of June 25th and titled as, "Reminiscences of "H." - Article No. 8":
"Lyman Munger was one of our best and most reliable and respected citizens, and had a paint shop on Elm Street, over Abner Bridgman's, now Jessup's harness shop. He painted the sign, "The Metropolitan," that was used on the front of the building until it was replaced in 1879 by the present sign. We remember seeing him apply the gold leaf on the lettering; in what is now the carpet room, the sign seeming much larger arid longer than when in place on the building. There were three sons, George, Orett and Pliny, and our family relations were intimate. Occasionally, and as often as our good mothers approved, Orett would spend an evening at our house, and another time we would go to Orett's. We will never forget those times and can almost taste now the "Seek-no-Further" apples we obtained in Mr. Munger's cellar. George had a military company, mostly composed of the older boys, such as Charles and George Hamlin, James Oliver, Wm. S. Oliver, George F. Hopkins, A. Oliver Lewis and several others. As recruits were needed and greatly desired, we were permitted to enlist, although not as tall as regulations required, and were given a position at the end of the line. George Munger was captain and we do not recall there were any other officers, as privates were not plenty enough to spare any from the ranks! Our equipment consisted of very nicely painted wooden spears, and our evolutions were confined to single file, and trying to keep step. We had no music.

During the Civil War, Orett enlisted in Co. C, 44th Inf., under the captaincy of an uncle, Bennett Munger. Our fellow townsman, George W. Hobart, was a member of this, company, also Lieut. Charles Kelly, deceased. Orett was promoted to second lieutenant, first lieutenant and captain. Some years later all three boys engaged in the laundry business in Chicago and became wealthy. "Munger's Laundry" is well known in Chicago and neighboring cities, and there is a large plant in Los Angeles. Orett now resides in Chicago, George in Los Angeles and Pliny died a few years ago. The two daughters, Ione and Agnes, we believe reside in Pana, Il. where Mr. and Mrs. Lyman Munger, resided until their decease. Their residence in Penn Yan was on Liberty Street in the house afterwards owned by Charles Hewins and later by Solomon Crittendon, a few doors above Maiden Lane. We think Mr. Munger built the house. Their removal from Penn Yan was a distinct loss to the village."

Merrick Munger was a brother of Captain Bennett L. Munger. From the *Ontario County Journal* dated June 23, 1876 we have the following: "Mr. Merrick Munger, a prominent citizen, died at his residence in this place last Friday evening (6-16-1876), after a long and painful illness. He was about 70 years of age. He came to Canandaigua about forty years ago from Somers, Conn., where he was born. He leaves a wife, two daughters and one son -- M. Dwight Munger, of this place. Two brothers, we believe, survive him--Lyman Munger, formerly a prominent business man at Penn Yan, now in the West, and Captain Bennett Munger, of this town."

George M. Munger of Penn Yan, New York was a brother of Captain Bennett L. Munger. In the early part of the war George enlisted as a private in the "Guthrie Grays", a Cincinnati, Ohio, 3-months organization that was part of the 6th Ohio Volunteer Infantry. The "Guthrie Grays" were organized at Camp Harrison, near Cincinnati, and mustered in on April 27, 1861. The unit was on duty at Camp Harrison till May 17th, and then moved to Camp Dennison, Ohio, on the same day and saw duty there until June 18th. The regiment was then reorganized for three years' service on June 18, 1861. At this point the three months' men mustered out on July 24, 1861. George served 4 months and was mustered out on August 21, 1861. Upon returning home George wanted to continue to serve his country and at the age of 25 years old he began recruiting for an infantry company that eventually became Company G of the 85th NY Infantry. George M. Munger officially enrolled on October 29, 1861, at Penn Yan, to serve three years and was mustered in as first lieutenant, Co. G, December 2, 1861. He was officially commissioned first lieutenant on January 7, 1862, with that rank backdated from December 2, 1861. During his service, he was wounded in action on May 31, 1862, at Fair Oaks/Seven Pines, Va. In this battle, several advances and withdrawals were made by the Federal forces that were being flanked by the enemy in places along their lines, and in the prolonged fighting George became separated from his regiment after offering assistance to one of his wounded comrades. While under fire from the enemy he attempted to make his way back to his regiment but soon realized that they were either scattered or not to be found. He eventually wandered into the command of the 98th New York Infantry who were in a state of confusion and mixed in with members of several other regiments who were in a state of retreat. The following is a partial account that appeared in the *Yates County Chronicle* of June 12, 1862: "I then undertook to find the remnant of the regiment but did not succeed. Just at that time I came up to the 98th N.S.V and Col. Dutton requested me to help rally his regiment. I took four of my men as a nucleus, and formed a company of stragglers who were leaving the scene of action for different regions, and placed them on the left of the regiment. The regiment was then filed off to the left to help prevent the enemy from again flanking us, which he was trying hard to do. We halted and lay alongside of a fence in support of a regiment which had succeeded in driving the enemy back, as we found by the dead and wounded rebels that lay thick around us. We found that it was a necessity to "lay low" to save our heads. At this time, I was going up to the right of my new company, I received a musket ball in the fleshy part of my forearm. It bled very freely and an officer standing near volunteered to take command of the company and I went to the rear and there found our regiment or about a hundred men of it. The loss of the regiment in this action, including killed, wounded and missing amounted to near seventy-five…. My arm will be as well as ever in ten days – perhaps sooner. The men are almost finished, having not had one complete day's ration in three days, which, in addition to standing three or four hours in cold water and laying on the ground these cold, dreary nights without a thing more than our clothes to cover us, is sufficient to weaken the stoutest man…." George M. Munger would eventually resign his commission on account of physical incapacity and was honorably discharged from the 85th New York Infantry on April 24, 1863, at Newbern, N.C. Several letters accounting his war service exist in the *Yates County Chronicle,* from1861 to 1863.

Orett L. Munger was the nephew of Captain Bennett L. Munger. Orett was born on July 7, 1843 at Penn Yan, New York. His parents were Lyman Munger (1811 - 1906) and Martha S. (Whitney) Munger (1811 - 1902). He enlisted at Penn Yan, New York on August 11, 1862 to serve three years in the service of his country. He was voted in as 1st Sergeant and served in Company C, under the supervision of his uncle, Captain Bennett L. Munger. Orett was promoted to 2nd Lieutenant to rank from January 31, 1863 and was then promoted to 1st Lieutenant of Co. G, August 4, 1863 and as Captain on September 19, 1864. He served as acting Captain from January 1864 to August of the same year. Orett also served as acting Adjutant of the regiment in 1864. He was engaged in the battles of Fredericksburg, Gettysburg, Wilderness, and every major battle or skirmish that the regiment participated in. He was captured by the enemy on May 8, 1864 near Spotsylvania along with 350 to 400 other Federal prisoners and was eventually rescued by General Custer's Cavalry on the 9th near Beaver Dam Station. He returned to the regiment just below the North Anna on the Richmond and Andersonville Rail Road. He was engaged at Petersburg and Weldon R.R. and went north sick sometime in August of 1864 and was in the hospital at Philadelphia September 8, 1864.

At Spotsylvania, he was slightly wounded and had five bullet holes through his clothing. Orett L. Munger was mustered out of service on October 3, 1864 near Petersburg, Virginia. He was a charter member of the Military Order of the Loyal Legion of the United States (MOLLUS) that was founded by Federal Officers of the Civil War the day President Abraham Lincoln died on April 15, 1865. Orett served as the commander and as an officer in the Illinois Commandery of the MOLLUS and as a member of the Grand Army of the Republic and the Western Society Army of the Potomac until his death. At the end of the war he worked for the First National Bank of Mercer, Pa. for fourteen years when he resigned his position in 1881 to go into business with his brothers and helped found Munger's Laundry service. The brothers made a considerable fortune in this business having branches in Chicago, Illinois and Los Angeles, California. Orett L. Munger died September 19, 1925 at Chicago, Illinois and is buried at the Oak Woods Cemetery at Chicago.

After the war Orett L. Munger wrote an account of his capture and rescue called *The Adjutant's Story*, which appeared in the 1911 publication, "*A History of the Forty-Fourth Regiment, New York Volunteer Infantry, in the Civil War, 1861-1865*", by Eugene Arus Nash. While at Spotsylvania, Virginia the 44th New York made two charges against the enemy who were thought to be a small contingent of dismounted cavalry. To the surprise of the commanding officers of the Federal forces a whole Confederate army was in line of battle behind their breastworks. On the second charge of the 44th against the Confederate works we have the following account from Orett L. Munger. This is only a partial account of his story, Munger states: "Once again the word, "Forward Forty-Fourth!" rang out, and the distance-not more than forty feet from certain parts of the line would have been covered speedily had strength been sufficient, but with lessened numbers and formation broken, there was little chance to dislodge the enemy. The reader, it is hoped, will excuse personal reference which now seems essential to the tale. In this last attempt to carry the enemy's works, the

Adjutant at once discovered that without semblance of a line of battle and with only little bunches of men, or single individuals, here and there, constituting the forward movement, the effort could not succeed. Impelled by the instinct of self-preservation, he made speed to reach a tree in front about half way to the enemy's line. A few vigorous jumps brought him to the desired haven, and although not half big enough to cover his body, the little tree became at once the basis of operation and a point of defense. Immediately in his front, perhaps twenty feet distant, was visible a little stretch of the enemy's breastworks, from behind which three rebel heads at once dropped out of sight.

To the right and left, trees and bushes so screened other parts of the enemy's position, that for the moment this was all of the enemy's line within the Adjutant's sight. Standing with left shoulder guarded by the tree, the Adjutant found the revolver an essential part of the situation, and it became the agent which prevented either of the men in front from taking careful aim which could not have failed to kill. Enemy number one, first resting his musket on the works, showed for an instant his head to note the position of his target, and in another instant raised his shoulder and fired. The Adjutant's pocket on the right side of his blouse was torn by this bullet, and at the same time the compliments of the revolver were extended to the Confederate. Enemy number two then imitated his mate, but more cautious, did not expose so much of his body and his fire was high. He was, in turn, made the target for cartridge number two from the revolver. So centered was the Adjutant's attention on the business in his front that he saw nothing of his comrades, for to turn his head was to invite death, but in the early moments of that particular situation he was cheered by the sight of a corner of the regimental colors which were held by Corporal George W. Wing as he lay, with knapsack and blanket protecting his head, waving "Old Glory" from side to side. 'Enemy number three tried his hand next, but fired high, and the third shot from the revolver was discharged in his behalf. Right here an interruption occurred, for, to the Adjutant's surprise, a ball from the left chipped through the top of his hat. He thought perhaps this might have been a glancing ball which had first struck a tree, but, unwilling to trust that kind of an interpretation, dropped on his knee for safer position.

In another instant a second bullet went through his hat and the tree itself was hit a number of times, convincing him that he was being made the target of Confederates more to the left. Watching for further activity in front, shot number four from the revolver replied to one from a rebel, and almost at the same instant a bullet cut through the coat over the Adjutant's left shoulder. Making himself as short in stature as was possible by crouching low, an outstretched leg was suddenly stung, and the Adjutant called out, "Colonel, I guess I am hit." A few moments later it was discovered that the Colonel was not there, neither was the regiment.

Then came the fifth chance for the exchange of compliments, and cartridge number five answered the fire of a man in front whose shot was high, and like those of his predecessors, did no harm. One cartridge remained, and what was to be done after it had been used was an open guess. To this day the Adjutant has been unable to explain a sudden impulse which caused him to jump to his feet and turn around. There stood two Confederate soldiers with muskets pointed at his head, while a quick glance discovered our fleeing regiments making speed to get back to their supports, and the enemy, in much greater numbers than they, in hot pursuit. Quick decision was imperative, and the first thought, which was to shoot one of the men in his way and disable the other by a blow with his sword, and then try to make his escape, gave way to conclusions more sane. The enemy were swarming from both flanks trying their best to overtake the 83d and Forty-fourth, but with little success, for our men were soon back to their starting point, and with the support of other regiments of the brigade were too strong to tempt the Confederates to attack.

To the demand, "Come in, you d-d Yank," the reply was made-"I think I'm in." Thus, the Adjutant found himself a prisoner, while his two captors appropriated the revolver and sword. A few strides brought us to the enemy's breastworks and, stepping over, the prisoner was confronted by a Confederate officer who jumped up, the still damp dirt clinging to his uniform, and called out, excitedly-"Surrender, Sir! Surrender, Sir!" Seeing scabbard and belt which my captors had failed to remove, this doughty officer busied him-self in taking them off, so that they became the trophies of his prowess. By his direction, one of the boys-for, like most of our soldiers, they were still young - started to the rear, having his captive in charge. The hurt leg bothered, and the guard agreed to a halt when a shady grassy spot was reached, so that an examination of the wound could be made. It was an agreeable surprise to find only a strip of skin gone and the black and blue marks of a bad bruise, albeit the bootleg itself was badly wounded. The fear of a more serious hurt having vanished, the lameness became less apparent and the disability was disregarded. The guard seemed in no hurry and was willing to rest, until one of Griffin's Battery D shells, passing over the breastworks, struck nearby, and ricocheting, went over and beyond. The prisoner's sentiment that he did not care to be killed by Yankee shells was heartily seconded by his companion, and the tramp was resumed to the rear.

This trip revealed to the Adjutant facts that made him yearn for the wings of a bird, so that he might inform General Griffin that the "few dismounted cavalry" against whom we were sent, had developed into a mass of infantry numbering thousands, with a half dozen batteries within easy call. The fences on either side the narrow road or lane through which we passed, were lined with artillerymen and other idle soldiers, who enjoyed the sight of captive Yankees. The Adjutant said to his guard, "I suppose you know your duty," and the reply came, "What do you mean?" The answer was, "You are my guard, and your duty is to deliver me to the Provost, and in the meantime to protect me. I do not want to be robbed by these men." The young fellow said: "I know that; I'll take care of you;" and so he did, pushing back with his gun a man who grabbed for the Adjutant's hat, which, though bullet torn, had some of its freshness left, and possessed the added attraction of a 1st division, 5th corps badge; and another man who crowded up, saying: "Give me that watch, you d-d Yank!" Thus protected, the headquarters of the Provost Guard were safely reached, and under the gentlemanly care of Major Ryals, in command, the prisoner was safe from further annoyance of that sort. The Adjutant soon discovered that he was not the only prisoner, and on the assumption, that there would be given him an opportunity to communicate with the Commander of the Forty-fourth sooner or later, he proceeded to take the names of his comrades who had been captured....

A fine grove of trees was our resting place for the greater part of that hot May day, but food was not to be had. The prisoners were informed that on the next day they would reach a point where supplies would be furnished, a statement that proved literally and liberally true, though not in the fashion anticipated. Let me state, by way of parenthesis, that this grove and resting place was identified by the writer during a visit to Spotsylvania Battle Fields in 1907, and is now the site of the Goshen Baptist Church. While a prisoner here the Adjutant had the pleasure of his first and only sight of Robert E. Lee, Commander of the Confederate forces, who rode up inspecting the condition of affairs at the front.

All through the remainder of that 8th day of May, at intervals of an hour or two, volleys of heavy musketry informed us that our uninformed Generals were repeating, with other regiments, the experiment at first tried with the 83d and Forty-fourth. Following each of these futile attacks on the enemy's position, other captives were added to our squad, until when night came 350 Union officers and men were claiming Confederate hospitality.

The thought of dead and dying comrades whose sacrifice was a sad mistake and had its own reward in the satisfaction of duty bravely done, added to the heaviness of our hearts as we anticipated a turn in rebel prisons. The night was spent a mile further to the rear in pleasant woods, the blue sky visible between the leaves and branches above us, as we lay without blankets on the ground. The bright stars twinkled kindly, undisturbed by "man's inhumanity to man," while happy dreams came to some and the night wore away. The morning of the 9th came early, and gnawing stomachs made their demands as, waking from the sound sleep of growing manhood, the consciousness of our situation again asserted itself. No time was wasted for breakfast, since there was nothing to eat, and when soft-voiced Lieut. Cunningham in command of the detail which was our conduct, gave the order to "fall in," those able to march were ready to proceed. I think all of the Forty-fourth squad, except Rosenkranz, started with the rest.

Proceeding in the direction of Richmond, we met, after an hour or two had passed, a large force of the enemy's cavalry going toward Fredericksburg, and concluded, from remarks by our guard, that for some reason a demonstration by Sheridan was expected, with which the Confederates proposed to interfere. A bad guess it was as to Sheridan's route, but fortunate for us, as the sequel will show. The annoying activity of the enemy's cavalry had given trouble, and about the time of our engagement at Laurel Hill, a conference between Generals Grant, Meade and Sheridan was in progress, as a result of which Sheridan was given the permission, so much desired by him, to cut loose from the army and deal such blows to the Confederacy as he might find possible. All was accomplished that he had promised, and the rebel cavalry found that they were more needed to protect Richmond than to chase after Meade's wagon trains. All this was of course unknown to our party, and the march was monotonous enough until, a little before noon, when the column halted and filed into a large enclosure, where to our joy was located one of the largest and most copious springs of cold water it has ever been my lot to see.

The writer is reminded of Gideon's Band when he thinks of the eagerness our comrades showed and the various postures assumed, as they quaffed nature's most delicious beverage. Nothing could have been better. Some, lying flat, put their faces in the water; others on knees used their hands as cups, and drank and then drank again, for it had been more than twenty-four hours since most of the men had tasted water. It was refreshing, and the men lay down in the grass, happy for the moment, and glad to rest. A group of the officers agreed, for the sake of the few slightly wounded men in the party who were suffering from the unavoidable chafing of their hurts, that Lieut. Cunningham be requested to permit his prisoners to rest in this delightful spot for an hour. Before the Committee of one, chosen to make this request, could discharge his mission, the sudden arrival of a mounted messenger, who excitedly addressed the Lieutenant, put an end to the plan, and the order came immediately, "Fall in." There being no alternative, this beautiful green spot was regretfully left behind, and the tramp resumed. The main road was taken for but a short time, when to our surprise, our route lay through fields and woods. In reply to questions as to the reason of this, we were told that the bridge over a river had been destroyed, and that we were making a point where the stream could be forded. Thus, the afternoon wore on, and the fact that we did after a while ford a stream, gave some confirmation to the statement. Water was arm-pit deep and swift, so that some of the shorter and less vigorous men required help of the sturdier ones, but the writer believes all crossed in safety. Between four and five o'clock, after passing through a strip of woods, the tired men again reached the Richmond road, when their ears were greeted by the sound of shrieking locomotive whistles impatiently but plainly saying "Hurry up." A messenger came, telling Lieut. Cunningham to be "quick," when another sound greeted our ears-a shot from the rear. Strange as it may seem, every one of the 350 men marching toward prison pens, tired and hungry, but with senses acute, measured correctly the meaning of that shot, and to the command, "double-quick," responded by instantly clearing the road and with common impulse, sidling off into the woods on one side and into the corners of the rail fence on the other. The clatter of hoofs was soon heard, and memory still pictures three horsemen, who, with speedier beasts, led the advance of the gallant Custer's Brigade of Sheridan's Cavalry, as it appeared in view. These three impetuous riders, almost lying on their horses' necks, with carbines extended, crowded so closely the now fleeing Confederate guard, that three of its number were brought down while the others escaped.

On came the troopers, receiving as they passed the wild and vociferous welcome of 350 liberated men, whose voices, raised in loud cheers, proclaimed their joy and gratitude.

"How the" prisoners "shouted when they heard the joyful sound," Of Custer's gallant troopers as they sped o'er rebel ground! "Glory, glory, Hallelujah!" was the song most appropriate, and the sentiment was felt if not expressed by all our men.

(BATTLES & LEADERS)

CUSTER'S VANGUARD CHARGING THE CONFEDERATES

The half mile to Beaver Dam Station was so quickly covered and the surprise was so complete that three trains of cars were in possession of our cavalry before the engineers could get them out of the station. Supposing this to be his safe point, General Lee had concentrated supplies, and there was food in abundance for man and beast. Vast stores had been collected and, the prisoners found, literally fulfilled the promise made them the day before that at the end of this day's march they should be fed. Were we hungry? Young fellows scarce out of their teens, after two full days without food, hungry? Were we hungry? Well, here was food in plenty, and one had but to help himself. Right opposite the station, in a log house suddenly vacated by the family which had occupied it a moment before, Capt. Bradford R. Wood and the writer found ready to hand a promising fire of coals in the fireplace, and the necessary utensils for cooking supper close at hand. A reconnaissance by two had discovered at the station some barrels of hams and lemon-box-looking packages which upon more intimate inspection proved to be filled with eggs packed in saw-dust. No objection to ham and eggs was to be offered on this occasion, and in a short time voracious appetites were being rapidly and satisfactorily appeased, at the expense of the Confederacy.

During the night, after men and horses were fed and had loaded up with as many rations as could be conveniently carried, the sky was brilliantly illuminated by the fires which consumed the station with its contents, as well as the trains of cars which were to transport the prisoners to the Capital of the Confederacy. The cavalrymen busied themselves also in tearing up railroad tracks, burning ties, heating and twisting rails and interfering as far as possible with Lee's communications. With happy hearts and weary bodies, we lay down for rest, but were not permitted to sleep late, for early in the morning the enemy's cavalry, after its fruitless trip toward Fredericksburg and a long, forced march, appeared on our rear, and the sound of their guns was our reveille. We recaptured, unarmed men constituted, of course, an impediment to our rescuers, but with veteran rebel cavalry pounding in the rear, and the front defended by home guards, guerrillas and other irregulars, whenever a cut through a hill or a narrow road in the woods afforded an opportunity for a barricade, the progress was not so rapid, but that the infantrymen could maintain the pace…..

Enemy in front and rear made the work of our cavalry severe, and the progress was slow, but the march was continued on the main road until one night the Adjutant was told that Richmond lay but two miles further on, and he wondered, as he saw the lights twinkling in the distance, if Sheridan would risk an attack on the enemy's Stronghold, which seemed possible because of the absence of the main body of its defenders. That was not to be, and shortly after, a turn to the left brought us to the Chickahominy River. It was rainy and muddy, and the route lay across a corduroy bridge, while over the river swamps extended on either side of the narrow road, which seemed the only point at which passage could be made. The Adjutant, unattached, approached as near as he dared to Sheridan's headquarters flag where a number of officers were grouped about their General, and watched with much interest their movements. Across the Chickahominy were concentrated several hundred of the friends of the Confederacy, who with such arms as they had been able to gather together, proposed to assist the Home Guards and Guerrillas in disputing Sheridan's crossing. The main body of the enemy's cavalry was crowding behind in the evident thought that now was the time for their harvest and that when the crossing was attempted there would be much confusion, and that a portion at least of the Union forces would become their prisoners. Sheridan's grasp of the situation was complete, and the enemy's plans were frustrated, Rebellion's most masterly cavalry leader, General J. E. B. Stuart, meeting his death in the attempt to thwart the purpose of the Union General….

When the order came, our cavalry in apparent retreat before the enemy, turned about and rapidly galloped for the bridge. Now was the enemy's chance, and confidently his troopers rushed on in pursuit, unconscious of the trap laid for their discomfiture. Batteries which they had not seen belched out their fiery welcome with great effect, and the onslaught was turned into a rout as men and horses, surprised out of their self-possession, turned about in confusion and made haste to the rear. Needless to say, before they had sufficiently recovered to try again, Sheridan's Troopers, with every piece of artillery, and his wards, the recaptured prisoners, were safely across the Chickahominy. The enemy's cavalry did not follow after the crossing was made….

Reaching Malvern Hill, overlooking the James River, on the historic field where in 1862 the Forty-fourth greatly distinguished itself in battle, the opportunity came for the transfer by General Sheridan of the recaptured prisoners, to General Butler, whose army lay at Bermuda Hundreds, across the river. One of Uncle Sam's gunboats nearby, gave assurance of protection, and after communicating with Butler, who promised to send boat for us next day, we bivouacked near Haxall's Landing. The cavalry proceeded on its way with our hearty God speed and sincere thanks for delivery. At Bermuda Hundred we were supplied with clean underwear, which was eagerly received and greatly needed; thanks to that grand association of good men and women called the Sanitary Commission.

The following day we were taken by boat to Fortress Monroe, where transfer was made to another steamer, arriving at Alexandria on the 17th day of May. On the 18th our party reached Camp Distribution, and the next day the writer secured pass to Washington and provided himself with sword and belt and sundry items of wearing apparel. On return to camp, orders were received directing us to report to Col. Tally, who was to command a provisional battalion and march to the front. On the 20th the march was begun. On the 21st a detail of 50 men was made to guard a wagon train, with Capt. Bradford R. Wood, Lieut. Edward Bennett and the writer, in charge. Starting at midnight, we reached Fredericksburg about 7 A. M., Sunday, May 22d, remaining during the day and visiting hospitals where a number of the Forty-fourth men lay wounded. On the 23d the train was started, and the rest of the Provisional Battalion joined in guarding it. A march of twenty-two miles brought us to Bowling Green, and three miles more the next day, to Milford Station. On the 26th, the wagon train having been safely delivered to proper authorities, we started for the regiment, where the glad reception by our old comrades, who had supposed some of us dead, made our hearts warm. Here for the first time, information reached us of the wounding of Col. Conner and Major Knox at Laurel Hill, and of the fact that Capt. Nash had been thereafter in command until the arrival of Capt. Allen, who, because of seniority in rank, assumed command. At the request of the latter, the writer resumed his duties as Acting Adjutant, and the work went on."

The Diary of Captain Bennett L. Munger

Page 1 – Herman Stiles 10 Cav., Capt. Johnson C R

Page 2 – A. J. Cole Emery Hospital Ward E Washington

R. C. Phillips Camden St. Hos. National Ward. Bal.

A. Perry Emery Hos. Ward L. Washington

J. K. Giddings. Emery

Page 3 – Bennett Munger Capt. Co. C, 44th Regt. N.Y.S.V. 3rd Brigade 1st Division 5th Army Corps

Com of Capt. Allen Cross Provost Marshall

Memoranda in pages following relate to periods just prior to battle of Fredericksburg, Va. to that battle to Camp and Picket duty – to

Burnsides "Stuck in the Mud" to Battle of Chancellorsville to Return to old camp at Stoneman's Switch.

Page 4 – **Camp near Falmoth, Va. Dec. 1, 1862**

Ordered to be ready at 9 A.M. for corps review by Majr. Gen. Butterfield. 4 miles from camp, were called into line and already to move when an order came countermanding our services – very cold.

Sunday Dec. 7

I slept poorly, was cold the night, was as cold as we often have at the north at this season, this day was clear and sun shone bright but scarcely thawed at all, it was one of the most cheerless days we have seen. N. Ackley sent to the hospital, the Dr. feels he will not recover, wrote to L. No. 3 recvd a letter from him and two black books. This one, and one from Kelly.

Page 5 – Monday Dec. 8, 1862

Ordered to be ready at 8 A. M. with two days' provisions for picket duty, Kelly officer of the guard and remains at camp. Arrived at our post at 11 ½ A. M. about six miles from camp north west and farther north than the old picket, found the ground occupied and rough houses built and everything comfortable, rec'd a letter from sister Sophia and one from Jane, commenced an answer.

Tuesday Dec. 9

Slept poorly, have taken cold, moved picket line and was on duty till 5 P. M.; again moved line, went to new camp at dark. Feeling most sick, took six grams quinine and although I did not

Page 6 – sleep well, feel much better, wrote Soph.

Wednesday Dec. 10

Feel much better, our provisions are gone and we are waiting to be relived, pickets taken up at 11 and we returned to camp, found the sick better, drew some clothing, rec'd letter from wife and Ida and wrote one to them. Rec'd orders to march at 5 ½ tomorrow morning.

Thursday Dec. 11

Up at 3 packed trunk left about 6, marched with frequent stops, about 2 miles; fire was opened at Fredericksburg at 5:10 and this continued without stop till noon. We were about a mile I suppose from the batteries. The roar was awfully sublime, since noon it had slacked, since 2 ½ P. M. firing has about

Page 7 – ceased. The ground, where are some hundreds of acres is covered with men, right in the mud as bad is the middle of the road, 3 ¼ came on a _____ commenced in again and continued till sunset. We left faced marched 100 rods and camped in a good place among pines. Reb did not join us and we must sleep without. The result of yesterday we do not know.

Friday Dec. 12

ARMY OF THE POTOMAC CROSSING THE RAPPAHANNOCK RIVER DECEMBER 12TH 1862.

Clear fine morning. It is said 40,000 troops crossed the river last night. This morning they are passing camp, 9:40 left camp moved 4 ½ mile to the front into the valley of the Rappahannock and near Fredericks and in sight of our batteries.

Page 8 – The atmosphere is very smoky and the day mild like our Indian summer, an old fashioned summer day and <u>I</u> dream, will the dream be realized (?) We can plainly see the batteries and hear the shell as they spin through the air and often see them burst; camped before dark near our last night's camp, had an opportunity to send letters and wrote a few lines home --------------

Saturday Dec. 13

Slept fair and feel well, 9 ½ firing commenced on our left with musketry, soon the artillery followed and kept up heavy firing, sometimes artillery alone and

Page 9 - both. We were immediately called into line and stood till about 1, the battle is getting in our front, in the rear of the city we are marched out in front in sight of the battle 1 ½ the battle is raging with the greatest fury. The musketry is terrific and continues 2 ½, we passed through the city and halted at the west side of it, near where the shells were flying uncomfortably near. Hunter was struck here near the eye and wounded slightly, (In the outer margin of the page Captain Munger wrote, "Hunter was the first man of the company to be wounded.") we formed line of battle and were ordered to advance to the front and relive the force.

Page 10 – that we encountered or were stopped by another Reg. filing in front of us, thrown into confusion, but rallied in fair order and moved in rapidly, as we ascended an elevation we came under the enemy's fire. 12 of our men were wounded there severely. Most of the men acted nobly, (penciled in very lightly and almost indiscernible is a name that looks like, "Norris" Possibly referring to William N. Norris of Company C. This is the best guess for this name.) failed. Our post was on the side of a hill protected from the fire of the enemy mostly, were obliged to lie close in the mud which we did for 30 hours under constant fire, towards now one of our regt. were hurt (In the inner margin of this page Captain Munger wrote, "Died of his wounds Fred Mitchell.").

Page 11 – It was a time that tried the nerve and we escaped it by a miracle. List of wounded, Taylor wounded his hand, also Mead Raymond in the head, Eaton on the shin rather severely. Giddings John in the leg bone shattered fear amputation 4 inches above the ankle. Mitchell knee pan shot off all these we have seen. Perry had his left leg shattered and amputated above the knee, J. T. Johnson was knocked down by the effects of a shell in the face either the powder or dirt in the face. Lewis Kelly also badly hurt in the same way, most of the men behaved well but some disgraced themselves.

Page 12 – 58 crossed the river waters with muskets, 46 started across the field, 11 were men of 1 Liut. wounded. 12 men whose absence not satisfactory. Cole wounded in the ankle, not seen him.

Sunday 14

And my God what a Sunday last night we reached the front at dusk and lay down as thick as we could with the dead and dying. The wounded were groaning and begging most piteously to be taken care of but it wasn't of the question, at 12 wagons came to take them off and I assisted in

Page 13 – removing them, found one who had been groaning just dead, I tried to cheer and encourage the living. I laid down again but could not sleep. Orett has the advantage, he can sleep. O that boy is getting dearer to me every day. Lieut. Kelly being wounded was not with us. We lost no men this day but were obliged to lie close to the ground, two were wounded during the day from other Regt. We laid till 10 O'clock and were retrieved without loss, marched to the city and camped on a brick sidewalk and told to make ourselves comfortable without fire,

This 1862 lithograph from Currier & Ives shows the Army of the Potomac marching toward the Confederate position at Marye's Heights. Nearly 5,000 Union casualties were reported in this battle.

Page 14 – we laid down at 1 A.M.

In a Letter that appeared in the *Yates County Chronicle*, December 25, 1862 Captain Munger wrote the following description for family and friends back at his home town. The following is his account:

Letter From Capt. B. L. Munger

Fredericksburg, Dec. 15, 1862

My Dear Friends: We still live and are well. Thursday at 5 o' clock 10 minutes a.m., the great battle opened. We were in our camp, but left a few moments after – went up to supporting distance – remained the day and camped near by night. The next day approached nearer and remained through the day and night. Saturday at 3 p.m. marched through the city – took refuge behind a bank and lay till 4 ½ o'clock, when we were ordered to the front to relieve a brigade. We formed in line-of-battle, and moved under fire of shell, but not severe. I forgot to say that one man (Geo. R. Hunter) received a slight wound in his face. And we left him behind.

It was a bad place for new men because the wounded and mangled were carried by with faces that only wounded soldiers from a fierce conflict can put on. I prayed for nerve and strength. We had moved but a few rods, when another regiment filed in front of the left wing of ours, stopping us while the right were able to pass on. This threw us into confusion, as we had to crawl through a fence to join the other part of our regiment. We however formed in fair order on the run, and as we ascended a hill, we were exposed to the fire of the enemy's fire of shell and musketry. Our men dropped like hail. Lieut. Col. Conner and Lieut. Kelly dropped at the same instant, one on my right and the other on my left – in all, nine of my men fell on the spot. We soon reached the position we sought and were in comparative safety. During this time, the whizzing of rifle balls and the rushing roaring sound of shell was almost deafening. The place we occupied was a side hill somewhat circular in form, and covering about one-fourth of an acre, and about thirty rods from the enemy's line of sharpshooters. The ground was muddy and we were obliged to lie pretty flat to avoid the balls. Those killed and wounded in the battles of the previous days were on the ground and the living, dead and dying were lying side by side, but I will not pain you by a recital of that night. It was such as I never wish to repeat. At midnight, the wagons came for the wounded, and I had the pleasure of assisting some poor fellows off the ground. Lieut. Kelly now made his way to us, his face was all bloody, and it was thought best for him to return to the city (about one mile) and have it dressed. He was probably knocked down by the bursting of a shell, as his face was powder burnt, (they will knock a man down as quick as a thunderbolt) and was detained by the doctor till morning, and by rebel balls till dark Sunday night, at which time he rejoined us. About 10 o'clock of this night we were relieved, making our stay at this point thirty hours, in which time I did not sleep much.

    We returned to the city and took lodging in the yard of a fine house at 1 o'clock a.m. on the 15th, and slept till morning. This day I have spent in looking up our wounded and getting a statement of their condition. I forgot to say that I sent men back as soon as safe to care for them. We have 12 in all. Lt. Kelly and J.T. Johnson were knocked down, as I have said, and faces burned. Alex Perry's left leg was shattered to the knee and is amputated above. J.R. Giddings by a musket ball four inches above the ankle, and will probably be amputated. J.A. Cole wounded in the ankle, can't tell how severely. Fred Mitchell's knee shot off. Taylor and Mead both through the hand, the last by himself in taking up his gun, G.C. Raymond in the head. The ball striking in the forehead and passing under the scalp, coming out at the crown (a close call.) W.A Herrick in the breast, I think not severely. A boy (Acton) who joined us at Albany a slight wound in the skin, and J.R. Rowel in the back, not severely. Perry, Mitchell, Cole and Herrick, I have not been able to see since they were wounded. H. Ackley, I learn tonight, is worse. I would like to go and see him, but it is out of the question. In the fight my men generally behaved well, some of them like heroes.

B. L. Munger

Monday Dec. 15

Recd. a letter from Pling and O. one from L. and Aggie; visited such of our wounded men as P, could find they are being removed from the city as fast as possible, at night we lay in houses or prepared to, in the evening wrote home thinking in all probability I should never write again, I lay down at 11.

Tuesday Dec. 16

Aroused and ordered to fall in at 12 ½ and marched to pickets' front and took our positions within 10 rods of the enemy's rifle pits

Page 15 – it on a level field and each party had a ditch and bank for protection. The dead lay in awful confusion in mud and dirt and the guns were as plenty (as) leaves on the ground. It was a horrid sight as a fearful place we lay flat and silent till 4 ½, recd. on orders to withdraw by the left flank, never were men more willing to obey. Our task was to cover the retreat of the army across the river, and a fearful past it was but it was executed safely and about 8 we camped the river, after a battle of 5 days of fearful fighting and

Page 16 – sustained a perfect defeat. At a cost of perhaps 10,000 lives and not a gain of one cent. It was raining and the mud was about 3 inches deep and very soft. We marched down to our old camp where we arrived about noon, put up our tents and at 3 P.M. had our breakfast having been under motion since 12 ½ without food. The boys feel disheartened and I don't wonder. I feel like (a) small children. I have some at school and "<u>I want to go home</u>". and "I feel I might tempt to cussing."

Page 17 – Wednesday Dec. 17

Forced to rest. Mitchell sent for me to come to him at the Division Hospital 4 miles to the front, walked, found him better than I expected, he wanted me to save him from amputation if possible, as one of the surgeons was anxious to take it off. Got back tired and most sick, Mandeville the son went with me.

Thursday Dec 18

Wrote most of the day to L and family. Felt badly, cleaned up a little. The army is low but I hope it improving a little. Mandeville is pushing his application for a discharge.

Page 18 – Friday Dec. 19

Had Reg. inspection, was officer of the day. Not well, finished letter home. One to Jane and one to (appears to say "Hawes") wife, recd. one from wife and I do feel somewhat low spirited and perhaps my letters partake of my feelings.

Saturday Dec 20

Went with Mandeville to see the medical director of this division. To Owen did not succeed in obtaining his discharge and he is to apply for a furlough, worked at clothing books, weather cold.

Page 19 – Sunday Dec. 21

Weather clear and cold, recd. word that Mitchell wants to see me, went down about noon and found him in good spirits, it is not yet decided whether he must suffer amputation. Returned at 5 P.M., tired and sick.

Monday Dec. 22

More mild, feeling poorly, under the Dr. care.

Tuesday Dec. 23

Feel no better not fit for duty.

Wednesday Dec. 24

No better feel <u>blue</u>, Col. Rice joined the Reg. tonight.

This Illustration is from *Leslie's Illustrated Newspaper*, January 11, 1863, front page. The Bright Side of War - Holiday Festivities of the 44th New York Volunteers, at Their Camp, Hall's Hill, Virginia. Drawn at the time of the Christmas Parade in camp on December 25, 1862.

Page 20 – Thursday Dec. 25, 1862

What a Christmas. O! ye dwellers at home may you never know the joys of a Christmas with nothing to eat and a prospect that you never will have no friends to visit and little hope for the future. The day is mild; Col Rice sent for me today, had a pleasant interview.

Friday Dec. 26

Felt very poorly we are fixing up for a more permanent stay. Have got out the papers for the discharge of E. Moon. H. Ackley is improving, sent letter to L, Recd. one from wife.

Page 21 – Saturday Dec. 27

Drew and fitted logs for raising our tents.

Sunday Dec. 28

Put up our log house with bunks and etc.

Monday Dec. 29

Had regimental inspection, felt poorly but went out with the men. Wrote to wife and recd. a letter from her and L, had sick head ache severely.

Tuesday Dec. 30

Our reg. ordered out on reconnaissance, started about 2 P.M. weather looked stormy, rained some in the evening, James and self stayed in camp.

Page 22 – Wednesday Dec. 31

Weather colder, not much storm, heard from the boys, 15 miles out and still going. At night sent rations to which were met and sent back with intelligence that they were on the way back and would be in tonight or morning.

Thursday Jan. 1, 1863

The morning is clear and cool. I am feeling sum better I think. The boys have not yet returned.

(**Note:** At this point in the diary the dates for January 2 – 14, 1863 do not exist. Page 23 is on the back of page 22 and starts out with the date of Jan. 15, 1863. In this situation, no pages were lost and it is not explained why Capt. Munger did not write in his journal for these days. He may have been too sick to write.)

Page 23 – Jan. 15, 1863

An order came this morning to medical departments to immediately send the sick away. I was included and had about an hour to get ready, got onto the cars about 11, crowded with sick of all grades and waited till after 2, sent down to Aquia Creek and arrived 3. Remained on the cars till most night but all the sick were on board at 6. 800 in all crowded almost to suffocation. 7 died during the night. Snyder was one. So death has kindly done what the authorities would not. This is the first man died of disease in our Co.

and we would have saved him if we could have got his discharge promptly. (In the margin of the page is written; "First death in the Company")

We are on board the John Tucker and have been lying at anchor in the river since 6 P.M. and are destined to a place 4 miles below Aquia at Wind Mill Point, when they say accommodations are to be made for 10,000 men. God grant I may not long be of the number.

This photo from the Library of Congress collection shows Aquia Creek Base of Supplies for Burnside's Army. Aquia landing became a large supply base for Union operations in late 1862. The landing also supplied more than 100,000 Union soldiers during the winter encampment of 1862-1863. The port was one of the busiest in the world. The port was also the site of the Union medical department and hospital for the 1862-1863 campaign.

Page 24 – Friday Jan. 16

At anchor off Windmill Mill Point, reached dock about noon, ¾ mile from Hospital which consists of tents just erected, some without floors or straw, none with fires and we are chilled through. I got something to eat about 8. Some of the men earlier and some not till 11 and some not at all. This is my first hospital experience and I shall try not to be sick again. I want to get well or die and it don't seem to make much odds which, this is the most black, forlorn place that can well be imagined.

Page 25 – Saturday Jan 17

Last night I laid down early and murdered a long, long night. This morning for the first time I tried to obtain leave of absence but of course in vain. I felt as if I could not stay, got breakfast at 10. The night was intensely cold today is a little more mild. Visited the sick, found Clark Reynolds and Sergeant Warner, E. C. Pelton rear of cook house Serg. Ackley, H. Houghton, Norman Harrington, P. Stran, William Adams, Sexton Co. E., Norris Fletcher, Stroup Moon, Cosscaden, Morse

Page 26 – Sunday Jan. 18

Slept with Ackloy and Sexton and rested well, spent a sad day, wrote to Orett and to Penn Yan, it is the darkest looking time I have seen not half enough to eat and everything without system or plan.

Monday Jan. 19

Slept with the boys but not well. It is said our army is to cross the river today, a part 7 miles below and a part 7 below Fredg. (Fredericksburg). At 3 P.M. the army had not moved. I have resolved to make an effort to get home.

Page 27 – Thursday Jan 20

Had a poor night. Wrote to Layman on the subject of furlough. Wrote to Orett. Spoke with a lady for the first time in 3 months. Many citizens are here to see their friends and to get the bodies of dead ones. Cold day, began to rain about 8 P.M. in the evening which to the general gloom. Our army is said to have moved today at 11. Lord pity them.

Wednesday Jan 21

Rained all night and blew a gale but I slept fair. O where are our poor soldiers (?) This is a gloomy morning. I have no place to stay. I eat with the Dr. of the 2nd Division and sleep with my boys, 4 ½ P.M. not a mouthful of food some mornings and so faint. I can hardly stand erect. The Surgeon in charge told me today that the object in coming here instead of Washington is to prevent any getting away. So that I am really a prisoner fed as a prisoner. Had a good dinner at 5 and it relished good. Had a talk with Dr. Clark and says if in his power he would give me

Page 28 – a furlough he would refer the subject to Dr. Lee. I told him with his decision I was his prisoner and no earthly power but the Sec. of War can release me.

Thursday Jan 22

Rained and blew all night, am weaker today, still raining, these are times to try men, the general discomfort and gloom exceed anythiny I have yet seen. Wrote to L but did not finish.

Page 29 – Friday Jan 23

Slept good, the night was still and mild. The Division Surgeon says he will make out my certificate of disability today and do all he can to get me leave of absence. My health is improving and today I have walked to the river in front and the creek in rear.

Page 30 – Saturday Jan. 24

The day passed as usual, cloudy and some like spring. My certificate of disability is made out and I shall go or send to Washington as soon as possible. Prospects seem favorable to my getting leave of absence still. I have but little hope. My impression that I shall never see home still clings to me. Toward night felt more poorly.

Page 25 Sunday Jan 25

Raining, had a poor night and not as good a day as usual, feel agwish (anguish), but on the whole am improving. Orett came down from camp, took letter from home and news from the reg. They left camp on Tuesday and returned on Saturday. They marched only 6 miles, had hard time, O left at sundown for camp and I intend to go tomorrow to receive pay.

Page 26 – MOnday Jan 26

Had breakfast and started at 9 for the dock, walked and got on the Fairy and started at 10. Dr. Hill is also going to camp. Cars left at 2 ¼, arrived about 4. Men well and apparently glad to see me missing, rather low it looks, rather blue for supper, eat with Sergeants Munger and Kinner. The paymaster has not yet paid the Reg. Find that I am to be paid only from Oct. 3rd to 31st. Fred is back with the Co., the Provost guard having been dismissed.

Page 27 – Tuesday Jan. 27

Waited all day for P M (Pay Master), settled mess and other a/co (account) with Lieut. Kelly, James and Russel. Kelly owed me $ 47, James $ 16 and Russel $ 9.18, many paid. About 7 P.M. I recd. $122.30. Recd. letters from home stating that Dwight would start for Washington, Monday the 26th to aid in getting me a furlough. Wrote letters home, also recd one from Julia.

Page 28 – Wednesday Jan 28

Not sleeping well. I got up about five. It has rained and snowed all night. Got breakfast settled with the men and left at 10 ½. The cars started at 11. Moon got his discharge papers and I took him to Aquia, we were over 3 hours in running down there cold and wet and I suffered some, got on board the Fairy at 3, wind blowing strong and snowing hard, met Dr. Hill at 5, started for this place, walked from the dock in mud 6 inches deep, was pretty much tired out, had but little wood

Page 29 – and could not get warm, so went to bed but did not sleep well. I've seldom have a more severe storm north, except it is not as cold. Things look cloudy. Have little hope of success in getting leave of absence and am at a loss whether to stay here or go to camp.

Thursday Jan 29

Morning clear and cold. I don't feel as well as common, bad tasting month, boys don't get food and wood rations yet. Petton, Reynolds and I think Ackley will get their discharge.

Page 30 – Heard nothing from my papers or Dwight. The snow is wasting away and is muddy and disagreeable getting about. Harrington returns to the Reg. tomorrow, wrote to Orett and sent it by Harrington.

Friday Jan. 30

A beautiful bright morning, clear, cold and exhilarating. The events of the day I suppose will decide if I have leave of absence to go home and if they do they have decided no. I do feel disappointed but must submit with the best grace I can. I feel humiliated that I ever wrote a word desiring assistance for I see they think at home I lack fortitude to bear the trials of my posting, all I have to say is let them do better.

Saturday Jan 31

A magnificent morning took a walk to the Potomac and along its shore, gathered some shells. The bank from the water up to 3 feet is composed of petrified shells and is very curious. After breakfast went down again found some shark's teeth which I gathered to send to the children, got very tired and went to sleep. At 4 while at dinner Lyman came in.

Page 31 - I was very much surprised but greatly pleased. I saw in a moment he had not succeeded but I was not disappointed. We have a most excellent visit, talked most of the night. L went with me and visited the boys and saw something of Hospital life. Joseph H. Fletcher died during the night.

Sunday Feb. 1

Fine morning, had breakfast at 9, took leave of the fort and started for the boat, got on board and started immediately. The cars were ready and we started for

Page 32 – camp about 12, Orett was expecting us but L was recd. by all very cordially.

Monday Feb. 2

Lyman stayed and visited, we enjoyed the visit much. I got out another application for leave of absence. L's visit here will enable him to gauge closer of one life than he could by any amount of writing and I rejoice that he came.

Page 33 – Tuesday Feb. 3

Layman stayed till most noon and saw our express box opened. The day is very cold and I took cold and am not as well as yesterday. Shipley's box came also, well kept. The good things cheer us, not only do we enjoy them for their own merits but the consciousness that they were sent by the hands of affection marked them doubly valuable. This is the coldest evening of the season and a high wind.

Page 44 – Wednesday Feb. 4

Last night was the coldest of the winter by far, did not sleep warm, we have little wood the Col. Has issued 4 orders in regard to wood today and will be obliged to continue for tomorrow, for we have not more than half enough to keep fire and as I am still weak it is difficult for me to get along. I saw the Medical Doctor of this division today and learn from him that my application for leave of absence is still in

Page 45 - his office. He asked how I was getting along and I told him I thought I could live where I am, but if he could consistently sign my papers I would be very much pleased and would try to get well as quick as I could. He complimented or tried to flatter me, some said he should like to be better acquainted me and if I did not go now he would remember me. I value that promise highly and conclude I am to get well here if anywhere. Capt. Kimble started for home today on leave of 21 days.

Page 46- Thursday Feb. 5

Cold and snow squalls, no wood and things look gloomy. Our tent is very cold and I lay in bed 12 hours last night to keep warm and think I shall be obliged to try it again today. My apatite is good but my mouth so sore I can enjoy but little in eating. The weather has moderated and rained all day hard. About 6 recd. an order to have my Co. in readiness with 3 days' rations to march on a recognizance at the shortest notice. Sent descriptive list

Page 47 - to H. Ackeley, Wm. Norris and Jacob Strauss.

Friday Feb. 6

Rained all night and thawed so that there is no snow this morning and continues raining. Our mode of life and this weather are powerful helps to laziness, the tendencies are bad. Cleared off about 3, the furloughs of 8 men from this regt. came back tonight approved. The men are to start in the morning.

Saturday Feb 7

Clear, frosty morning, I took a walk about sunrise. It seemed like the

Page 48 – last of March in our latitude. As such mornings remind of home and passed life. I can't divest myself of feeling of sadness and depression that are painful. O what a failure my life has been, no youth's aspirations realized, all my hopes sacrificed to others and without merit on my past. Here histories are seldom known even to our nearest friends, and our sorrows and disappointments canker in our own breasts. The present, destitute of pleasure and the future without hope. F. Halls letter from home this morning in which it is said there is little hope of Merrick's recovery. God pity him and his family. P. Jobin accidently cut off the forefinger of his right hand today. I wrote to wife and 1 friend. Orett recd. a letter from Agnes tonight. I am not feeling as well as common but still am gaining. The 9th Army Corps are leaving for N. Carolina it is said.

Page 49 – Sunday Feb. 8

Clear and frosty, took a walk before breakfast and feel sad but must not indulge. Had Co. and Regiment inspection, men appeared well, wrote to the children Plinz, Ida and Hattie and commenced a letter to Aggie. It is exceeding muddy and unpleasant getting about. The time of the 44th Reg. is half out today.

Monday Feb. 9

Morning clear and more mild, birds singing but not like our northern birds. Wrote letters, was just finishing one to Mother

Page 50 - when the adjutant came in with my long delayed leave of absence which made something of a revolution in things and on our feelings. I am nearly well but shall avail myself of the leave, it gives me thirty days and I start tomorrow morning.

Tuesday Feb 10

Started on the morning train at 8, arrived at Aquia at 9, got aboard the Zephyr and arrived at Washington about 2, went immediately to Baltimore Depot and I arrived at that city at 5 and left at 9

Page 51 – Accounting of expenses

Carrying trunk .65

Board .85

Fare from Washington to B.   1.50
"   "   Baltimore to E.   5.25
"   "   Elmira to home   1.35
"   "   Hack Hire   1.25

Snowed till afternoon and thawed some, wrote to Nancy, headaches tonight, no recitation.

Page 52 – (Note: This page is blank in Capt. Munger's Diary. There is no mention of his homecoming or the events at home while on his furlough.)

Page 53 – Mar. 9, 1863

Started at noon from Pen Yan for the army at Falmouth, arrived at Elmira at 4:20, J. Mc Bride with me, paid $2.70 to Elmira and $14.50 to Baltimore. Leave Elmira at 5:45. At Troy McBride left and as I had his ticket he is out to sea and I am out eight and a half dollars. I am not feeling well and if the weight of the universe was upon me I should not feel more depressed. The experience and events of the last few days have been too much for me.

Page 54 – At Williamsburg took a sleeping car and slept fairly but awoke with headache. I forgot to mention that at Watkins I was introduced to Capt. Chapman, brother of Capt. Coleman's wife. He is doing provost duty at Bell Plains and will go as far as Aquia with me. Got up at 6 and found the ground bare and but little mud. 25 miles from Baltimore, arrived at 7 ½ and left soon and arrived in Washington about _ got breakfast and went to the Provost Marshalls Office and obtained a pass.

Page 55 – Met Lt. Warner and retired to the National to bed, very lonely in a crowd. The boat leaves at 7 tomorrow for Aquia, fair from B. to W. $ 1.60, Baggage .60. The day is gloomy, snowing most of the day and as to keep one indoors, thaws as fast as it falls. In the eve went to the theater with Capt. B. H. Chapman of the 23rd N Y I. Returned at 11 1/2, slept well.

Wednesday May 11

Up at 6, Boat left at 8, Paid for baggage $1.45, Capt. Chapman 1st Corps

Page 56 – Arrived at the Creek at noon but did not leave till three and got to camp at 4. Paid for portage $1.75. Found the camp almost deserted, the regiment having just come out on picket and I do feel so lonely. I can hardly rest. Lt. Kelly is here but most of the Co. are gone, officers appear glad to see me. There is no snow here and the ground is dryer than I expected to find it. The roads are still muddy. I find that Kinner has not been fined as was reported at

Page 57 – home but Elwell has. Orett's Commission came tonight. He is with the reg. on picket. It is with the greatest affection that I keep off the blues and perhaps I don't quite succeed.

Wednesday Mar. 12

Slept well, morning clear and fine, birds singing, I am officer of the day. A wedding takes place today of a Capt. In our Div., weather is much cooler with high wind. Kelly's box of provisions arrived today. He visited the 50th NY and Lt. Robbins

Page 58 – returned with him, they the Engineers are under marching orders; wrote to wife.

Friday Mar. 13

Morning cold with snow squalls. Various rumors are afloat, one that we move with 12 days to Richmond via peninsula. Some think one Corps will remain here to guard this road and vicinity. The day is cold and windy and I feel gloomy enough, wrote to Lyman on the subject of my future course in regard to efforts for promotion.

Page 59 – Saturday March 14

Cold and windy, the boys came about noon and are looking well. I find there is some unpleasant feeling in the Co., Robert goes into the Co. and H. Houghton cooks for us. Lieut. Munger commenced messing with the officers.

Sunday Mar. 15

Cold and looks like storm, I am officer of the day again, snow squalls through the day and night. _____ was buried today.

Page 60 – Wrote to George Munger, attended meeting at our chapel, ground covered with snow, all officers ordered to recite twice a week to designated officers.

Monday Mar 16

Cold and cloudy, I weighed on Commissaries scales today 170 lb. and O.L.M. Munger 150 lb., thaws some, sent to Washington for sword and belt for Lt. O. L. M. by Mr. Downing, cost not to exceed $20. Our lesson tonight is to be 60 papers.

Page 61 – Our Brigade which is the 3rd of the 1st Division of the 5th Corps consists of 6 Regiments, vis, 44th and 17th and 12th N.Y., 16th Mich., 83rd Penn., and 20th Maine. The snow mostly disappeared today under a cold thaw, recited to the Col. An indifferent lesson.

Tuesday Mar. 17

Clear and cold, inspection and Co. drill A.M.; P.M. went to see the celebration of St. Patrick's Day. It was done by running up horses to turn a stake at which two horses were killed by collision and I fear their riders the Quarter Master of the 9th Mass. and the surgeon of the 62nd Penn. are so injured they cannot live. Invited to an officer's party in the evening; attended but stayed but a short time. Weather much more mild.

Wednesday Mar. 18

Had Co. inspections and Co. drill, our Co. drilled by Lt. Grannis. Wrote to Ida and Aggie.

Page 62 – The fatigue suits of the 44th were distributed to the men and worn on dress parade, making as fine an appearance as I ever saw. Our parade ground is dry again.

Thursday Mar. 19

Cold and clear, policed camp and prepared for inspection tomorrow, had Battalion drill the first time. I have been out since the battle of Fredericksburg and made poor work of it but I will get posted if I live.

Page 63 – Lt. O. L. Munger is Officer of the Guard for the first time, wrote to Nettie.

Friday Mar. 20

WINTER CAMP OF THE 44TH NEW YORK INFANTRY ON THE PLAINS OF VIRGINIA
Photographic History of the Civil War

Snows powerfully, Position of Co.s in 44th Reg. in camp near Falmoth, with the names of officers,

First - F. Allen, Capt. Zeilman 1st Lt. Graves, 2nd Lt.

Second - G. Fox Capt. P_____

1st Lt. _____

Third - I. Gibbs Capt. Johnson 1st Lt. Botckford 2nd Lt.

Forth - A. Boice Capt. Kimburg 1st Lt. Russel 2nd Lt.

Page 64 – Fifth - H. Danks Capt. Grannis 1st Lt. Kelly 2nd Lt.

Sixth – C. Munger Capt. Kelly 1st Lt. Munger 2nd Lt.

Seventh – D. Nash Capt. Wood 1st Lt. Dunham 2nd

Eighth – K. Bourne Capt. Mc Cormack 1st Lt. Thomas 2nd

Ninth – E. Kimble Capt. Hustead 1st Lt. Warner 2nd

Tenth – B. Larabee Capt. Pease 1st Lt. Hardenberg 2nd

Snowed till 2 P.M., wrote to Nancy.

Page 64 – Saturday Mar. 21

Snowed, Officers of the day, Orett recd. letters from home and Gertie Chamberlain, wrote to Sophia.

Sunday Mar. 22

Warmer, snow thawing off, taken a severe cold in head, attended meeting, Crane preached. Recd. letter from Nettie, she proposes to go to Addie's in Mich., answered hers (answered her letter) and wrote to wife and Hardy. Col. Rice presented the officers of this Reg. with a pair of white gloves each and recommends that the men be supplied with them.

Page 65 – Monday Mar. 23

Mild but cloudy, snow gone, my cold worse, Recd. letter from L and replied.

Tuesday Mar. 24

Morning mild but cloudy, no drill presentation for inspection this P.M., 100 men policing the camp ground, sick with a nervous headache, rained powerfully the first of the night.

Wednesday Mar 25

Morning clear and fine and looks Spring like.

Page 66 – Last night the peeping frogs had a fine concert, am officer of the day but am not feeling well, hope I rally soon, feel better, just recd. an order to have our command ready to fall in at a moment's notice.

Thursday Mar 26

Morning cloudy and cool, order for review this P.M. said to be a fine show. I made a blunder which mortified me exceedingly. Our Regiment was complimented on their appearance and marching. I feel almost discouraged. I am behind in drill and there is no opportunity to perfect myself.

Page 67 – There seems to be an old time with the officers, whisky is in fault I think. Visited at Doct. Townsend's, I saw his wife but he did not introduce her, wrote to Ida.

Friday Mar. 27

Morning cool and clear, studied a little, played some, Gov. Curtain is visiting our troops, saw him in company with Gen. Mead, we have had a good Battalion drill today. It has been a splendid day. C.W. Taylor recd. his discharge and he started for home today. M.F. Graham joined us today, lost 2 to weight, wrote to Taber.

Governor Andrew Gregg Curtin

of Pennsylvania 1861-1867

Page 68 – Saturday Mar 28

Morning very rainy, rained heavily during the night, study some, Recd. a request from the Ex Dept. of NY to furnish a history of our Co., wrote to sister, Julia and to Mother and Abigail.

Sunday Mar 27

Clear, cool, very windy. Had regimental inspection, had a Bible class the first since we were at Warrenton. An order is received today making Capts. responsible for all the property recd. by the Co., attended a meeting, recd. a letter from wife and replied; very cold.

Page 69 – Monday Mar. 30

Clear and cold, moderated and was a fine day. As Officer of the day I inspected the cook houses with the Field Officer, repaired the hedge around the camp, swept the color line and drew off at from rear of camp. Was visited by Capt. Sloan who is located at Bell Plain. The camp is in fine condition for inspection tomorrow. In the eve attended debate at the Chapel.

Tuesday Mar 31

Stormed since midnight, rain and snow and is now 9 A.M., storming hard. Wrote to Jane, Raymond returned to camp. Wrote to Lyman, cleared off toward night and the snow melted away, Col. Rice returned.

Page 70 – Wednesday Apr. 1, 1863

The morning is clear, cold and windy. The Col. just called the officers and stated that Gen. Hooker has sent in an order to have leaves and furloughs resumed, also that the _____ was to have moved tomorrow but it will remain sometime on account of mud. Cresceden recd. his discharge today and will leave tomorrow.

April 2 Thursday

Clear, mild and windy, wrote to wife, worked on Ordinance Report. Hardy arrived. The men are cleaning for Corps inspection tomorrow.

Page 71 – Friday April 3, 1863

A magnificent morning, we are very busy preparing for inspection. The Co. did fairly but the inspection was very critical and we were censured for wearing vest and jackets and were not perfect in drill. But the Col. subsequently can't murder us. Our regiment are (is) granted additional furlough to enlisted men and leaves to officers, one man to a hundred and one officer to the regiment. On the 10 inst a general muster of the army is to take place.

Page 72 – Saturday April 4

Clear, cool and windy, the roads and (are) dry and dusty. Had Co. drill on Review Ground A.M.; Geo. W. Wing recd. furlough of ten days. Lt. O.L. Munger recd. his discharge to date from Jan.31ˢᵗ. Also a letter from home containing one for me L. Wrote to L. and sent it by Wing. Snowed with high winds in a most tedious eve.

Sunday Apr. 5

Snowed all night and now 8 A.M. lies about six inches deep and very heavy, we seldom have a more tedious time at the north. Our tent is very open and we have very little wood, enough to last till noon. O. is officer of the guard, not a desirable birth today.

(In the top margin of this page is written, **"O.L.M. discharged an enlisted man so as to be Mustered in as 2ⁿᵈ Lieutenant."**)

Page 73 – Snow disappears slowly and the day is some cloudy and cold, one of dullest of this dull spring but a day for that, not aright, that's but of blasted hopes of unrealized aspiration. An abortive bliss and for this world a hopeless future and with such a present and such a prospect for the future it is humiliating. The mind can be diverted by the present trifles in as to forget themselves and their fate and even feel a sort of pleasure in passing events. Oh: if there is not another and better state of existence than this it were better never to have existed. Will the aspirations we now feel be realized in that world! God grant it! Amen.

Page 74 – Monday Apr. 6

Morning cool, hazy, had inspection and some drill, at 10 recd. leave from the Col. to go and witness the cavalry reviewed by the President and General Hooker. It was a fine sight and a much larger cavalry force than I supposed, estimated by some at _____. I saw the President for the first time, and although I was prepared to see and a homely man he exceeded my expectations. Recd. orders to report for three days Picket duty; that order was countermanded and (we) were ordered to prepare for Review by the President. Recd. letter from Wife, Ida and Sophia. At 9 P.M. rained.

Page 75 – Tuesday April 7

Morning fine. The last order yesterday sending us on picket was this morning countermanded after we had started. I had previously been appointed officer of the day, that was overruled and I started with for picket. We are now ordered to prepare to receive the President in camp at noon and hold ourselves in ready for picket. I was again notified to act as officer of the day and within two minutes (of) that (I) would be relived from that duty till after Review. Some changes to take place before 10 A.M. but we take it all coolly, wrote to wife. About noon the President and Gens. Hooker, Meade, Griffin and a host of other Gens came to our camp and passed in front of our Reg. The President looks care worn, poor (and) pale. Our Reg. made a fine appearance. Recd. a letter from E Pluribus Unum my Apr. 1 friend again notified that I would act as officer of the day at 11 P.M. ordered on Picket at 7 ½ A.M. tomorrow.

ON APRIL 7TH AND 8TH OF 1863, PRESIDENT ABRAHAM LINCOLN, ALONG WITH NUMEROUS GENERALS AND THEIR FAMILY MEMBERS, REVIEWS THE 75,000 TROOPS OF THE ARMY OF THE POTOMAC. TAKEN FROM *HARPER'S WEEKLY* MAY 2, 1863.

Wednesday April 8

Cold, cloudy morning, started for picket lines at 7 ½, our whole company. The clouds cleared away about noon. We arrived near our old lines and our Co. was held as reserve.

Page 76 – Lt. Munger was detached and placed in command of the night post. Had a nice game of ball, I am to be on duty two hours during the night.

Thursday Apr. 9

A magnificent morning, cool and forty, our camp is in a romantic place and I am now enjoying a stroll to the top of one of the hills, the prospect is fine but not extensive. We are to go to the outpost today. I relived O. that I took his place with a part of our Co. and was awake all night. Toward the morning, it was cold, all quiet along the lines, recd. letter from Nancy.

Page 77 – 1863 Friday Apr. 10

The morning is fine but I am feeling blue. We were relieved by the 12th N.Y.S.V. at 10 A.M. and retired to the Guard Reserve camp. (In the) P.M., O. and self took a stroll over the hills south, saw a cluster of half a dozen log huts nestled between the hills. They looked cozy and homelike but small and poor. The well trodden paths from one to another showed they were neighborly and they seemed so entirely isolated they appeared to be a world by themselves. We then went out to the point of the hill near our camp which ends abruptly with a ledge of rocks. It faces Potomac Creek Valley and is about 100 feet high. The view is somewhat extensive for this

Page 78 – country and very romantic. In viewing such places, we intuitively desire the company of friends to share the pleasure. 20 or 30 feet below the crest the rock shelves over so as to form a sort of cave which the soldiers use as tents. There are many curious things! Holes and nooks apparently washed into the rock, which is sandstone containing stones of various sorts and sizes, some as large as my head and of colors some white as alabaster.

Saturday Apr. 11

The morning is fine and I had a good night's sleep. We are to be relived this morning. The weather

Page 79 - has been fine for picketing but the nights are cold. I am feeling more contented with soldier life but perhaps it is because the prospect of an early peace are brighter. Recd. letter from Brun, Wife, Layman (and) Nettie.

Saturday Apr. 12

Fine morning and Officer of the day, had an introduction to Mrs. Rice. Our Corps was reviewed in Divisions today by Gen. Fogbardy (Captain Munger possibly means Major General Follarde, of the Swiss army who came as a foreign military observer under the supervision of General Mead. Mead noted in a letter dated April 12th that, "No sooner had the President left, then a Major General Follarde, of the Swiss army, comes down here, with orders to Hooker to show him every attention, and as he does not speak English, and I have some pretensions to speaking French, Hooker turned him over to me, and I have, to-day, been taking him all through my camps and showing him my command. He seems like all foreign officers of rank, intelligent and educated. He expressed himself delighted and wonder-struck with all he saw, and says our troops will compare favorably with the best troops in Europe, and he has seen them all.")

a Swiss, the day is warm and dusty. It is confidently expected that we shall move with (in) a week. The Cav. Belonging to this Reg. is ordered to move tomorrow morning.

Page 80 - (Top of page reads) 1863

Write to Jane, Wife and Nettie.

Monday April 13

Rained a little last night just enough to lay the dust, cloudy this morning. The cavalry passed this morning, said for Culpeper Court House. Wrote to Pluribus.

Tuesday Apr. 14

Beautiful Morning, Recd. orders to be ready tomorrow morning with 5 days' rations for a march, superfluous clothes packed and left with Q. M. We hope to be paid today. On the eve of movement,

Page 81 – (Top of page reads) Camp near Stoneman's Switch, Va.

THIS MATHEW BRADY IMAGE OF STONEMAN'S STATION, VA SHOWS THE LARGE DEPOT AND THE SURROUNDING CAMPS IN THE DISTANCE. LIBRARY OF CONGRESS

THIS LIBRARY OF CONGRESS CIVIL WAR IMAGE SHOWS STONEMAN'S SWITCH AND THE DEPOT LADEN WITH SUPPLIES (OFF TO THE RIGHT).

like the one in prospect, one is apt to think deeply of past and future, the prominent that is what will be the result of the coming contest. Shall I act well my part? Shall I get through unmarked? Not one of these questions can I answer. We have been most 5 months in this camp and it is sure like home to us and leaving seems like moving "at home". Our thoughts natural wonder from our own surroundings to friends and home, though that I will not record.

Wednesday Apr. 15

Rain, Rain, Rain and the most delugeous of the season.

Page 82 – Our camp is flooded and everything is wet. The storm will prevent our march perhaps. Recd. two letters from wife and one from Gertie Chamberlan. Wrote to wife and Nancy. Called by invitation on the Col. and wife in eve.

Thursday Apr. 16

The sky partially clear and the weather looks better but not good. (I am) Making our clothing report. Am down with head ache. Had battalion drill but could not go, Kelly took command. Still cloudy. All is uncertainty and excitement about our move, we are still making preparations, yet stay.

Page 83 - Friday Apr. 17

Cloudy, I am feeling better this morning but not well. Settled my a/c to this date, find my due $17.22; from Kelly, $12.22; Russel, $4.02; Orett, $1.28. Recd. letter from Abigail and wrote one to Graham. Barrowed ten dollars of Southerby. I still have a dull head ache. The order is repeated to hold ourselves in readiness with 8 days' rations to march.

Saturday Apr. 18

Morning fine. Am Officer of the day. No drill and a dull day, wrote to Ida Harrington, went to Hospital.

Page 84 – Made out Ordinance Report. Nothing new in regards to moving.

Sunday Apr. 19

A magnificent morning, as warm as May. Lieutenant Munger and I have permission to go to the 33rd N.Y.S.V. We are to the house of the Commissary Sgt. and Dr. Spencer. O. was disappointed and getting a horse and I went along and had a fine ride, the country is as wild as any I ever saw. I found Capt. Root, Lieut. Brennan, and Chaplin Lung well. I saw Chas Hyatt and G. Chidsey, their time is out in about a month. S. P. Dye and William Norris were arrested for straggling and put in the guard house.

Page 85 – (Top of page reads, "**Badges to distinguish Corps and Divisions**")

Monday Apr. 20, 1863

Rained during the night and is cloudy this morning. The Corps of this army are to wear Badges of Red, White and Blue cloth on hats and caps of different forms to distinguish one from another. Our corps for instance we are the Maltese Cross. The first division wearing Red, the second, White and third Blue.

Form of Badge for 1st Corps – A Sphere

2nd Corps – A Square Trefoil

3rd Corps – A Diamond (This was crossed out by Capt. Munger and a more exact description was then given.)

3rd Corps – A Square with a diamond cut from it.

4th (No description of this corps badge was given by Munger. The badge is a Triangle.)

5th A Maltese Cross

6 A Grecian Cross

7 (From the 7th Corps to the 10th Corps no description was given.)

8

9

10

11 Crescent

12 Star

13 (From the 13th Corps to the 16th Corps no description was given.)

14

15

16

Page 86 - Orders are recd. this morning prohibiting officers playing any games as ball with their men. Capt. Bouren returned today. (He) was married while home and is having a jolly time tonight treating the officers with wedding cake and ------

Wrote home to Aggie. Dull day.

Tuesday Apr. 21

Cold, cloudy, clear morning. We are living very short. Our Brigade Commissary is not efficient and we are on Hardtack and Pork. Got some beef and bread. Acted as officer of the day in place of Johnson in the P.M.

Page 87 – **Camp near Stoneman's Switch, Va,**

Wednesday April 22

Morning cool and cloudy, Recd. new orders to move at any hour. Dr. Townsend tells me he is morally certain I am not able to endure the fatigues and excitement of an active campaign, maybe I am not, we will see. Sent ____ of my men to the Guard house for *playing cards after Taps. Also ordered four of Capt. Dank's men to report to him for the same offence, wrote to wife.*

RAILROAD YARD, SUPPLY DEPOT AND CAMP NEAR STONEMAN'S SWITCH, VIRGINIA. (LIBRARY OF CONGRESS)

SIBLEY TENTS, WALL TENTS AND "A" TENTS ARE SEEN HERE IN THIS 1863 PHOTOGRAPH OF A FEDERAL CAMP NEAR STONEMAN'S SWITCH, VIRGINIA. (LIBRARY OF CONGRESS)

Thursday Apr. 23

Rain, Rain like a flood. My head aches this morning. Rained till noon

Page 88 – it is a dolorous day, our tent floor is all mud and water, everything soaking wet, myself most sick with headache, the Payrolls are recd. and signed.

Friday April 24

Pay Master here and paid Reg. I recd. $494.88 for four months' pay, Kelly recd. the ten dollars for commanding the Co. and c. one month. The day was rainy. I shall send to L. ____ dollars for safe keeping.

Page 89 – Saturday Apr. 25

Morning clear and windy,

Settled with Kelly on the following basis

Mess	a/c	$ 7	12.22
"	"	24	2.41

Paid for Hat	1.75
McBride's Order	10.00
Kelly Note	7.00
Paid Mc Laughlin	24.00
Paid Wilson	<u>29.25</u>
	86.63
By Cash of Linch	40.00
" " paid today	46.63

And gave him (Kelly) one plain talk which if not beneficial to him serves my mind some. Orett is down with Diarrhea. Recd. letters from L. and wife.

Page 90 – Afternoon walked with Lt. Russel to Rail Road bridge at Potomac Creek and to the fortifications. The view from the upper fort is beautiful. I enjoy it much. Taken with the Diarrhea.

Sunday April 26

A fine day with drying wind. Lt. Col. Connor joined us today as a citizen. I am about sick today. Wrote some, saw bank swallow.

Monday Apr. 27

Recd. Orders at 7 this morning to march at 11. Wrote to wife and Mother. Left camp at noon, marched nearly north about

Page 91 – (Top of page reads **"On March, Leave the Stoneman's Switch camp."**) ten miles and camped near the old camp of last fall where we struck and pitched our tents so often. O. and self stood the march well, bivouacked after dark. Recd. letter from wife today, all well. Saw today the first bat of the season. The day has been very warm.

Tuesday April 28

Up at 4 ½ troops moving in vast numbers. O. is not as well as I, fear he must give up. Our camp is about ½ mile from Hartwood Church. The 11 and 12 Corps are before us and perhaps some others. Our boys stood it well yesterday only one

Page 92 – fell out and he came up. The morning is cloudy and cool, left camp at noon, went about a mile and stopped till 2, then marched hard till after dark. Not half of the Brigade kept up. Orett being sick when we started fell out and I fear he will not come up. It is said to be as hard a march as the Reg. has ever had. I never saw such exhausted looking men. We marched perhaps 10 or 12 miles toward Kelly's Ford. I was nearer tired out than were before. Got a supper and went to bed at 11 and slept cold.

Page 93 – (Top of page "**1863**")

Recd. a letter from Eliza Booth stating that Ansel is one of the Sperrys was in 140th N.Y. that is in Sikes Div. and have been within 2 miles of us all winter.

Wednesday April 29

Up at 4 ½ and cold, to be ready in ¾ of an hour, poorly. Orett did not come up last night. Moved at 7 and crossed the Rappahannock at its junction with the creek of that name. Our Division Red, the Corps and our Reg. was next to the front

Page 94 – (Top of page states, "**44th the first regiment to cross the Rappahannock.**) Reached the Rapidan about five, were the first to ford the stream, ascend the bank about 80 feet high and camped for the night. We have two days of severe marching, the hardest we have ever done. But we safely passed both streams meeting no opposition but our advance saw and drove the Reb pickets from service the country below. Orett came up and kept with us all day.

Page 95 – Thursday Apr. 30, 1863

We had a rainy night and our tents leaked so that my head and shoulders were wet through, yet I slept much better the last two nights. Moved about 8, there is a Division in advance of us. Sykes. about 10 we halted an hour or more to have the front explored as there is a force of the army in front, at 11 we passed rifle pits (that) extended 51 rods or more and placed for planting cannon so as to command the road, said to be obstructed. We have been so successful in fording the streams that our

Page 96 - (Top of page reads, "**Arrives at Chancellorsville, Va.**") men are very much slated. The country here looks fresh, not having experienced the "Army blight" like the portions of Virginia I have seen before. The marching today is very heavy, the mud is so sticky, the road is lined with blankets and cloths thrown away by tired soldiers. This morning as Sykes Division was passing I found Ansell Booth, he is (in) the 140 Reg. 3 Brig. 2nd Division of our Corps. Sperry was in the same Co. but I did not see him as they were moving. Stayed at the spot referred to till night. It is called Chancellorsville, but the ville is but one house

Page 97 – (The tops of pages 97, 98 and 99 read, "Chancellorsville Battle")

The enemy are found to be in force, 2 miles distant toward the river. The 11 and 12 Corps are with us and it is supposed there will be a battle tomorrow. Camped after dark in a wood nearby. Our troops took about 100 prisoners yesterday. They camped fairly with our men. I talked with a Mississippian of fair intelligence who says if the Constitution can be restored he is willing but if not he is for fight. Saw Booth and Sperry, Orett is not as well tonight. All but two of the men that fell out came up last night.

Page 98 – Friday May 1, 1863

Slept little, lay cold, up at 3 ½, so cold I could not sleep. The morning is clear, the clear weather since Monday. Moved at noon toward the left, which is toward the river. Marched rapidly about six miles and nearly to Banks ford. The battle had commenced on the front about noon. We were ordered about and marched rapidly almost back to the front of starting, halted. Countermarched and re-countermarched, formed in line and c, the skirmishing was sharp and (we) were advanced right under the fire of the Reb Battery. One man in Co. E,

Page 99 – was struck by a piece of shell and dangerously wounded in the head. At about 10 P.M. we took a portion in front, sent our skirmishers and held the line till 1 ½ A.M. Marched back to Chancellorsville, the back to a road paralleled to the one just occupied and 2 miles or so from it and laid down at just daylight, after a day of hard marching and some excitement. We know nothing of our success or prospects but taking a new position in the rear, may look bad. The country on which we are fighting is covered with wood and thick underbrush and very difficult to pass through.

Page 100 – (Top of page reads, "**Battle continued, Co. C on Picket duty**")

Saturday May 2

Fine morning, the battle is not opening this morning as vigorously as it could. We went to work at 10 to fortify by Abuttis and Breast Work, took till near night, very little firing and no marching. It is supposed we have the enemy penned and we hope to compel him to come out and fight or do the other thing. About 5 the battle opened again with terrific furry on our right and about a mile from us. Our company went on picket at noon and remained till 6, the (battle) raged till late in the night at intervals. Our position is a good one. We can hold a force of twice our number.

Page 101 – (Top of pages 101, 102 and 103 reads "**Battle of Chancellorsville Continued**")

Sunday May 3

Called at 4, ordered into line, instantly moved to the front, on the right at 5, the day's work with a furry indescribable and raged till about 8 and slacked a little but kept up till noon. The enemy rallied for a time. About noon there was an artillery duel. We think we are giving them fits. We have again put up breast works to protect ourselves and are awaiting an attack. 5 P.M., It is said the enemy are forming in front and we are expecting a most obstinate change back to our lines. Rumor says our troops occupying the heights of Fredy' (Fredericksburg), and if so we may hope. The day passed off and on, more firing except between pickets. Today was clear.

Monday May 4

Clear morning, we had no engagement during the night. I laid down ½ hour all night, feel tired this morning. We passed quietly till just night. Gen. Griffin ordered a regiment into the wood on our front to learn the passion and strength of the enemy. They lost one man killed and 8 wounded, took over 40 Rebs prisoners and it stirred up an awful time, the muskets and artillery made the earth tremble!

Page 102 – Tuesday May 5

On duty from 1 A.M. till morning. At ½ past 2 ordered to be ready to march at 3, called up the men and waited, no prospect of a moving, little fighting, rumor says Fredy' (Fredericksburg) is retaken. 6 P.M. We are possibly to move across the river tonight, it rains like a torrent and the roads are bad. We are feeling somewhat sad of all our toil and hardship has been for nothing it is too bad.

CHANCELLORSVILLE INN – 1863 – LIBRARY OF CONGRESS

WHEN THE CONFEDERATES OVERRAN CHANCELLORSVILLE, THEIR CANNON FIRE DESTROYED THE CHANCELLORSVILLE INN. UNION GENERAL HOOKER WAS INJURED ON THE PORCH OF THIS HOUSE WHEN CANNON FIRE ALMOST KILLED HIM. THE PHOTOGRAPH, ABOVE, SHOWS THE CONDITION OF THE INN ABOUT ONE YEAR AFTER THE BATTLE. THE SITE OF THE INN IS LOCATED ON WHAT IS NOW STATE ROUTE 3 (THE OLD ORANGE TURNPIKE).

Page 103 – (Top of page reads, "*Union Army Retreats. 44th goes back to old camp.*")

Wednesday May 6

Rained hard last eve and during the night, called at 2 and ordered to move in half an hour with the utmost silence. We were 4 hours in reaching the river ____ miles, as we had to cover the retreat, crossed at United States Ford on Potomac. The mud was unfathomable, words can't describe it, march till 11 and had coffee and moved on to old camp, arrived at 5. Marched ____ miles. Our tents were gone, it was raining hard and things had a dolorous look, got a super off the Suttler and slept in Hospital tent.

Page 104 – (Top of page reads, **"George M. Munger is now at home having resigned as 1st Lieut. Co. G, 85 N.Y.V."**)

Thursday May 7

Cloudy, or to put the arms and c in condition, have inspection and be ready with 8 days' rations, to move at 2 ½ O clock. Recd. letter from home Geo. Has resigned and at home. Wrote to wife.

Friday May 8

Rainy night and Blue morning, nothing of particular importance occurred today. Clothing was issued to the men. Pay Rolls were made out. Wrote to Lyman, perhaps rather blue, I certainly felt so, and I think the feeling is general, but I always (am)near writing my feeling s as there is no one who can in turn (attest) to my feelings.

Page 105 – Saturday May 9

O and self went to Aquia for bread, milk and a dinner. It was a beautiful day. I saw Wm. Booth who is after his son who was mortally wounded at Fredericksburg. Returned at 4 P.M. and was mustered.

Sunday May 10

A magnificent day, finished muster rolls and fix clothes. Visited Sykes Division and saw Sperry and Booth. They are well and like all of us are anxious to see the war closed. The news today is more creasing, and the men are perhaps less desponding. The Herald today was suppressed at Aquia by order of the Provost Marshal.

Page 106 – (Top of page reads, "**1863 In camp at Stoneman's Switch, Va.**")

Monday May 11

A fine morning, hired a black boy and let him go again, Kinner and Ackley and Shiply went to Aquia. Kinner is ordered under arrest for not taking the Co. to bathe today. This is the warmest day of the season. Some of the officers are getting quite discouraged at our war prospects. Maj. Knox expressed his utter discouragement today. Says, he can't see the end, those at home little appreciate what a sacrifice it is to endure this life of exile, in fact so far as enjoyment is concerned it is a negative life <u>we have</u>, that is all; and life without <u>hope</u> is half a life, and if there is no better on the <u>other side</u>, then our creator

Page 107 – (Top of page reads, "**Recd. letter from Jane**")

seems to me a great mistake, for so far, this is made up of hopes blasted. <u>Aspirations</u> <u>unrealized</u> and an agonizing longing for as got unattainable happiness. O blank and abortive life, if endured here it is ended in accordance with the past. Without <u>enjoyment</u> and <u>with little use</u>, not understood even by my friends, a stranger at <u>home</u>. Wrote to wife.

Tuesday May 12

A bright morning, but warm. The 14th N.G. has passed our camp on their way home and our Brigade was out to salute them as they passed. Our reflections we will leave to the imagination. Recd. letter from wife.

The end of the Chronicles of this book

The next 12 pages of Capt. Munger's Diary contain his daily notations concerning bills paid, bills due, Quarter Master acquisitions, Mess accounts, debts settled, and addresses of men and officers in the United States Army.

Page 108 – Apr 17, 1863 Mess a/c

To Bread, Beef and Sugar	1.90
18 Bread and paper	35
20 Potatoes, paper and ink	60
21 Beef, Rolls and paper	1.30
22 Ham, Bread, Sugar and c	4.30
" Fish	.50
24 Sugar of Harrington	51
" Cash to Houghton	20

Page 109 –

300 Lb. S. Pears

 80 " Soap

 66 Gal. Vinegar

160 Lb. Soap

282 Lb. Rice

288 "   "

301 "   "

May 16 Recd. of Q.M.

6 Pr Pants

3 " Shoes

2 " Drawers

4 " Shirts

1 Blouse

2 J. A. Tents

4 Lanterns

1 Haversacks

7 Pr Socks

Page 110 –

Mess Account

A list from first page   20.70

L Cash to for form   1.15

Mar 25 Sugar   75

 27 Candles and Paper   35

28 Potatoes, sugar and c   145

30 Ham and c   160

Apr 2 - Ham, candles, bread and c   190

"   4 - Sugar and c   135

"   6 - Candles   50

Apr 7 – Oysters   100

"   11 – Flour, Bread and Sugar   130

"   13 – Hard Bread and Sugar   200

April - Purveyors' Bill   324

Mess a/c Settled to Apr 17, 1863 and balance changed

Apr. 17, C. Kelly ok

To Balance on Mess a/c $12.22

         20   O.L. Munger

In Cash   25

24 Cash to balance all a/c   25.40

     "   "   "   Mess a/c   2.41

Page 111 -   1863

Mar 7 - C. Kelly ok

     12 – Cash rcd. for H at   1.75

     15 – O. E. Watkins   ok

          In Cash   1.00

     16 – F. D. Hills ok

Buy 1 Pair of Gloves	.75

O. L. Munger   ok

For 1 Flannel Shirt	2.25
" 1 pr Drawers	1.00
" Cap and Bugle	3.57

Mar 19 – a/c M. A quires ok

To Cash	1.00

" 21 – Matt Fety Patrick   ok

To Cash	1.00

" 22 – O. L. Munger ok

To Cash for sword	16.00

Page 112 –

John McLaughlin ok

Cash Lent	1.25

O. L. Munger   ok

Mar. 27 ½ Box Pens 12/-	.75
½ Bunch Collars 6/-	.38

Mar. 28   --------------------

Apr 1 F. D. Hills ok

Cash   40

14 M. F. Hardy

By Cash   2.07

April 17 O. L. Munger ok

Balance on Mess a/c   1.28

Apr. 17 James Russel ok

Balance on Mess a.c <u>Paid</u>   4.02

24 By Cas to balance a/c   2.04

Page 113 – (In this section of the accounts paid, the book has been flipped upside down and the month of January has been noted. It is assumed that this is for the month of January of 1863. There is also a section with the accounts of late 1862 noted.)

Jan 15 – Lt. Kelly

Cash   3.00

O. L. Munger

Cash   1.00

The Butter on hand at James Mess article   8.15

Geo. W. Francis

For Pr of Boots   50

Russel

For pr of Boots   62

J. G. Neal

For Freight on boots   50

F. D. Hills

For freight on goods   1.00

Page 114 – Co. Mess ok

Cash paid Rob   2.25

   "   Provisions   3,00

Dec 27 Cash for provisions   2.09

    29 "   "   "   2.00

Settled   75

                                    1.05

Jan 14   Cash for Butter   2.00

Officers Mess for

Feb 1   Cash pd. for butter   60

     3   14 lb. Sugar   7.00

     4   pd. for paper   .10

     6   pd. " Robs boots   7.00

     9   pd. " Beef, Tea   1.10

18 By Cash of James 2.00

Mar 19 " Mess   1.90

To 6ᵗʰ Butter 4/-   <u>3.00</u>

        $2.00 $20.70

Page 115 – Blank page

Page 116 – Falmoth Va. Dec 11, 1862

Lt Kelly

Cash   10.00

Lieut Russel

1 for boots   2.50

Dec. 29 A. Horton

To Cash   50

L. L. Osgod

Cash Ck 501   75

H. Ackley

Cash   1.00

Jan 6 Lieut. Kelly

To Cash   10.00

Capt Royce   <u>Paid</u>

Cash   10.00

Page 117 – (It should be noted that this page has very light pencil lead and in some cases the information cannot be read completely. This page also shows foxing and has smudges. The following is the most accurate rendition that could be read.)

January 6th as to 11 (This is the best guess on the transcription of this line)

Owen M. Noreaton

J. P. Chamberlin

Corps so long think 5th, 3rd, 6th, 1st, 2nd, 9th, 11th

150.00

220.00

<u>128.00</u>

578.00

Clendennan Lt. Col.

Regiment 8th Ill. Cav. (Note: Lt. Col. David R. Clendenin of the 8th Illinois Cavalry would later capture the battle flag of Company F, "Night Hawk Rangers" 17th Virginia Cavalry at the battle of Monocacy, Maryland on July 9, 1864.)

E. S. Smith Lt. Col. of Cav. Finally put in Co. K, June with

K. Stiles 10th Cav. Co. M.

Qr. Master Sec. Thomas Boaner

The 1865 Diary of Captain Bennett Munger – Co. C. 44th NY. Vol. Inf.

The 1865 diary of Captain Bennet Munger was provided through the kindness of Shelly Case of West Chester, Pa. She is Captain Munger's great, great granddaughter. This diary covers Captain Munger's trip from Elmira, N.Y. to the Great Kanawha Valley in West Virginia to invest in land & to speculate in possible natural resource opportunities such as salt, oil, coal & timber in January of 1865. This diary also covers similar investments made in Ohio, Pennsylvania & New York. **Note:** To separate the Case collection from the Kesterson collection of Captain Munger's letters the Case letters will be transcribed in New Roman Times font to differentiate the two collections. Page 212 also gives more information on the discovery of the Case Collection.

Page 1 – B. Bennett Munger – Jan. 1865

Page 2 – Mary Sheredan – Somerset Co. – O. Perry

Page 3 – January 1, 1865. Sunday

At Brother Layman's. Penn Yan. L in Oil City.

Monday Jan. 2nd

Returned to Elmira with Dr. Hammond to assist him in obtaining the appointment of Post Surgeon.

Tuesday Jan 3rd

Saw Col. Tracy in relation to Dr. Hammond & wrote to the Dr.

Wednesday Jan. 4th

Went to Penn Yan to finish my collections.

Thursday Jan. 5th

Saw Hacssending in relation to going to the Kanawha Valley. Went to Canandaigua at night. Bought cloths of Smiths.

Page 4 – Friday Jan. 6th

Visited at Mothers & Merrick's. Went to Bloomfield to see Nettie. Found her well. Deposited in the Trust N Bank of Can. $633.xx. Snowed. Heard Prof. Anderson lecture in the evening.

Saturday Jan. 7th

Returned to Penn Yan, finished collections, took remainder of suit of clothes of Smith. Reg. coat, vest, pants & over coat & paid him $90.xx therefore.

Sunday Jan. 8th

Went to church (Berchus) the first time since July last.

Monday Jan. 9th

Visited prison camp to obtain information in relation

Page 5 – to the mineral production of the Great Kanawha Valley & c.

Tuesday, Saw Dr. Morse. Paid him $45.xx & of bill for proof services. Visited prison again.

Wednesday Jan. 11th

Went to Penn Yan with Dr. Morse to make an arrangement for going to Western Va. Agreed to go with Harper during next Tuesday. The Briggs & Prosser Co. give me ½ a share ($500) to see to their interests. Returned to Elmira found letter from Maj. Colt.

Page 6 – Thursday Jan. 12th

Visited camp with a pass from Col. Tracy. Saw two more men from Kanawha & secured the privilege of taking letters to friends of prisoners.

Friday Jan. 13th

Recd. letter from Layman. He has decided to sink the well "Little Yates" deeper. Visited camp, obtained some information in relation to salt wells of Virginia. Bought boots. Made arrangements to start for Western Virginia on Monday to buy land.

Saturday Jan. 14th

Maj. Colt returned. Approves of what I have done.

Page 7 – Layman arrived at noon from Oil City, gives a fair account of prospects there. Will return about the 1st of Feb. Major Colt spent the eve with us. Monday, we are to conclude our arrangements with Demorest & Maj. will superintend business in my absence.

Sleighing excellent.

Sunday Jan. 15th

Cold, attended church A.M.

Monday Jan. 16th

Obtained letter of introduction to citizens Kanawha Valley. Harpending arriving on the morning train. Made arrangements

Page 8 – with Demerest & c. Left at 7 P.M. Fare to Cincinnati $17.20 by way of Buffalo. Reached it at 2 ½ A.M.

Tuesday Jan. 17th

Left Buffalo at 7 A.M. Reached Cleveland at 11 P.M. & left immediately & reached Cincinnati at 5 A.M.

Wednesday Jan. 18th

Crossed the river & walked to Daniel Ruffner's. Found Mrs. Ruffner absent in city, returned with son, saw her at 3 ½, took letters to friend. The boat does not go up tonight as we expected & we

Page 9 - took passage on the Ohio #3 at 7 dollars & staid on the boat. It is a magnificent boat. The weather is very cold for this latitude but little snow.

Thursday Jan. 19th

Cold & cloudy, wrote and mailed a letter to wife, snowed, bought paper, ink & c. Stayed on board all day. Night foggy & we don't start.

Friday Jan. 20th

Started about 7 A.M. The river is really full of floating ice & the day cold. We move about 7 miles per hour. 4 P.M. the ice is increasing but the weather is not so cold.

Page 10 – Saturday Jan. 21st

Mild 7 rainy, staid still 4 hours during the night for the fog. Find many of the passengers are bound to Kanawha.

*Jehu L. Gregory

Reached Gallipolis about 7 P.M. Put up at Richardson's where wife has a brother.

*Jehu L. Gregory a prisoner at Elmira obtained a pass & went on board the Gen. Crook a government boat to leave for Charleston at 2 A.M.

P.M. Rained but little & mild, no snow.

Page 11 – Sunday Jan. 22nd

Boat left Gallipolis at 2 A.M., at 9 passed Winfield where the boat (the steamer B. C. Levi) we are on was once captured by the Rebs (at Red House on February 4, 1864) with Gen. Scammon & staff. Arrived at Charleston about 2 P.M. found it muddy & dilapidated. Called on Mrs. Parks, Messrs Wilson & Smith. At Bell went on to camp & H. & I staid *Feb. 1st.

Monday Jan. 23rd

Up at 8 A.M., ground covered with snow & still coming, melting as it falls. Dined at Mr. Wilson's. Saw Mrs.

Page 12 – McFarland. Had a pleasant time. Wrote to wife, snowed all day, no boat for camp.

Tuesday Jan. 24th

Cold, ground frozen so to bear a team. Started at 9 A.M. for Camp Piatt on foot. Took dinner at Malden & rode in an ambulance to camp. A Godforsaken place. Called on Col. Platner.

Wednesday Jan. 25th

Went up Lens Creek to see the property bought by Asbell & Sheppard. Had to walk over the roughest road in the

Page 13 – imaginable – returned and went to Malden, had good quarters.

Thursday Jan. 26th

Had a good night's rest. Saw Brace & Fitch. Floating ice in the river. Weather cold. Bought boots at $8.50/100 dollars, mine being so small I could not wear them. P.M/ went to Charleston. Took supper at saloon. Wrote to Layman.

Friday Jan. 27th

Cold, river so full of ice that boats don't run. Doubtful if we can get up the Elk.

Page 14 – 3 P.M. started on foot up the Elk. Crossed to the right bank near the mouth & traveled till dark. Stopped at Widow Jacob's & staid all night. Harpending tried & concluded to go on further.

Saturday Jan. 28th

Broadhead & I started about 9 A.M. Traveled to Coopers Creek, up the creek one mile, crossed to Little Sandy, up Sandy three miles, then up Wills then Cooper to Elk & down Elk to Higginbotham Hotel. Staid all night.

Page 15 – Sunday Jan. 29th

Started for Charleston at 10 A.M. Crossed to the left bank of the Elk at Coopers & arrived in town about three P.M. Found H. all sound. Went to church in the eve.

Monday Jan 30

Staid in town A.M. Went to Malden P.M. on horseback saw oil in an old salt well on the premise of Walker & Shrewsbury. Called on Mrs. Parks, had a pleasant visit with the Miss Wilson & Miss Parks.

Page 16 – Tuesday Jan. 31st

Remained in town, weather mild & roads muddy. Took dinner at Mr. Wilsons & spent the evening at Mrs. Parks. Navigation is still closed. No letters from home.

Wednesday Feb 1st

In town, weather mild, called at Wilsons P.M., sick headache. H. & B. visited at Wilsons. I remained at home. Mud plenty but dear.

Js. Arthur Neal, son of B. F. Neal of Texas in Elmira.

Ready to start for home as soon as the river is open.

Page 17 – Walker & Shrewsbury's

Have made during 10 months of the year 140,000 bush of salt at a profit of 10 c per bush. Will sell their entire interest at 150,000. Own in front 100 acres. 300 yards on the river & in the rear ¼ of 200 acres, & in rear of this ¼ of 150,000acres. Work 35 hands at one dollar & boarded or one & half without board. Average 600 bush per day. 4 engines 15 horsepower each. Salt water at 10% or 9 by the hydrometer. Works cost 20,000 dollars. Use 700 bush coal per day.

Page 18 – Thursday Feb. 2nd

Spent the day in Charleston. Called on our friends.

Friday Feb 3

In Charleston. Weather mild. In the visited at Wilsons with friends of theirs. A pleasant time. Introduced to Dr. Comstock in charge of post.

Saturday Feb. 4th

In town. Recd. notice at 2 P.M. that the ice is out of the river. Called on our friends, took leave and went on board of the Gen. Crook at 9 ½ P.M.

Page 19 Sunday Feb. 5

Started at 6 A.M. & arrived at Gallipolis about 1 P.M. Put up at the Garnett House. The Ohio #3 is expected up to night. The results of our investigations in the Kanawha Valley is the conclusion that oils has not & will not be found in paying quantities. We made no purchase. Coal is abundant & land is cheap.

Monday Feb. 6

The Ohio No. 3 arrives about 6 A.M. Took breakfast at the Garnett House. Went on board & started about 9 ½ for Parkersburg.

Page 20 Laid up most of the night to repair wheels. Weather cool.

Tuesday Feb. 7

Cold, snow, boat machinery out of gear. Arrives at Parkersburg at 1 P.M. Put up at Swan House. Oil men are abundant.

Wednesday Feb. 8th

Snowed, decided to go to Marietta this P.M. Oil in this vicinity is "Von Grand Hunburg". Wrote to wife & Maj. Colt.

Thursday Feb. 9th

Started on the Balt. & Ohio R.R. at 7 P.M. for Wheeling via of Grafton.

Page 21

Edn d L. Bill

1190 acres   Spencer

Right hand   Roane Co.

Fork of Triplet   W.Va.

Run of West Fork

8 or 9 miles above Burning Springs

He has also a tract on the Big Sandy of Elk of 1445 acres for which he asks $15 per acre – It is six miles from Elk.

Page 22 Arrived at Belair about 7 P.M. & left for Wellsville at 10. Arrived about 1 & slept till 4 A.M.

Friday Feb. 10th

Took the train for Ravenna about 5 7 left at 9 A.M. for Meadville where we arrived about 2 P.M. Had some grand singing on the train. Left for Franklin at 5. Arrived at 8 & took a sleigh for Oil City. Arrived at 10 found Layman & Orett at home & Gev in Cincinnati. No news from home.

Saturday Feb. 11th

Layman, Harpending, Broadhead & myself took

Page 23 horses & went to Panther Run & down the stream to city. Orett went to Clarion to look at a piece of land.

Sunday Feb. 12th

Cold & foggy, at home.

Monday Feb. 13th

Concluded to go back to Cincinnati to sell some lands. Started at 2:30, arrived at Meadville at 8 P.M. Last night was the coldest of the season. Mercury at 26 below zero at sunrise.

Page 24 Monday Feb. 14

Left Meadville for Cleveland at 1:30 A.M. Arrived at 7. Left at 8 for Columbus, arrived at 4 P.M. & put up at the American. Left at 12 for Cincinnati, arrived at 7 A.M.

Wednesday Feb. 15

My last night at Columbus a sister of Gen. Sheridan & escorted her to Cincinnati & sent her to Hamilton, is a rare woman. Put up at the Burnet House, found George, heard his plans, declines to act in the case of the property on Larkey Run. Introduced to Miss, Susie O., his prospective wife. – Rainy

Page 25 Thursday Feb. 16th

Am to return to Oil City tonight. Started at 10 P.M.

Friday Feb 17th

Foggy & unpleasant. – Our train being 2 hours behind time had to wait 12 hours thus prevents my reaching home this week. There is very little snow in southern Ohio & not much here. Left from Meadville at 11:30 & reached it at 4:30 A.M.

Saturday Feb. 18th

Left for Oil City at 7:45 A.M. & arrived about noon. L. had left for Detroit on Tuesday & would remain

Page 26

at Penn Yan a few weeks. Saw Allen & co. Found Harpending at O.C.

Sunday Feb. 19th

Took a walk & ride with Orett – Day Mild – Attended church in the eve.

Monday Feb. 20th

Started at home at 7 A.M., cold frosty morning but clear. 3 ½ P.M. 20 miles west of Corcey, our train collided with a freight breaking their engine & damaging ours, no one hurt, got another engine & started at 8 ½ ran all night & reached Elmira at 12 noon.

Page 27

Tuesday Feb. 21st

We were 12 hours behind time, found the family comfortable. Our selling scheme is/has collapsed. Demerest refusing to fulfill so the prospect of business in this town is is not flattering. Saw Dr, Morse & Maj. Colt.

Wednesday Feb, 22nd

Thorn & Isbell presents a rug to Mrs. Munger as a keepsake of Linh bury. Investigated

Parks money a/c.

Thursday Feb. 23rd

Saw Maj. Colt who proposes to form a co. partnership for the purchase of Government

Page 28

Vouchers & c. Have seen & been introduced to the Confederate officers sent here to distribute clothing to prisoners. Col. Price of Memphis & Maj. Printoss of Rome, Georgia.

Friday Feb. 24th

Harpending not arriving as arranged. I shall go to Penn Yan tonight. Mary & Ida go to Sadlers on a visit arrive at P.M. at 9 P.M. friends well.

Saturday Feb. 25th

Decided to embark on in the oil business & go to Oil City, Monday

Page 29

In the evening made a report to the Co. in relation to their Kanawha purchase. Shall stay in Penn Yan till Monday. Weather warm & snow going rapidly.

Sunday Feb. 26th

Attended church A.M. & evening heard Mr. Buck. Am not feeling well.

Omega

Monday Feb. 27th

Left for Elmira at 8:30, arrived on time, found all well. Wrote to L & treasurer of Sten Co. Unable to find Maj. Colt. Bought ½ ton of coal. Started about 7 P.M. for Oil City.

Page 30

Tuesday Feb. 28th

Arrived at Meadville at 6 A.M. & at Oil City at noon. Found Geo. Had gone to Cincinnati. Wrote to Layman, Geo. & Mrs. Parks. Orett at home.

Wednesday Mar. 1st

Orett went to Panther Run. Harpending is still at Oil City. Has not yet bought anything. Orett & self, start at 3:25 for Mercer via Meadville. Detained all night on the road.

Thursday Mar. 2nd

Arrived at Greenville at 5 A.M, found the Mercer Stage, did not leave till

Page 31

Note in a squared off section at the top of this page Captain Munger wrote the following: ("Tuesday Feb 28, 1865 – Divide interest as far as possible. Buy to cancel my demands. Tell George Gibbs to cancel his. If necessary buy enough for present emergencies.")

3 P.M. Went to bed & laid till noon. Arrived about 8 P.M. at Mercer. Found Jane & John at home & well. Warm & rainy.

Friday Mar. 3

Visited with Jane at. With John at Bank & School & c. Had a pleasant time. Weather cloudy & unpleasant. Wrote to wife.

Page 32

Saturday Mar. 4th

Stormy. Visited & read at the house till 11 A.M. Went to Bank. Union Inauguration. Prayer meeting & to Aunt Hanna's. In the eve Mr. & Mrs. Small called.

Sunday Mar. 5th

Attended church, heard Mr. French. At home reading. Bushnell the remainder of the day.

Monday Mar. 6th

Clear, cool morning, ground some frozen. Saw the first robins of the season. Started at 10:15 A.M. for Franklin by stage. Arrived at 6 P.M.

Page 33

Walked to O. City, found a letter from Maj. Colt am near sick.

Tuesday Mar. 7th

At the office the forenoon. Went to see the Farrel Farm on Slate Creek P.M. got in at 8 ½. Layman came at 9 O.C. Has purchased this Richmond property. The first steamboats arrived. Rained at eve.

Wednesday Mar. 8th

Layman & Orett went to Panther Run. Gibbs brother-in-law came while Gibbs was absent. Gibbs returned at 12:15. Wrote to wife & Sophia & c. Ice left the river at Panther Run.

Page 34

Thursday Mar. 9th

No letters. Weather warm7 cloudy. Wrote to J. Hanna. Estimated the amount of our several interests

(L's, O's, My own) in the oil business.

L. Munger's capital   6500

B. Munger   "   2500

O. L. Munger   "   2000

Drew articles of Co. partnership to date Jan. 17, 1865. Concluded not to go to Ohio at present but return at once to Elmira. Left at 7 P.M., Meadville at 11. Cold & snow.

Friday Mar. 10th

Left Meadville at 3:40, Salamanca 9:15, Elmira at 3:30. Found family well. Ground frozen.

Page 35

Saturday Mar. 11th

Saw Maj. Colt & Prentuss. Found draft for Stenbon Co. Bonds ready for me $160.50 – Cold

Sunday Mar. 12th

Attended Church & S. School.

Monday Mar. 13th

Settled with Bronson. Visited prison camp & attended to various matters pertaining to removing to Penn Yan.

Tuesday Mar. 14th

Took leave of officers at No. 1. Hired horse & buggy & carried family to ride.

Page 36

Wednesday Mar 15th

Took leave & left at a noon for Penn Yan, left baggage by mistake. Arrived at 4:30 7 put up at Tuel House.

Thursday Mar. 16th

Warm, wife sick, wrote to Merrick. Visited at Mr. Bridgeman. Had sick headache. Staid all night.

Friday Mar. 17th

Snow 3 inches deep. Our trunks & goods came on the train due last night. No mails.

Page 37

Saturday Mar. 18th

No mails till night on account of damages to R.R. by flood.

Sunday Mar. 19th

Went to church. Heard Mr. Buck.

Monday Mar. 20th

Left at 10 A.M. for Canandaigua. Found our friends well. S. F. & Julia Kent were at Abigail's. Visited with them during the day & evening. Julia had a telegram that her little daughter was sick & she started immediately to Merrick's to stay overnight. - Warm

Page 38

Tuesday Mar. 21st

Extract from Olano Rep & Messonger of Mar. 4th, Oil Struck at the mouth of Big Sandy. A tributary of the Elk, W.Va., at the depth of 125 feet, yield 230 barrels a day.

Staid at Merrick's, went to see Nettie. Visited at Abigail's P.M. Staid at M's. Bought – off F. M. $22.50

Wednesday Mar. 22nd

Visited at M's & Abigail's. Left for home at 8 P.M. Found family well.

Page 39

Thursday Mar. 23rd

Cooler, snowed last night. Investigated the boarding question.

Friday Mar. 24th

Visited, assisted Mother some. Cloudy, some snow.

Saturday Mar. 25th

Took tea at Mother's. Recd. a letter from Frank & answered it. Wrote to Wilson of Kanawha Valley. Attended temperance lecture at Baptist Church.

Page 40

Sunday Mar. 26th

Attended Presbyterian Church A.M. M.E. in the evening.

Monday Mar. 27th

Contracted with J. Bridgeman to board my wife & daughter, furnish them a room at $7.00 a week.

Tuesday Mar. 28th

Packed clothing & finished preparations for leaving. Paid J. Bridgeman $50.00 in advance on board. "The last time"

Wednesday Mar. 29th

Started on the morning train for Oil City. Settled with & redc. pay ($100) of

Page 41

Dr. Morse. Sold company bond to Maj. Colt at 10 percent discount. Had sick headache & stayed overnight at Elmira. Slept with Colt.

Thursday Mar. 30th

Rainy – Started for Oil City at 9 A.M. Lodged at the M. House, Meadville *

Friday Mar. 31st

Started at 7 A.M. & arrived about 9, found L. & O. at home. L. not well. Did nothing but purchase blacksmith tools & provisions & wrote wife.

Page 42

Saturday Apr. 1st

Collected tools & provisions loaded onto steamer 7 sent to Panther Run. Recd. Letter from Frank Munger & answered it. Sold horse to the man of which he was purchased for $160.

Sunday Apr. 2nd

Beautiful morning – Attended Presbyterian Church & wrote to Ida & Sophia & attended the M.E. Church in the evening

Richmond taken at 8:15 A.M.

Monday Apr.3rd

Layman went to Panther Run & O. & self to Cherry Run. Took lumber to the new lease. Visited the Hicks Well.

Page 43

Tuesday Apr. 4th

Rainy. O. & self, went to Rousville & Hicks Well. Hired a new man to draw the lumber. I left at 3 ½ O. staid till dark. Layman came down from Panther Run. Wrote to wife.

Wednesday April. 5th

L., O., & self, went to Panther Run. Took up tools for L. & helped take down derrick & c. Felt well, staid all night.

Thursday Apr. 6th

Rain – Danhoiel (**Note: this name is hard to make out & the transcription of the spelling is probably incorrect**) returned worst shape ever & I am clear down. Cleared A.M. Returned to Oil City on a raft.

Page 44

Friday Apr. 7th

Sick from the effects of medicine & diarrhea. Kept the house most of the day. Wrote wife.

Saturday Apr. 8th

Feeling better, went to Franklin to buy lumber & c. for L's Panther Run well, found none to suit. Met Geo. & returned to Oil City.

Sunday Apr. 9th

Pleasant, went to M.E. Church in the A.M. Wrote to Ida.

Monday Apr. 10th

Started Columbus, O. for two engines. Cold & cloudy.

Page 45

Tuesday Apr. 11th

Arrived in Columbus at 4 A.M. Saw the freight agent & found the engines had been to Cleveland. Started on my return at 10. Arrived at 3 P.M. Found both engines had been recd. by A. & G. W. R. W. Co. One had been sent on the other lying at their depot. Rainy – Staid at the American.

Wednesday Apr. 12th

Took breakfast at the American. Took the 9:50 train from Meadville & from M to O. City. Found the engine had been delivered to Orett. Found Geo. At office. L. at P. Run & Orett at Franklin.

Page 46

Thursday Apr 13th

Went to P. Run on tow boat of coal with Orett. Went over to Little Yates. The torpedo has not been of any use apparently. Staid at Panther Run all night.

Friday Apr. 14th

Went to pit hole with L. Bought lumber & floated it to P.R. - Health not good.

Saturday Apr. 15th

Explored the cave at Panther Run with G. & O. found it a home by only a fissure. Bound to O.C. on a raft. Recd. two letters from wife & Ida. Took supper at office.

Page 47

Telegrams announcing the assassination the assassination of President Lincoln & Seward were recd. today.

Sunday Apr. 16th

Attended M.E. Church with O. in A.M. Afternoon wrote to wife & Ida. Cloudy & gloomy day. We are somewhat effected by the blues.

Monday Apr. 17th

Clear & frosty – Ground frozen. O. & self, went to Franklin for engines. Found but one there a Blandies & had it sent to Raines for Cherry Run.

Page 48

Sent provisions, pipe & c. by the advance to Pan Run. Walked to Oil City.

Tuesday Apr. 18th

Geo. Started for Mercer. O. & self, started for P. Run. The Richmond well has a good appearance on drawing the tubing. Concluded to go to Can – on business & start tomorrow.

Wednesday Apr. 19th

Left O. City 8:40 A.M. for Penn Yan. O. came to Reno for an engine and at Mead 11 A.M. Left at 3

Page 49

Thursday Apr. 20th

Arrived at Elmira at 3:15 A.M. & left at 7 A.M. Home at 9:20. Found all well, family at Wesley Boarding House.

Friday Apr. 21st

Saw many members of the Union Co. all seem satisfied.

Saturday Apr. 22nd

Settled with D. Wagner & took his note for $41.00. Bought chair for wife of Curtis at $9.00 Helped Martha.

Sunday Apr. 23rd

Attended church at Presbyterian, heard Starr's farewell.

Page 51

Took dinner at Martha's.

Monday Apr. 24th

Went to Can. with Ida. Visited Nettie, found all well. Checked & $635.00 from 1st National Bank.

Tuesday Apr. 25th

Returned to Penn Yan on the morning train. Settled with Bridgeman & recd. $34.25. Left with wife $70.00.

Wednesday Apr. 26th

Left for O. City at noon & staid at Elmira all night. Left by the train.

Thursday Apr. 27th

Eft Elmira at 8 & reached Mead at 7 ½.

Page 52

Friday Apr. 28th

Breakfast at Meadville & left for O. City at 6 A.M. Found Geo. & O. left for Cincinnati – Thursday morning L. was at P.R. I walked up A.M. found the well pumping water freely with some oil. Came down on a raft. Took supper at the Petroleum at 50 cents per meal. Rained.

Saturday Apr. 29th

Raining hard. Went to Franklin for water line & box of machining.

Page 53

Sunday Apr. 30th

Attended Church & Bible class. Wrote to wife & Hallie Parks.

Monday May 1st

L & self, went up to Reno. Got box of machineries. Went to Cherry Run.

Tuesday May 2nd

Went to Franklin of 66L water line L. started for home. Sent letter written on Sunday to wife. Wrote to Capt. J. Leonard.

Wednesday May 3rd

Bought Sand Pumper No. 29, waited Water Line to arrive. Wrote to Bruce C. & W. Ainsworth. No line.

Page 54

Thursday May 4th

Took belt, bull rope, sand pump & box of machinery to Cherry Run. Orett arrived on the evening train.

Friday May 5th

Orett Left for Penn Yan on the morning train for a stay of two weeks or so. Not feeling well. I stayed in office, wrote to freight agent foe engine & Emma Day & received one from Frank.

Saturday May 6th

Deposited G. M. Munger's & Co., Wrote with Lambertol & paid interest $10.00 – Went to Panther Run. Well improving, think doing finely.

Page 55

Rained powerfully last night & day some.

Sunday May 7th

Attended M.E. Bible class & church. Wrote to D. W. Adams wife. P.M. of Granville, Ill. & Julia Rose.

Monday May 8

Clear, recd. bills for Fox's engines & paid also Bland's box of fixtures. Sick with headache. Box ½ in gas pipe for C.R. Leare 29.

Tuesday May 9th

Went to Cherry Run. Fox the Buffalo engine man came today.

Page 56

Wednesday May 10th

Contracted with A.R. Fox of Buffalo for a 10 H.P. engine for $1,500. Fox to set it up & we pay expenses. Went to Cherry Run, will probably start that drill on the 12th. Went to P.R. well doing finely. Rained Hamlin goes home tonight. Wrote to wife.

Thursday May 11th

Rainy, in office all day. Wrote to Nancy & Nettie.

Friday May 12th

Clear, went to Franklin, found one of Foxe's engines.

Page 57

Paid freight $137.85 & had it shipped to Reno. Easton & Sheldon left for home. Sent line to wife. Had P.R. deed recorded. Wrote to Frank & Abigale.

Saturday May 13th

Gibbs returned. Paid Marquis $275 & Gibbs $10. Hired a horse & went to C.R. & P.G. At C.R. the drill was started today & will commence work. Monday, P.R. doing about as usual.

Sunday May 14th

Attended Bible class & church. Wrote to wife. Hathaway of N.Y. called.

Page 58

Monday May 15th

Saw Broadhead & went to Franklin for engine. Found it at Reno.

Tuesday May 16th

Contracted with Hunger to draw engine from Reno to Cherry Run for $100.00. Saw race on the track.

Wednesday May 17th

Orett came on the morning train. Went to Cherry Run at Hicks well. Lease No. 29 is being drilled. Engine for the upper well was put on the ground today.

Page 59

Thursday May 18th

Went to P.R., found the well yielding 5 bbls per day average. Wrote to wife by Bogart. Looked over accounts & was credited $757.56 on Co. books.

Friday May 19th

Bought tools & fixtures for Cherry Run Lease No. 29, cleaned beat & c. Recd. letters from wife & Frank M.

Saturday May 20th

L. was expected this morn but did not arrive. Drilling tools for Cherry Run finished & sent up. Wrote to Frank & Soph.

Page 60

Sunday May 21st

Attended Bible class & church. Rainy dull day, headache a little, wrote to wife.

Monday May 22nd

Went to Panther Run & Rowley well. Progressing finely. Orett went to Cherry Run, second well will commence drilling on Thursday. Warm.

Tuesday May 23rd

Recd. telegram from Lyman dated 22nd, he is sick abed (in bed). Went to Franklin & Meadville. Found the Blandy at Utica & the other is to be forwarded soon. Letters from wife & Jone.

Page 61

Wednesday May 24th

Took down stove & cleaned up room. Went to Cherry Run, wrote to Ida & recd. letter from wife.

Thursday May 25th

Went to P.R. wrote to L.

Friday May 26th

Took belts to C. R.

Saturday May 27th

George arrived bringing $1,000 from Layman, who is sick with typhoid fever. Went to P.R. bought Little Yates tools & c.

Sunday May 28th

Attended M.E. Church

Page 62

& Bible class. Wrote letter to wife.

Monday May 29th

Recd. letter from Frank Munger. Went to Panther Run. Found on examination that the Richmond well had produced bur one bbl per day. That the engine had consumed 24 bush coal per day & we at once <u>shut down</u>.

Tuesday May 30th

Decided to go immediately to Penn Yan & announce the above facts to the Co. Started at 8:40 for home.

Page 63

Wednesday May 31st

Arrived in Penn Yan at 9:20. Found Layman very low. Saw the Pres. of lumber Co. Mary & Ida well as usual.

Thursday June 1st

Met the directors & reported.

Friday June 2nd

Met again. They proposed to employ me to superintend the sinking of the Richmond well 300 feet deeper. Layman improving slowly. Layman's services closed with Union Co.

Page 64

Saturday June 3rd

Sick with headache.

Sunday June 4th

Eli Sheldon was buried. My self not well, took tea at Ls.

Monday June 5th

Agreed with Pres. of Union Co. to superintend their well for $6.00 per day.

Page 65

Tuesday June 6th

Started on the noon train, O. City.

Wednesday June 7th

Arrived on the morning train, found O. at office. Wrote to Richmond.

Thursday June 8th

Went to P.R. & C.R. Bought 700 bush coal at $1.00 per bush. One of the wells at C.R. is delayed by a prior waist all being thrown into it.

Page 66

Friday June 9th

Went to P.R. The engines arrived & one unloaded. One load of coal arrived. Wrote to C.C. Sheppard.

Saturday June 10th

At office sick.

Sunday June 11th

At home sick. Wrote to wife & Abigail.

Monday June 12th

Wrote to Layman, am feeling better.

Tuesday June 13th

Not as well, wrote to wife by Strowbridge. Letter from wife.

Page 67

Wednesday June 14th

Little better. Recd. telegram from Sheppard to buy or repair tools & crowd the work. Wrote to wife by Dunning. Recd. letter from wife.

Thursday June 13th

About the same. Bought tools of Martin except temper screw for $3.20. Fox of Buff arrived to set up engine. Wrote to wife & Nettie.

Friday June 16th

Sent drilling tools to Richmond well. Went to P.R. Fox commenced setting up engine. Staid all night.

Page 68

Saturday June 17th

Worked at engines. Went to Oil City in skiff. Recd. letter from Sheppard & replied. Found tools for Richmond well too large. Sold them & ordered others.

Sunday June 18th

In the office all day. Wrote to wife & Ida. Recd. letter from sister, Jane.

Monday June 19th

Went to Panther Run & worked at putting up engine. Staid all night.

Tuesday June 20th

Recd. letter from wife.

Page 69

Fired up the Fox engine. It ran well. Finished the water connection. Burns & his men came on this noon. Fox left for home. O. & self, went to Oil City after 6 P.M. Recd. letter from wife.

Wednesday June 21st

Mr. Hazen a director in Union Co. arrived this morning & went with O. & self, to Gen. Lane well & up C.R. s far as the Hicks & across to P.R. & staid till Thursday night, O. returned to the city. Tools for the Richmond well on the ground. The jars had to be sent back.

Page 70

Thursday June 22nd

Commenced Drilling the Uncle Abe well. Sent Nugent to city with jars repairs. Recd. letter from wife. Hazen returned to city.

Friday June 23rd

Drilled the U.A. well & worked at the Richmond gilting, found the derrick 3 feet too short, put on addition & hung tools, found the bits would not fit. Blew off the engine at U.A. to fix chick valve.

Page 71

Saturday June 24th

O. & self, with three men took tools in a canoe to Oil C. for repairs.

Sunday June 25th

Wrote wife, Layman & Mr. & Mrs. Hanna, cleaned & moved beds.

Monday June 26th

Went to P.R. found the tools would not go into the Richmond well & decided to ream it 5 inches.

Tuesday June 27th

Mr. Hazen came to see us again & left at 2 P.M. for home.

Page 72

Pling came about noon with O. & Nugent brought a letter from wife.

Wednesday June 28th

Worded at the Richmond well which we commenced reaming yesterday. Pump at U.A. doesn't work, broken flange to air compressor & O. took it to O.C. Pling went also & both staid all night. Nugent & self, run the drill from noon to midnight. My first drilling.

Thursday June 29th

Pumps in the R. engine would not work, took out valves & found them

Page 73

Stuck with oily matter. Engine cannot be stopped on a/c of the leaking of the throttle valve. Broke Temper Screw. Heavy shower in the night. Letter from wife in 14 days from writing.

Friday June 30th

Worked at the R. well with no accidents or hindrances till 9 P.M. when Burnes injured a box by putting a dirty tap into it & we were obliged to shut down. O. went to O.C. The engine at the U.A. well is not yet repaired.

Page 74

Saturday July 1st

Boat gone & poured. Took auger stem & bit the throttle valve to O.C. Valve repaired but tools must remain till Monday. Recd. letter from wife & Chas.

Elmendorf came.

Sunday July 2nd

Cool & cloudy, went to church. Wrote to wife, Ida & C.C. Sheppard. C.E. staid with us all night.

Monday July 3rd

Took tools & base grates to boat & staid for powder. O. & P. went up at about 6 A.M.

Page 75

The throttle valve would not work & we ground on it all day. Run the Fox engine a short time & shut it down to fix water connection.

Tuesday July 4th

Fox engine works well. The valve to R. engine will not work. Took it out & brought it to city. C. Elmendorf goes home in the morning. Wrote to wife.

Wednesday July 5th

Took old valve to machine shop. Had a new one put in, cost $25.00. Took it to the boat. Recd. letter from wife & Abigale

Page 76

& wrote to Nettie, J. A. Booth, wife & Abigale.

Thursday July 6th

Went to P. Run this morning. Put in new valve. Nugent went to city for his daughter, got back at 4 P.M. I cleaned engine.

Friday July 7th

Nugent & I run the reamer, made but about 12 feet, burdened some with tools sticking, ran 15 hours.

Saturday July 8th

Run the well till noon. Hired Mart to take my place & O., P. & self, came to

Page 77

city. Have reamed about 125 feet. Cleared up & feel better. Recd. letters from wife & Richmond, wrote to Sheppard.

Sunday July 9th

In office. Messrs Sheldon & Sualow called. Wrote to wife & Lyman. Went to P.R. in the evening with Pling. Saw Mr. Harris former chaplain at Elmira & was introduced by him to Jerome Munger.

Monday July 10th

The U.A. well started 6 A.M. the boiler leaked. The Richmond at midnight, the tools stick badly & progress slow.

Page 78

At eve I went to O. City with cracked reamer. O went to C. R. A broken bit is in the wood & well. The Wadsworth well is 400 feet deep.

Tuesday June 11th

Took reaming to Martin who says it must be new steeled & it can't be done so as to go on the boat today. Wrote to wife. Went to the Run, found the well not running. Burns & Newman straightened jars & Nugent & Newman work till midnight reaming the hole they reamed last night.

Page 79

Wednesday July 12th

Nugent, Wilcox & self, run the engine during the day only making about 8 feet. We have made little progress this week, tools have stuck badly. Pling ran a trick from midnight.

Thursday July 13th

Run the Richmond well with better success. Orett returns from the city & C. Run. Dick Counsell runs with from midnight. Recd. letters from Sheppard. Richmond's brother (with draft $200) Lyman, wife & Abigail.

Page 80

Friday July 14th

Run with Dick from midnight till noon, did fairly. Run 4 center bits & 4 reamers. Lost tools in Uncle Abe well & took them out.

Saturday July 15th

Run with Dick till noon. Paid hands & went to O. City. Letter from Nettie & wife. Wrote to Sheppard. Richmond well down 205 & U.A. 175.

Sunday July 16th

Got up at 9 breakfasted at 1 P.M. Cold & rainy. Wrote to wife. Went to P.R. in eve, dark & rainy.

Page 81

Monday July 17th

Commenced running at midnight, run 8 reamers & fixed Bull well by noon.

Tuesday July 18th

Things work well. The Richmond well is down 270 at noon & the U.A. well 206. Weather cool & clear. Recd. letters from Lyman.

Wednesday July 19th

Rainy. The drilling goes badly & everything is perplexing. O. has gone to O. City.

Page 82

Thursday July 20th

Jars broke & auger stem in U.A. well taken out readily. Richmond well down 285 feet at noon & working badly. Ream broke & sent to Oil City packet with jars. Both wells shut down. Went to O. C. found O. there. Letter from wife & Ida.

Friday July 21st

Took reamer to Martin's, had it repaired & took it to packet. Jars not sent. Wrote to L. Checked $100 from 1st Nat. Bank. Went to P.R. at 3 P.M. Started the Richmond engine, works well. Heavy rain.

Page 83

Saturday July 22nd

Both engines shut down last night at 10 o'clock on account of the rain. Broke nut on wrist of pitman crank & sent to the bend for repairs. Started again at 1 ½ P.M. Richmond well 300 feet, A. U. 255. The P & S well ready to start. Left for O.C. on a raft at 2 P.M. Orett has not been to P.R. since Wednesday night.

Sunday July 23rd

Wrote to Sheppard & wife, went to church, could not get in. Day fine, feeling well. Wrote to C. H. Richmond.

Page 84

Started for P.R. at 6 P.M.

(Note: The rest of this page is blank.)

Page 85

Note: The rest of the diary has bookkeeping expenditures for payment of wages, repairs on machinery & supplies.

June 6th 1865

Recd. of J. Burns for Union Co. 1000.00

"   " L. Munger   603.16

June 2 O. L. Munger   500.00

    13 " " "   L. Yates   106.85

June 15 " Richmond   199.00

Aug 5 " Ocean Bank N.Y.	125.00	
1 " L. W. Gage	175.00	
19 " W. A. Richmond	200.00	
	2909.01	

Page 86

May 29th 1865

Paid Nugent	60.00
31 "	15.50
" "	2.50
Bradshaw	143.00
June 14 Telegram	1.60
" 15 Coal	700.00
May 25 Nugent, P. Cartridges	1.50
June 19 Paid for cable	97.24
" 21 Paid for tools	320.00
" 22 two derrick L.	1.00
Two balls wick	.50
Rope coupling	17.50
Carting tools	10.00
Gudgeons	1.00
Sand pump	12.00
2b carpenters	150.00
July 1 Paid Martin Re	23.00
" J. W. Mc Cleery	9.00
" B. Minger	13.00

$1427.09

Page 87

Amount brought up	$1427.09
July 1 B. Isaac Graham	21.50
" Repair on Te. Screw	4.00
July 1 J. P. Mulligan	18.00
" Thos. Barns	5.00
" I. Nugent (9Days)	27.00
" " ", Smith's board	2.00
" " " supplies	20.95
" Repairs on valve	3.00
" Rope (loring)	.75
" Jo. Smith	6.00
" Chas. Black	9.00
July 5 Throttle valve	20.00
" Setting & freight	7.30
" 15 Dick Counsel	6.50
" I. Nugent	24.43
" Alan Bell	1.50
Repair on Lemper Screw	20.00
A. S. Wilcox	19.50
	1660.52

Page 88

	1660.52
July 15 Paid I. Graham	1.75
" " J. Milligan	1.50

"	" Mart. Roney	1.50
"	" David McKee	3.00
"	" B. Munger 11. L.	35.75
July 20	" D. McKee	9.00
July 21	Boiler bolts	1.15
July 21	Paid Repairs of reamer	9.50
"	" Repairs on Ream last week	1.00
"	22 " Nugent	19.50
"	" R. Counsel	17.88
"	" B. Munger	19.50
"	" Nugent old acct.	11.00
"	24 " Rep. Put. Wrist	.75
	" 1 gal. Oil	2.80
	" Rep. on Len. Screw	.50
"	29 " Belts	31.95
	" Labor	22.25
	" Pitman Crank	15.52
		$ 1866.30

1865

July Amount brought over		$1866.30
" 24 Paid for nails & etc.		2.00
Aug. 7 " Flax seed		1.99
" Seed Bag		5.00
" Solder		1.70
" Twine		.65

" Packing valve	.75
" Nugent on old a/c	60.00
Aug. 12 " R. Counsel	15.00
" 19 " " "	15.00
" Lube Reducer	6.00
August 19 Paid R. Burns	20.00
" B. Munger	4.50
" R. Counsel	10.00
	2008.89

Page 90 – **This page is blank.**

Page 91

1865

Apr. Amt. brought from right paper $ 3063.07

Apr. 8 Recd. of Lamberton	$37.05
9 " " "	100.00
12 " " "	137.85
13 " " "	275.00
19	3612. 97
Paid out	$3612.97
June 3 Recd. of L. Munger	50.00

Page 92 – **This page is blank.**

Page 93

Oil City Mar. 7, 1865

Paid expenses to H. Creek	3.10
8 Paper & postage	.15
9 Paid Bill at O. City	4. 50

Fare to Meadville		1.35
Supper at "		1.00
Fare to Elmira	3.15, 2.20, 2.50	7.85
Incidentals		.20
10 Rail Road Guide		.30
11 Meat		.30
11 Rubbers for Ida		1.25
Bill Book		2.00
12 Contribution		.50
13 Paid Bronson		25.78
" for camphor, ice & c.		.50
14 Paid for prescription		1.25
" " Postage stamps		1.00
" " Horse hired		2.00
" " House rent		6.00
" fare to Penn Yan		2.80
		1,228

Page 94

Amount brought over	1,828
15 Paid hack hire	.20
16 " Perkins bill	1.25
17 " Freight on goods	2.05
" Cartage	.25
" Apples	.10
19 " Contribution	.10
20 " Fare to Canandaigua	.75

21	" Horse hire	3.00
	" F. M for watch	22.50
22	" Fare	.75
	" Papers	.25
24	" Maple Sugar	.37
	Paid mending satchel	.15
27	" Boots & slippers	9.00
	" Blacking	.25
	" Books	2.13
28	" Bridgeman	50.00
	" School books	2.00
	" cartage	.50
		163.93

Page 95

Amount brought up	163.93
29 Paid fare to Meadville	7.75
" Cartage	1.00
" Coloring Coal	2.00
30 " Breakfast Elmira	.75
31 " Bill at Meadville	3.00
" Map	.25
" Fare to Oil Ciry	1.35
" Balance of Co. share	157.00
" Mrs. Page for board	24.00
Apr. 3rd Lent Layman	100.00
4th Paid for Map	10.00

5th " Board		7.50
6th " Ferriage		.30
7th " Lemons		.25
10th " Fare to Meadville		1.35
" Lunch		.50
Paid fair to Cleveland		4.00
" Supper		.50
" Fare to Columbus		5.75
		$48418

Page 96

Amount brought over	484.18
Apr.11 Paid for Breakfast	.75
" Papers & apples	.25
" Fare to Cleveland	4.50
12th " Bill at American	2.75
" Fare to Meadville	3.50
" Linen HJK	.75
" Lunch	.50
" Fare to Oil City	1.35
15th " Ferriage & raft ride	.45
" Eatables & paper	.75
18th " Fruit	.50
19th " Board at Sheriff	2.50
" Fare to Elmira	8.90
" Dinner	1.00
" Papers & Fruit	.20

20th	"Fare to Penn Yan	1.40
	" Collars	.25
	" Paper	.10
21st	" W. R. Long & Co.	5.40
		51998

Page 97

Apr.	Amount brought over	51998
21st	Paid for Book	2.00
	" Fruit for family	.60
	" Cartage	.25
	" Cravat	1.00
24th	" Fare to Canandaigua	.75
	" Horse & buggy	2.00
	" Fare to Penn Yan	1.13
25th	" Wife	70.00
	" Collars	.50
26th	" Fare to Meadville	7.75
27th	" Bill at Elmira	1.75
	" Book	1.75
	" Breakfast	.75
	" Papers	1.15
	" Fare to O. City	1.35
28th	" Edding Tool	30.00
	" Board & tickets	2.00
	" Lime & hauling	1.00
		650.71

Page 98

Apr. Amount Brought over	650.71
29th Paid fare to F's & back	.70
" A. J. Watkins	200.00
" Eddington	35.40
Paid L. Munger	100.17
" Lemons & paper	.25
" Contribution	.10
	987.28

May 1st

Paid expenses on box for Cherry Run	1.50
" W. H. S. Rent	125.00
" Winsor Bro. C.R.	57.42
" For board & tickets	10.00
" " Bolts & P&S	.60
" " Fare to Frak C.R.	.70
" Ferriage	.10
" Dinner	1.00
" Sand Pump for C. R.	7.00
	20332

Page 99

Amount brought up	20332
May 3rd Deposited in Bank	600.00
4th Paid cartage to Cherry Run	1.00
5th " O. L. Munger	100.00
" Lambertson	400.00

6th " Interest on G's note	10.00
" for belt Panther Run	1.13
" Paper Since May 1st	.30
7th " Contribution	.10
8th " Meal Tickets	5.00
Paid Edington	35.00
" Bridge Tickets	.50
" Telegraph to L. M.	2.70
" Fox & Co. Engine	1700.00
" Blandy for Fixture	37.05
" Robson bill for P.C.	30.84
" for S. P. Pulley C. R.	3.25
" Fruit	.50
10th Paid for Horse Hire	4.00
Over	3134.59

Page 100 - 1865

Amount Brought Over	3134.59
May 10th Toll & Paper	.15
12th Paid Freight Bill C. R.	37.85
" Record of Deed P. R.	2.50
" Dinner	1.00
" Fare from & to Frank	.70
" Fruit & Papers	.75
PS. 13th Davis & Marguis	275.00
Paid Frank Gibbs	10.00
" Horse Hire	3.00

	" Steel & Fuse P & S	2.20
	" Crackers	.30
14th	" Meal Tickets	5.00
15th	" Dinner at Franklin	.75
	" Fare to & From Franklin	.70
	Paid Revenue Stamps	.50
	" Papers	.25
17th	" Copperas	.15
	" Bell for C. R.	1.25
	" Fruit & Toll	.70
		3577.34

Page 101 – 1865

Amount Brought over	3577.34
18th Paid Fugle C.R.	20.00
" Meal Tickets	3.00
" Bridge "	1.00
" Telegram	1.65
" Sugar	.56
	3605.55
19th Cash on Hand	7.42
	$3612.97

Page 102

Cash on hand May 20th, 1865

	7.42
24th Recd. Orett	20.00
30th " "	30.00

June 3rd Received of L. Munger		50.00
7th " of O. L. Munger		5.00
18th " Bank		2.00
July 2nd Orett paid back		6.82

Page 103 – 1865

May 24th Paid for Meal Tickets		5.00
25th " " Steel		4.75
" " Pistol Car		1.50
" Papers since 15th		.50
" Ferriage		.10
" Fare to Mead		1.30
" to Elmira		7.55
Fare to Penn Yan		1.40
June 3rd Paid for repairing boots		1.50
" " Watch		.50
" Wife		50.00
5th " Ida's tuition		5.50
May 31st Bill at Elmira		1.75
Dinner at Meadville		1.00
Paid for Photographs		1.00
" " Lemons		.25
" " Papers		.25
June Fare to Meadville		7.75
Paid for Supper at Elmira		.75
Breakfast at Meadville		.75

Page 104

June 20th I. Nugent Cr.

By ½ day's work N.A.

21st by 1 day's work

Davis & Marquis Cr.

20th To 3 ½ days on Bull Wheel

24th Nugent, Adams & Graham

One day each to O. City

Nugent 21st to 24th, 4 days

27th to July 1st, 5 days.

Page 105 – 1865

	Amount brought over	$9315
	June 7th Paid fare to O. City	1.35
	" Papers	.15
	" Gibbs	10.50
	" Telegram	1.98
11th	" Doctor	1.00
	" Prescription	1.25
	" Telegram	1.00
	" Postage Stamps	.75
	" Syrup & Bread	.45
	" Berries	.35
	" Papers	.15
18th	" Meal Tickets	1.00
	" Medicines	.50

	" Toll & Papers	.20
20th	" Bridge Tickets	.10
	" Berries	.35
24th	" Two Bundles of Straw	1.00
26th	" Tin Pail	.60
Paid	Milk	.30

Page 106

June 26th Paid Lean & A. Packing		.80
	" Bridge Tickets	.15
27th	" Milk	.10
	" Meal Tickets	1.00
	" Lemons	.60
	" Suspenders	.90
	" Sugar	.50
	" Castings	5.00
	" Hauling	2.65
	" Freight	3.00
	" Hasp	.50
	" Bridge Tickers	.10
June	" Doctor	4.00
	" Prescription	.80
	" Meal Tickets	5.50
	" Padlock	.75
	" Hat	.45

Page 107

Meal Tickets	5.00

Postage Stamps	1.00
July 20th Milk since date	1.60
Watch guard	.25
23rd Meal Tickets	5.00

Page 107 & 108 – **Note: These pages are blank.**

Page 109

Cady Supr of B. Class

S. D. Howard barrowed the jars from Little Yates.

<u>May 8th per L. Lowell</u>

Length of belt for Richmond engine 35 ½ feet.

Diameter of Pitman Crank 2 5/16 inches

Key seat 5/8 inches

Page 110

May 6, Saturday

Present G. M. Munger's note at Lumberton's Bank & take up his pay interest.

With money from Horing & Easton pay self $150.00

George Hess for coal & work. Pay Berlin, Burnes, Hadley & Pegdrick.

Paid for O. L. Munger & Co.

For plank	1.72
Rich Counsel & Tom Raften	82.00

O. L. Munger No. 19

Paid for irons	10.00
" " nails	1.40
	100.12

Page 111

John Lovette

Greenville Bond Co. Ill.

See farm of 40 acres 5 miles south of the village, ascertain its value.

Note: At the bottom of this page is a note that is written upside down:

At Salineville, Ohio is a coal bank containing 320 acres owned by Mr. Kirk & offered for $170 per acre cash, Crawford & Co., Chamberlain & ------

Coal bank 1mile south corner of Saline on the west side of R.R.

Page 112

Agent of Daniel Rufner

Geo. Runnion corner of Central Avenue & Seventh St.

Feb 24th Expenses to P. Y. & c.

Fare 2 ways	2.80
" from Elmira to Oil City	10.55
Breakfast at Meadville	.75
Expenses to Mercer & back	10.50
Board at Sheriff House	1.50
	26.10
	87.40
	113.50

Page 113 **Note: This page was written upside-down.**

Stop at Conner's & ask for Steel's Survey. The track reaches from Will's to Jordon on Elk & running north to Pocatalico, 14, 000 acres. Oil is said to exist. Straight & Green Creeks. John Frail is a gent on Song Ridge.

B. Parker Account

Walter Holt West Henrietta S.B. Lork Westfield, N.Y.

Nature & the Supernatural

By H. Bushnell

Christ & his Salvation

Page 114

From Parkersburg to Wheeling

By River .96

By Rail via Grafton 2.04

Wheeling to Pittsburgh

Danial S. Printuss

Rome Geo. May 5 5 Inf.

Mrs. M. M. Richardson

Gallipolis, Ohio

Page 115

Expenses to Kanawha

Jan 16th, 1865 – Paid for ticket to Cincinnati	17.20
Paid for Breakfast at Buffalo	1.00
" " Sleeping Car	1.50
" " Passage to Gallipolis	7.00
" " Stationary	.75
" " Passage up Kanawha	2.50
" " Bill at Charleston	2.50
" " " " Malden	.50
" Koontz	1.70
Paid for Ferry	.20
" " Supper at Saloon	1.50
" Bill at S. & W.	5.00
" " " Mrs. Jacobs	1.00
" " Straton's	1.50

"	" Higenbothem's	.80
"	" Ferrying	.25
	" Slack & White	13.50
	" Bill only Crook	2.50
		60.90

Page 116

Fare to Parkersburg	8.50
Bill at Parkersburg	9.50
" " Bellaire	1.50
Fare to Ravenna	7.50
Bill at Wellsville 27.20	.50
" for Horses	8.00
	35.20
Bill at Oil City	6.00
Bill at Meadsville	3.00
" Supper	.75
Fare to Elmira	7.55
	52.50
	60.90
	113.40
Breakfast	.75
60.90	114.15
27.20	99.20
7.55	12.95
.75	23.20

96.40   58.15

 2.80   64.00 + 3.50   26.10

99.20   3.15

          B 200 + 300   87.40

Page 117

Feb 14th, 1865 For Turkey Run

Paid for Fare from Meadville to Cleveland	3.75
Breakfast	.75
Fare to Columbus	4.50
" " Cincinnati	4.00
Supper & Bus	1.50
Expenses in Cincinnati	.75
Fare & Portage & c.	9.90
Breakfast	.75
Dinner	.75
To Meadville	4.80
" Oil City	3.75
Billet at Oil City	4.00
Fare to Meadville	3.00
Dinner	1.00
	23.20
	113.40
	155.60

Page 118

P.O. Box 131 O. City

4 Bolts 5 ½ Lory

4 ½ diam.   24850

                    9953

                   14900

L Tax 52.65

COLONEL JAMES CLAY RICE - HARPER'S WEEKLY 28 MAY 1864

DURING THE FIGHTING AT LITTLE ROUND TOP ON JULY 2, 1863 BRIGADE COMMANDER, COLONEL STRONG VINCENT WAS MORTALLY WOUNDED AND COL. RICE OF THE 44TH NEW YORK, ASSUMED COMMAND OF THE 3RD BRIGADE, 1ST DIVISION, V CORPS AND LED IT FOR THE REMAINDER OF THE BATTLE OF GETTYSBURG. FOR HIS SERVICE AT GETTYSBURG, RICE WAS PROMOTED TO BRIGADIER GENERAL OF VOLUNTEERS ON AUGUST 17, 1863. IN MARCH, 1864 GENERAL RICE WAS IN COMMAND OF THE 2ND BRIGADE, 4TH DIVISION, V CORPS, WHICH HE LED INTO ACTION AT THE BATTLE OF THE WILDERNESS. RICE WAS MORTALLY WOUNDED AT THE BATTLE OF SPOTSYLVANIA COURTHOUSE ON MAY 10, 1864; HIS THIGH WAS SHATTERED BY A RIFLE BALL, WHICH NECESSITATED AMPUTATION OF HIS LEG. HE DIED SHORTLY AFTER THE PROCEDURE. WHEN THE SURGEON ASKED HIM ON WHICH SIDE HE WOULD REST MORE COMFORTABLY, HE REPLIED, "TURN ME OVER THAT I MAY DIE WITH MY FACE TO THE ENEMY." HE WAS BURIED AT ALBANY RURAL CEMETERY, MENANDS, NEW YORK, IN SECTION 42, PLOT 11.

The Letters

In introducing the Kesterson collection of letters for Captain Munger it is important to realize that his letters pick up where his diary in the Kesterson collection left off. Captain Munger's last diary entry is dated May 12, 1863. His letter grouping begins with a password for the day addressed to Colonel Rice of the 44th New York Infantry, dated March 21, 1863. Unfortunately, all of the letters that Captain Munger received from his wife and friends have been lost to time, and in this case, this is the only known documentation of his exploits as a soldier to the end of his discharge. I have endeavored to maintain Munger's writing style and intent. I have only modified the text where it needed proper spelling or punctuation. I have also modified Munger's paragraphs, as many of these letters are one long paragraph. Aside from these modifications, Munger's letters appear as he wrote them and his first-person voice is preserved for the reader to interoperate. It is also believed that there were other letters in this collection that were lost with time and that these will probably be lost forever unless they are discovered at some future date.

Note: In a try-folded note addressed to Col. Rice 44th New York Volunteers we have the following note.

Col. Rice

44th N.Y. Vol.

Head Qrs 3d Brigade

March 21, 1863

Countersign

"Vienna"

Offical

W. Jewett

Lieut & A.A. DE

Camp near Falmouth, Va. Mar. 22, 63

My Dear Wife and Daughter,

    I recd. your letter Friday also containing one from Layman, I am sorry to hear you are all so poorly, the health and hope you will soon be better instead. L's letter to me last says Ida is much better at which I rejoice and that his family he thinks are a little better. I recd. a letter from Nettie saying Abigail was sick. I wrote to L the day after I wrote to you which you probably saw. I would like your opinion on the subject contained in it. I don't know as anything can be done in that direction, all is good now if accomplished it would probably take me south unless I got into a regiment of New York conscripts. I believe I told you Fred was appointed Sergent to date from January 31st and Kinner as first Serg. from same date. Ida, I suppose, has received her letter on this and hope to get my pay. Those Kisses were very <u>Sweet</u>.

It has stormed here the last two days. Snowed, but it is nearly gone, consequently muddy. I have no news to write but that just a line would not be unacceptable and my passion for writing has fully returned. This is the ninth since I returned. I do sympathize deeply with Graham. Comfort him all you can. I wish you would ask

Beam to send me in the next letter a black neck tie such as he wears. He will know what I want and you may pay him or he may wait till I come. I think finally you had better pay him. I am studying hard but cannot confine my mind to study as I could once. 2 O. clock P.M. the clouds have cleared away finally and the sun is shining brightly but if I were not a soldier I should think it dull and lonely. It is too muddy to walk and I am tired of staying in my tent, but tomorrow will bring work enough in drills and to keep me busy. I was obliged to be out in the storm and got some wet. _____ is trying hard to get an office in a colored regiment. Holmes and Cleveland are aiding him. This storm will increase the mud so that we cannot well move for a week or so, the roads were getting good. The bugle sounds for meeting and I will go. I have this moment recd a letter from Nettie saying she is disappointed in obtaining that school at Boynton and proposes to go to Michigan with her sister and wants me to furnish her the means to go. Things here are looking like an early move, we to have two reviews and one inspection this week. Today white gloves are ordered for the Reg. and with the new fatigue suit presented the men look finely. Kisses as sweet as they can be; your affectionate Husband and Father,

B. Munger

Camp near Falmouth, Va. 11 P.M. Mar. 25, 1863.

My Dear little Birdie,

I believe it is your turn to have a letter. I write so often lately I hardly know who to direct to. I am officer of the day for the fourth time since my return just two weeks. I think they intend to make me pay for lost time. Well, perhaps you would like knowing what an officer of the day has to do. So, I will tell you what I have done today and that will give you some idea of the duties. First at 8 & ½ O clock A.M. we have guard mounting (& that is quite a show) the night previous the first sergeant of each company selects the men for guard & tells them. At the time appointed the bugle sounds & the sergeants call out the men detailed for guard, they form in the Co. streets in four ranks & at another signal march out to the color line, then they form in two ranks, are inspected by the Adjutant and officer of the guard & when this is finished I (as officer of the day) step to the front of the center of the guard behind the Adjutant and facing the guard he commands, "Present arms" then turns to me, salutes & says, "Sir your guard is formed." Returning the salute I say, "March the guard by the flank to their posts." I have forgotten to tell you that (the) guards were dressed in their new uniforms with white gloves & I with sash & sword. That being done the officer of the previous day gives me any orders he may have & reports to the Col. for further orders. Today as it had been raining hard, during the night there was nothing particular to tell afternoon, then I took twenty men with shovels and three teams (& sometime I must tell you about mule teams) to clear up & carry off the refuse that has accumulated during the winter. You have heard I presume that soldiers are proverbially lazy & ours are not an exception. So, I told them I knew soldiers were apt to overwork themselves unless restrained, but that I should allow no such thing. They must take it moderately. They look at each other as much as to say, "He is an old one." And I had no trouble with laziness.

We worked till night and I had the pleasure of seeing a dress parade without practicing in it and it was a pretty sight. At dark, we have a countersign which is some word, usually the name of some city (I will enclose one in the form we receive it), it comes from headquarters and is given to every regiment. Tonight, ours did not come to us and after waiting till nine O'clock we went to another regiment and obtained it. After dark no one can pass without having this word. When a man comes along to a sentinel the sentinel says, "Who comes there!" The man replies, "A friend" with the countersign. He says, "Advance friend and give the countersign." If it is right he lets him pass. If not, or he has none, he sends him to the guard house. It is now most 12 O'clock. I have been out several times to see if I can pass them. Some I could as they knew me; others would stop me but very reluctantly, while others would do it with a vengeance. Once I got sent to the guard house & the Corporal sent with me was one of my own men. At 12 we expected the Brigade officer to make what is called the Guard Rounds & I am to set up till after he has been here or I must visit the guard at least once after 12.

It is now just that hour & so away I go & will then go to bed & finish this another time.

Tuesday morning,

I have got through being officer of the day & will tell you something of myself as myself. In the first place, I am recovering from a severe cold & day before yesterday I had one of my old headaches of the worst sort but am about well now. Yesterday was a pretty day, a real Spring day, birds sing a little but not such as we have north. But peeping frogs of the old sort have been singing the last two evenings. It is raining again today, consequently unpleasant and Orett is Officer of the Guard today. That is different from officer of the day and harder work. Tell Uncle Syman I fear that we shall not be able to get Lts. pay for Orett till the 12th of the month the day assumed the duties of the office. If he had entered upon its duties as soon as appointed, he would have pay.

6 P.M. we have had one grand review this afternoon. Gens Hooker, Mead & Griffin were there. I suppose it was a grand affair. I had little chance to see & then I am so much behind the other officers in knowledge of tactics that it mortifies me exceedingly. Today I made a mistake that spoils my comfort and the tents of the old regiment are heard to bear. I am resolved to get posted or resign. The majority of the officers who sneer, in all modesty I

consider my inferiors in all save military knowledge & it is humiliating to be criticized by such men but enough of this. I suppose we shall soon be on the move it is that next week but we cannot tell. I have written very often since my return partly because I cannot probably write much after I start. Our Col. is now absent in Baltimore.

Charles W. Taylor has recd his discharge papers today & M. F. Graham returned to the Co. from Baltimore Hospital. I want my little Darling, you should remember all I said to you when I was with you, for I do feel so anxious you should be a good girl & if you live grow to be a model woman. Tell me little One in your next letter if you have any trouble in being as good as you want to be if sometimes you don't fail when you want to be good! & maybe I can help you for I have felt just so. I am alone this evening the Lieuts. Kelly and Russel are visiting I guess & Lieut O.L. Munger is as I told you, Officer of the Guard and stays at the Guard house. I am so seldom alone I am glad of a little quiet. I can think better. I would love to dispense with two of my family very much. You must now kiss Mr. Graham for me & tell him I am very sorry for him & will write to him if we do not move too soon.

The officers are pretty noisy tonight and I think I can guess the cause O (my) little (Birdie) this is not a good place to live, "too wicked" but I must bid good bye & may God bless you & mother.

Your affectionate father & Husband

B. Munger

Camp near Falmouth Va. Apr 1st 1863

My Dear Wife and Daughter,

Although I wrote you a few days since the time of our moving appears to be so near I thought I would commence a letter & write as events transpired. We have no knowledge to where we go. Tomorrow was fixed as the day of our start but the recent storm has made it necessary to postpone the move. I will now give you extracts from diary since I last wrote. Monday Mar. 30 was visited by Capt. Sloan who is located about three miles from here. He says about two thirds of his Co. whose term of enlistment expires next month will reenlist. Thursday Mar 31 stormed since midnight, snow and rain. Cleared off toward night and the snow mostly melted. Raymond returned to us and Co. Rice is back. Wednesday April 1 the morning is clear, cold and windy. Col. Rice has just communicated the fact that the orders suspending leaves and furloughs has been revoked and we accordingly sent in Geo. W. Wings.

Orett's promotion prevents him from obtaining a furlough but he may get a leave by and by, he is well, Fred also, and all the boys with whom you are acquainted. We have been inspected today and the men appeared well. They were never in as good as trim but a march of a hundred miles will take the shine off us I suppose. Old Billy Crescaden received his discharge today and will leave tomorrow.

We have now been in this camp about 4 ½ months and leaving it especially for a march seems like leaving home. I expect we shall have a rough time. Ever this reaches you I suppose you will be keeping house and if you are well enough to do your work enjoy yourself better than to have no care. Although my cares are many and annoying yet I would not be without them to occupy my mind to bear with fortitude whatever may occur. I feared you schooled yourself sufficiently to bear unmoved the chances and incidents of war. You must not expect too much but prepare your mind for the dark side.

I don't mean that you should feel gloomy and sad but the reverse, meet cheerfully or at least partially the events as they transpire. And to that little darling all I can say is be good, be good always, love truth, love God, don't be selfish with being ordinary but excel in goodness and God will ever bless you. Since my arrival, I have written to every friend who corresponds with me, and I think about twenty letters. This is probably the last I should write from this place.

I have received a ring for Ida presented by Robert Shipley and made by him and Kinner from a beef bone. It is with the tools he had a great labor. You must thank him in your next letter. I will enclose it in this.

April 2nd, the prospects of an immediate move are stopped to have blown over and now it is that we shall stay some days so that you may hear from me again from here. Still it is uncertain. Today is mild but windy for the two weeks it has rained for a day or so and then cleared off and blow a hurricane till the ground was pretty dry and then rained again. We have no drill today but are preparing for a Corps inspection. In other words, we are having a general house cleaning.

I'll tell you a little incident showing some of the little annoyances I have. I have two boys who have been sick a long time and are just able to get around, one with diarrhea and the other rheumatism. I went to the Dr. yesterday and asked if something could not be done more. He seemed interested at once and came over to their quarters. On a close examination one was found to be dirty and ordered to the hospital, the Dr. remarking he'd be damned if he would not give him one washing. The boy did not want to go and was allowed to remain. In conversation, I told the Dr. his tent-mates were not of the right sort, and that I had some difficulty in making them keep clean, that one of them had notified me that day by appearing on inspection with a dirty face. I talked with him just as I would with a brother. Shortly after as I was writing in my tent the Col's Orderly came in and said the Col. wanted to see me. I went to his tent and after a little hesitation he said that he learned from the surgeon that my Co. was filthy and proceeded to instruct as to the responsibilities/duties of captains in relation to their men. He talked well, said few understood the duties and responsibilities of a Capt. Who strove to do his duty and etc. I asked him if the Dr. said my Co. was filthy or that I had filthy men in my Co. He said he spoke of two particularly, one sick and who was out at inspection duty.

I suppose I did not feel some indignant but I went straight to the Dr. and said, "Dr. did you report to Col. Rice that my company was filthy?" "Why no Captain." said he. I told him the Col. had just sent for me and said that was the fact and described the case we had conversed about during the day. The Dr. was embarrassed and said he would relate the whole conversation which was that the Medical Inspector complemented this Regt. for having the cleanest quarters of any in the Division and the men were generally clean, that there were some exceptions as for instance I found said Dr. to have one or two men in Co. C today that are filthy. The Dr. protested that he had no idea of injuring me or the Co. and did not think the Col. would mention it. But all the explanation did not remove the impression that the smallest circumstance is seized to bring this Co. to censure. The afternoon is very fine but windy.

We are all in good health. As an evidence, O and myself were weighed this afternoon. He weighs 132 Lbs. and I 173 by our Commissary scales. 155 was my average weight at home. I think I may in time get so reconciled to soldiering as to do quite well. I want to gain 2 pounds more then I will be satisfied for that part. You say I am in your debt as to letters. My book shows a different state of things. I have written you and Ida five besides this and have received four from you, one last night containing necktie suits me and etc.

Yours affectionate husband and father,

B. Munger

Camp near Falmoth, Va. April 6, 1863

My Dear Wife and Baby,

I recd. your letter today and will commence my answer tonight as tomorrow will probably be a busy day. I wrote you on the 2nd inst. so I have little news to write. Today we have been to witness a cavalry review by President Lincoln and Gen. Hooker. It was a splendid affair. Some estimated the cavalry at ten thousand. The review took place on the ground on which our army stood the first day of the battle of Fredericksburg. It brought up some thoughts not pleasant especially when the artillery fired the salute to the president. I was prepared to see a homely man but Abe exceeded my expectations. He looks pale and care worn.

Today Orett was mustered into the U.S. service as 2nd Lieut. to date from Jan. 31st so that the question of pay is settled. He receives pay as Lt. from that date. The Paymaster has not yet called on us and we are getting anxious to see him for we cannot all raise the dollars and that will not last long. We were ordered to report for picket tomorrow at 9 A.M., then countermanded and ordered to prepare for Corps review by the President and Gen. in command, Hooker, but now at 9 ½ P.M. it rains hard and has for some time so perhaps the review will be given up and we go picketing. I'll stop till tomorrow and see how things work.

Thursday morning – The review is countermanded and I am going on picket. Kelly goes and Orett stays. It is muddy but mild and clear. I have not another moment.

Good bye,

As ever,

B. Munger

GEORGE A. CUSTER AND GENERAL ALFRED PLEASONTON ON HORSEBACK – FALMOUTH, VA, APRIL 1863

Library of Congress Prints and Photographs Division

Camp near Falmoth, Va. April 14, 1863

My Dear Wife and Baby,

Yesterday the cavalry connected with the army moved up the river. Tomorrow morning, we start with 8 days' rations. The men are to carry 5 days' rations of Pilot Bread (hard tack), coffee, sugar and salt. 3 days will be carried by the baggage train. Officers are the whole 8 (in impossibility). Today all is bustle, all superfluant clothing and c is to be sent back to Washington.

In short everything of baggage is to be reduced to the lowest possible figure. Of course, we know nothing of our destination. My opinion is that we are to cross the river and as military men say feel of the enemy. I think the calculation is to return but can't say positively. The boys are well and feeling well. My health is excellent. We hope to be paid today as there is not one dime in our mess. We paid out the last cent yesterday. I sent for 20 lb of butter I will probably be lost if sent now. I think I shall send one blanket to washing as I shall not need it here anymore. I shall not mail this today but keep it till the last moment.

5 P.M. We have just recd an order that the officers must carry in addition to their 8 days' rations, their blankets and tents. It looks like said orders and rumors are conflicting and indefinite. No one seems to know just what is to be done, and I would be surprised if we did not move. We, that is our mess, are in a fix, no money to buy our provisions with and none in camp that can be barrowed but I don't feel much trouble about it for if I don't buy it I shan't have to carry it. Our Paymaster don't yet make his appearance although other paymasters have paid some regts in this brigade.

Thursday morning April 16, yesterday we had the heaviest rain storm of the season. It was rather a blue day. Our tent leaked, the floor or ground was covered with water and most of the day we were without fire but we lived and did nicely. We're busy in making out reports. In the evening, I had an invitation to call on the Col. and lady. Had a pleasant talk, more like home than anything.

I have experienced here no one else was here so it was a sort of a family visit. Remember especially to all friends inquiring after me, particularly Mr. and Mrs. Miller family, Graham and family, and Fannie. Tell Fannie, I would be pleased to receive a line from her. A Kiss for Katy, Maty, Miener and as many others as call for them. The weather is clearing off and the world looks more pleasant. I am still ignorant of our destination, but we are to leave this place not to return.

Love and Kisses,

Your affectionate Husband and Father,

B. Munger

The Paymaster has not been here and I wish you would send me twenty dollars <u>Green Backs</u> by mail.

THE 1862 UNITED STATES TREASURY NOTE WAS OFTEN CALLED A GREENBACK DUE TO THE COLOR OF GREEN INK USED IN THE PRODUCTION OF THE NOTE. THIS NOTE'S PRODUCTION BROUGHT ABOUT THE NATIONAL BANKING ACT OF 1863.

Camp near Falmoth, Va. April 26, 1863

My Dear Wife and Child,

It is Sunday and a clear day with high wind. The camp is very still. Orett is asleep not being well. This is the 4th day he has complained. Today I think he is a little better. Diarrhea is the trouble. He has not been on duty the last two days. Kelly is also asleep (which I do not regret) and taking all things it <u>is</u> <u>as</u> <u>still</u> <u>as</u> <u>Sunday</u>.

I am not quite well today with the same complaint as Orett and it weakened me very much as I have little appetite, but I am still on duty and hope to bear it though. It is fortunate we are not on a march. I think I will be well again in a day or two and Orett also. We have had another Virginia rains cleared of yesterday morning. Lt. Col. Conner has this moment returned and that makes a stir. He was wounded in the last battle you will recollect and has not been with the Regt. since. James Kelly and Jack Wickham have been here today and Kelly relates a story which if true shows how the news has reached the Rebs heretofore. One of our soldiers at Falmoth went to the shop of a citizen to get a book mended and while waiting heard a faint ticking of a clock but faster his suspicions were aroused so that he gave information to the Provost Marshall who found in the cellar a telegraph apparatus and Operator in full blast. The wire hid under the surface of the ground and sunk in the bed of the river, so that our plans, so far as made known here were at once safely transmitted to the Rebs. It is said this discovery has something to do with this delay but the weather alone is sufficient for that. But if this story is true the whole plan of march and attack will be abandoned. I am not in a writing mood today and as my head aches too. I will stop awhile.

I have been to Col. Conner, he is looking well. I believe he is not restored to the service. I wish you would ask Layman to send in the next the enlistment papers of Sylvanus Eaton, they will be found in the Japanned trunk at the store. I have just a little from Nellie, she is in Brockport, intends to leave for Michigan soon. Zunna is at Brockport sick with chill and fever. Perhaps it is not best to stir you up with any more reports of moving. We expect an order tomorrow or next day but I can't say whether we shall get it or not.

The army is not living as well as formally. So many orders to move disadvantage the Commissary Department. Stoneman's Cavalry have not yet returned but we do not know positively where they are, perhaps near Warrenton. It was supposed here that one of the objects of that move was to draw the Rebs off up the river while we should cross way below. But I think if they had been successful they would have crossed the river, gained the rail road between Fredericksburg and Richmond, destroyed the bridges and joined us near Urbanna. Perhaps that is all a guess. Remember me kindly to friends especially to Mr. Miller's family, Graham and family and don't feel troubled about my health.

Your aff' Husband and father,

B. Munger

In an undated note:

Monday 7 A.M. We have marching orders for 11 O'clock. I feel better this morning but not well, hope I shall stand it. Ida, enclosed you will find a peach blossom from the sunny South. Orett is better and will march. Although we are mostly ready there is much to see to this morning and yourself to be worried about me and may God bless you both. Good bye your affectionate H & F,

B. Munger

Banks Ford, Va. May 29, 1863

My Dear Daughter and Wife,

This must be considered Ida's property and you will see as the boys say, "We don't live where we do now", but have moved. Yesterday till after dinner all was quiet on the Rappahannock but a little after there was a rumor that we were to move, which I did not believe it. At 1 ½ the Brigade bugle sounded "Strike tents" without any order, so we paid little heed to it. At 2 we were summoned to the Col's tent and told to be ready in one hour to move with all our baggage and tents probably to Banks Ford. We started at 3 ½. We have been in our new camp 8 days and had not finished our improvements and did not like to leave but they did not consult our wishes.

When an unexpected order to march is given it is a question of some interest to us where and for what we are going. I am trying to be entirely unmoved at anything and this I had succeeded but caught myself feeling <u>some</u> anxiety but not much. We reached this place about a mile from the ford just before dark at 6 or 8 miles from the old camp, some tired for it was hot. We lay down in the pine woods without tents, took our supper and I cut some cedar boughs for a bed and had just laid down when Capt. Laribee came up and said, "Captain I've had news for you." I told him I was ready for anything. "Well," said he. "I want you to go on picket and take your Company." I told him I would be ready in 10 minutes. It was a beautiful moonlit night. Two other Co.'s went but both only as large as our one. We started under the lead of Col. Rice and a guide went a quarter of a mile. The two companies were filed to the left and we were ordered to march on to a house and lie down in the rear of it and keep perfectly still for we would be in 50 rods of the enemy's lines. The house was in a beautiful spot and in the moonlight, did look magnificent but it was deserted.

We laid down and soon I was confident I heard something coming and a cavalryman rode out of the bush and I went out to meet him. He said the Capt. of cavalry wished me to march my Co. to the river. It was just exciting enough to be to be pleasant after getting to the river, 8 men with Lt. Munger, Sgt. Kinner and myself moved on with a guide and the remained with Lt. Kelly laid down as a reserve. After proceeding a little further Lt. took 4 of the men to the right up the river and I, the Sergt. and the other 4 down. A cavalryman was on duty said they had been there a week, that the pickets did not fire on each bother but that a large force was over there, probably under Longstreet.

I put 2 men on his post with instructions not to fire unless the Rebs did or should attempt to cross with arms in their hands and not to converse with them and if anything transpired to let me know immediately. I was directed to establish a new post 20 yards down the river as the best point I could find. The brush was so thick I could not see ten feet in front and poked around till I was tired but found no place that suited me so I took up with a poor one. I was in easy range of their rifles but they were good and did not fire after seeing all was right. I went back with Lt. Munger to the reserve and laid down about 11 but the insects and ants crawled all over me and made one nervous and I did not sleep well, got up between 3 and 4 and went around to visit the post and discovered what I could of the enemy. The country is not fertile but very romantic. I enjoyed 2 hours very much. It has been said the Reb picket would fire on officers and I thought I would see, so I stood out on a bank so that they could see I was an officer but they evidently thought that I was too good a fellow to shoot. I had a good bath in the river. Our picket was relieved and we returned to camp and I am now curled up against a tree writing to my little one. You perhaps will want to know what we came out here for, so do I, but they won't tell me. It is said to guard the ford permanently and perhaps it is time but it was said our Reg. only would be stationed here. The 83rd Pa. would guard Richardson's Ford and the 16th Mass. and the 20th

Maine would guard Kelly's Ford. That all looks so reasonable I could easily believe it for it is much more sensible than lying idly in camp and keeping cavalry here when they are so useful for other purposes, but today Gen. Mead is here with one or two batteries and it is said the whole Corps is coming and our pioneers are ordered to the front to dig rifle pits so it is difficult to tell but being a Yankee and having one eye open and I <u>guess</u> we are to stay and the whole Corps is not coming but a sufficient artillery force to assist us in keeping the Rebs on their side of the Jordon.

Mrs. Rice just came to ask me to fix her tent so it would shade her better, she being alone and I have been sitting in her tent and had a pleasant talk. After dinner orders to move camp to the front and we did so to a mean place. The regiment is divided and the right wing in which we are, guards the dam and the left wing of the ford.

We were ordered to dig a strong line of rifle pits in front of our line but as we have a canal along the shore so we are going to cut the bank and drain the canal into the river and use it as a rifle pit and as it was at my suggestion, I am ordered to do it. Night is the time chosen for, as the Rebs are in easy rifle range. They may make it "uncomfortable" for us. So, at 9 O'clock I took a squad (of 12) men and commenced work.

The Rebs did not interfere with us, though we expected it. Worked till 2 and I was so sleepy having been up most of the previous that I would go to sleep standing. I did not succeed in draining off all the water but think I can at another trial. We see a great many Rebs and although against orders our boys talk with them, it is said. They are sharp on both sides. Reb asks, "Where is fighting Joe?" Our boy answers, "Gone to Stonewall's funeral." And so on. Some of their jokes not being polite. My opinion is some party of this army is going forth but I do not know, not this Corps probably.

Today is Saturday, May 30. I did not give the date when I ought. The Field and Staff officers move their camp further to here so that the Reg. has three camps and the poor line officers don't live anywhere. Our mail facilities are not good, and it will probably take letters at least one day more to reach you. I am trying to rest today for I am very tired and am aware that I am writing a dry letter but will do better sometime if I live. You need not feel at all troubled about me. I am doing well: love much love to all but the main portion to yourselves. Husband and Father – B. Munger

Manassas Junction June 16 (1863)

Dear Wife,

We reached this place yesterday noon. There is now no fight expected here. Yesterday there was a prospect we are bound to Centerville, I suppose and perhaps into Maryland and can't now tell you of our march. However, yesterday will be remembered, many were sun struck and several. I came so near failing that one mile more would have finished me, I think. It was a day of extreme heat. This morning I feel better. Took 10 grains of quinine yesterday and am going through if passable. I think there is no prospect of a fight for sometime I think. Orett stands it well. Ford fell out the first night but has since felt better. Yesterday we started with 39 men and have 18 when we arrived here. This morning is much cooler and I hope we shall stand it better.

I have not received mail since Saturday and don't know when I shall send this but will be ready, perhaps will add some tonight.

4 P.M. we are still here in camp, but the most of the army has moved on, all I think but our division. I am feeling much better and feel now able to march which I suppose we shall do tonight. I am feeling rather sad today, perhaps in part owing to so many casualties yesterday. Very many were stricken down with heat, none in our Regiment but today a man at play injured his spine so as to be utterly helpless. Another was bitten by a poisonous insect or reptile and is numb and I have seen today a worse object still, one of the Diarrheas. I will not describe his case.

Men die so easily, and in such a variety of ways and seems as if powder and ball were unnecessary. But I will not distress you by another.

We are within 3 miles of Bull Run battlefield. It is naturally a pleasant place. I would much like to visit the field but cannot. Yesterday we expected to act a new play on it but probably shall not. It now looks as if we were to take a walk into Maryland by way of Washington.

We have no mail since Saturday and have heard nothing from the <u>world</u> and I do not know when I can send this. I am in hopes in this present trial the enemy will be soundly punished and I am glad the struggle did not take place here. The army has a dread of this place and cannot fight as well here as on a new field. You need not feel anxious about me. I shall do well enough and feel better soon. We all have our <u>blue</u> days.

Your affectionate Husband

B. Munger

Note: On the back of this letter Bennett Munger pens the following: "Near Centerville, June 17th 11 A.M. Well and on the march."

FEDERAL SOLDIERS AT CENTERVILLE, FAIRFAX COUNTY, VIRGINIA DURING THE CIVIL WAR

Library of Congress Prints and Photographs Division

This 44th New York Infantry envelope was recovered from Captain Bennett L. Munger's personal effects. The envelope contained the letter that Captain Munger sent home to his wife after the battle of Gettysburg. In the lower right hand corner is printed the word, "Camp" and then in very light pencil is written, "Near Gettysburg, Pa."

Near Gettysburg Pa. July 2

(1863)

My Dear Wife,

I sent a letter to Lyman from Hanover last night at 7 and at 8 we moved toward this place where fighting had been going on all day. Our troops said to have been the winners. We marched till 12.9 miles. We were rear guard and on such a march it is laborious duty. We laid down with (out) tents and as our baggage was in the wagons and they ordered to the rear, we had no tents or blankets but burrowed so as to get along. Aroused at 3 ½ and moved at 5, at 8 got into the vicinity of the town and after various moves laid down at this place at 10 A.M. and still remained 1 P.M. We are 2 miles east of the town. 6th Corps are said to be here and that we took 3,000 prisoners, 11 pieces of artillery, 7 battle flags yesterday and that one of the Lees is among the prisoners. There is but little fighting done so far. The reason I do not understand. The boys are very much worn out but only 2 have fallen out, Stroup and Henderson. Blistered feet are the order of the day and some are obliged to go barefoot.

Last night it was announced that McClellan was in command of the armies in place of Halleck and as the news was carried along the column and reached the different regiments their cheering could be heard first in one as far as we could hear and passed on. When it reached us the old 44th gave such a shout as they have not uttered since I have known there and on it went till it was lost in distance. I do not think it true but hope the army will think so till after this fight.

The fact that we are on northern soil almost inspires the men so that every counts one and a half at least I think I will fight with desperation. We have rested but one day since leaving Aldie. It is now 2 O'clock and the day seems a yawning eternity. There will probably be no fighting. It takes time to handle such an army but if the Rebs stand we <u>must</u> whip them here.

Oh, I hope this engagement will decide the struggle and in our favor. I need not say I am tired for that gives you little idea of our exhaustion. I can't give you details at present for I write under too great difficulties.

July 4th noon. We have had a desperate fight and we are victorious. We have suffered severely, 25 killed, 76 wounded and 8 missing in our regiment. 2 killed and 8 wounded in our company. I am sorry to say I am one of the wounded though slightly. I was lying on the ground, the ball struck my left thigh, just grazed it, passed up and to the right, struck my pocket knife checking the force and turning it a little so that it struck me in the left going but not penetrating the flesh. The bruise is severe but the only damage done lies in mortification. As the internal injury is considerable; I can walk some but am in a good deal of pain. I think there are 9 chances in my favor to 1 against me certainly if we can have care at present we are in the woods on the ground and nothing to do with. I'll write more if I can by and by.

B. Munger

On the same letter Munger writes:

6 ½ P.M. I feel a little better but we are still in uncomfortable quarters. I have not eaten a mouth full today. My stomach is out of order so that I cannot keep food down.

B. McElligott, Francis Griswold were killed yesterday. W. M. Norris knee wounded amputated above; M.F. Graham shot through breast from right to left just back of the bone, R.C. Phillips through the left shoulder. I think W. Smith in about the same place, J. Dansenburg through the left arm below the elbow. H. Houghton back of his head slightly and George W. Holbart thigh slightly. All the others here and well and behaved well enough to make their friends proud. The friends of the two killed I am not acquainted with, they were <u>true soldiers</u>. Orett has been down to see me today, 2 miles and F is well. Kinner loves to shoot Rebs.

(July) 5th Morning, I am not as quite as well this morning, hope to get to hospital soon. Our troops are successful. I have a chance to send this by a citizen. I will write when I can.

B. Munger

A VIEW OF LITTLE ROUND TOP AS IT APPEARED IN JULY OF 1863. NOTE THE HARSH TERRAIN, PROTRUDING ROCKS AND THE SPORADIC, TANGLED TREES THAT COVER THE RIDGE. THE 44TH NEW YORK WAS PLACED TO THE RIGHT AND ABOUT 100 FEET FROM THE TOP OF THE RIDGE.

THE OFFICERS OF THE 44TH NEW YORK INFANTRY WHO HELPED SAVE LITTLE ROUND TOP

Both Photographs by Timothy H. O'Sullivan - Library of Congress Prints and Photographs Division

Note: It would appear that Captain Munger was able to get a leave to go back home for a short period of time as witnessed by this letter where he is returning back to his regiment. Munger complains of depression and poor health in this letter to his wife and daughter.

No. 1 Bealeton Station August 19, 1863

My Dear Wife and Daughter,

I reached Elmira at 4 without incident, but I failed to find Dr. Wey or any of the officers of our Regiment and left at 5 1/2. I will not describe the journey but I failed to throw off the feeling of gloom that sometimes comes over me and to owe that I felt intensely sad don't express it <u>all</u>. But I lived, reached Baltimore at

7 and Washington at 10. My appetite was poor and I ate nothing but two tea cakes and a cup of coffee after I left home till 2 O'clock next day. Had the headache and felt blue generally. I wish I could control my feelings as well as I can their manifestation.

I met a member of our Regt. wounded in the first Fredericksburg fight in Washington who wanted to join the Regiment and could not without help and I assisted him and he helped me carry my valise. We cross over the Alexandria and took the cars at 4 on the ferry boat. I met a lady right from Gettysburg who had been out with the army two years as nurse, she has a son in the 6th Maine and remarks that her headquarters she has been on all the battlefields and in many cases help dress wounds right on the field. I helped her in getting a pass through to Warrenton where she is going to see her son who is sick, though her name is Mrs. Harriet Sinson.

(Captain Munger may have meant to use the surname, Simmons. There was a George F. Simmons who appeared on the roster of Co. K, 6th Maine Infantry. This may be the son referred to by the lady that Captain Munger helped get the pass to Warrenton.)

Reached Warrenton Junction all <u>right</u>. I see a writer in the Tribune thinks we need not look for the fall of Charleston at present and talks rather discouraging about it. I hope still to hear of its fall during the month. 150 conscripts were brought into our Brigade last night for the 83rd Pa. but some of them left before morning. The weather is now as cool certain if not cooler than with you when I was there, but has been much warmer than the night, average quite cool. It is almost 11 and I must close. Now keep up good courage and we will all be home someday yet.

Your affectionate

Husband & Father,

B. Munger

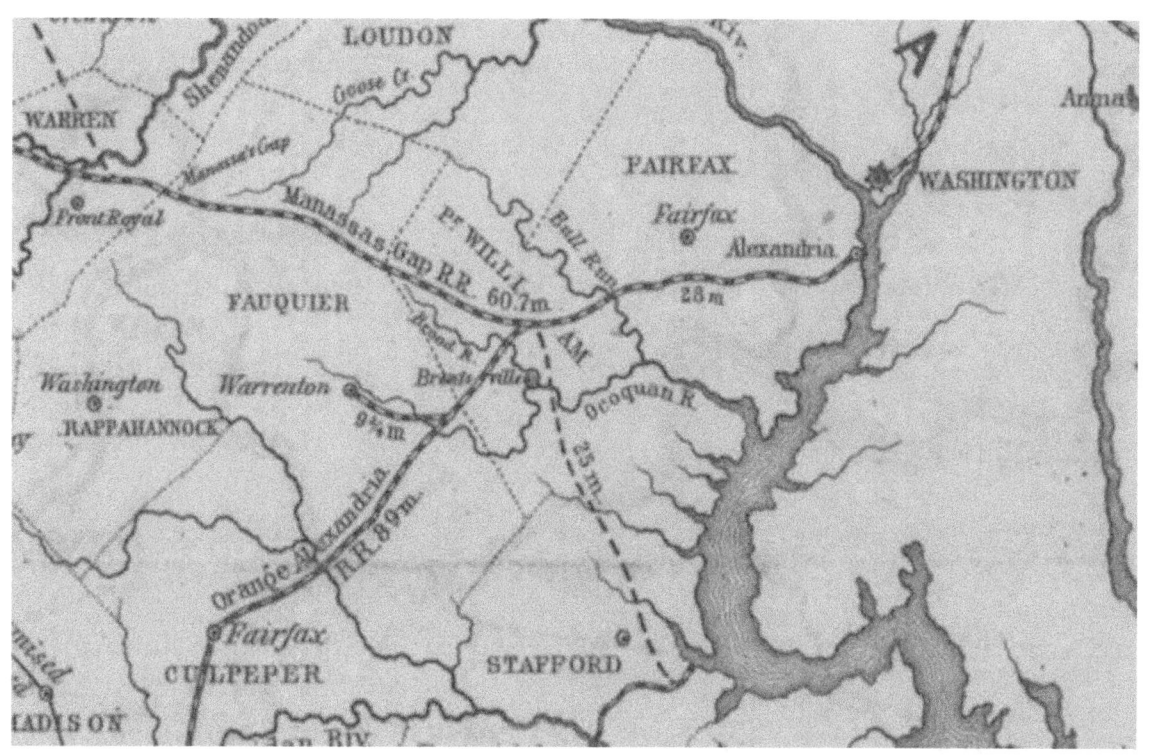

PARTIAL MAP OF THE 1852 ORANGE AND ALEXANDRIA RAILROAD

A WARTIME SKETCH OF BEALETON STATION, FAUQUIER COUNTY, VIRGINIA

Beverly Ford, Aug 26, 1863

My Dear Wife and Daughter,

I wrote you on Saturday last and some on Sunday. I will quote from my diary to give you some idea of our everyday life in camp.

"Sunday, Aug 23, Had Regiment inspection at 7 ½ A.M. Day very hot. Wrote to sister Julia. Had religious service at 5 P.M. Chaplin Clark of the 83rd Pa. preached from John 4 and 13-14. Bathed in the river, a beautiful sunset and pleasant evening. This is my first day in camp since return. How different from the last.

Monday, Aug 24, Morning cold and pleasant. Studied tactics and read most of the day. Battalion drill commanded by Captain Allen, Lt. Munger Officer of the Day, Lt. Kelly on picket. Showered in the evening. News from Charleston is encouraging.

Tuesday Aug 25, spent the day in reading, writing and study except the time occupied in drill and the ordinary labor of the day. This day, Wednesday is very cold the night and morning were cold.

I slept cold and this morning put on woolen socks and drawers. Rained hard the fore part of the night. The day is clear. Fred has been over to see us today also received official notice of his transfer to Signal Corps. He is highly pleased with his position.

There is no indication of motion with this army. I have written to Cleveland a report of the present strength of our Co. and a sketch of its members for publication. The mail is just in but nothing for me except some official ones. The execution of 5 deserters was to have taken place today but is postponed to Saturday. 8 ½ P.M. Since writing we have had dress parade, supper and a visit from Capt. Royce, have discussed tactics & c. The news tonight is cheering. I think Charleston must soon be ours. I sometimes almost think this army is to see no more fighting and that perhaps we may see home before spring but all is uncertain.

I am trying to fit myself for duties if I remain here. The old officers of the regiment have had so much better appointments than I that I have always felt under restraint. But I am determined if any present opportunities continue to become entirely posted. Noah Shultz who was sent to hospital from Fredericksburg the 16th of Dec. last has joined us this evening. I have not yet seen him. I must give you our bill of fare tonight. Fried beef, boiled potatoes, coffee, sugar, condensed milk, and last but by no means least, boiled corn & salt (no butter). Corn from Rebeldom across the river, the men wading it to their necks to <u>confiscate</u> it. That is not a bad supper. But enough to eat is <u>not</u> <u>all</u> one wants. I frequent feel the shallowness of the argument made to slaves. What if they have enough to eat they should be content. Enclosed I send you the photograph of Gen. Mead without his glasses, imagine them on, his beard white, his face thinner than it shows, & you have the commander as he is. When you write tell me if you have heard from Sophia, and if yes, how she is & if Bruce has been there & c, also how Lt. Lawrence is. Lt. Munger has this moment been notified that he will have command of Company K for the present it is Capt. Bowin's Co. his absent, his 2nd Lt. killed at Gettysburg & the 1st Lt. goes home tomorrow morning on leave of absence for ten days. His mother lies at the point of death. There no prospect of leave being granted at present excess in such cases. It is late and cold. I must return to my <u>downy</u> <u>bed</u>. If I have time I will add a word in the morning.

Good night

Your aff. Husband & Father

B. Munger

Beverly Ford Va. Aug. 30, 1863

My Dear Wife & Daughter,

I recd yours of the 25th yesterday. I wrote you last on the 26th. I fear you looking on the dark side of things as you were feeling somewhat "down in the mouth" as so you say. It is Sunday evening; I have been very busy lately. As I wrote Lt. Munger is in temporary command of Co. K and the close of the month brings a large amount of writing and figuring. The clothing account for the whole Company is to be settled in addition to the ordinary work. This month completes the year. Most of the men have been in the service so that their account must be settled with the Government. In addition to my Co. labor I am a member of the Court Martial which convened on Saturday and may continue a week or more. So you see I have enough to write to you to keep me busy all night but can but little tonight.

I would like to tell you of the execution which took place yesterday, of the changes in our Co. officers & c. Strouss who left was a man from Frederick City in June was brought in last night by the Provost Guard in citizens' dress. He was arrested near Harrisburg. His case looks dark and he will fare hard I think, unless he can make a better case than appears at present. He threw away his gun and equipments which cost 27 50/100 ($27.50) dollars, the expenses of arrest were 24 40/100 ($24.40) & his lost time amounts to 26 dollars. 66 dollars and a suit of clothes are (the) only items in the account. The Government determined to put a stop to desertion & it is high time, this keeping ½ the army to watch the other don't pay. Shooting 50 or 100 will cure it. We have no tidings of Davis or Henderson. Shultz has returned to the Co. Only Francisco is now off duty. Morse is still in arrest for going to Baltimore without leave. Tomorrow we are to be mustered for pay, though we may not be paid in three months. I learn an election for Mayor will take place tomorrow also. We are living well. Our cook improves every day. This noon we had a veal pot pie & considering we have no butter it was good. My blankets I found safe but the nights are so cold now. We are not quite warm enough. I have today ordered some. The weather is clear, cool & dry. We see no indications of a movement of this army. I presume I shall not be able to write much this week but will do what I can. Love to all. What is George going into! Your affectionate Husband and Father

B. Munger

Beverly Ford, Va. Sep 8, 1863

My Dear Wife,

I wrote you Tuesday last & I do on Saturday. But have not heard from you since a week last Saturday & we have had a mail every day. I can't imagine the cause but fear you are sick, if so get someone to write a word & let me know. I have received but two letters from all sources (& those were from you) since my return three weeks & you may well imagine I feel somewhat anxious. I wrote to Graham Sunday. I have no news to write for we have spent the most quiet 3 weeks I have experienced since I have been in the service. The weather has been very uniform, clear, dry, & cool for the season & you can scarcely imagine a life more monotonous. But I keep off the "Blues" by work, study, reading & writing. I think I am making progress in military science, though as member of Court I am unable to drill with the Co. or Regt. It is almost time for court to assemble & as this will not go out tomorrow morning I will stop.

4 ½ P.M. Court adjourned early today and I am not sorry. The day is what you would call hot. The Regt. had gone out for Brigade drill under its new commander, Col. Welch. It is very warm at this hour for drilling but <u>soldiers</u> can stand it. The mail is not yet in & I shall defer writing much till that arrives as I hope to be able to acknowledge the receipt of a letter. 8 P.M. I have just read your letter of the 3rd your previous one was dated Aug 26th & was recd just ten days since. I was much relieved to learn you are not sick as I feared but I am still unable to conjecture why you remained so long silent.

    Your aff Husband

    B. Munger

COLONEL NORVAL E. WELCH OF THE 16TH MICHIGAN VOLUNTEER INFANTRY WAS GIVEN COMMAND OF THE 3RD BRIGADE, 1ST DIVISION, 5TH CORPS AFTER THE PROMOTION OF COLONEL JAMES C. RICE ON AUGUST 17, 1863 TO THE RANK OF BRIGADIER GENERAL OF VOLUNTEERS. RICE HAD BEEN PROMOTED FOR HIS ACTIONS AT LITTLE ROUND TOP AFTER TAKING COMMAND OF THE BRIGADE AFTER THE MORTAL WOUNDING OF COLONEL STRONG VINCENT. WELCH WAS LATER KILLED IN ACTION AT THE BATTLE OF PEEBLES FARM, POPLAR GROVE CHURCH, VIRGINIA ON SEPTEMBER 30, 1864 DURING THE SIEGE OF PETERSBURG.

THIS PHOTOGRAPH WAS TAKEN AT CULPEPER, VA, SEPTEMBER 1863. FROM LEFT TO RIGHT ARE THE GENERALS OF THE ARMY OF THE POTOMAC: GOUVERNEUR K. WARREN, WILLIAM H. FRENCH, GEORGE G. MEADE, HENRY J. HUNT, ANDREW A. HUMPHREYS, GEORGE SYKES.
TOP RIGHT: MAJOR GENERAL GEORGE G. MEAD – MATHEW BRADY COLLECTION (LIBRARY OF CONGRESS)

MAJ. GEN. ALFRED PLEASONTON, CAVALRY COMMANDER OF THE ARMY OF THE POTOMAC. PLEASONTON IS SEEN HERE WITH HIS STAFF AT WARRENTON, VIRGINIA JUST BEFORE THE BATTLE OF CULPEPER COURT HOUSE, FOUGHT SEPTEMBER 13, 1863, NEAR CULPEPER, VIRGINIA. THE UNION CAVALRY OF THE ARMY OF THE POTOMAC ATTACKED THE CONFEDERATE ARMY OF NORTHERN VIRGINIA. THIS BATTLE OPENED UP THE CULPEPER REGION TO FEDERAL CONTROL AND WAS A PRELUDE TO THE SUBSEQUENT BRISTOE CAMPAIGN IN OCTOBER AND NOVEMBER OF 1863. MATHEW BRADY COLLECTION (LIBRARY OF CONGRESS)

Beverly Ford Va. Sep 15, 1863

My Dear Wife & Daughter,

I have just returned from court & recd your letters & one from Lyman all marked the 12th. I wrote you last Sunday 13th & recd one from you on that day. I should not write you today but there is a prospect of a move. I suppose we are to cross the river and cooperate with the force over there. We have not yet recd orders to move & as yet it is uncertain but as I am off so much I will ignore the present.

Yesterday Capt. Rudgers called to see me. I was at Court but he came up to see me. He is at Rappahannock Station about 2 miles south of us. He is still complaining & thinks he will offer his resignation again. It is 5 P.M. Lt. Kelly is officer of the day & Lt. Munger is out on Brigade drill. The camp is very quiet. The daily papers bring us no news today. The reconnaissance I spoke of Sunday was under Pleasanton, supported by the 2nd Corps which was at Culpepper when last heard from. They (captured) 3 pieces of artillery and 40 prisoners. Last night I secured council from Strouss to assist him in his company trial. It is not common for the soldiers to have help but I thought where a man's life was at stake all what could be done should be in his case. I see no possible hope for him except in the mercy of the General. I shall not sit upon him. My oath would compel me to do what I don't want to do. We have been trying a man today who will probably be sentenced to death. Two years ago, my conscience would not have allowed me to pass the sentence of death but times have changed and I have changed. This is stern work.

Friday - 18 are to be shot in this army, one of them in this Division. Don't think we have lost all feeling of humanity. You can't appreciate the necessity. Hundreds are arriving daily and some of them the most sickly men in the whole country and they must be awed into obedience. It is from this class mostly that desertions occur. This crime has been treated lightly so long that men have come to think they can commit it with impunity. It will sound hard to you if I say that when there is a clear case of desertion I am decidedly in favor of shooting till this evil is checked. So I won't say it.

The battalion is just in from drill so I will stop awhile and go to the river and take a break. 1 PM. Orders are received to have our baggage packed and loaded tonight. It really seems like old times. In camp property a c cumbrous and in a move like this many things must be left which are almost indispensable. I can hardly carry all my goods.

We suppose we are to move toward Gordonsville. I am not at all confident of the success of the movement. My experience across that river has not been pleasant but I will hope for the best. It is not certain we shall go, for this is uncertain business. "<u>Uncertain</u>", that word has peculiar meaning here if among the uncertain you should never hear from me again remember (me) as one who <u>tried</u> to do his duty. I may add more but will close for the present to be sure to be ready.

Your affectionate Husband & Father,

B. Munger

I also intend to write my old Diary. (Note: The diary that Captain Munger speaks of has been lost to time. The last entry in his diary that appears in this publication ends on May 12, 1863. There was obviously at least one more diary that Captain Munger kept.)

On the back of this letter is written a short message:

Sept. 15, 4 AM. We move at 5.

B. Munger

Camp near New Baltimore Oct. 22nd, 1863

My Dear Wife & Daughter,

I have just recd a mail and I got a letter from you on the 14th. We recd but 2 mails between the 10th instance and yesterday and one letter from you on the 8th and the one just received. In that time, I have written 2, one from Fairfax and one from Bull Run Battlefield. I see that the date of your last you were not aware of our movements and I was rather glad of it for you will not have so long a time to worry about it. I expect we shall rest a while now but not in this place. I will commence where I last wrote you and continue the account of our marches.

Reveille was sounded next morning (Tuesday) at 1 ¾ A.M. I had not slept well and the roar of our supply train passing on the "Pike" ½ a mile distant disturbed me some so that I got up little refreshed. It was bitter cold, we got our breakfast hastily but were not called into line till 4, then we marched ten rods and halted without being minute, we were till 6 in going 1 mile that was to Groveton. You will see it on the map south east of Centerville 6 or 8 miles. From here we moved very rapidly over a muddy, bad road to

Gainsville, 6 miles which we reached at 7 1/2. This you will see on the Manassas Gap Rail Road.

Our cavalry had an engagement with the enemy here yesterday and lost all the horses belonging to 1 squadron and the enemy were supposed to be between us and the Gap. We laid here till one and moved toward the place about 8 miles. I can't explain the reason of all the moves. Some of them I do not understand. The enemy are now supposed to be across the river. I am not in a mood to write today.

We arrived here night before last 4 P.M. not expecting to stay but camped for the night. Such relaxation of such excitement and labor is exhausting and depressing and yesterday and today I have <u>felt</u> its full weight. I don't know as we have all our back mail or shall ever get it or whether you have got or will get all (of) mine. Since the commencement of our march in addition to the 2 from you I received one from Mother and Abigail and today one from Frank Munger and one from James and one from Nettie. But as a rule I find the old proverbs true, "Out of sight out of mind". I forgot to say I received one from Beam, for which please give him my thanks.

In many respects this has been a much more severe march than that of last summer. We marched 11 successive days with one exception, carried 8 days rations. The officers were not loaded as heavily as on the Chancellorsville march but the soldiers were and if ever such a set of men were entitled to the eternal gratitude of their country it is the private soldier in our armies. "Gratitude" is a word now nearly useless. I held out well and have never ridden or rode on any march since I joined the army. Of the prospect of peace, I have done thinking and expect to serve 3 years on duty. My exhaustion makes me feel blur today "but I shall get over that" and feel better someday.

5 P.M. We are still in camp, shall move to a more roomy place tomorrow and probably stay in this vicinity some days till the Rail Road from Manassas Junction to Washington which the enemy destroyed is repaired. Our future will depend much as here to for on Lee's movements. I am resting and feel much better tonight. Perhaps you do not appreciate the difficulties I labor under in waiting (besides having no peace) for want of subjects I see nothing, know nothing but what pertains immediately to myself and fellow soldiers.

Our excessive fatigue even prevents our seeing the country as we pass along through. I have done my best to profit by my <u>travels</u> in this state. It was said of Judea, "it is a course country". The reverse is true of this. It is a vast country especially its valleys. I think I mentioned the view from the crest of that range of hills <u>we charged up and took</u> (when no enemy was near) between Culpeper and Rappahannock. Another equally grand is to be seen from the heights of Centerville.

When we last passed over there our army was crossing the valley between the heights and the Bull Run Mountains. I can give you no idea of the indescribable magnificence of the view. A column of such magnitude is a wonderful sight. In the distance, it looks like a living, moving monster stretching miles, winding, curving and swaying with the bright flashes of light reflecting from the bright arms. Then the wagon trains no small item in the picture. You know they are all covered with canvas and in the distance, looks like a continuous line of white. I think you have little conception of the vastness of an army like this.

Mead has shown himself a master in the movement of armies if nothing else. In such a move as ours it required more talent to keep the trains, troops and so on in a position to defend themselves and save their supplies than is usually supposed. 6 ½ I have just received letters from you and Ida and part of one from Lyman dated 18th & 19th instant you will in this be advised of our moves and whereabouts. The 5th Corps was not engaged, we were back to support the 2nd and engage the enemy if necessary but we were too late. Sykes is blamed for not supporting that Corps promptly and it is said we might gain great advantage if he had done so. I reject it for we have the labor without the <u>glory</u> as usual. Our prospects look bright but not for a speedy peace, we must make up our minds this is to be a long war. By the way if I should be so fortunate as to be promoted I shall be obliged to swear into the service for three years from the date of my new commission which I am willing to do if you are. At present, there is no prospect of promotion. I will write to L soon and to Ida. Next Sunday is my birthday. It will be pleasant without doubt. Robert Shipley is quite sick with fever but <u>plucky</u>. Harvey is well and the Co. generally but so <u>tired</u>. You have not answered my inquires about your home. O writes today. Fred, I have not seen since the first of the month.

Your Husband, B. Munger

Note: This is the longest letter written by Captain Bennett Munger to his daughter and wife at home. There are no letters for the month of November in the collection.

Dec. 14, 1863

In Camp at Rappahannock Station, VA.

My Dear little Daughter,

I think I promised in my last to give you a description of the field and defenses of Mile Run (Captain Munger probably is referring to Mine Run in this section of his letter. The Mine Run Campaign lasted from November 26 through December 2, 1863. The 44th New York was engaged in this campaign.) on which the armies of Mead and Lee were lately in line of battle. Also, something of the country through which we passed and etc. Please have the map before you as you read and you will about be able to see us on our way. We left our camp at Mountain Run you are aware on the morning of Nov. 26th, your birthday and marched south west. About 11 O'clock we reached the old road at Ely's Ford on which we marched to Chancellorsville and I recognized the spot when I threw away my overcoat and where Orett (who was then sick) had the nose bleed and I got the Dr. to let him ride his horse a little way. The road was mostly woods. On reaching the place about two miles from the river we were halted, filed off the road to the right in a bridle path and the old officers we were to form line of battle.

By the way cannonading had been heard to the front for some time and we were in momentary expectation of a fight. By this move you will see we left Ely's Ford on our left. We moved up the river at some distance from it to about opposite to and a little above the mouth of Wilderness Run. Here we were halted in a valley and at first forbidden to build fires. A hill covered with oak shrubs hid the river from our view. We all dreaded the crossing of this river as the south bank commands the north. That is, it is much higher giving the artillery a great advantage and then being wounded in a swift stream is almost certain death for a gun that paralyzes for a moment so that the wounded man is most sure to drown. I think we lay here to 4 P.M. getting our dinner and in the time I went up the hill found the pontoons already laid, the place a very favorable one and some of our cavalry already across and no enemy in sight. We crossed just before sundown, halted on the south side at an old gold mine and quartz mill called by some, Wycoff's Mill and by others, Gold Mine Ford. It is a wild place covered with the never failing oak bushes and pits or shafts where dug or sunk as they call it, (that were) so deep we could not see the bottom.

This is the beginning of the "Wilderness" of which I presume you have read in the papers and we did not get "out of the Wilderness" till we re-crossed the river. Here we loaded our guns, sent out flankers and commenced our march through the bushes. In many places the only way to get along was to take hold of the brim of my hat, raise my elbow, let it project forward and then push my way through. I can't tell you how far we marched in this way but we struck the Plank Road leading from Germania south east across Wild Run. It was long after dark and we marched almost at a "double quick".

FEDERAL SOLDIERS CROSSING AT GERMANIA FORD- HARPER'S WEEKLY- JANUARY 2, 1864

On reaching the run we filed to the right without crossing it and camped on the Orange and Fredericksburg Pike. Our regiment was set out on picket. I was out from 11 till 1. A mounted sentinel was in sight a little beyond our lines and as it was a bright night I could see him at a distance. I saw him ride slowly up to our line and talk with one of our sentinels about a quarter of a mile from me; I went out to see what he wanted. He said he was placed there 2 hours before dark, that the squad that he belonged (to) were (was) then bivouacked nearly a mile beyond our lines and that he had seen no one till we came. (He) asked if I was in command of the infantry picket and if he might go in to Corp H.Q. I told him to ride back to the place where he left his company and if they were gone to come back again. He soon came back and I sent Sgt. Hobart with him to H.Q. He was an Irish boy about 18 and I related the incident to show you how the forgetfulness of an officer will sometimes make a poor soldier suffer (he had been forgotten) he would have staid till morning (and it was a severe cold night) if he had not been relieved. In the morning, we moved toward Fredericksburg and all supposed we were going then we halted every little while and at 9 O'clock were not 2 miles from where we started.

At one time, we stopped near a little farm house that looked a little "northern" something like the houses of the Dutch in the suburbs of our cities. Some of the officers said to me, "Let's go."

Then we went to the door but it had no latch, only a keyhole, so we went around the house, a crowd of soldiers were around it and at a window inside sat a woman crying as if her heart would break. I went to the door, raped softly, she opened it, I told her I had observed her crying and came to see what was the matter. She said she was afraid. I asked her of what. Soldiers she said. So, I told her not to cry. Soldiers would not hurt her. They might talk rough but keep her door locked and she would be safe. She wiped her eyes with her apron as if she thought her life was lengthened and locked her door.

We then moved rapidly down the pike to the first right hand road (see map) filed down that still in the bushes and so close to the road in many places wagons could not pass. Then the question was, "Where are we going?" I took out my compass and decided we might yet be going to Fredericksburg. Soon we came to a plank road crossing this nearly at right angles and we filed to the <u>right</u>. Then we bid good bye to Fredericksburg and guessed very close where we were going. We had not proceeded far when an order was shouted along the column, "Take off to the right!" Which meant that the troops must take the right hand side of the road. Soon a train of supply and ammunition wagons, ambulances and horsemen came rushing down the road as if "Mosby was after them" and sure enough the train had been attacked. Our Division H.Q. wagon; that is the wagon in which Gen. Bartlett our Div. command carried his personal baggage and food was taken. Our medical supply wagon and some ambulances with several drivers of other Co. wagons and the rascals were off so quick we did not catch them. All this time cannonading was heard in front, rear and both flanks and we began to think we were indeed out in the wilderness. This affair hindered us about 2 hours.

The 16th Michigan a regiment in our Brigade was sent back to guard our supply train. When the road was straight we could only see a black column of troops before and behind, all else thick bushes. Toward night we neared the cannonading and finally came in sight of the church which the papers called Oak Grove Church but it was called the Coopers Church. You will see on the map a mark for church near the Co. H. in Spotsylvania Co. that is probably intended to represent the place but the map is not quite correct.

As we approached they were having a sharp artillery fight. We passed a house they were using as a hospital and saw wounded being taken in. It looked like old times and we hurried toward the front and passed the usual scenes in rear of battle. I can't describe it. But imagine the largest collection of people you ever saw increased a hundred fold and a thunder bolt to knock a few thousands of them into "fire" and they trying to get back to a place of safety. Wagons, gun carriages and horses knocked into all shapes accompanied by all shouts of swearing and you have some idea of the picture. Sometimes a poor fellow all torn to pieces will attest the attention but usually little attention is paid such things. Jokes and witticisms are indulged in as if it was a show. Some inquire anxiously about the state of things at the front and generally the answer is an encouraging answer to such a question by one of our boys the reply was. "O we have got a splendid position. Give it to them boys!"

Just before marching (to) the field we were filed to the left, marched to the rear of our artillery and halted. The shells were bursting a few rods from us but not near enough to be very dangerous. One however burst so near as to make us draw down our heads a little and although pieces made the dirt fly finely, no one was hurt I believe. We had eaten no dinner and were so near the enemy it was not safe to have fires. So, Nast went to the rear and made us some coffee and we feasted on Hard Tack and coffee. The night was cold, cloudy and looked like snow.

Our generals expected a flank movement and we were assigned our work to repel an attack on the left. We were protected by a rail road bank. It was a strong position and we were confident we could do it. This was the night I slept between 2 rails and I made them rails ache some. I apprised you they were glad when morning came. The battle or skirmish was not renewed in the morning and about 8 O'clock we moved rapidly back. Then I that sure now we are going to Fredericksburg but we soon filed left and sent our skirmishers and we were ordered to move as silently as possible and not speak. It now rained hard. We were on a cart path and in the never ending scrub and oaks.

We were marching about north. Firing on our left, I knew that direction would lead us back into the pike we had picketed on the first night but much nearer Orange C.H. About noon we suddenly came into a clearing and found it to be Robinson's Zouaves. Mead's H.Q. were there and our whole army close by, and still it rained, the ground was too wet to sit down and we too tired to stand up. Some troops began to pass and form line of battle. The 3rd and 6th Corps passed and afterward learned the 2nd was already in line. Here I saw a lot of prisoners and the place where the 2nd Corps (I think) had met and repulsed the enemy. Toward night it stopped raining. We had a fine supper and I tore a shutter off a barn and Mort got a board and we slept as dry as kings. This was the only good night's rest I had on that side (of) the Rapidan. Next morn we were up at 4, cooked some coffee and moved at daylight down the pike toward Orange C. H. The road was one perfect jam of troops. Some mistake was made in the order of starting and two columns were moving one way and one the other, to add to our comfort the mud was about six inches deep and so that it would run together as we raised our feet. We marched a mile and half and filed right into the woods. I have our coward in our Company and he has always managed to get out of our fights and this time I had determined he should fight if we did and told the file closer to watch him and if he attempted to run, bleed him a little. But as we approached when things began to look squally I looked through the ranks for my fighter and he was gone. No one knew where. I was vexed bad and feared if I could have found him that he might have had a wound to show when he got home but he was safe and I saw no man of him till we were ten miles this side the river. We moved forward ½ mile, halted and ordered to relieve the 2nd Corps who were to picket at the front. The three companies on the right were ordered to remain as a reserve and the remainder move one Co. at a time. Then a sharp firing of musketry was commenced and kept up till the picket was changed and although the balls passed far beyond our line only one man was seriously hurt and a few slightly. One poor fellow was hit where soldiers are not proud of a wound and although the balls flew like hair, they laughed at him till I believed he would have rejoiced at a severe wound provided it was not in the rear. Many had their cloths pierced. After getting into position the men were pretty well positioned by rails piled so as to form a breastwork. We advanced to the picket line through a thick pine wood and about one half the length of it (the right) was in the wood the left extended to the pike 20 rods from where it crosses (Note: Munger called it Mile Run) Mine Run. Our picket line as well as that of the enemy was nearly parallel with the creek. Then, Little One, I have been most as long talking to the position of the enemy as we were but never mind, you will get away to safety as we did. But as I am to go on picket in the morning, I must postpone your introduction to the Rebs till I returned for it is now 12 O'clock and my family have long been in bed. So, wish one hearty embrace and fervent kiss. I will bid you good night.

Tuesday morning 6 O'clock.

I thought daily I would write a while before the lieutenants got up. The change of picket I spoke of took till about 10 A.M. This was Sunday. A little after midnight I received the left of the line resting on the pike with the three reserve companies and remained on duty till Wednesday morning at 3 O'clock.

THE ARMY OF THE POTOMAC AT MINE RUN-GENERAL WARREN'S TROOPS ATTACKING
SKETCHED BY A. R. WAUD – HARPER'S WEEKLY- JANUARY 2, 1864

Monday morning at 8, Gen. Warren on the left was to attack the enemies' right, turn their flank. Gen. French was to follow the move as Warren advanced and as their; the enemies' lines were flanked and gave way. We were to advance and so on from left to right of our line. The attack for some case was delayed till 9 and as something happens in war the enemy would not let us turn his flank. As to explain Warren found their right so strong he could not turn it. But at 9 our batteries opened. The lines of the enemies' fortifications were parallel to Mile Run (Mine Run) and as the center where we were posted ¾ of a mile from it, but varying in different places according to the surface of the country generally on the crest or brow of the hill rising from the stream on our right they extended to the river then up the river I don't know how far and to our left it was said to Gordonsville. Part were old defenses thrown up on former occasions strengthened and extended.

These fortifications consist mostly of the way of trenches 3 or 4 feet wide and 2 or 3 feet deep with the earth dug from the banks up so as to form a breast work as high as shoulders. Sometimes they are strengthened by logs and brush. In their trenches, they stand as thick or near together as possible and fire over the bank which protects them from the balls of their enemy. On commanding positions, that is the higher elevation and such as command a large extent batteries are placed at such points the fortifications were much strengthened and in our immediate front 42 pieces of artillery were in position. Here the works were much heavier and the banks of earth from 4 to 6 feet or more thick on top and so huge as to cover or hide the men working the gun. A place is left called an embrasure for the muzzle of the gun, and the men who load are exposed only when loading. In front of this a breast work they had fallen trees with the tops toward us cut off the brush and sharpened the ends of the limbs and were there were no trees, brush was carried and piled in front. This is called abates and as the men charge their works they are much hindered in getting over this and after a severe charge you will see at such places piles of dead.

In our front and from 20 to 50 rods from our picket line was the Run, a stream 10 to 15 feet wide and the channel from 10 to 15 feet deep worn down by the action of the water much like a ditch the water was from 6 inches to 2 ½ feet deep and banks perpendicular. On the other (South) side the hill or second bank ran about as steep as the back of the house where you are and about as high then for

¾ of a mile was a general assault to the enemy's lines. Their artillery could rake every rod of the space as well as their musket. A bridge crossed this stream at the pike but their artillery commanded it. In making an attack the first obstacle was to cross the Run. Many places were devised but none seemed more practicable than to wade through and climb the bank as best we could.

Some of the objections to this even it would take a long time to get a sufficient number across and the severity of the weather was such, that if wounded after being wet they would die in a few hours. Next advancing so far under fire is murderous business and if successful must lose a vast number of men. After I had been out on the line 2 or 3 hours and looked carefully at the position. I went back to the reserve and some officers asked when I thought the attack would commence. I told them <u>never</u> at that point, that unless the flanks could be turned we should get away some night in a hurry. I thought no sane man would attack this night.

Our position also a strong defensive one and we had nothing to fear but starvation or a flank move if Lee was strongly reinforced. We were cut off from all communication with Washington and our trains carried all the rations we had except what were in our haversacks. The enemy were at work till the last day strengthening their defenses. The last day they watched us. Many exciting incidents occurred during the time we were there. During the first day a dozen ball were seen to whistle near the careless head that was put above the breast work. The next day but little firing was done. Word was passed up the line that 2 artillery officers were interfering with the men and I passed the word back to send them up to me in arrest but they started off the other way. I went down the line and the Rebs fired several shots at me, none coming near than a few feet. I found the officers were drunk but very polite and respectful, glad to go with <u>me</u> but, "Would not go with a corporal no how Captain." I took them to the Col. and he sent them to their command and they were so grateful that I had represented their case no worse they wanted to "treat" me. Perhaps you don't know what that means, if so you may ask. I have very many such offers.

Friday December 18th – Well, Darling, I have been picketing and a good time we had of it. I went out with a bad cold, lived outdoors, laid on the ground, was up most of the night, visited the outposts alone in the night, right in the teeth of the Bushwhackers a distance of 4 miles, stood seven hours in a powerful rain that froze as it fell, then waded hours through the mud and found myself cured of my cold and as good as ever. So, you see, I am <u>tough</u>. But a little more of Mine Run and its incidents. One day about a dozen sheep came in sight. In an instant, all that danger was gone, for the boys were hungry and gave chase. In an instant the Reb pickets poured in a volley at our boys and our boys a volley at the sheep. The balls fell like hail and strange to say not a man was hurt. A man would clinch a sheep and drop flat to the ground to avoid the balls and lie till the storm was over. Our Regt. caught 8 I think but I got none (soldiers are selfish when hungry).

At another time a party of the 1st Corps was sent up the creek to our left to cross and dislodge the enemy from the rifle pits and as it is called feel the enemy's strength and if possible to draw on an engagement. From our position, we could see both parties but they could not see each other. It was very interesting to see our men advance cautiously till they arrived at the point where the Reb pickets could see them start at double quick firing as they advanced. Then to see the rascals run and once in a while a poor fellow would drop, his fighting done. If our men advanced too far they would have to fall back.

8 P.M. Lieut. Kelly and Mr. Southerby have just received their papers and will start for home in a few minutes. So, I will close my letter and tell you more another time. It almost makes me want to go to see others leave for home. It is said today that our Corps is ordered to the south west and will leave soon. If so, it is perhaps as well, though, if I could have my choice I would not go. But if I do go Mother and you must be brave and stand it like a good soldier. I send by L's for another pair of boots. Love lots of love to Ma, your own little self and <u>all</u> friends. Goodbye and God bless.

Your affectionate Father,

B. Munger

This is the last letter in in the Kesterson collection of Captain Munger's letters to his family. In early 1864, Captain Munger would be reassigned as the commanding officer of "Drafted Men and Substitutes" at Elmira New York for a short time and then assigned to the post of Inspector of Elmira Prison for Confederate prisoners of war. Captain Munger would be released from his duties at Elmira Prison and further obligations to the 44th NY, by Special Order No. 275 dated October 11, 1864. The 44th New York Infantry was mustered out of service on October 11, 1864. The men who did not muster out with the regiment were transferred to the 140th and the 146th New York Infantry regiments.

SERENDIPITY! A MYSTERY SOLVED AND A CHAPTER ADDED! – THE MISSING LETTERS FOUND!

After nearly seven years, from the time that I first started the Captain Bennet Munger project in 2009, to January 2016, I was finally ready to publish the story of Captain Munger's military career, or at least I thought that I was. On January 30, 2016, I was starting to put the Captain Bennett Munger book to rest and was working on the process of getting the cover for the book ready to print when I received an email from Shelly Case of West Chester, Pa. Shelly had been doing family research on Captain Munger and noticed that I had posted a message about preparing a book on the captain back in 2012 on an internet site. Emails were quickly exchanged and I sent Shelly my contact information and shortly thereafter she contacted me by telephone and resolved the mystery of how Captain Munger's letters got to Marietta, Ohio. The fact was that her family lived in Marietta for many years and that part of the letters that I had purchased had once belonged to other relatives in the Marietta area. Shelly further informed me that her father, Philip Benham Case had been the keeper of a great deal of family history and lore but had passed away a few years ago. Her father had been the guardian of five boxes full of family documents and letters pertaining to Captain Munger & the decedents of the Munger family. Upon hearing this exciting news I was overjoyed as I hoped that some of the missing letters of Captain Munger's early association with the regiment and some of his later letters detailing his appointment as Chief Inspector of Elmira Prisoner of War Camp might still exist, not to mention possible letters from his wife and friends!

I asked Shelly if she would be willing to share her information for possible inclusion in this small publication on Captain Munger. She stated that she would need to sort through the material and get back to me but she had no problem with sharing her information for inclusion for the book. I think that we were both excited about the prospect of adding one more chapter to Captain Munger's life story and I am thankful that she was so generous in her offering. On February 5, 2016 I received a parcel in the mail from Shelly that had four folders containing photocopied letters and documents written by Captain Munger and a few fellow officers. Two of these folders were of no use as they contained material that I already possessed but the other two had letters from early 1862 through late 1863 that were not in the collection of Captain Munger's letters that I had purchased back in 2009. Several of these copies were extremely light and at least one had been copied where the last line was cut off. Aside from these minor annoyances I set out once again to transcribe Captain Munger's writings and add one more, small piece to the puzzle. In Shelly's letter to me she stated that she had four more boxes of original letters that needed sorted and that she would send those as soon as possible. I could only hope to imagine what sort of tantalizing content these aged pages would contain. Shelly started sending me the originals in small groups of twenty or so letters & I slowly started the task of transcription.

As I continued the task of transcribing letters & diary entries I discovered an amazing story in Captain Munger's 1865 diary entries & letters. It would seem that the Captain was very familiar with the Mid-Ohio Valley as well as that of the Great Kanawha Valley. This was of a great surprise to both Shelly & myself as Shelly had lived in Marietta, Ohio for a number of years with her family & I live in the Parkersburg, West Virginia area. Captain Munger had visited both of these towns in 1865 & mentions them in his diary entries on a number of occasions. Captain Munger also talks about many of the locations in the Kanawha Valley that I have visited while doing previous research or visiting friends in the region.

Another revelation was the fact that Captain Munger & his male family members were speculating in property & natural resources in West Virginia. It would appear that a number of Confederate prisoners from the Kanawha Valley who were imprisoned at Elmira had talked to the Captain about the vast possibilities of gaining one's fortune through land, timber, oil & coal speculation in the state & elsewhere in Ohio & Pennsylvania. These facts were unknown to both of us & seemed strange in the ever-growing web of coincidence that this project has taken. The reader should understand that during the telling of Captain Munger's story it is important to realize that his health was a continuous issue for him but he continued to soldier on through adversity & misfortune.

The reader will also take special note of how I have set this book up as far as text font. In the case of the letters that came from my collection I have use "Bickley Scrip" which very closely mimics Captain Munger's own writing style & in the case of the letters provided by Shelly Case, I have used "Times New Roman" when dealing with the letter & diary sections of this publication. The reason for this differential usage was to allow researchers in the future to understand the division of the letters & the importance of each collection. Farr too often such letters are separated, sold or lost to time. This collection is very unique in the fact of how it came to be reunited & how it came to be published.

In this publication, I have also chosen to make minimal corrections in Captain Munger's usage of language/grammar, tense & punctuation but I have corrected spelling when applicable & I have amended run on sentences & fragments when necessary. In many of Captain Munger's letters the use of paragraphs is nearly nonexistent & I have modified these letters to reflect a more coherent break in the subjects that he relates. In this way, Captain Munger's first person voice is preserved for future generations using this publication for research. It should also be noted that Shelly's collection contained a great number of monthly returns of clothing, camp & garrison equipment, muster in & muster out rolls, pay rolls, receipts of issuance to list of stores received & ordinance & ordinance stores as well as personal loan receipts for men & officers of the company & the regiment. These documents are of interest but have not been added to this publication as they would better be served for specialized research on the company & the regiment by future historians. The letters owned by Shelly Case were donated to the Manuscripts and Special Collections New York State Library New York State Education Department Cultural Education Center, 11th floor Albany, NY 12230 on December 5, 2016 and can be located for research at that location.

The following transcriptions are from the Shelly Case collection:

Albany Barracks Oct. 5, 1862

My dear wife & daughter & friends,

It is Sunday eve & a magnificent one too! I am in our barracks with few conveniences for writing, still I have written a long letter to Layman, the first I know sent to Penn Yan. (I've) Been to the city to church with Lieutenants, Nephew & thirty others attended service in camp & the other duties ensue ant to camp & intend to write you plenty liberal one since writing before we have been mustered into the U.S. service & the men have been paid $29.00, each have got a part of their clothing and I think we shall leave this place one week from tomorrow though it is uncertain. Yesterday we had a grand washing time both of our person & the house. We have yet drilled but little. The weather is better than when I wrote before & the place seemed pleasant today. We; that is the Lieutenant F & O have been upon the brick building with a glass & have a fine view of the surrounding country & a partial view of the city & river. It is a magnificent view & the mountains remind me of New England.

We have here an extensive hospital that is it seemed so to me, a building 520 feet by 20. There are now but about 100 patients under treatment but there have been many wounded here & some remain it hardly strengthens our hearts to hear & see them. Some with a leg off, some with an arm. One case with both arms & one leg. Still I have not heard one complain. They think the rebels poison their balls (as) the wounds will not stay healed. We have one poor fellow in there & I fear he is to stay there a long time, S. P. Dye of Italy. I suppose you will naturally inquire if I enjoy myself. If I do it is in the discharge of my duty to my Company. I work hard, stay with them, sleep with them & am trying to make them a model company. They think me strict but that is not strange. They are unused to such restricts but I impose on myself the same restricts. Profanity is one of their besetting sins which is difficult to cure. There is no drunkenness for they have not the means. I have one man who makes some trouble & is reckless talking mean to say the least but I have but little fear on the score of government. I will be obeyed. These difficulties although unpleasant have a tendency to divert the mind from home & grief as an illustration when I left you in Geneva. My heart was too tender for a soldier when I went to camp. I found some of them needed the sternest treatment & the effort I had to make was calculated to eradicate tender feelings & it is more or less so constantly. But sight of a little child & the consequent that of my darling will fill my eyes in spite of me.

                                        Albany Barracks   Oct 8, 1862

My dear wife,

The lieutenants & myself have just returned from the city where we have been to secure our commission but did not succeed & learned that they date only from our mustering which is the 3rd of Oct. & if it is true we lose most 2 month wages to make money. A man should be a private & to live easy. I am unusually well & have the best appetite I have enjoyed in a long time & our living is good but not neat. I am now eating my fifth peck of dirt since I left home but am fattening on it. I think we shall leave on Monday & join our Regiment which is near Sharpsburg in Maryland guarding a ford on the Potomac. We are complimented somewhat on the appearance of our men it is good and I believe it. This letter to Ida & I had forgotten it. So from this point it is hers.

Dear Little Darling,

You can't imagine how much I think of you & if I could see you (I) could tell you much that would interest you. I will first give you a description of the duties of a day. We get up at 5 ½, call the roll at six & to give you an idea of our strictness I give but just 60 seconds to obey the order & if a man is out of place at that time he is punished without respect to any this morn three were tardy & their punishment was to do all the sweeping for the Company which when done as a punishment they think a disgrace.

After roll call wash & prepare for breakfast at 7 & at about 8 we go drilling for two or three hours then play or anything else till noon & if not too warm drill again, supper at 5 & amusement till nine when all the men are to be in their quarters at half past nine, lights are to extinguish & still sometimes they get so full of fun that it is hard for them to stop & I have to be severe occasionally for 80 men are not as easily governed as a few children. Some of them must have stern discipline. I go to the city now most every day it is a long walk. On the way, lots of little children on the walks & say "good bye soldiers." Some out to shake hands not more than 3 years old. Sunday at church a little (one) passed me and I was sitting in my seat & the congregation were passing out & looking up in my face so much as you do that my eyes filled with tears in spite of me & in writing it they are quite dry darling. I was pleased with your letter & wish you would continue to write me every time mother does. We have just received an order to leave today but I still, we will stay till Monday. It seems to be a part of military strategy to keep men always excited & in suspense but they didn't succeed in disturbing me much for I didn't care. I am in a glorious state of indifference. Perhaps it is because I can't help myself.

Baltimore Oct. 11, 1862

My Dear wife & baby,

We left Albany at 9 P.M. of Thursday arrived in New York at 8 A.M. left at 10 A.M. got to Philadelphia about 1 O'clock & staid till five reaching this God forsaken place at 2 A.M., staid in the cars till morn & shall probably proceed to Washington at 4 P.M. & I don't know where we go or what we do there for there seems to be the last known on this subject of any which with I ever had to do. No one knows where our Regiment is here but the powers insist on our moving on. I am writing in the Baltimore & Washington Depot & have material for a long letter but don't know when I can write it. Our order to leave Albany came at one O'clock & of course all was hurry till we were off. My transportation papers were handed me after we were boarded. The steamer which was the New World said to be the largest on the river. Nothing of note occurred on our passage down which was pleasant considering it was in the evening. Twas a fine eve last daylight, were forty miles from N.Y. the scenery hardly equaled my expectations but with 80 men in care one has a poor chance to see a country favorably. Friday was a drizzling day & the country which we traveled low, sand, barren, & more swamp but in Philadelphia my heart was really cheered. We were on the ferryboat and invited to dinner by the Relief Association & it was bestowed with such hearty good will & all seemed so kind that it made my hearts feel light for it can't be denied that our isolated position tend to make us feel that we are forgotten by all human kind. We left amid cheers, shaking of hands & blessings but one reception in this city is far different if we received at all but were not. We came here & they left us & although we have been fed by an association similar to that in Phil. the spirit is so different that it loses half its value (it still rains) but a little better than that north of P & when I get time will describe it as well as I can but I have come to the conclusion that God never made another such country as western New York. I have received but three letters from home & only one from you while I suppose you have five times the time & convenience that I have. I probably shall not write as often here after as I expect to go immediately to the field. As you were at Penn Yan one letter would do for all but now. I must divide them. Layman is a glorious brother, you don't know how much he has done for me since I began this enterprise. O the suffering & misery we see here as the result of this rebellion. My darkest conceptions if God could relieve I think he would. You need not write till fetch up some when. Love to all, kiss that <u>loved</u> <u>one</u>.

As ever yours,

Bennett Munger

Camp near Antietam Oct. 16, 1862

My Dear wife & daughter.

  I have but a few moments to write now but as we are under marching orders we may leave at any moment& may stay all winter. There is heavy firing to the <u>south </u>west of us about 10 or 15 miles & with a glass we can see a camp of the enemy about 3 miles across the Potomac. We are close to them evidently. I had forgotten to tell you where we are it is 8 miles from Harpers Ferry on a mountain ½ a mile from the Potomac & 1 ½ from the battle ground of Antietam we have not yet recd. our arms but hope to soon. The boys feel no fear & are in good spirits. I wrote to L. yesterday& should not have written to you in now in haste but for the uncertainty of staying here. We are ordered to disperse with trunks & take but 25 lb. in satchels. It seems like parting with friends to let our few conveniences go but it is a necessity. I want you to keep up good courage.

  4 P.M. Orett has recd. a letter but I am still without one. I have no time to give a description of country, you can see L's letter when you get to Penn Yan. The firing of which I spoke ceased soon after but has commenced again. It is supposed Burnside's Division is over there after the enemy. You spoke in your last about a life insurance. I had no time to attend to it then & was ordered off soon after, perhaps it would be well but it would be expensive for me while in the army. My health is good & the men are mainly well. When I see you I can tell you what I cannot write. I recd. yesterday a letter from Noys of the 148th & he says the regt. George is in is encamped near them having left Newport News a few days sense. We are in Porter's Corps, Butterfields Brigade. There are about 2,500 men in this camp. I shall send my trunk to Washington till it is wanted. I don't see anything to hinder you writing of ten. Still, I have recd. but one letter from you since leaving Geneva & I have written you three. Little darling must write. O how I want to see her.

Good bye & may God bless you both from your affectionate husband & father,

B. Munger

Direct your letters to Washington, D.C.

44th N.Y.S.V.

Antietam Ford Oct. 23, 1862

My Dear wife & child,

We are still in our old camp & in all respects as we were when I last wrote you it is so monotonous in camp that there is little news to write but since I last wrote I have been to Sharpsburg & the battlefield. Seen James Hanna & spent the day pleasantly yesterday. The Norman School company arrived & we were glad to see them. They come with a perfect outfit while we are destitute of everything but good <u>grit</u>. I hurt my hand a few days ago, & have to write with a glove on & make rather poor work of it. If I can judge closely we are esteemed as highly as we could ask by our fellow officers. Day after tomorrow is my birthday & I confess I hardly feel reconciled to spend it here but I must never the less. There are few enjoyments but if any good is to be gained I can stay cheerfully. Tonight, our camp is in a stir in consequence of an order to prepare three days' rations & sixty rounds of cartridges & a team was sent to Sharpsburg after the ammunition. This evening still, I can't tell what it will amount to perhaps nothing but if anything, it possibly is to attack Lee's army. As everything is so uncertain here. I thot I would drop you a word although I hear nothing from you.

Sunday, Oct. 26, yesterday I rec'd a letter from you & perhaps it did not do my heart good. I was obliged to read it in company with officers & in my efforts to control my feelings the blood started from my nose. Sunday morning & raining still. We are feeling pretty well, getting accustomed to our mode of living. The monotony is tedious & the want of society & reading I feel deeply I am perhaps too old & habits too firmly established to make a good soldier. At any rate I long for home & friends & the subject fills my mind almost constantly. You don't know how anxious I feel about Ida. I have great confidence in Layman's judgement in such matters. I wish you would consult him but use no extreme means or medicines. Don't send her to school at present & especially try to divert her mind from the gloomy side of my position. I say again at present we have no privations worthy of the name of suffering to a man of wealth. What a march or battle may be we have got to learn sufficient into the day is the evil there of. Yesterday being my birthday I wrote to mother, the day before to Sophia. We dined with officers of the normal School Co., had a good time & a good dinner. I presume you may often wonder why we write so much about our food. The reason may be we have so little change & so few of the comforts of ordinary life that our living is an important item in our estimation. Jacob Stroup acts as our cook at present but we shall be under the necessity of hiring one or losing the wages of a soldier. One will do for us all. Some of the officers have one aspired. I would prefer to do my own cooking if I could. Things look some as if we were to move from here soon but I can't tell. You need not worry. Continue to direct your letters as at present and they will find. Yours Aff. B. Munger

The next letter in the Bennett Munger collection needs a note of explanation:

The envelope along the outer edge written in period pencil "Antietam Oct. 25 & 26, 1862" but the post mark dates from "Washington, D.C. Nov. 12, 1862". This letter is only partial and the introduction & ending have been lost or this letter is part of another letter in this collection. The partial letter is as follows:

(**Page missing**) when I told Orett, I would write you. I have just been to the pinnacle of Blue Ridge & enjoyed the most magnificent view I ever saw & you know how I enjoy such things & I intend to describe it to you but hard marching since has for a time knocked the romance out of me. I stand the fatigue of duty well. You would be surprised to see the immensity of this army. I can't tell the number of men it is so large we never see either end of it & it is camped over miles of ground. It is not a pleasant sight a large camp except at night then it is splendid & an army on the march is a sight that would fill you with awe. We march 4 a breast & the line reaches farther than one can see & as the line ascends a hill or winds around a bend in the road it is a sight not described easily. Such a living moving mass looks like a monster serpent winding himself around the hills & through the valleys but the reality is not so beautiful. Perhaps one in every hundred is just ready to faint & are only kept from falling out by their pride or the stern commands of officers & many on one hardest marches are obliged to yield. One of our men went till he was so near exhaustion that he lay nearly 24 hours before being able to move on. Others are cheerful & stand it well with the exception of the 6 that are left in hospital at Antietam. All our men are with us in camp of which I feel a little proud. We are 18 miles from Manassas & don't know our destination. Today when we were but into camp I supposed we were forming for battle there was a camp in sight & I thought from the (**The letter ends here**.)

Antietam Ford Oct. 26, 1862

My Darling little <u>Boy</u>,

      This letter is all for you & I must tell you of some of the odd things we see here as you saw our camp at Geneva, you have some idea how a camp looks. This one is on a field about 20 tents as large as that & little regularity but we are not scattered over the whole field but in groups. There is no grass on the ground but is trodden & dusty or was till last night (it has rained since till now). Perhaps the first thing you would notice after the tents would be the great covered wagons, covered with tent cloth & the teams of four mules with the driver on one of the hind ones & driving with one line & then the way they talk to them would make you laugh. All our food & the food for the mules & horses is brought in these wagons over the hills from Harper's Ferry. You frequently meet trains of these teams more than ½ a mile long then when you get into camp you will see scattered all around half a dozen men squatting all around their camp fires cooking their suppers, each boiling his coffee in a pint cup & frying his meat on a tin plate & for a handle a split stick if one has a frying pan he uses it for plate as well. I dined at another camp the other day & the host brought in his frying pan of beef all smoking hot, put it on the ground, handed me a loaf of bread & politely asked me to take hold with knife, fork or spoon so with my pocket knife I cut the bread, used the point for a fork & had a good meal. (It is now about dinner time & I would like to dine with you today.)

  Almost all the houses here are built of logs but better than log houses at the north sometimes of stone & well finished but the oddest quirk of all is they don't build their houses by roadsides but away on the farm usually near a spring & if you find a small creek the houses will be as thick as on roads as the north. Then there are no orchards here & I see very few signs of berries & another thing that would strike you as new is the ledges of rocks in one place. Near the ferry there is a precipice rising over 200 feet in some places. A mass of rock will project 15 to 20 feet & look as if it would surely fall onto you. The mountain rises 600 feet, so steep & rocky that one could hardly climb it & still covered with trees growing out of the scars in the rock. You write that sometimes you want to fly to me, much as I want to see you, darling I would not have you come here if I could. I fear if you should you would not be favorably impressed with our fare for it seems worse to the observer than a resident & I want you to think of me without pain or dread. I wish you would write often. Suppose you keep a diary on paper & send it to me in form of letters. You don't know how much I think of you daily & may add nightly. It rains hard & is cold, the worst day we have had. Our tent leaks so that there is hardly a dry place in it. We have not yet had any dinner. The men are feeling blue & I must stop & go around & cheer them up. I have just found that my rubber blanket wets through which is misfortunate you cannot appreciate. I must close darling, be cheerful & good & God will keep you. Pray for me love that I may always do my duty.

From your loving father.

B. Munger

                   On the march near White Plains Nov. 7, 1862

Dear Little Ida,

  I promised though Orett to write you that day if I had time but we received marching orders within an hour, we struck tents at 3 P.M. & marched 5 miles to Division Headquarters. Reached camp at dark, slept cold, eat in a hurry & we're off at 7 ½ this was at Snickers Gap. Next day, Saturday we marched 16 miles & camped near Middleburg this morn off at 6 ½ marched 5 miles to this place & camped in a piece of woods. It began to snow as we halted & snowed all day and is really cold freezing all day. We expect to stay here a day or two but I learn we are to march at 5 in the morn. When I told Orett, I would write you I had just been to the pinnacle of the Blue Ridge & enjoyed the most magnificent view I ever saw & you know how I enjoy such things & I intended to describe it to you but hard marching since has for a time has knocked the romance out of me. I stand the fatigues of duty well. You would be surprised to see the immensity of this army. I can't tell the number of men but it is so large we never see either end of it & it is camped over miles of ground. It is not a pleasant sight, a large camp, except at night, then it is splendid & an army on the march is a sight that would fill you with awe. We march 4 abreast & the line reaches farther than one can see & as the line ascends a hill or winds around a bend in the road it is a sight not easily described. Such a living moving mass looks like a monster serpent winding himself around the hills & through the valleys, but the reality is not as beautiful. Perhaps one in every hundred is just ready to faint & are only kept from falling out by their pride or the stern commands of the officers & many on one (of their) hardest marches are obliged to yield. One of our men went till he was so near exhausted that he lay nearly 24 hours before being to move on. Others are cheerful & stand it well with the exception of the 6 that we left in hospital at Antietam. All our men are with us in camp of which I feel a little proud.

We are 18 miles from Manassas & don't know our destination. Today when we were brought into camp I suppose we were forming for battle. There was a camp in sight & I thought from the peculiar evolutions of our brigade that we were forming in line of battle & I afterwards found it was the opinion of most of our men. You will want to know how I felt but I will only tell you how I acted. I think I formed the company with as much accuracy as if on dress parade but war little girl is not pleasant business & I think if I live to get home I shall know how to enjoy its blessings as I never did before. What would I give little one, to take you in my arms tonight? Still I would not have here & I do not want to come home till I get through with this war for I could not enjoy a visit with the thought that I must return to camp again. I wish you would tell Uncle Layman that I wish he would get me a pair of heavy calf boots pegged long legs & for hard tramping. He will know the size by the pair I let him have. I want them large. Send by express. Love to all.

Your loving father,

B. Munger

Envelope reads: "On the March" 3 O'clock A.M. Nov. 8, 1862

My Dear wife,

Received your welcome letter last night after finishing Paws containing to NY, all safe for which I think I also received one from Mother & Abigail. The boy's mail was not distributed last night so we do not know what they received in our marches. I slept with Orett, & last night although the coldest was the best night rest I have enjoyed since we have joined the Regiment mostly to having straw to sleep (on) and you can't tell how tough I am. I don't carry as much load as the boys but am up earliest & have more care than a married woman. You naturally want to know how we feel. There is not a man who loves the business but all bear the hardship with cheerfulness or most all and want the war to close before they come home but when you read of the troops being eager to fight you may set your mind to newspaper talk. We are human still and not anxious to die but I am ready to do our duty. I think you all have the impression that I am sick which is not the case, but I will write back if I write anything thing & the oft separated opinion that there is great enthusiasm in the army is a lie & I say again that duty & pride are the prevailing motives in the minds of 99/100 of the army & if it is homesickness to say so (as Merrick seems to intimate) then the old officers & soldiers are the most homesick men here. If I could have a furlough today I would not accept it & yet we are making sacrifices than as never can or will. The bugle sounds &

I must be up & doing wright after, while we are on the march we cannot but will embrace every chance. Orett sends love. God bless you all good bye.

B. Munger

P.S. My boots are most gone & I wish Layman would send me a pair as soon as possible. Large ones. B.M.

Warrenton, Va. Nov. 10, 1862

My dear Wife & Daughter,

We have been in camp since yesterday morning today Gen. McClellan passed here & our brigade & others were out to see him. Gen. Burnside takes command today, his headquarters are about ½ a mile from our camp. There are a large number of troops in this vicinity & it is said the enemy are concentrating their forces at Warrenton Junction, 10 miles from here. The old soldiers are indignant at the change of commanders & there will be many resignations in consequence. Porter our corps commander & Butterfield our division commander besides many inferior officers are said to be of the number who ready to resign. One certain in our regiment is marking out his, I learn. What the effect will be on the coming battle I cannot tell but hope for the best. I have been to the village today which is about ½ as large as Penn Yan. The stores & shops were closed & I saw but few citizens. I saw a few ladies & some children did my heart good. One thing that I noticed that looked odd a door yard full of flowers as fresh as May many of the apple trees are still green which reminds a northerner is in a new latitude. The village does not show thrift of our towns but is far the finest I have seen one thing that gives. - Nov. 11, morning – It is very fine weather again & perhaps we shall remain in this camp some time. I learn this morning that our forces rolled the Junction & it is probably true as a train of cars are said to have reached this place last night which will be a great advantage to us in relation to our previous prices are famously high here for everything not furnished by the Gov.

Tapping a pair of boots 10/100 (Captain Munger means 10 cents to re-peg or put on metal heal plates on the boots), a pair of ordinary boots $12.00 & so on. We have had no mail since the 8th but hope to get one today. I think we do not receive all the letters sent on this side but don't know. You don't mention the receipt of all I sent. I received one from you on the 8th & one from mother. Have written you a word since on the 9th. I think when on the march I have no time & but little when in camp as there is nothing private in these, I want them to be shared by L's folks. I feel deeply the obligation I am under to them & the more as I cannot repay it. If L has not sent the books I requested ask him to hold on for the present as no express can reach us at present & the future is so uncertain. I have a pair of shoes which I was compelled to buy. My feet swelled so & they are very easy to march in so that my feet are well again & I am tough as a knot. Someone from home (I have forgotten) who expressed apprehension for the morals of the boys on that score they have nothing to fear at least while we are out of the way of cities. The good boys are just as good as ever but perhaps the profane ones are more profane.

Evening – You can see I don't write long as a line. I left at noon to visit Lieut. Atwood of the firm, Munson & Atwood. He is quartermaster of the 32nd & is looking well, has matured more since he left Yates than some men do in five years. The company officers were called to the Cols. Tent & received instructions in regard to discipline which is to be more strict. One of our sergeants was reduced in rank today for disobedience to orders. It is John O'Neil. Lieut. James is not well I fear. He is going to be sick. We have no servant & get & do our own work. We are obliged to certify that we employ a servant & therefor we want one.

It is generally supposed that we are to have a severe battle soon. We have an immense army here, probably 150,000 men & still they gather in & though some think we shall have no battle this fall. I think otherwise. If this marching is all a farce it is an expensive play both in muscle & money. I never write home without thinking perhaps it is my last letter & if this should be the one all I have to say is forgive the errors I may have committed although many& remember only my visits if I have any & I pray that I may die in the discharge of my duty. Don't think that I feel fearful that is not the feeling, still seeing the endless marching of war as we do here. No one can fail to be impressed with the fact that if these two great armies meet there must be an immense slaughter. I think the hope of promotion in the Regiment is so small that there is not one chance in one hundred. Perhaps we made an unwise choice in coming to this regiment but it cannot be helped now. Good bye for the night.

The mail is just recd. & although a large one having accumulated since the 8th I have no scrap from friend or foe. Lt. Kelly recd. five letters & two papers. Perhaps you may guess my disappointment. I'll try not to tell it. O. & F. recd. two or more each & have gone to read them. I'll not blame for perhaps no one is to blame & I never want a <u>friend</u> to write to me unless they choose to. I was stopped at this point by the entrance of Orett with a <u>line</u> from you & I see by the date it was written on the day of our severest march. Such a day's experience as I never wish to have repeated. It was a beautiful day however & God, I guess intended we should be happy. I will try to write less about myself & more about other things. The officers who have been absent from the regiment are returning to us& everything looks like preparation for work & I do hope the struggle may come soon if a certain amount of fighting is to be done. I say the sooner we do it the better & even if I knew we must fall I rather it would be tomorrow than next year & I see no hope for favorable settlement but in fighting them to the death. I have been reading a report of the commission on the Harpers Ferry defeat & although I thank God that I was not in the 126th. I have little confidence that the same blunders will not be repeated for every battle for there is no wisdom or generalship in the management of this war, but if I have little hope to inspire ambitions I have pride enough to die by inches rather than be disgraced. You asked if I have recd. a letter from Soph. No, nor from anyone except yourself, L., Netti & Mother. I don't think I am in a good mood for writing today & as this must be mailed in an hour. I will close & finish a word I began to Ida.

Yours as ever,

B. Munger

My Dear Ida,

I will begin where I left off which was where my meal was cooked as the Lt.s were not up & ready. I ate alone sitting on the ground & ground for table. By that time came questions & c. First the Orderly from the Col. with an order that our Co. come out for Co. drill at 9 A.M. & Battalion drill at 2 P.M. Then a man wants a pass to visit it brother in a cavalry regiment & I write it. Another one wants to visit a cousin in the 34th & I have to explain to him that the other has to return, two more want passes as soon as the last returns. A man comes who is sick, hurt himself at Antietam & thinks he will never be able to do duty again, pity him some, encourage more & give a little advice. Time for drill which lasts one hour, by that time news comes that we have a mail. All is excitement. It is a large one & takes time to sort it. The mail for each Co. is put by itself & I went to my trunk learning directions to have it sent then found men under arrest waiting for me whose offence was talking in the ranks, talked to them & let them go. Mail comes & as a call over the names on the letters you can't tell with what eager joy they answer but the poor <u>disappointed ones</u> not satisfied with the evidence of the sight linger around with the Capt., "Ain't there any for me?" and go off sad. Well as I had none to read I went to writing & this is the result. It is now noon & the mail will close soon & as I want no dinner I will close this, put it in the mail bag, walk out by myself & think. Be a good little girl always. Do what you think right & & God will bless you which I pray. Good bye, love to all.

Your Father.

B. Munger

I just learned the mail has closed & perhaps I may add a word before another goes.- 4 P.M. Well we have just been out to take leave of this old commander, Gen. Porter of the change of officers you of course know as soon as we do so that I will leave out. Our whole division was out today the first time I ever saw them together. I have command of our first (that is of the regiment) & my want of familiarity with military tactics mortified much. Maj. Knox promised to competent instructors is hardly fulfilled. I have resolved today to go work more zealously than ever if we have an instructor. The bugle sounds for dress parade & I must stop again.

6 ½ I try again. The next letter I write I will mark the interruptions I have. We now (have) the Baltimore papers & are better posted on matters in general & another thing we are now within hearing of a rail road engine which sounds like civilization. The Col. sends for us so I stop again.

8 P.M. Received instruction in battalion drill.

Nov. 12 & 13, 1862

To: Ida M. Munger

Nov. 12th –

Well little Ida good morning. I feel rather lonely this morning & that I would visit with you a moment. It is a cloudy morning but warm & as usual I was up early & the first thing to do was cut wood & build a fire then superintend roll call & next get breakfast & I'll tell you how I did it. One stove is a hole dug in the ground just in front of our tent, 3 feet long & 1 wide & deep 1. Our furniture a frying pan, stew pan, coffeepot & kettle. Our breakfast consisted of coffee with sugar (no milk) fried pork & beef & pilot bread softened in water & fried in the meat fat. Pilot bread is in form & size like soda crackers but extremely hard & although much despised is really the soldiers best friend. It is light & easy to carry on a march & is so nearly tasteless that one never tires of it soaked in water & eaten with sugar is a nutritious dish & not bad to the taste. It is good in coffee also. I have almost filled my page without finishing my mornings work & must leave.

Thursday Nov. 13

As I failed to get my letter into the mail yesterday I will add a word this morning. There is no order yet for march. I suppose the change of commanders involves some delay but I feel anxious for every days dealing increases their strength more than ours. We had an addition to our family. A young lieutenant just returned from a furlough was wounded in the battle of Balls Run. I would prefer being alone but must submit as the wall tent which we occupy is granted us as a favor & not as a right, so we must share it. I don't know whether I mentioned that John K. Giddings, who left is at Washington has returned. He came in last Monday, says he was asleep in a car back of ours & it was detached & left while he was asleep & he was sent to Alexandria. We are in good health & spirits. Our rations are a little short just now but it is (a) vast multitude to feed & it is no wonder that stores run short something. Again farewell. B. Munger

Rained a little & I fear it is to be a big storm. The roads are now dry & dusty. I don't know but I have told you that our Lieut. Col. (who is acting Col.) makes me think of Dwight most of any man I ever saw. I never look at or speak to him without thinking of Dwight & the Man reminds of war pending. Most of the officers I like but there is no kindred spirits here. I value Orett's society more than all the regiment beside & I do wish he was Lieut. We made one great mistake but it is too late to remedy as there is a rumor that we move tomorrow but no order as yet. The morning we stopped here (Sunday) we expected to be in Gordonsville before this time but all is uncertain if that scripture, "None knows what a day may bring forth." is true anywhere. It is the army but I am so accustomed to it now I don't mind it much though I still hate to get up in the night & march but I can do that. I think if you get this letter you will not need another at present. Keep up good courage, love to all & etc. Where is Fannie Waite?

Good night. As ever, your affectionate,

B. Munger

The mail is just received & although a large one having accumulated since the 8th I have no scrap from friend or foe. Lieut. Kelly received five letters & two papers perhaps you may guess my disappointment. I'll not try to tell it. O & F received two or more each & have gone to mail them. I'll not blame for perhaps no one is to blame and I never want a <u>friend</u> to write to me unless they chose to. I was stopped at this point by the entrance of Orett with a <u>line</u> from yours & I see by the date it was written on the day of our severest march. Such a day's experience as I never wish to have repeated. It was a beautiful day however & God, I guess intended we should have been happy. I'll try to write less about myself & more about other things. The officers who have been absent from the Regiment are returning to us & everything looks like preparation for work & I do hope the struggle may come soon if a certain amount of fighting is to be done I say the sooner we do it the better & even if I knew we must fall I rather it would be tomorrow than next year & I see no hope of favorable settlement but in fighting them to the death. I have been reading a report of the campaign on the Harpers Ferry defeat & although I thanked God that I was not in the 12th I have little confidence that the same blunders will not be repeated at every battle for there is no wisdom or generalship in the management of this war. But if I have little hope to inspire ambition I have pride enough to die by inches rather than be disgraced. You asked if I had received a letter from Soph. no, nor from anyone except yourself, L., Nettie & mother. I don't think I am in good mood for writing today & as this must be mailed in an hour I will close & finish a word I have begun to Ida - Yours as ever – B.Munger

  My Dear Ida – I will begin where I left off which was where my meal was cooked as the Lieutenants were not up & ready I ate alone sitting on the ground & ground for table. By that time came questions & etc. first an orderly from the Col. With an order that our Company come out for drill at 9 A.M. & Battalion drill at 2 P.M. then a man wants a pass to visit his brother in a cavalry regiment & I write it, another wants one to visit a cousin in the 34th & I have to explain to that (see third page) the other has returned, two more want a pass as soon as the last returns. A man comes who is sick, hurt himself at Antietam & I think he will never be able to do duty again. Pity him some encourage more & give a little advice. Time for drill which lasts one hour by that time news comes that we have a mail. All is excitement! It is large & takes time to assort it. The mail for each company is put by itself & I was to my tent leaving directions to have it sent there. Found 4 men under arrest waiting for me who's' offence was talking in the ranks. (I) talked to them & let them go. Mail comes & as a call over the names on the letters you can't tell with what eager joy they answer but the poor <u>disappointed ones</u> not satisfied with the evidence of sight linger around with Captain, "Ain't there any for me?" & go off sad. Well as I have had none to read I went to writing & this is result. It is now noon & the mail will close soon & as I want no dinner & I will closet his, put it in the mail bag, walk out by myself & think. Be a good little girl, always do what you think right & God will bless you for which I pray.

Good bye, love to all, your father B. Munger

A note in period pencil on the outside of this letter's envelope notes the dates of this letter as:

                             Nov. 15 & 16, 1862

Note: The first part of this letter is missing: We camped on the side of the mountain on the road to Rock Ferry. We laid at this place till Wednesday about 4 P.M. We had a pleasant time here & enough to eat without heading Blackston on the rights of property. I think I wrote you from this place but am not certain. On leaving this camp we marched down the mountain & then south to Snickersville, here we joined our Brigade which had been guarding the gap & searched it on Sunday night just before the Rebs reached it from the other side & this was the reason why we were marched so on that day. We bivouacked late that night & had a cheerless time, rained some during the night. The men felt down hearted. I must cheer them whether I feel it or not. Aroused at 4 in the morning got into line at 6 ½ & stood in a piercing wind one hour to wait for troops to pass. We marched 16 miles this day & our communication Harpers Ferry closed today & we were ordered to let no man fall out on any account. The baggage & artillery were sent to the front which looked like danger. The men stood it well. Today we camped near Beaver Dam Creek. On the map, I have made a dot southeast of Snickersville. Started at 6 ½ marched till about noon camped in a wood from which place I wrote to Mary of the snow storm & etc. Up at 3 next morning & made a rapid march till about noon & camped there. I lost the handkerchief you sent me, this was near White Plain as a dot. Up at 3 ½ & marched to within 3 miles of this place & Sunday before daylight it came to this. Waited 2 hours in the cold & then ordered to pitch tents. The pitching & striking of tents is about as agreeable business as household moving & a new camp seems dreary. It will be one week tomorrow since we came here.

Summers Corps are moving this moment & we expect our time will come tomorrow or next day. Today at 1 ½ we are to be reviewed by Gen. Hooker. There are an unusual number of sick this morn. One man took part of his medicine & threw the balance away for which he was reported to the Col. (He was) sentenced to wear a heavy knapsack & march in front of the guard house all day. It grieved his heart & he cried to me like a child but there is no remedy. There are so many such vexations, little matters to settle & cares to attend to that sometimes it seems as if I should care but I <u>shan't</u>. Returned from the great review, Gen. Hooker is about 50, good sized, light completed <u>red face</u>, & looks like an earnest go ahead man, but when a nation is as deeply humiliated as ours such holiday shows are disgusting. I feel anxious to do what I am to do & be done with it.

The day is a very bright one & if one was visiting the country on a tour of pleasure there would be many things of beauty to enjoy. The face of the country is very rolling & everywhere mountains in the distance but there are so many drawbacks with us that it falls somewhat short of a pleasure trip. Still, there are prospects so beautiful & sublime & loving nature as I do I forget everything for a moment, but there is nothing I have seen in varied beauty that equals the scenery around Penn Yan. One thing that was apparent of everything is the destruction of fences. It would astonish you to see how quick 100 rods of fence will vanish when our brigade halts for the night. The companies vie with each other in getting into line, calling roll & stacking arms that their men may have a good chance for rails & in ten minutes it is all on the motion. The troops leaving this place are taking a southeast direction which looks like going to Fredericksburg. I am anxious to be on the move. The roads are so good & if it should rain or snow, poorly shod as I am, marching would be tedious.

Sunday, North last night was cold but I suppose it seems more so to us living as we do we have just had a sermon by one of the enlisted men. It is warmer, there are signs of a move so I will be ready to close at a moment. Has Mape's wife called for the money sent her? Have you received Lieut. James trunk? If so please store it away till you hear from us. It contains Company property. The name of Corps commander is Joseph Hooker, Division Gen. David Butterfield, Brigade Col. Stockton acts as Brigadier Gen, one Col. F. Coremer is acting Col. although ranks as Lieut. Col., J. C. Rice the Colonel is in Albany. Mail again but nothing for me. There are several things I want you to send me when I get to a stopping place but no express can reach here.

Orett has just mailed a letter to Pling so I think I will wait to see if we move. Yesterday we engaged R. Shipley as cook with consent of the Col. & he makes a good one & I think we shall be more comfortable. I wish I could write as I sometimes feel & all I feel but I can't, so let it go. I forgot to say I received yours of the 9th on the 14th, give me credit in yours.

8 P.M. orders just received to march in the morning at 6. I have felt in my bones all day & are prepared but it begins to storm & I fear will have a hard time but don't worry about us, we are tough. You shall hear from us at the first opportunity. Good bye may God bless & keep you.

B. Munger

On The March Nine Miles from Fredericksburg: Nov. 20, 1862

My dear wife,

I wrote a letter directed to Layman, Sunday night saying we were to leave camp next morning but I learn this morning it with all the mail from that place is still in the brigade & that there is a prospect of sending it today. You may have been anxious about us but you will see the fault is not ours. We have not had a very hard march, lost one man, Bassett who fell out & I suppose was sent to Washington. Fred fell the past day but is well now. It has rained & been raining since Sunday night but not much water fallen till last night when it came down freely. It has been nasty unpleasant march & now it is worse than ever. This is as bad as soil for mud as I have ever seen. Yellow loam & clay with a heavy subsoil & as I have only shoes it is not comfortable walking. I don't know when or where we are going from here. I think the whole of our grand division under (Note: Captain Munger wrote the name, Hooker and then crossed it out in this part of the letter) is in this vicinity. It is the largest camp I ever saw & covers several hundred acres. It is now 9 A.M. and no sign of moving, still we may be in motion in 30 minutes, it is the uncertain life you can imagine, sometimes get a meal almost ready & the bugle will sound out the note for marching & everything must be left & jump for life & perhaps get into line & stand two long hours before we move but that is not much, only annoying. I have always been ready but once & never lost a meal on that account. I have received no letters since my last to you & can't guess when I shall. Perhaps at Fredericksburg if we go there. This is Abigail's birthday & next Wednesday is Ida's. I think of home some especially the anniversaries. Perhaps I would like to be with you one week from today. I could be a soldier with perfect composure & cheerfulness if the sacrifices I make provided a corresponding good for the country but to be made such an object slave as we are here to aid the personal ambitions of a few is too much to bear with patience & I like uttering Grahams saying, "I feel nigh to cussing." but you at home don't understand & never will understand the real sentiment or the entire want of sentiment here. There is nothing that will create such a general laugh as a newspaper account of the devotion of the army. I want Ida to write me on her birthday, stories to make her a thoughtful child, be patient with her & may God bless you all.

As ever, B. Munger

Enclosed you will find a rose I had plucked day before yesterday. The weather is mild, last night the warmest in two weeks. This morning the quails whistled as with us in spring but give me my own home. Yet in nothing have they the advantage except in climate. On paper I can't give you all the points of difference in the country. Perhaps the most striking is the fact that the highways are not the building points here but the springs of water. So we travel all day & pass but one or two houses then the roads are very crooked & seems more like a deserted country than an inhabited one.

Noon – Rained like a torrent & O how muddy. Mail leaves at 2. It seems we are going to Fredericksburg but we don't know when. I have seen no paper for several days & do not know anything of the position of the army or the plans of our generals. Tell me all the news from home anything is of interest. Tell Graham I would like to hear from him & I sometimes wish he was here just one day but with the idea he was elected for the war. I would be satisfied. James wilts under it but his health is poor. The boys are well & take things very coolly. Love to all friends if I have any.

B. Munger

Camp near Fredericksburg Nov. 20, 1862

My Dear Ida,

Rumor is your birthday & as everything is so uncertain here I will secure the present have to write you. Some of the friends say I am not particular enough. I'll try to correct that fault this time. First I'll acknowledge the receipt of letters on the 21st containing hers & yesterday in part from yourself. I wrote last on the 22nd. Sunday morning I was up at 5 and Robert had breakfast most ready & I suppose to be minute. I must tell you what we had for breakfast. First, fried pork then we baked up pilot bread – the boys wickedly call it hard tack – put on cold water & let it soak overnight after the meat was fried, pour off the fat & fry the prepared bread then our never omitted coffee & sugar and as you know I am fond of a desert, I have a dry hard tack & sugar. When we want anything new we change the order. Now little fellow don't feel sad & think that is all we have to eat. No, we have pretty good things but it is true that when on the march bread, coffee & sugar are all we can have as a rule, for we carry 3 days rations & of course it must be light nutritious food. You see little one I have forgotten Sunday march already. Well, we ate our meal, packed our goods, struck our tents & carried all to wagons about ½ a mile, came back to camp & I went to visit the sick. John O'Neil is the sickest with swelled face & fever. I got him into an ambulance. John McLaughlin the next is down with severe cold on his lungs. The Dr. says he must try & walk. Mandeville is down with diarrhea. By the way I am disappointed in him. He makes me more trouble than any other man in the company. Just as I had finished with the sick an order came that we were to be rear guard of the brigade & that today is in the rear of the corps. 8 ½ the bugle sounds to form in line & an order for Capt. Munger with ½ of his company to march over the camp & arrest all stragglers. So away we go with an additional order to hurry the camp. Covered about 25 acres & groups of men scattered over it. I took six I think & marched them in & we had one man under arrest from Capt. Kimble's company. My instructions were to let no man fall back unless he had written permission from the commander of his company countersigned by the Dr. All others to prick into the ranks. That means force them to march even if I had to use the bayonet to make them. Perhaps that will sound harsh to you darling. It is a hard post this rear guard, especially when we are abandoning the post we leave. Uncle L will explain that to you & tell you why it won't do to let them fall to the rear when the enemy is following us. Now how do you think your father would feel ordering a squad of men to push a poor tired soldier with the point of a bayonet? Well, he <u>didn't</u> do it. About ½ a mile from camp I came up to poor woeful looking fellows living beside the road & I spoke to them, "& well boys have you a pass?" Yes they answered. I told them to let me see them. They were genuine & entitled them to a ride in the ambulance. So I told them they must try to keep up till that train joined ours which would be some distance or they would be left to the tender mercies of the wicked. One replied, "Captain if there is anything or anybody more wicked than I have seen for the last 18 months I'd like to stop & see it." I asked, "Have you had it tough my dear fellow?" "O", said he, "It makes all difference who your officers are, they can make it hard or pleasant for us. If you had ordered me up. I would not have stirred but I kind'a liked your way." & they kept up most of the day. I can't recall all the incidents of the day. One however I will tell you a little after noon we were passing through pine shrubbery & an old grey Negro was standing beside the road & appeared utterly astonished at the number of troops passing called out, "Well I guess you cotch dem dis time massas but if you don't for de God Almighty's sake go home & give um up." It raised a general laugh & all that is pretty sensible advice for we have men enough to eat through to give you some idea little one of the size of this army. I suppose it would take it three days & nights to march past a given point with their wagon trains, artillery & all marching as we do four men abreast, but I have not finished my Sunday yet. There was an immense wagon train before us & toward night another behind us from some other road but next us in rear was a battery which consists of six cannon & six each drawn by six horses. Toward night we were hindered by the train & it was growing cold. We halted on a cold hill nearly two hours till we were chilled through, went on a mile or so into a pine wood & halted in a wet spot a long time, then moved again ¼ miles & halted in a deep cut in a hill where the cut was just wide enough for a wagon. It was dark, we were cold & our patience was taxed <u>some,</u> after a while I went forward, found a place where my men could climb up the bank, called them & told them they might build fires. That diverted us until we had fires enough to make us comfortable. In about an hour the adjutant came back to us & called out, "Captain Munger make your men as comfortable as you can. We shall have to stay here tonight." That was about 8 O'clock. Some of them had been to supper, that is had eaten hardtack enough but the officers had not so. We selected a place for our fire in a pine grove on a side hill, built a fire & some had pork, hardtack & coffee but not feeling well myself that I would not eat a <u>rich</u> supper, so took only hardtack & water as I did for dinner & if you think that was hard I can tell of a worse case. I passed a man& asked the usual question, "Have you a pass?" "Yes Captain but I can't keep up." I asked why he had no food & he said their brigade was out entirely. Fact I had before learned so I gave him a tack & he was pleased as you would be with a new dress. Now let me caution you not to get too dark an impression from that incidents in the main. We have enough to eat & suffer no more than men do in new countries in the accumulation of property with the exception of a home & family to sympathize with us when the day's trial is done. I say as I have said before. Let others complain as they may. My physical suffering doesn't compare with my mental & even this is mostly negative. It is not so much what I suffer a want I <u>don't</u> enjoy. So, don't let your lives be saddened by the idea that we suffering severely though you don't know how we miss your sympathy as expressed in your letters & when I come home I will tell you more about it than I can now. It is past 2 O'clock & the boys have long, long been asleep & I will bid you good night with an imaginary kiss hoping to be able to add something to this in the morning.

Camp near Fredericksburg Nov. 25, 1862

My Dear Ida,

Tomorrow is your birthday & as everything is so uncertain here I will secure the present hour to write you. Some of the friends say I am not particular enough. I'll try to correct that fault this time. First, I will acknowledge the letters on the 21st containing (**this word not readable**) & yesterday one in part from yourself. I wrote last on the 22nd.

Sunday morning I was up at 5 and Robert had breakfast most ready & I supposed to be minute. I must tell you what we had for breakfast. First, fried pork then we break up Pilot bread (the boys wickedly call it <u>hard</u> <u>tack</u>) put on cold water & let soak overnight. After the meat was fried pour off the fat & fry the prepared bread then our never omitted coffee & sugar & as you know I am fond of a desert. I have a dry hard tack & sugar. When we want something new we change the order. Now little fellow don't feel sad & think that is all we have to eat. No, we have many pretty good things but it is true that when on the march bread, coffee & sugar are all we can have as a meal, for we carry 3 days' rations & of course it must be light nutritious food.

You see little one, I have forgotten Sunday march already, well we ate our meal, packed our goods, struck our tents & carried all to the wagon about ½ of a mile, came back to camp & I went to visit the sick. John O'Neil is the sickest with swollen face & fever. I got him into the ambulance. John McLaughlin the next, is down with severe cold on his lungs. The Dr. says he must try to walk. Mandeville is down with diarrhea (by the way I am disappointed in him. He makes me more trouble than any other man in the Co.). Just as I had finished with the sick an order came that we were to be rear guard of the brigade & today that is the rear of the Corps.

8 ½ the bugle sounds to form into line & an order for Capt. Munger with half his Co. to march over the camp & arrest al stragglers. So, away we go with an additional order to hurry the camp, covered 25 acres & groups of men scattered over it. I took six I think & marched them in and we had one man under arrest from Capt. Kimble's Co. My instructions were to let no man fall back unless he had written permission from the commander of his Co. counter signed by the Dr. All others to prick into the ranks that means force them to march even if I had to use the bayonet to make them. <u>Perhaps</u> that will sound harsh to you darling. It is a hard post this rear guard especially when we are abandoning the post we leave. Uncle L. will explain that to you & tell you why it won't do to let them fall to the rear when the enemy is following us. Now how do you think your father would feel ordering a squad of men to push a poor tired soldier with the point of the bayonet? Well, he <u>didn't</u> do it! About ½ a mile from camp I came upon two poor, woeful looking fellows living beside the road & I spoke cheerfully to them & "Well boys do you have papers?" "Yes!" they answered. I told them to let me see them. They were genuine & entitled them to a ride in the ambulance. So, I told them they must try to keep up till that train joined ours which would be some distance or they would be left to the tender mercies of the wicked. One replied, "Capt. if there is anything or anybody more wicked than I have seen for the last 18 months I'd like to stop & see it." I asked, "Have you had it tough my dear fellow?" "O", said he, "It makes all the difference…." **Note: The letter is missing the closing page & ends here.**

Wednesday morning Nov. 26, 1862

Good morning my Darling & a happy birthday to you. I am officer of the day today & you must read this with dire respect. I will resume my day's narrative. We were ready to lie down at 11 O'clock. Seven of us had three rubber & three woolen blankets. We laid the rubber on the woolen (& the woolen) over us. Orett & I lay together, it was a cold night & we built a good fire. A little before 12 I got up for the blanket was too narrow on my side. Covered Orett up good, fixed the fire & laid on the ground close to it. Then I enjoyed all the pleasures of heat & cold while one side smarted with other side with cold so I changed often to see which was pleasantest & came to the sage conclusion that the best is in passing from cold to heat. At 3 I got tired of that I laid down with O a piece till five when O got up I told him if he always looked out as well for himself, I'd risk him but he complains that I was a very unfair bedfellow & that I took pretty much all of the blanket. So I was obliged to compromise & call it even but I took cold & paid a severe penalty next day with sick headache. The first severe attack since I left Geneva. Our greatest discomfort now is the ground is cold & we do not of course sleep warm as you do in beds for it is impossible to with the means in our reach to keep off the ground so that the cold will not make the lower side smart some. We lay a rubber blanket on the ground & a woolen on it so that the moisture kept from us pretty well. I slept very little after that & I lie & think & think & think and what do you suppose it is about. There darling I have given you some particulars of one day's marching day, sometime if I live I will give you a camp day. I would (like) to write to you much more but our writing facilities are like our other matters, not of the best.

Your loving father,

B. Munger

Nov.30, 1862

On Picket 10 Miles from Falmoth

My Dear Wife & Daughter,

It is Sunday & the last day of autumn, mild & happy & were 5 or 6 miles from camp & in the woods. I believe you like particulars so I will give you the events of the day. We moved our camp a few rods into a piece of pine woods which we cleared & swept so that it looks like a meadow. Yesterday at 4 P.M. we had everything about finished & were cutting our Sunday wood, expecting dress parade at 4 ½ when an order came to get ready for picket duty with 2 days' provisions in haversacks immediately. I rolled up my blankets, filled my sack & was ready in a twinkle but the men had a thousand questions, first, "Where we going Captain?" Which by the way we never know. Officers know more than men but they love to ask. Some wanted to know what to carry & few could go straight to work in a few minutes. An orderly came saying the Major wanted me to hurry up my men. Rob had just got our supper ready but eating was not to be. Though & I left everything to get the men ready. Kelly was on guard duty at camp & therefor excused from picket & James got out after the men were in line. Soon another order came from the Major to have my men in line as soon as God would let me. I was then about ready & was in line in time & the second company ready, we moved off, joined the brigade & in a short time were ready & we started at a rapid step. It was now dark & we were well loaded. I had not the least idea where or how far we were to go. We marched rapidly till about 7, turned every corner & toward every point of the compass, halted on an obscure road through woods & bivouacked in the woods. We had marched about 6 miles. I ate a hard tack & sugar & laid down, was wet with perspiration & not comfortable enough to sleep soundly. I had got most to sleep when a little reptile of some sort close to my head squeaked out much like a young rat. It was possibly a harmless lizard but I could hear him crawl among the leaves & squeal about once a minuet. I got so wakeful I could not well sleep but did at last. Waked at 2 with the cold got up, built a fire and sat by till morning. Ate 3 hard tack with sugar for breakfast, went to a stream & washed and with Orett took a short walk. I came back & he with others went to a little log house & bought a chicken & if we had the needful for cooking it should have a good meal as it is it will be a great thing for us. As near as I can judge we are northwest from our camp & the object to prevent surprise. Why our armies are literally still here I do not know unless it is to obtain supplies for the army. This rail road was useless on account of the destruction of bridges. They are now rebuilt & cars run day before yesterday so if that is the cause it will soon be removed. There is more sickness usual in our company. 18 were reported unfit for duty & some of them are pretty sick. Ackley started with us last night though complaining some & had to fall out but came up with us & I have just given a pass to return to camp. His complaint is diarrhea & bad very. I am not as well today. I took some cold last night. You asked if we have anything to take when we are sick. Yes, we have a first rate Dr. & frequently take a dose from his stores. It is past 1 & I must close for the present it is a dull day & I am duller than the day. If I would allow myself to express a wish, I could make an earnest one but <u>know</u> it will do no good.

   Monday, P.M. - Last night I received letter No. 1, enclosing one from you also one from Graham. I was cheered to hear from you but am sorry to hear that you worry so about us. I wish you would not. We are doing well enough & shall be so happy when we get home.

 Orett & I share your letters & I wish you to do the same. This part however is to Lyman. James is sick as death & told me the other day if he could get out of service now he would be willing to lose his wages & his expressage since the first of August. I only quote his languish to show how sick he is now. If the acceptance of his resignation can be secured with the strong possibility of Orett's promotion I am anxious to bring it about & I <u>trust </u>you will find some interest in it. I only suggest it but am going to sound James more fully, also the Colonel & Lieut. Kelly. James is an estimable man but he can never be a soldier & he knows it. If you have any suggestions or advice write without delay. Answers to your questions as to bills are on the way. I will add that the barn of Starks was done by the yard at the usual rates. I think perhaps if you can sell Billy for 90 or 100 dollars unless you can get him kept for his work or unless you want to use him, you better do so.

   You will see I have made a mistake in filling these pages but read by number & you will make it out.

   Was Gaylord's Charley sound at the end of the six months & has Resner paid that board bill & did C. Stark settle this matter fairly? If I get time I shall write to Graham in a few days. It is one of my chief sources of enjoyment to write home & if I burden you, hurt is I dreamed of home last night but you were not glad to see me & I felt it so keenly I awakened immediately to lie awake to think it over. I had one advantage however. I <u>was</u> <u>not</u> <u>there</u> so I went to sleep again. I do no not understand our new move in picket duty today. The number of men has been greatly increased. We sent out a brigade & today I think there are at least four times as many & took a corps of ambulances. It looks suspicious though we saw nothing war like.

Last night I slept finely & feel well today. At 10 A.M. ordered to fall in to return to camp. We returned by the same road over which we traveled last Saturday as related to Ida the impressions of that day were revived & were not pleasant. Today I received the Chronicle of the 27th. The quickest paper yet. Ido hope in future our mail matter will come more regular. The sick men left in camp were glad to see me. Some of them are pretty sick. I believe I wrote to you that Bassett fell out on our first day's march from Warrenton without a pass. Today I learn he was taken by the Rebs, paroled & is now in the parole camp at Alexandrea. I am sorry, he was a good boy. I have not had any tidings from my boots but hope to as soon as the army supplies are received. Their transportation occupies the road at present.

The day is cloudy with a little rain but mild. The climate here is agreeable but nothing else is half as good as with as at the North Country is at least one hundred years behind the times. I hardly dare prophesy again as to the immediate future. I must confess that the signs don't look like fighting just now but I can't tell. We live in such constant don't know witness that we learn to be ready for anything & accept nothing in particular so that we don't feel as anxious about our personal safety. As you seem to. It is not a reckless feeling but the constant thought of battle has so accustom us to it. We are fairly indifferent. Noe don't worry any more we are tough & can stand most any human & some things inhuman. When we come home we shall know all the better how to appreciate friends, home & comfort. I am writing a part of this on a table for the first time in months. If I don't write tomorrow take this as a good bye.

Your affectionate husband,

B. Munger

Tuesday Dec.2, 1862

Last night was cold again but not as cold as north. 4 P.M. A rumor is just circulating in camp that Burnside is being ordered to cross the river & not thinking it prudent has resigned. It creates some excitement & much speculation. The prevailing opinion is that Gen. Hooker will take his place & fears are expressed that he will err on the side of rashness. It is said if ordered he will cross or loose every man in the attempt. I hope the rumor is not true. I have great confidence in Gen. Burnside's judgement & in Hooker's fighting ability. But it is astonishing how patiently we can wait when we are obliged to. Now I say to you again, "Don't make yourself unhappy about us". I'll write you tomorrow if anything new transpires.

Yours,

B. Munge

Camp near Falmouth, Va. Dec. 7, 1862

My Dear Brother & friends,

I am under the necessity of exhibiting the shady side of soldier life a little. By a recent order of the department no sick can be sent from camp nor can their friends visit them here. The only hospitals we have is a large tent with a fire in it with cots made by driving 4 crotched sticks in the ground 18 inches high, 2 ½ feet apart one way & 6 the other two poles six feet long are laid on these & covered with barrel staves a little hay if one can get it or a blanket makes the bed. The weather is as cold now as it usually is at the north at this season of the year. Of course, there is some suffering here but what I intend to write most particular about was the case of H. Ackley. He has been down sometime with diarrhea & rheumatism & suffers severely this morning. I had him removed to the hospital. The Dr. me he possibly never would be fit for duty & the prospect was that we should lose him. I can't feel reconciled to it. It seems next to murder & I have a greater responsibility than I want to bear. It appears sometimes as if I should sink under it. I do not get the support in such burdens from the Lieutenants. I ought to indeed. I feel almost alone in so far as care and responsibility are concerned. I don't mean to complain of them it is not in them. James is good & amiable as a woman but had no confidence in himself & breaks clear down under our hardships. Kelly is a much better officer but is entirely destitute of fatherly qualities. This morning I could hardly summons resolution to go around & visit the sick but I found them more cheerful than I expected & with the expectation of Harvey doing well considering the severity of the weather. We have about three inches of snow & the roads frozen so as to bear our heavy wagons & our breath froze to our beards as we lay in bed & for sick men to lie on the ground is not comfortable to say the least. Perhaps you will ask why we do not build log houses, it is because we are hourly expecting marching orders. It is said that Gen. Butterfield told an officer that we should move tomorrow or next day if the mud did not prevent. You will see by what I have said how little I can do to make my men comfortable. I stopped to see if I could get some hay for Harvey promised. At 2 O'clock had dinner, called to see a man taken suddenly sick (Pelton). Have been to see the Dr. & am waiting now the climate & our exposures render it necessary to take such cases by the foretop & I think the little knowledge of medicine I have has saved more than one severe fit of sickness. The doses given here are large. I took six grains of quinine a few days since & an officer in the next tent 9 grains. I have just received your letter of the 3rd instance & not numbered but I guess it is genuine and our diaries for which we are grateful & you don't know how a word from home cheers us. Sometimes we need it for we don't always feel alike even under the same circumstances but I believe that the responsibility I feel does a great deal to keep me up and cheerful. I have just been out again to see about some hay for Harvey & O'Neil. It is quite a process here to get a lock of hay.

I hope you will not worry about us. Those who are well can stand it & I am one of those, but it is time we <u>suffer</u> some this weather but if it will do good I try to stand it. The only good that I can do at present is to take care of the men I in this I don't express to satisfy everyone & presume that already complaints have reached home but that is to be expected if I can satisfy myself I think I shall do well. Company A, had a man die last night in the hospital & his body still lies there side by side with the living. He was the only son of wealthy parents yet he dies & is buried like a dog. God grant when <u>I</u> die it may be at home with friends. I am willing to toil & <u>suffer</u> but at the end I do want to die in peace. Writing has become a perfect passion with me. I could write all the time but I have to do it under difficulties, usually called off at least twenty times & of late it is so cold as to make it uncomfortable, well not quite as warm as your barn. Still I write more than ever before. I have just returned from backing up wood & am warmer than I have been before the day. Maybe you will think it beneath the dignity of an officer to carry wood – it is not a necessity of course, we are free to do without it, hire it out, or do it ourselves. We <u>choose</u> the later.

It is now about time for dress parade which is our last duty for the day except roll call. It has been a very bright day, sunshine all day yet scarcely thawing and in the shade has frozen all day. I have forgotten to mention the case of Elisha Moon of Benton. He is more idiotic than I suppose & is not capable of taking care of himself. I am obliged to see that he washes & changes as you would a child & what is worse he is sick, growing poor & I heartily wish he was at home.

Orders read on dress parade tonight look some like going into winter quarters but as I have often said we don't know anything of the future, but in any view the prospect is not pleasant, but there is one grand comfort we are only to do the duties & endure the sufferings of a day in a day & I guess we can do that. Tomorrow we intend if not too cold to build a fireplace in our tent. There are no stoves here & bricks are obtained with difficulty but we must do something to make ourselves more comfortable. It is intensely cold tonight. I mean considering we live without fire except as we build it outdoors. I must soon stop writing for supper. My principal object in writing about our circumstances is that in all probability some of our men must die here & it would appear strange to you & their friends that something more was not done for them, but if I were taken sick I could neither go to you or you come to me but I hope it will soon be different. I am not low spirited at all but I do feel as if I was taxed all I am able to bear. I hope circumstances will brighten up before I write again but I intend to do as the boys often say here, "<u>Hold up my/your head</u> & be tough". Now don't let this make you feel more sad. I (write) it due to myself or ourselves to let you know a little more than I had done of our situation in view of the future. I wish you all the happiness you can enjoy (this means all of you). I have not so much as a shadow of envy but would like to make you happier if I could & if I live to see home, one I hope to enjoy a little myself. Fred is still at headquarters & more comfortable than he would be here. Orett is the same faithful fellow he ever was & really for advice would prefer him to my <u>legal</u> advisers. Much love to all friends & untold depth to yourselves a thousand to the kissable with good wishes & earnest prayer.

Your affectionate Brother, Husband, Father & Uncle,

B. Munger

Camp near Falmouth, Va.   Dec. 10, 1862

My dear wife & friends,

The reserve just returned from picket duty of two days. We had a rough time there & a muddy walk back lying on the frozen ground with 3 inches of snow in the open air sounds tougher than it is perhaps but it is not comfortable though we <u>stood</u> good. When we arrived in camp found that Kelly &

Rob had built us a fine fireplace & chimney & it looks really like comfort but alas for earthly comfort. We have orders to march tomorrow morning at daylight. All is hurry for we are to take 3 days cooked provisions. The rumor is that the Rebels evacuated Fredericksburg. We don't know whether it is true or not. I received letters from sister S. & Jane on Monday have answered L & shall not have time to write to J. I that I could not go without writing a word & yes, I have nothing especial to write but considering the uncertainty of the future I feel as if I must say one word. I can't say that I feel indifferent no I feel deeply anxious about the future but as I cannot change in the least the events. I am resolved to go along do my duty & hope for the best. I hope living or dead I shall never disgrace my friends. I know nothing of our future moves but suppose we are to cross the river & perhaps match to Richmond I hope for the best.

   Stand up bravely in case of misfortune. <u>You</u> with stern duties to do bring up that that darling child to be true to her conscious & you will have enough to live for. You may think I write despondingly. I do not feel so at all, but do feel as if I ought not to shut my eyes to the fact that I am likely to fail as others. As to my funerary affairs leave all to L. I of course hope to see you all & enjoy something yet in <u>this</u> world. You can scarcely imagine how intensely I long to be with you just an hour tonight but I ought not to indulge in such feelings, my duties require a stern heart. Though I do not believe a soldier may & ought to be a feeling man especially an officer. As an officer I may have failed often in judgement but I can think of no case where I have not <u>tried</u> to do my duty. I wrote a letter last Sunday directed to Layman & numbered 3. I learn this will not go tonight so perhaps I cannot send it for some days & if so shall add to it as I have opportunity. I have not received my boots which I regret, as my shoes are very poor but I guess I can get along. I am not half as badly off as some of the boys. Many are next to barefoot & you can imagine the care in such a time as this something of the care I have one & another with, "Capt. what am I to do my feet are right out to the ground?" I tell him," My poor fellow you must do the best you can. I hope to get some soon." Another, "My pants are most off me what can I do?" & so on to the end of the chapter. I have an opportunity to send this now & good & all & may God bless you is my prayer.

            Yours ever,

            B. Munger

            In front of Fredericksburg, Dec. 12, 1862

We commenced shelling the city yesterday at 5 A.M. continued till 12 noon. It began about 3 & stopped at sunset. We have not been in danger. Our troops now hold the city & are I should think moving cautiously. We are in the best of spirits & hope to cross tomorrow. There are 7 bridges thrown across, some have been killed. The firing was <u>awfully</u> <u>grand</u>, beyond anything I ever seen & I am writing under difficulties & must stop. The boys are well & feel well, Much love to all. I'll write as often as I can, mail uncertain

Affectionately Yours,

B. Munger

Noon - I have just received orders to be ready to march at 6 P.M. & as an obedient man I suppose I must go too. So good bye for the present & may God bless & keep you. From your affectionate husband & father.

B. Munger

Noon – I have just recd. an order to be ready to march at 6 P.M. & as an obedient man I suppose I must go so good bye for the present & may God bless & keep you.

From your affectionate husband & father,

Bennett Munger

                                                       Fredericksburg Dec. 15

Dear Wife,

        We have been under fire & are all alive. 11 are wounded. A. Perry, most severally, lost a leg, J. Giddings I fear will lose one. The rest not severely, Kelly was knocked down by the explosion of a shell but is on duty. Myself & boys are unharmed thank God. F was not in – O was a <u>man</u>, the battle is not over.

B. Munger

                               Written at Fredericksburg, Va. On the battle field Dec. 15, 1862

I have forgotten the number. I guess No.4

        Fredericksburg Dec. 15, 7 P.M. 1862

My dear friends – We still live & are well today. I rec'd a letter from Pling and sent a hasty word to you. Fearing you may not receive it I will recapitulate. Thursday at 5:10 the great battle opened. We were in camp but left a few moments after we went up to supporting distance and remained through the day and camped near at night. The next day we approached nearer and remained through the day and night. Saturday at 3 P.M. marched through the city took refuge behind a bank and lay till 4 ½ when we had an order to move to the front & relieve a brigade. We formed in line of battle and moved under fire of shell but not severe. I forgot today that one man, Geo. R. Hunter rec'd a slight wound in the face and we left him behind. It was a bad place for new men. The wounded & mangled were carried by with faces that only a wounded soldier from a fierce conflict can put on. I prayed for nerve and strength. We had moved but a few rods when another regiment filed in front of us – that is, the left wing of our regiment stopped while the right were able to press on. This threw us into confusion as we had to crawl through fence to join the others. We hurrious formed in fair order on the run and as we reached the hill we were exposed to the enemy's fire of shell and musketry. Our men dropped like hail. Lt. Col. Conner and Lt. Kelly dropped at the same instant, one on my right and one on my left. In all, nine of our men fell on the spot. We soon reached the position we sought and were in comparative safety.

During this time the whizzing of rifle balls and the rushing, roaring sounds of shell was about deafening. The place we occupied was a side hill somewhat circular in form and covering ¼ of an acre perhaps and about 30 rods from the enemy's lines of sharpshooters. The ground was muddy and we were obliged to lie pretty flat to avoid the balls. Those killed and wounded in the previous day's battle were on the ground and the living, dead and dying were lying side by side. But I'll not pain you with a recital of that night. It was such as I never want to repeat. At midnight the wagons came to take the wounded and I had the pleasure of assisting in doing it.

One mere boy who had been groaning during the evening I found just dead – but don't think of it and I won't write any more about it. Lieut. Kelly got up and came to us but his face was all blood and it was thot best for him to go back to town (about a mile) and have it dressed. It was probably the bursting of a shell as his face was powder burnt. They will knock a man down as quick as a thunderbolt. The Dr. thought it not prudent for him to come back that night and he could not safely next day for Reb bullets. So we did without him till dark next night.

We were relieved about 10 P.M. making our stay 30 hours in which time I did not sleep much though I did some even right under the whistling of bullets. We got into the city at 11 ½ and to bed on the ground in the front yard of a fine house at 1 and slept till morning of today which I have spent looking up our wounded and getting something of a statement of the condition and conduct of our company as some of them I am sorry to say did not behave well. I forgot to say I sent men back as soon as safe to look after our wounded men and take them to the city. We have twelve in all. Lieut. Kelly & J. F. Johnson were knocked down as I have said & faces burnt. Perry's left leg was shattered at the knee & is amputated above. J. K. Giddings by a mini ball 4 inches above the ankle & will probably be amputated. A. J. Cole wounded in the ankle can't tell how severely. Fred Mitchell knee pan shot off. Taylor and Mead both through the hand slightly. The last by himself taking up his gun & yesterday in another regiment which he got mixed when we were coming onto the field. George C. Raymond by a ball by a ball in the forehead & passing between the skull and scalp and coming out at the crown (a close call). W. A. Herrick in the breast, I think not severely. A boy, Acton who joined us at Albany a slight wound on the skin & Geo. R. Hunter wounded as I have said. Perry, Mitchell, Cole and Herrick I have not been able to see since they were wounded and I suppose all or most all are removed as we expect this city to be shelled by Rebs.

As to the success of our arms the paper will give you a better idea than I can. Only I think the storming of the enemy's batteries by infantry is given up. I think it can't be done & I think that Franklin's success is to be taken advantage of and our forces pushed in that direction. Ockley, I learn tonight is worse and has been insane a day or two since we left camp. I'd like to go and see him but it is out of the question. I supposes you would like to know how one feels under fire or how I felt. I can hardly tell you. It is trying to the nerves but I was as cool as I expected to be and on reflection can't think what I would have done more. I speak this not in boast. You are aware that receiving a fire which you cannot return is very trying even to old troops and the boys of old regiments say it was as severe a time while it lasted as they have passed though. Fred you know was detailed for guard duty and of course was not in. O as usual was a man. By the way Layman, if we live and get home I shall owe that boy. I am not contented from him ½ an hour in the day.

I ought not perhaps speak of individuals but Sargent Kinner & Powell behaved like heroes and some of the men from Italy were cool as veterans. The battle is not yet over and I may fall but God grant I may pass through unheard. Pray for me. Yesterday morning I did not expect to live to see the sun go down and today the position we occupied was taken with great slaughter. The Rebs planted a new battery that raked it the whole length. O is writing also and perhaps we shall both sometimes write the same thing and we shall send them separate so that if one fails the other may reach you. I seems solemn to write when there is some possibility it is the last time but I don't know what I can add unless it is to commend to your care anew. L., my loved ones and to each one a fare well blessing & to my little one in far & each fidelity and truth. Kelly wishes me to say if he falls sell his property as quick and favorably as possible. Remember me to friends.

Your affectionate Husband, father, brother and uncle,

B. Munger

P.S. I will answer Pling when I can. B.M.

Camp near Falmouth, Va. Dec. 21, 1862

My dear Wife & daughter,

  It is Sunday as you will see as the date. The weather is clear & cold & although I wrote you on Friday. I feel like writing again. I received your affectionate & welcomed letter Friday night. Letters are the bright spots in our experiences, if we have any. I believe I told you I had received a letter from Sophia & one from Jane & have answered both. Jane writes she has a boy. I think I know now about 2 months old. I also wrote to Nancy sometime since & must soon write to Julia. In a line from Abagail, she says Nettie has been to Canandaigua & was going to Webster & then to Brockport. I am very sorry. I think from your letters you are enjoying yourself at L's as well as you can in my absence & if it is not too much of a burden to them I rejoice at it & although I appreciate your intense anxiety about me as it cannot effect any good. Strive to throw it off as much as possible & divest your mind from the subject. I had hoped if there was a prospect of an indefinite continuance of the war I might get a furlough this winter to visit you a short time but I find it is hopeless. You ask in one of your letters if we shall be discharged when the old soldiers of the 44th are. That is a point not settled. I think we shall but that will be a year from next August which is equal to five years at home but I find whatever a man must do he can do. Necessity sometimes makes heroes.

  I have much recovered from my fatigue and prostration & am more like myself again. It was one of the most tests of my power of endurance. I was ever subjected to. We were out on picket duty in another direction two days before the battle so that we were on duty for Monday morning till the next Tuesday noon. I think very few stood it better than I did. I see by your letters of last Saturday & Sunday that you understood our movements better than I supposed & a thousand times better than the papers that reach us describe them. Everything in camp here has assumed its old monotonous course. We know nothing of the future. I have heard nothing from the wounded since I last wrote you. Most of them have been just off passage to Washington & Baltimore but do not our own. I am going to make an effort soon to get several of our men discharged. They can never be of service ever & it will be a mercy to them to be sent home. Reverend Mandeville is still here and will probably succeed in getting his son a furlough of 3 days. I am anxious to hear how my accounts & debts foot at home. I fear not favorable. I have estimated from memory & it looks bad. I am living cheaply as I can here. It costs including the wages for our cook 20 to 24 per week & we live poor enough at that. I have bought very few cloths, 2 woolen shirts, a blows, pair of shoes, 4 pair of sox & 2 blankets I think is all. A messenger has been in to say that Fred Mitchell wants to see me again & I shall try to go. In truth Mary, my principal enjoyment is in trying to do good to someone to make them more happy as I can't do it directly to myself I can only make myself happy by helping others& I am not sure but it is partly selfish.

I ought to write to that little darling of mine but perhaps I can't today. I wrote to you if you asked questions as to indicate what you would most like to hear about. It would help me some in interesting you. I wish to avoid as much as possible writing of my own feelings & other subjects sum day. I suppose you forgot the question I asked you as you seldom answer any. I will repeat a few & ask some new ones. Have you paid Abigail for your board? And if not please do so. Has Remer paid Francis bill? & where is she & do you correspond with her? What is Graham doing for a livelihood? What are his prospects for the future? Has Ogden obtained an office of any kind & what is he doing? How are Migner & Gould doing in the business? I am just called to inspect my company so must leave probably too toward night as I must go see Mitchell which is an 8 mile walk which at home would be that quite a job.

7 P.M., I have been to the hospital & seen Mitchell. He is cheerful & bears his pain with great fortitude. It is not certain yet whether the leg must be amputated. He wants if it is done I should be with him & our new surgeon should do it. I am quite tired with my walk. Tomorrow our Dr. is going farther to the front where he hears there are two men of this regiment wounded & one bears the description of one of our men & if I can get a horse I am going with him. Harvey is better today & I have strong hopes of his recovery. As I can do nothing at drilling I am trying to see the men are as comfortable as possible. I wish Layman or you for him if he has no time would give me the opinion of thinking candid sum on the present & future prospects of this war. How the Emancipation Proclamation is to effect it? Where the blame lies for this defeat or this attack for that was the error & so on. I hear no opinions here & I long to compare notes with someone if the opinion I have expressed are false in your judgement say so & point out why. The papers we get here are not worth reading. The Tribune is never sold here. The few that I see received by mail. I hope by this time you have received my first letter after the battle for you might be anxious about us. I hardly think we shall winter here but can't tell. It is now cold & the ground frozen & pretty dry. We can make more mud with little water here than in any country I ever saw.

Thursday morning, I am not feeling well today. My walk yesterday was too much for me but I shall be better soon. I have just been with Rob to have a tooth pulled which has troubled him. It came hard but he bore it well. Harvey is better this morning. The weather is more mild & still clear. Dr. Townsend our new Surgeon is from Bergen Germany, Co. & I like him much! Mandeville will probably succeed in getting James a furlough & if so will I think leave tomorrow. If he should visit Penn Yan you will be able to learn more from him than you probably can by letter as he has had an opportunity seldom granted to civilians to see soldier life in all its beauties & if he has the talent may interest an audience with his narration of things he has seen. As I said, I intend to go with Dr. Townsend today if I can get a horse but will close this & if I find anything worthy will write again. The Holidays are close by but all days are alike here. Only the memory of past pleasures on those days sometimes saddens us a little but the wise man says of all things there is an end. But the question is whether I shall not <u>end</u> before my term of service does. I guess not for I am <u>tough</u>.

With much love your affectionate husband & father,

B. Munger

Camp near Falmouth, Va. Dec. 23, 1862

My dear little Daughter,

It is a most magnificent day, warm enough for a comfort & this morning the birds sang a little but not such as we have as the north, though they sang prettily. I thought if a good set inhabitants were to occupy the country it would be the finest in the world. I am not well today, no appetite & very much prostrate but in good spirits, still little rest. I would prefer to be home till I got better. I fear if I should be sick long the company would not do well. I fear I have spoiled them. Nothing seems to go right if I am not around. It would pain your little heart to tell you of <u>awful</u> things. I saw Fredy so I will tell you how the city looked. The river there runs nearly south & the city is built on the bank about 1 ½ miles in length & ½ a mile wide. The first street next the river is dirty, the buildings old & irregular & looks like the mean suburbs of some large city. The first evidence of battle was the holes in the sides of buildings. It makes no difference whether it be structure brick or wood. The ball don't stop but the hole made by a ball is not as large as you would suppose, not larger than a paint basin but I saw no buildings but more or less of them some with 20 or more. They do not tear a house as I supposed but make a clean hole except when they burst. The streets look as if the people had all been moving on the same day & not quite finished. Beds, broken furniture, books, papers almost everywhere you can think of lay in the street. When we marched through the first time we did not look around much but as we neared the battlefield the road was strewn with soldier's blankets, knapsacks & clothes of all descriptions & looks as if there had been a commotion. Our men had thrown them off so that they might march & fight better. I went into but two houses except those used as hospitals. One was a fine dwelling of brick in old style, solid mahogany doors, heated by a furnace & lighted with gas. A good piano stood in the back parlor on which our soldiers were playing. The house had been used as a hospital & the usual evidences of in such cases. It would pain your little heart darling even to go into a house from which wounded men have yet been removed. Words of sympathy & pity are far less common than oaths. I have been from one house to another where the wounded were laid in rows on the floors as thick as they could lie & as a rule the most patient subdued set of men I ever saw. It was painful for it seemed the patience of hopelessness. So far as I was able to judge the city is not as large as Canandaigua & not one tenth as pretty. There are few blocks of buildings but each built by itself. Sometime I must tell you what passes here for a house or so in other words may experience in camp.

Wednesday morning, I think I am a little better this morning but still feel quite poorly. Our boys are very busy in fixing their tents with fire places. A large number are on the sick list/ 15 are excused from duty today. Tomorrow is Christmas but oh it will be a sad day. The boys are thinking of home & friend & what they used to enjoy & the contrast is so great they are more sad than usual. It does really seem out of place to be mirthful here. I wish I could see you today little one. We have received excusing us from drill today & instead the streets are to be cleaned & decorated with ever green. Rob has been to the commissaries to see if we could get anything to pretend Christmas with but there was nothing. While gone he saw some soldiers under guard with boards tied on their back with the name of the soldiers on top & the words "Skulker" in large letters below & they are made to walk to & fro in public streets all day & perhaps every day for a month. I saw two men the other day sentenced to carry a log of wood 10 hours a day for disobedience.

   Orett leaves us today to go to his tent. He has been with us since we returned from battle. I am sorry to have him go but can't avoid it. Major Knox & our new surgeon just called for me to talk about our cooking arrangements. The Dr. says we must have a Company cook & our men must be made more comfortable. I certainly like that & if he will carry out what proposes it will be a help to us. I also consulted with the lieutenants & we have agreed to try John McLaughlin & George Henderson for cooks. Perhaps I may as well give you my hour experience now. I am of course in my tent & since I commenced the line about an officer has been here to inquire if we want an ax for our Company. I told him yes, 3 of them but he has but one & no helve. A man comes in & asks if he may go & get the ax. Yes! Rob comes to know if I can't send for a load of evergreens, cedar & pines boughs to put around our tent. I ask Lt. James to see to it. The man returns with the new ax & thinks he can make a helve quiet for a moment. James returns to say there are brush enough & wishes me to go & see about it. Well I have been out & found there are not half brush enough & ask James to take a squad of men, go & back up some more. The Major calls again to say that he wants my men to put a row in rear of their tents. James says the men are mostly at dinner. I think J shall be obliged to take hold myself at last sick or well. I have asked Lieutenant Russel who tents with us to help & he has gone with Rob to get some for our tent. Perhaps you think it ought to be an hour by this time but it is only 30 minutes I have been out to witness the distribution of food for dinner in one of the companies which has a company cook. The dinner was beef soup thickened with rice & looked pretty good. Mr. Mandeville came up & thinks he will get his business completed today. It now lacks 3 minutes of an hour but as there seems to be an unusual quiet. We will let it go.

   Now little fellow my letters are written in such a stew only I have not been called away as long as a time as common today. It is everything & since I stopped writing our Col. Rice has arrived but it makes but little stir. Mitchell has sent for me to come & see him again. Poor fellow, he has had his leg off since I was there & I learn Perry is there too. If I am possibly able I shall go & if not get Lt. Kelly to go. I am no better tonight but hope I shall be soon. Mandeville has been in to say good bye. He failed in effort to get his son home. A man may as well get rid of death as to get away from here. It is too late to send this tonight so I will write a little tomorrow. The wishes are freely expressed by officers & men that they were at home tonight. While I am sadly writing, you are enjoying your festival at church I hope. I love to think you're feeling happy but sometimes when all alone you <u>think</u>. Tell me in your next what you think about. Love to all.

Your loving father,

B. Munger

Camp near Falmouth, Va. Jan 27, 1863

My Dear wife & friends,

It makes little difference to whom I direct my letter as they are for all. You will see by the heading I am back at the old camp. I came yesterday & shall return tomorrow. Our regiment returned to the old camp Saturday & on Sunday O. came down to see me with the intention that our regiment was to be paid yesterday. So, I summoned all my strength & came up. It is now 3 ½ & we are not paid. Well L., I am still better I do contend but I will tell you honestly just how I am. It is now over five weeks since I gave up duty 7 am very, very weak. There is a great temptation here with soldiers to make themselves sicker than they really are & perhaps in my disgust at that I have ended on the other side and then I have only on the days I felt best & I naturally wanted to make as good a case as I could. My appetite up to yesterday for a week was better. My trip here exhausted me so that it is not as good & I didn't feel as well today but I think I finally got well here if I can get away indeed I am resolved not to die here. I believe determination is almost omnipotent, still it is not much of a place where one is as weak as I am to gain much. This camp is infinitely perforable to our <u>Hospital</u> & if I can't get home I shall back here by hook & crook. I regret that I wrote so hasty to you for help. It is not with the intention of <u>exciting</u> <u>your</u> <u>sympathies</u> & I fear you have incurred expenses that will prove fruitless. I can easily excuse myself for suffering my self-reliance to forsake me for the moment & I think <u>you</u> could if you had been there but five minutes, if you have done nothing it is not best to. The only thing you can do is to prompt Chamberlin as he has the necessary papers & I can put them through if he will. I need not say I should rejoice to get home for a few weeks I think I could get well fast but if I can't I can do the other thing. It is next to impossible to get a furlough now. But now my hand is in. I shall <u>try</u>. James papers are not through & I don't know when they will be.

It is just announced we are to receive our pay tonight. We, the officers of our Co. got only 29 day's pay from the 3rd of Oct. to the 31st include liberal very. In regard to the grain fed to Scheetz's horse it was all Graham's & estimated by Clark at 10 bushels. The shipping feed was for myself & the little I fed to his horse of shipping feed I exchanged mess for mess to avoid two a/cs. You say Mary, you think I am not a tough fellow in some respects & want my opinion. I don't understand in what respects you mean but will confess in general that I had weak points & may perhaps confess particulars if you will point them out but I feel as My Shuts did when he was drunk. I shall get over this & will then be ready to look at those who are tough all over. O. will write tomorrow & send some money. Yours & B. Munger

Camp near Falmouth, Va. Mar.12, 1863

My Dear Wife,

Once more in camp & well. I arrived yesterday about 4 P.M. found the boys well with the exception of Squires of Italy moderately such with diarrhea. I think the report of better rations is true for those I have seen are getting very fleshy. I will copy from my diary. At Nimrods we stopped & McBride got some whisky & was quite troublesome. At Watkins, I was introduced to Capt. Chapman, brother of Capt. Coleman's wife. & we were together until we arrived at Aquia Creek. At Elmira I got our tickets to

Baltimore, $7.25 each but at Troy some 20 miles from Elmira he gave me the stop weather intentionally or not I can't say. He asked permission to leave the car a moment & did not return, it being dark he had all the advantage he could want. At Williamsport I took a sleeping car. I am not well tonight & if the weight of the universe was upon me I could not feel more desperate. The experience & events of the last few days weigh heavily. Thursday Mar. 10, Got up at 6 & although I slept fairly have a headache. We are 25 miles from Baltimore. The ground is bare & much drier than I expected to find it but I see but little difference in temperature. Arrived at Baltimore at 7:30, left immediately & got into Washington about 10. Put up at the National, got breakfast at a saloon & went to the Provost Marshall & got a pass. It is snowing & thawing nearly as fast as it falls & is a disagreeable day. Stayed indoors most of the time. In the evening went with Capt. Chapman to the theater, was not very well pleased with the thing it dis not come up to my expectations. To bed 11 ½ slept well.

Wednesday, Mar. 11, up at 6, boat left, arrived at Aquia at noon but did not leave till 3. My big box is a constant partner & hindrance to me. I lost the noon train on its account. Arrived at camp about 4 found our Brigade had just gone out on picket duty. Lt. Kelly & a few of boys only were left & I suppose it looks some lonely to me. O the contrast between this & northern life but I must put up with it. It is best for me all things considered & I accepted it. The officers appear glad to see me. Our camp has been improved by pulling out everything around it so that it looks like a young forest. The ground is drier than I expected to find it but now dry enough to move an army & there is no evidence of an intention to move at present. I find the report that Kinner was fined for disobedience to orders is false. Elwell was fined one month's wages for disobedience to orders issued by Kinner & that is probably what the report grew out of. Orett's commission came tonight & I shall send him word tomorrow as Kelly says he is feeling very anxious about it for Kelly's came some time ago. Orett ranks as Sgt. From Jan 31 & probably will get pay from that date. This is a blue evening but I am tough.

Thursday, Mar. 12, Slept well considering my new bed for I was very sleepy. The morning is clear & fine but cool. The birds are singing a little. I am appointed officer of the day. You see they seem disposed to set me at work. There is a wedding in our division to which our officers are invited but as officer of the day I cannot leave if I wished to which I do not. Kelly received a box of provisions by express today which had been opened & two oyster cans & whisky confiscated at which he is some angry & has gone to the Provost Marshall to see about it. My ham is not as great a treat as I supposed they get them here now & Kelly says they have three in their mess. It is now 3 P.M. the weather has changed & is now windy cold & cloudy. I am not in want of cool fresh air now. I have a large supply & my hands are numb with cold as I write. I have lost Kelly's gold pen but how & when I do not know. I have not yet opened the big trunk & shall not until the boys come in & I hope to feel a little better then for it is lonely here now. I reported to the Col. last night. He said but little, seemed satisfied, spoke of Orett approvingly & Kelly has written to Cleveland. Holmes Neeland & Harpending to aid him in getting the command of a colored regiment. Had I better try? Ask L., his opinion of the continuance of the war, are as various as with you from 3 months to as many years. I think we will wait & see. A boy belonging to this regiment was just killed by being thrown from a mule & dragged by the stirrup. Layman will perhaps remember him as the little cook at Wind Mill Point. His name is Wienstien. The mail is about to close & I must do likewise. Love to all.

Your affectionate husband, B. Munger

Camp near Falmouth, Va. Mar. 18, 1863

My Darling Daughter,

      I think I must make a letter for your benefit today. This morning is mild & spring like but the weather here since I arrived has been about as cold as it was there while I was at home. My health is good & I weigh by our scales 170 lbs. & Orett 150, Fred 163 & the men generally are very fleshy. The truth is this is a pretty idle, lazy life we are leading now & as we are living well we ought to be fat. It is probable our easy life is about over. I think we shall move soon but where I do not know. The army is in first rate health & in as good trim as it has ever been. There are a thousand rumors in camp as to what is to be done with us. One is that we are going to Baltimore, another that we are to stay in this vicinity & guard the rail road, another that for the present we are to act as guard of Ge. Hooker's headquarters, still another that we are to march to Richmond perhaps. Neither is true but I think there is to be a stir soon. Kinner was yesterday appointed First Sergeant. Fred, Sergeant & Mc Elligott, Corporal not without opposition. There is a good (bit) of enthusiasm in the regiment in regard to drill & discipline & the hope of promotion is constantly held out to the men.

      I am sorry to say that two of our men, P. Hubbard & Dansenburg are each fined two months wages a few days since so in one case I think I must tell though contrary to my custom. Our first sergeant was ordered to detail two men with axes to work for the regiment a little while. We had no company axes but several of the men had axes they are Government property but the men have got them by the other means than through the Quartermaster. Some bought them, others picked them up where they had been left & c. knowing Dansenburg to have one I sent the sergeant to have him lease his ax. He said he would not. I then sent to have come to my tent with his ax. He told the sergeant he would be damned if he would. I put him under arrest & sent him to the guard house. The officer of the guard took him to the Col. who fined him as above. Yesterday was St. Patrick's Day & was celebrated by some regiments from Mass, us & some of our officers & among myself went to see them. There were a great any officers present, some mounted & some on foot. Gen. Griffin & lady both on horseback were there. The sport so far as I saw was running horses & mules, climbing greased poles & it was to end with a race after a sheared pig. There had evidently been some whisky drank & the men were running horses through crowds of men. The kind of running was what is called turning the stake. A stake or other object is chosen & two or more horsemen start run to the stake turn round it & run back & the one who reaches the place of starting is the winner. Two horsemen had turned the stake & were half way back when four officers started at full speed. I expected in a moment there would be trouble, one of the four instead of turning to the right as he ought took the left & the horses seeing they must meet swung their heads one side & struck their breasts together with such force as to throw them into the air. I should think ten feet & killed them so dead they never kicked but strange to say the men were not killed & I hear they are alive this morning. One was a Lt. Master & the other a surgeon & about 60 years old. I had seen enough of St. Patrick & came home.

      In the ___ I had an invitation to an officer's party. I guess you would call it. I was asked to call into a certain & told the Adjutant wanted to see me there. I found most of the Captains & first

Lieutenants & some others. I soon found that the Adjutant proposed to treat us with raw whisky & I think I was invited on purpose to see if I could be induced to drink. It was offered me first and urged with every possible argument that at least in compliment to the new Adjutant, I would go through the form of drinking & where they failed a captain told unerringly he would get me some bread & then I could take as a sacrament. I told him he acted unmanly & wicked. I stayed half an hour or so & left them to enjoy themselves in their own way. You know our society is not just what I would like. We have now a new attraction in camp. Three ladies, one is the sergeant's wife & the others are starting with her but I don't know who they are but must find out for they are quite pretty. I suppose you & mother are at your new home before this I wrote your mother the day after my arrival & shall expect an answer about Saturday & I also wrote to Uncle a day or two after which you will see & let & let them see this. When you write tell me how you like soldiering there & all about your morning. The day is not as warm as the morning promised. You must not worry about me for I am well & if I live I can do better here than at home & if I die in the service I shall leave a pension of twenty dollars per month to you & mother so it is best in many respects that we make ourselves contented. I may stay longer than I anticipated when at home.

I shall write again on receiving a letter from mother if I can. This is a long letter & before you get another I may be on the move, Anyway, God bless & keep you both, love to all. I don't know as I said a word about H. Ackley in my other letter. He is so fat! He looks like a pony & I think will stand soldiering now. You must let mother share in this although you are the owner. Good bye from your affectionate father & husband,

B. Munger

Camp near Falmouth, Va. Mar. 29, 1863

My Dear wife & daughter,

I have just received in your letters of the 24th & learn with some anxiety that you were not to board with Wolcott. I fear you moving & consequents labor & fatigue will be too much for you. I just will worry too much. I am tough enough to make myself while here & no anxiety will protect me in action so we may as well perish eventually & find joy where we can. I will quote from my diary of Mar. 20. Weather mild but cloudy. My cold is worse. Received a letter from Layman. Tuesday, mild & cloudy. O noticed to prepare for general inspection. No drills today. Cleaning camps, tents & putting everything in order. Sick with nervous headache of worst sort. Rained till the first of the night. Wednesday morning, clear & fine, looks spring like. Last night the peeping frogs had a fine old fashioned concert. I am officer of the day again. Am not feeling well, hope to soon receive an order to have my company ready to fall in at a moment's notice. Then a report that the Rebs are crossing the river above us. (Proved to be false. / Thursday, order for review this afternoon. I think I wrote of it to Ida & Mandeville about it. Spoke with Doctor Townsend tonight & he urges me to stay. Mrs. T was present but was not introduced. Several officers were there it was the pleasantest call I have but the want of an introduction made it embracing. Wrote to Ida.

Friday, cool & clear. Studied tactics & had a game at ball, the first for some years. Gov. Curtain just passed, he is visiting the army. Had a battalion drill today & I learned more than at any drill before in days, life having been sick so long I have had little opportunity to practice battalion movements. This is severest I think I have been in. C. W. Taylor of Benton received his discharge today & started for home. I have lost 2 pounds weight since my return.

Saturday, very rainy, received a request from the Ex. Dept. N.G. to furnish a history of company its formation & a sketch of the lives the officers & men. Wrote to sister Julia & Mother.

Sunday, clear, cold & very windy. Had a regimental inspection as usual. Had a Bible class today, the first since leaving Warrenton. Attended meeting, this endeth my diary. We are living rather poorly. I think that I never told you that Rob went back to the company the day the boys returned from picket & we have a new one, his name is Harrington. Harrington, good boy but not as smart as Rob. My cold is still bad but tomorrow I am to be officer of the day.

It is severely cold today & Monday morn I am some better. The morning is clear but cold.

Yours,

B. Mung

Camp near Falmouth, Virginia Apr. 12, 1863

My Dear Wife & Daughter,

I received your letter yesterday on my return from picket duty & one from Lyman I was glad to hear you & Ida were so well. I also recd. in due time your letter containing Kelly's pen. it was safe & unharmed. I think I have recd. all of your letters but the reason the account doesn't foot up right. One or more is on the road all the time. We are expecting to move very soon now. Gen. Stoneman's Division it is said to move tonight. It is said we are to cross the river above us & of course whip them there. The army is in prime health & condition & I think we move with much more spirit than when we attacked before. The opinion is it will not pay to attack this city, but I can't tell. I suppose something must be done. We have lain still a long time & should be willing now to do our part. I feel entirely calm & ready to do my duty & as I have before written, you should school your heart for trial. I have this moment heard that all the cavalry belonging to this army will move at sunrise tomorrow morning with 8 day's rations, destination unknown. Mrs. Rice is here & will stay till we move. She arrived while we were on picket. This morning I had an introduction to her & talked half an hour. She is easy in manner, not brilliant but good, apparently is all over camp distributing books or tracts & has been out to see our Division. Reviewed today by a Swiss officer. You may think it strange that we have reviews on Sunday but we have so many now there is not time weekdays. I shall not be able to probably to write to L. You will show him this. Tell him O. recd. a letter from home this afternoon, dated 5th & 8th. He is well & in good spirits. F. also. O. is going to write now so he can tell all. I have written so often that there is no news except little matters such as experiences on picket & the like & I feel in no mood to write that today. Remember me to Mr. & Mrs. Miller & the children. I am enjoying myself better than formerly. Or at least I am contented to stay here till we get through with this war. Still I have no society here. There are but 4 Co. officers I think in this regiment who are strictly temperate, refrain from profanity & c. Indeed a man who wishes to gain position here & be admitted to full communion must drink, swear & play cards so I am outcast.

I wish in case I fall that Netti have $100 when she is married or in case she is not then on her 23rd birthday. Bring up Ida at best you can. I must leave all to your judgement. Be cool, be calm & be true. I think I shall conduct so you need not blush for me, that is, I will try to do my <u>duty</u>. Kiss that darling child for me. Remember me to Graham & family & all friends. You need fear nothing if you don't hear from me as soon as usual.

Your aff. Husband & Father,

B. Munger

Camp near Falmouth April 20, 1863

My Darling little Ida,

Today I am officer of the day again & as I usually have some time for my own I will devote the spare moments to you only suggesting that you <u>let</u> mother share it. It is now 8 A.M. and I shall have no duties to perform till 9. The morning is pleasant & warm, the first fine morning since the big storm. It makes me think of my boyhood & early life. There is one point of contrast. Here there are no singing birds although a few robins are seen. Not one musical note have I heard from one this spring & the little brown grass birds are occasionally seen. They maintain a <u>dignified</u> silence. One bird only sings, that is a little fellow like our northern wren but two or three times as large he sings very prettily but very seldom. I do not blame the poor birds & if they know how to cry I have no doubt we should hear from them. The frogs peep like our good northern frogs & that is the only familiar spring sound we hear. But instead we hear the incessant braying of mules by day & by night. I believe I told you that most of our orders or signals were given by sound of the bugle. We are first called up by the bugle, next the sick are sent to the Dr. by it, then guard mounting, then drill call, next dinner & etc. each a distinct sound or tune. Last Tuesday the ominous officer's call was sounded, we all repaired to the Col's tent & received orders to have our commands in readiness by next morning to move at the shortest notice. Each man to carry 8 day's rations but no clothing but one extra shirt, one pr. Of drawers & one pr. Of sox, blanket & overcoat all over that to boxed & sent to the Quarter Master. Commandants were to see the men were fully equipped, had all necessary clothing & 60 rounds of ammunition & we were cautioned to see that the orders were carried out to the letter & the remark was added, "Hooker never makes false motions." So we concluded that we had <u>work</u> to do. Well we got ready & the orders have been repeated several times so that in the morning we expect to move before night & when we go to bed we expect to be called before morning. You will think it must be somewhat exciting to live in such a state of uncertainty & it is but like everything we <u>get</u> <u>used</u> <u>to</u> <u>it</u>.

Mother asks if we live well & comfortably. As of late we have not quite as comfortably as formerly. Our cook is not a rugged boy & can't do for us as Rob died & of late we have been so short for money that has embraced us but I barrowed some yesterday & will do better now. You need not worry about us. We can get along well enough. I sent to Mother for $20 which I hope she will send for I will not depend on the Pay Master in future. Day before yesterday I had one of my headaches, am much better but but not quite well. Mother says I don't write particular enough so I will now tell you particularly what my experiences have been the last two hours. It is now 11 A.M. & I am through with my morning duties. At 9 the bugle sounded for Guard mounting & I put on sash & sword & proceed to the Col's line. I have not time to describe the form of guard mounting now. But as soon as it was over I am called to the Col's tent. Knock, he says, "Come." & I open the door. He greets me very cordially which I return with a salute & doffing my hat (that hurts me) I ask, "Have you any orders this morning Col?" He told me what he wanted done viz. the grounds in front of the field & staff officer's tents. (You would laugh if you see how I write this letter. I stopped at the word "officer's" in the line above, was absent half an hour seeing to our ordinance report, came back & wrote the word "tents" was called off a gain, came back, wrote one line to the word "letter" then dinner was ready since which I have been seeing a sick man taken to the hospital & cared for.) – swept & the ordinary camp cleaning which we call "policing". I went to the Sergeant Major told him I wanted a "detail" of six men with brooms to report at my tent. I took them & did that job with a good deal of watching for men will do very little unless someone is with them. Just as that was finished one of the doctors came & asked, "Have you examined the camp thoroughly?" I told him, "No". He said there was much offal outside the camp needing removal. We went round & there was wagon loads of old meat, bread & all kinds of filth so I called on the Sergeant Major again for 8 more men with shovels & two sergeants to order them, divided into two squads & set them at work raising the filth which we completed at 11 as I said . Then I visited the guards (Orett is officer of the guard today.) When they see the officer of the day coming he calls out, "Guard Fall In! Officer of the day." They form a line & present arms just as I arrive in front of them. I answer by raising my hat.

Usually after once turning out the guard of the day on approaching the guardhouse & hearing the order, "Turn out the guard." answers, "Never mind the guard." & passes on to his duties. On leaving my tent after dinner I met one of my boys, Norman Harrington who has had the diarrhea since the battle was at Wind Mill Point with me. He is poor as poor can well be. I asked if he was improving any. He said he was growing weaker. I went to Dr. Townsend & told him he could not be cured. I wanted him sent home & not have another man die here on my hands. He came up to see him. Harrington says his bowels move about 9 times in 24 hours. The Dr. ordered him to hospital. (By the way this is the boy I got called before the Col. for) He cried he did not want to go but I think his life is at stake so I sent him, promised to see him every day while he stayed here & tried to cheer him all I could & if he does not get better I shall try to get him discharged. The ladies have all left camp except Mrs. Rice. She is the most agreeable one we have here I think. More citizens are visiting us than usual. There is a great deal of playing of late of ball & chiefly with which I frequently engage. On the whole the men are more cheerful than formally. My sheet is most full & I must close. I wrote to Mr. Graham yesterday but you must pay him one more kiss for me. Give my love to all friends & don't forget that oft separated request to be such a model little girl for me to meet & kiss, if the Rebs let me come home someday.

From your affectionate father,

Bennett Munger

Camp near Falmouth, Va. Apr. 22, 1863

My Dear Wife & Daughter,

It is 3 O'clock P.M. The regiment is out on drill & being officer of the day I am at home alone. We are again "stirred up" today with the prospect of a move tomorrow but as we are pretty much ready there is little to do & little excitement. The 20th Maine Regiment belonging to our Brigade left this morning on account of 12 men having been taken down with small pox from using bad matter in vaccination. The weather today is quite fine the second good day in the week. The roads of course are not good. Our doctor talks rather discouragingly to me. I have not been quite as well as usual of late. He asked me into his tent today & said that he ought to tell me before we march that in all probability I would not stand active duty & advised me if I should be taken down again to leave the service at once.

I see no reason why I may not stand it as well as last year but I could not shake his opinion. I hope I shall be well. You need give yourself no undue grief about me. I have good friends here so that if anything serious does occur I shall be cared for. It is one week today since I received a letter from you or I think any one the longest period since I returned to the army. Today I did expect one but was disappointed. I received yours by Wing on the 15th & another by mail the same day & answered it on that day & Saturday, 18th I wrote to Ida. The health of the company is good. Harrington's case is the worst. We that is the officers of our mess are well provided for. The men have returned from drill so that a line at a time is about all I am able to write. An order is just received demanding a report of the number of cartridges necessary to give 60 rounds to each man. One hour later, and I have made my report & also seen that every man still has his 8 days rations.

You can hardly imagine the amount of care and perhaps I don't take care as easily as some. I can't avoid a certain amount of anxiety which my nervous temperament wears on me. I think sometimes I will not write about our orders to move and our counter orders & etc. but I only wrote what seems true I if you are misled by my letters I can answer I am mislead by our orders & I can only advise you to take it coolly as we do. O & F are well & all the NY boys. I visited the 33rd Sunday, saw Brennan and Capt. Root. Mr. Lung & I had a good visit, found all well. 8 P.M., I have been turning over to the Q. Master our surplus tents & other property, so we look as if we had broken up housekeeping. We have not yet received our pay & probably shall not. Of course we are ignorant of our route whether we are to cross the river above or below. It now appears below but I am tired of guessing. After we move you can continue to write & the letters will find me if I am findable. I shall leave this letter till morning to add what may transpire before the mail closes.

I don't but I told you in my last we were living poorly. We did for a time but are doing well now, as usual. It is an old saying, "On earth" that "everyone must eat his peck of dirt" but that saying is not applicable to soldiers. I have already eaten over 4 bushels of real filth & am still alive & & doing nicely. Am convinced that, "That which goeth into the man defileth not a man", but it is exceedingly unpleasant to eat so much of it. The early close of this does not seem as probable as two months ago. The soldiers & officers all expect to serve out their time. There is some dissatisfaction in the two year segments. The companies were mustered at different times. The terms of some companies is out tomorrow morning. 11 ½ P.M. I am obliged to keep up till after 12 to visit the sentinels & see that all is right. I have several men arrested tonight for playing cards & having lights after taps. Nothing new has transpired since dark in relation to move.

April 23rd – This has been one of rigorous rainy days & to us full of discomforts. Our tents is all water & mud & the country is soaked. It will probably postpone our move a day or two. I have not been well today, some headache but am about. I recd. notice of the discharge of A. J. Cole today from hospital. So you will perhaps see another of our maimed boys.

April 24 – 8 A.M. The storm has ceased & the morning is partly clear & windy. I am well again this morning. We were all disappointed in not moving yesterday. Everything was ready. This is the second time we have had such a storm Justas all was ready. I have received no letters since a week last Wednesday, but the mails are as regular as ever. The boys are well, only two are excused from duty on our prospective march which I suppose is to be the most severe one we have ever made on account of our loads & the distance. Remember to all friends generally & particularly much love from your affectionate Husband & Father,

B. Munger

In a small note dated April 24th, 1863 we have the following: Recd. of Capt. B. Munger fifteen (15) dollars in full of all demands to date.   Moses F. Harvey

Camp near Falmouth, Va. Apr. 24, 1863

Received of Capt. B. Munger fifteen (15) dollars in full of all demands to date.

Moses F. Harvey (This short note was found among Captain Munger's letters)

Ten Miles North of Fredericksburg, Va, May 2, 1863

My Dear Wife,

We left camp last Monday noon, marched 8 miles & camped after dark. Stood the march fairly, the roads were bad. Started next day at noon. Marched a mile & waited till after 2 – rained. Marched that afternoon over 15 miles in rain & mud. Orett had been down with dysentery 3 days & this day his exertions were so great that was taken bleeding at the nose & the Dr. advised him to stop. I think about 5 we marched till after dark. The reason for starting so late & camping so late is that large bodies of troops are moving & we being in the rear have to wait for them to move. I slept poorly both these nights.

Next morning moved at 7 as we lead today. Reached the river about 9 & crossed at Kelly's Ford on pontoon bridges the 11 & 12 Corps crossed before us & took a road to the right of ours. We marched about south & with great rapidity. O came up to us near the river. About 5 miles from it we forded a stream abought thigh deep, stopped ten minutes to wring our socks & moved on. The men were most exhausted. The night before only 20 out of 47 went into camp with us & today they fell out again. We marched this ford on the Rapidan about 5. The river here is about 15 rods wide & 3 feet deep. Our brigade was with the advance & one regiment 2nd.

Gen. Griffin wanted a regiment to volunteer to lead in fording the river. Col. Rice did, so I being next to the front was among the first to cross. The current is very rapid. Our cavalry had crossed before driving the enemy's pickets & held the high bank. We expected to meet opposition at this point but did not. This was the hardest march we have ever made, Next day we moved about 7 miles exploring carefully as we advanced, halted at noon with the enemy two miles in front. Next day the battle commenced. Saturday & yesterday there was most terrific fight & at near as I can ascertain the result is to our advantage. The fighting has been mostly in wood with think underbrush. We have not been actively engaged. Our regiment has lost a few men by random shot & etc. Our company all safe at yet. Today 30 hours we have lay at this spot momentarily expecting an attack. We are well but so tired. I slept none last night & but little for several. The spirits of the reg. good.

I received a letter from Libbie Booth informing me where Ansel & Beachr Sperry were & I found them next day. They were well, have since been in battle with what resulted to themselves I do not know. Rumors are all in our favor & I hope it is true.

Yours affectionately,

B. Munger

Morrisville seven miles from Kelly's

May 5, 1863 - 8 A.M.

My Dear Wife,

We left Banks yesterday at 11 ½ & arrived at this place at dark. You can see this place on the map I sent Ida. We are only bivouacked & expect to move again soon. It is said we are bound for Beal's Station but I do not know. We were relieved at Banks by Sykes Division after working night & day for a week to fortify it & get our tents livable. Yesterday's march was somewhat severe being warm & dusty. Only about half the Co. stood to keep up with us. We marched 13 miles. It is 9 to Beals but they are Virginia miles of no definite length but much longer than Yankee miles. The Rebs it is supposed intend to come around there & we are going up to give them a reception. I don't feel quite as much enthusiasm as when we went to Chancellorsville but hope it will result better. I may as well stop guessing what we are going to do one thing is certain our commanders of divisions are ignorant as we & our order are unexpected to us to you. The Rebs are said to be informed at Culpepper & say they are going to Maryland. Since going to Banks Ford we have no daily papers & gets the news after it gets old but I much fear Grant will not be able to take Vicksburg. The leaving of our quarters at Banks often enjoying our night & day was rather trying to the flesh but we are soldiers & have no sight to have a home. As it is too late to send this today. I will wait & add this day's experience.

Saturday Morning May 6th, in camp at Crittendens Mill. I wish you would go to the book store & buy Lloyd's Official Map of Virginia & by its aid I can tell you very nearly our marches & camps. I will assume you have it. You will see west of Falmouth 6 miles the river bends south opposite the mouth of Golin Run. That is Banks Ford & our late camp. We marched mostly on roads laid down on this map paper Hartwood to the north about 8 miles then North West & bivouacked at Morrisville. There commenced this letter at 10, moved nearly west to this place on Summer Duck Creek which you see crosses this road. Our camp is on a fine green field & we were again told by the Col. that it was to be permanent but we have learned to believe as much as we know to be true & our skepticism was strengthened before night by a general order from Hooker to hold ourselves in readiness to move at the shortest notice, send all extra baggage to the rear & keep 3 days cooked rations on hand.

I had no heart to fix up again but as we must have some place to stay finally that we would make ourselves comfortable so worked all the afternoon hard. Perhaps you wonder that it is so much work to put up our tents. I believe I told you we were obliged to turn over our wall tent to take the little shelter. It is so hot nothing human can live "comfortable" in one down on the ground. So, we set them up 2 or three feet to let the air circulate & this building up is the tug our tools an ax, dull & our lumber the woods. Teams our own shoulders, stakes, crotches & poles do everything. Our tent is now comfortable & O. & I are its sole occupants. As to our family living & cooking our family that is our mess is the same as usual. Our living not as good, our cook, Houghton no such a boy as Rob, I assure you but as good perhaps as they average. If you reflect for a moment you can form something of an idea of our comforts in food & furniture when we are regained to carry all on the march & to always to be in such present readiness as to be able to pack & be in line in 30 minutes. I don't complain. I am answering your questions.

Kelly is on picket, Orett has gone to call on a family with whom he stayed all night on our march to Chancellorsville. They invited him to call if in this vicinity. I don't know as I ought to use up space & time in giving rumors but there is one of so much importance "if true" I will give it. It is our forces attack Fredericksburg yesterday succeeded in crossing & took 3 of the 4 lines of defenses in rear of the city. I need not say we do not believe it although firing was heard in that direction yesterday & this morning. I recd. yours of May 31st last & Graham of the same date & if we do not move too soon will answer. The sample of Ida's dress is pretty & I hope you will be as good darling as the dress looks. Don't let it make you proud but good & when you put it on. Imagine you have a kiss from your soldier father. I must not say that sometimes I feel tired of this kind of life for it would not be patriotic but it is a sacrifice some don't comprehend. We seem to accomplish so little I am not satisfied. O we need better officers here, men of principles who would exert a good influence over the men & I think if our army were addressed occasionally by the Generals & others it would do an untold amount of good. There is little to no sympathy between officers & men & no enthusiasm in the ranks. It need not be so. The men are intelligent but have little to inspire them. I don't want to say anything against our officers but I would be ashamed to have it known at home that I am associated with such men. Many of them are naturally &

some of them smart but they are spoiled. Our Col. doesn't swear or use low obscene language as I know of but "on reliability" I always believe what I <u>know</u> to true but who will write it.

One of ours from Division Headquarters has just been here & says the report that Fredericksburg is ours is believed there. It is too good to believe. I wish it was. For however strong I may be in refusing to go home, now I would be <u>entirely</u> <u>willing</u> to if the war was over but we will want & see. I am surprised at the tone of the Democrat of your village that young men of such personal worth as the proprietors of that paper should allow themselves to be held responsible for sentiments uttered in it, is to me astonishing they are selling themselves quite too cheap. The acts of the Govt. may not all be wise but there is a vast difference in the spirit manifested by its friends & its foes. Soldiers who take little interest on the local quarrels of parties are quick to detect opinion to the Govt. The Govt. is the only power that can act against the Rebels & to weaken that power is to prolong the war & multiply its honors. I think if 100 soldiers to each town could go home for 30 days it would do more good than a victory it <u>would</u> <u>be</u> a <u>victory</u> over our worst enemies too. I think I mentioned the fact of Gen. Blain's visit to our camp to see the 16th Michigan & that I saw several New York men of note. In speaking of the criticisms of the people & the press of the north particular on the insanity of the army I told him my patience was completely exhausted that they did not seem to use common sense. Said Capt. Munger, "They don't know your situation. I did not know I had learned more in one week <u>seeing</u> the army than in all the reading I have ever done & my answer in future to fault finders will go down then yourselves." Our northern men seem to think that all the talent remains north & an editor that knows enough to take charge of a Picket squad can instruct our best commanders in all the intricacies of great battle. Their wisdom consists in saying, "Whatever is done might have been done better." Perhaps you will think this not much of a letter for a woman & wife. My apology is I have no one to talk with & I get full sometimes & must free my mind & every word that brings the Govt. into disrepute strengthens the enemy, prolongs the war & increases the sufferings of soldiers.

B. Munger

Camp near Falmouth May 11, 1863

My Dear Wife & Child,

We are still in the old camp & it is one of the warmest mornings of the season. Our Corps I should now think would not move for some days. A portion of the Corps have been mustered out & more are to be soon. The news is a little more cheering & I am feeling a little better in <u>mind</u> & shall stand it all, but at first to think all our toil & effort was so nearly lost was disheartening. Saturday I went to Aquia & although there is little there to see or get it was a change that diverted my mind some. I saw & conversed with men of intelligence & that which I cannot do every day. Yesterday I visited Booth & Sperry the later a sergeant & the former a corporal. You would not know then, they look like soldiers. I have hardly a heart to describe our late march & battle. Perhaps I will sometime. I was much less effected than at the first battle amounting almost to indifference. Such musketry I never dreamed of from 5 to 8 A.M. last Sunday week. The contest was most fearful but after being in it awhile it doesn't seem "much" to die or be wounded. The most awful thing was the wood in which the battle took place took fire & I suspect thousands of the wounded were burned to death. Soldiering in this heat will be oppressive this summer but as I am good to stand heat think I shall get along well.

This morning at Guard Mounting a man was sun struck & fell from the ranks & I suppose this is only a beginning. I receive very few letters now so that camp life is a little more dull than formerly & as we have no tent my facilities for writing are not good. It is astonishing how one gets accustom to circumstances. This life is mental, moral & social as well as physical starvation still we live & are cheerful comparatively. I can think, think abundance of time for that. A regiment the 2nd New York is just at the Depot on their way home & their shouts of joy ring again & know some who would like to be in a like situation. There is a new rumor in camp that our regiment is going to Aquia to do Provost Duty but in all probability, it is as groundless as most of the rumors circulating here. My opinion is that we are to move across the river & fight!, fight! I am ready to own that. I am willing to go into a place where our duties would be less severe & dangerous but still am ready to do my whole duty. Perhaps my life is of less value than that of younger men. I have less to hope for & if I can do good here I ought to be willing to do it.

I saw Mr. Root at Aquia, Saturday on his way to see his son who you know was mortally wounded at Fredericksburg. I saw him but a moment & when I got home found that Capt. Root was at Alexandria. I got a severe reproof a few days since from the Col. that my Co. were not more tidy. It is quite as difficult to make men keep clean as a family of children. I suppose the world is looking pleasant at the north now. Here everything is blasted by the army so that nothing looks fresh & green, still reviewed under favorable circumstances would look fine & pleasant. Kelly has gone to Aquia & there is little to do today. An incident has just occurred, very annoying & trying. This morning the three best appearing men on inspection were to have passes to go to Aquia & Kinner was one of them. Just before they were ready to go the Col. called the 1st Sergeants & told them they might take the men to Potomac Creek to wash & swim. He (Kinner) probably forgot it & I knew nothing of it. One of the men who dislikes him went to the Col. with the complaint & he the Col. has just been here & ordered Kinner arrested as soon as he returned. It will hurt Kinner's pride very much but nothing more will result from it. The Col. has been particularly crusty for a few days.

Today a colored boy came & wanted to work for us. He left his master one month since & has been chopping says he, puts up 2 ½ cords of wood a day & I advise him to go back & earn all the money & save it, possible keep out of bad company & try to be a man. So he is back with new courage. The poor fellows appreciate freedom even in its lowest form. The idea of making their own bargains & receiving their own pay seems to inspire them. I am now writing in Fred's tent as I have none as yet except a place to sleep. The Washington papers contain nothing of interest today & the New York papers are not allowed here.

Tuesday morning, Mat 12th - It is a fine morning, clear & bright. The evenings & mornings in Virginia are beautiful at this season but the middle of the day is oppressively hot. Our magnificent evenings "reminds me of something I can't think of." I frequently walk along at such times & <u>think</u>. There seems less probability of a speedy move each day. I received a letter from Jane yesterday. All is well as usual. The mail is about to close & I must close this. Give love to all inquirers & take a quantity yourself & baby.

Your affectionate Husband & Father – B. Munger

Camp near Falmouth, Va. May 13, 1863

My Darling Ida,

I think it is now your turn to have a letter for we are now sitting again in our old quarters but in a new tent having recd. one last night & shall now have a place to write. I will give you some sketches of our late march & some of our experience. The marching was as severe it is said as any ever done by this regiment. The roads were muddy & the first days rainy. Monday & Tuesday we marched only ½ of each day. The first, marching 10 & the second, 13 miles with heavy loads. More than ½ the men were so tired they fell out the second day but most of them came up at night. Do you suppose I was tired any? <u>No</u>, only at times things looked misty & dark. I felt faint & that I was going but I would arouse & think I would not falter. I will endure & it seemed to give me strength & I kept on & now I <u>guess</u> I can stand anything. The third day in the marching we came to the Rappahannock above its junction with the Rapidan & crossed on the pontoon without opposition to this place. The country had been barren & desolate but between both these rivers it is mostly very fine & it really seemed as if we had got into a civilized part of the world again. This Thursday was very warm. About 11 we forded a stream called Mountain Run, the first we have forded, water about 2 ½ feet deep. About noon I threw away my overcoat as my load was too heavy to bare in the extreme heat. This left me with a woolen blanket, rubber blanket & tent cloth, two haversacks of rations, canteen & coffee & sword. We reached the Rapidan about 5 & I was among the first to cross. We camped on the opposite side, marching 22 miles.

It rained hard during the night & morning so that in the morning I found my shoulders in a pool of water & wet through. This day the enemy were near so we moved with caution. Passed in the morning rifle pits occupied by the Rebs the night before & about noon arrived at Chancellorsville & perhaps you would like a description of the village. Well, it is just one house & its outbuildings nothing more. It is or was a large one to be sure but a small affair to make a village of. When we arrived. It was occupied. I saw a half dozen ladies in the Piazza looking at the Yankees. Next noon the fight began & although we were ready in the fight we were exposed to fire more or less from Friday noon till Tuesday night. I felt much less nervous this time than in the first fight, almost indifferent. I enclose a map cut from the Tribune to assist in describing our route & battleground & our position as a regiment. Figure #1 near Hanover Church was our first night's camp ground. Next took the road to Morrisville, then Orett had the nose bleed so badly & being very weak, he stopped. We took the road to Kelly's Ford & camped after dark in the woods. At #2 from Marsh Run I have marked our route as nearly as possible to Ely's Ford. We camped at #3. Thursday before noon arrived at Chancellorsville & lay in a field in front of the house at a dot. The 11th & 12th Corps came in on the Plank Road from Wilderness having passed to our right since leaving Kelly's Ford. Our lines of battle I will mark as near as I can.

This whole country except the Chancellorsville farm & a little on the road back to Ely's Ford is forest of oak & pine & filled with brush called Chinquapin which grows in clusters or bunches & spreads out so the tops which are as high as the head meet. At first our lines extended around the C. House as I have marked with a pencil & it was near this road where I have two faint dots that the 11th Corps routed & your wise little will perceive at once that gave the Rebs possession of the Plank Road to Fredericksburg. Thursday night we camped in the woods near the head of Mine River, which is a small brook. Here we lay till Friday noon where we were called into line & marched rapidly to near Bank's Ford found no enemy countermarched at the same speed & at dark halted a mile from C. House. This road was a cart path through wood & the battle began just as commenced our march. The fight was on the left or southeast of us. The point of our lines at figure #4 is called the front & imagine yourself facing it & you will understand the positions when I say right, left, front & rear. When we halted, the woods were full of skirmishers & shot flying about carelessly.

Here we were marched in all conceivable forms & directions, finally halted & ordered to fix bayonets. This usually means something & at this moment a battery opened on us no more than 50 rods off but the wood being thick & the darkness complete. They did through their shell directly toward us but our officers anxious to correct their error apparently marched us directly under their fire & halted us. This was a trying spot. The shells screeching like demons just over our (heads) & bursting just behind us & the fragments flying in all directions. One of Co. E, men was struck by a fragment penetrating his brain & driving the figure 4 on his cap & strange to say he is alive and doing well. After a time, the Rebs seemed to be tired of their labor & stopped. We were moved further toward the enemy & laid down silently on our arms about 200 yards from the Reb pickets. It was 10 P.M. at 1 ½ we were called without noise & moved up to near figure #5 & laid down till morning, then ordered to fortify our line & make it as strong as possible & we went to work with a will, cut trees & made cribs of logs 3 feet wide & filled in with dirt dug so as to make a ditch & beyond fell trees with tops out or toward the enemy called "Abbattis" so that in approaching us the Rebs would be obliged to cross through & over this brush under our fire & we protected by our defense could mow them but they would not come. We felt good over our defenses & supposed we should occupy them but next morning, Sunday at 4 we were ordered into line & moved to the front & the 11th Corps which had been so badly routed that they were worthless & put into our trenches. They were the most frightened set of men I ever saw. We went to a point between the figure #4 & the corner made by our line & the road at two little dots. As we were getting into line the most terrific fire I ever heard was opened at our rear & left from the C. House to the point of the bend in our line & it continued without abatement till 8 & the artillery till 12. We were entirely unprotected & expected our line attacked every moment. After waiting 30 minutes or so we set the men to bringing old logs & making a rude breastwork for it was a weak position in a valley & we facing northwest toward the #4 where was the crest of the hill or rise. At noon, the firing slacked & we began to fortify again. The enemy were said to be determined to break the line at that point & we were determined they should not, so we made our defense very strong & then longer for the rascals to try it. We waited & watched but they would not come. Our picket line was along the right hand line of #4 in the edge of the wood & on the crest of the hill the Rebs in firing at our men sent their balls over into our lines & quite a number were struck & some killed

& the shells pommel the C. House would occasionally visit us. We lay here from Sunday morning to Wednesday morning 2 O'clock.

It was a cheerless night, rained hard, we were wet through & cold & as our brigade covered the retreat we moved painfully slow & at every 50 to 100 rods were drawn up in line of battle across the road & waited for stragglers & the odds & ends to pass on. About 8 we arrived in sight of the river & halted, ordered to cook coffee but before we had fires built a battery down the river opened & old Col. Stockton of our brigade commander, did not want to stay any longer & he started us off with little ceremony crossed the river 7 we did not stop long enough to eat till 11 O'clock & the mud so deep that I dare not state it, but our pants were muddied above the "junction" & raining most of the time. We came into camp about 5 tired & I don't know darling but I was <u>cross</u>. I certainly felt sad & I fear impatient.

Our tent was sent away, the ground was muddy, our clothes wet, no place to sleep, & <u>hungry</u> doesn't begin to express the conditions of my stomach having had but ½ pint of coffee & one hard tack & been on the march since 2 ½ in the morning & toad to my discomfort boots were worn out, feet wet & full of sand, & aching like tooth aches. But it was no time to lie down in despondence. We had nothing to eat & I am a pretty good forager & soon found a Suttler who had some boiled pork & coffee & secured a meal for Orett & myself that tasted as delicious as any I ever had. I also found a place to sleep, hooked some of Uncle Sam's hay, had a good wash, went to bed & slept well. I am still alive & think I am <u>hard</u> to <u>kill</u>. There are many incidents & scenes that would interest you & if I live to return can tell you many things. I cannot write it.

It is not probable that my description of positions is exactly correct but real enough to give you an idea of our lines. It is the worst country to map I ever saw. No straight roads & usually wooded & the point of the compass in a cloudy day is out of the question. Then consider that I cannot leave my position in column to see anything. My information is gained under difficulties you will understand. Let Uncle Lyman see this & map if he wishes to & tell him my own opinion is our line extended to the northwest so as to enclose Mine River & is described by a line of dots. But the Dr. I consulted thinks the line southeast of the river is near correct. Uncle Lyman & Mr. Graham will explain to you why we occupied so odd shaped line. It was so we might obtain supplies from the river at the ford. You may ask them all the questions you can think of about it as to where the supplies came from, how carried & c. for I would like you to understand it all. You will see also why the Rebs made such desperate efforts to break the lines at one point. If they had got in at that place we would not dare fire on them for our lines would be firing on each other & we would be obliged to depend on the bayonet alone. We repulsed the enemy in every encounter except on Saturday night when the 11th Corp shamefully gave away. A thoroughly frightened soldier is a painful sight. They will encounter ten times more danger in running away than in the discharge of duty. They seemed perfectly wild, crass and mad. You can't reason with them & nothing but the certainty of instant death will arrest one. I saw several stopped but sometimes not till the point of the sword touched their breast would they heed. I guess I have written enough of war to so little a heart as yours. There are some <u>awful</u> <u>things</u> about it I don't want you to think of.

Our Brigade has just gone out on picket & strange to say I am not detailed. I can hardly credit my senses. None of the officers of our Co. go & it looks as if we were to have 3 lazy days. This is your letter little one but you will <u>lend</u> it to <u>mother</u> you know.

One of the greatest trials of camp life is its painful monotony, no variety, you can't tell how a letter breaks the tedium of this prison life. My correspondents are few & don't appreciate our utter starvation & my <u>friends</u> that are only friends when I am present. I'll remember or rather I'll forget for I shan't always be a soldier. This is a cloudy day & not uncomfortably warm but I am just notified that I am officer of the day so I must stop & attend to the duties. - I am here again but clothed with the badge of authority (a red scarf). Yesterday Orett received by express a box of eatables from Jone & we are now living well but expensively. I would recommend my darling that you buy a nice little book & keep a diary in ink. I think it will improve you besides being a great pleasure to me to have you send me extracts from it. I wish mother would buy some good flannel plaid or blue fast colors & make me two good shirts & send them the first good opportunity. Sale shirts are of little worth. The length of neck can be reassured by my cotton ones, no larger.

Well little girl it is 3 O'clock & we have just had a refreshing shower but the sun now shines hot. No news in the daily paper. Fred has been to Hooker's Head Quarters today to get a position in Signal Corps, perhaps will succeed. Capt. Pierce, Graham's nephew starts for home tomorrow. The mail is in but nothing for <u>me</u>. A sound just greets my ear that reminds me of the past. It is the song of Martin Bird & I think she learned it north for it tweets the same cheerful one I have so often heard there but good. Share all this with Mother. Your aff. Father,

B. Munger

Camp near Falmouth, Va. May 17, 1863

My Dear Wife,

It is Sunday A.M. & a warm debilitating day & the sun reflected by the white sand of this soil is oppressively bright. Our regiment is out on picket & will return today. I have remained in camp & have had three of the most leisure days since I joined the army. Not enough to do to make the time pass pleasantly. Night before last I recd. your letter of the 11th inst. written while you supposed Richmond to be in our possession. You must have sadly been disappointed. We were saved that disappointment not having believed the rumor. We believe little that we don't see for there are many lies in circulation that we got disgusted & don't believe anything. The time here for the 9 months & 2 years' men is expiring now & several regiments are leaving daily. They are a happy set of men. The 33rd left day before yesterday. They suffered severely in the last fight. It peculiarly had just started as they were expecting to go home. Our corps will be much reduced by the 2 years' men & it is rumored again that we are to do garrison or guard duty but I can't be fooled again with that story. We shall probably stay here till the army is reorganized & reinforced. So far as my observation extends the confidence of the army in Gen. Hooker is not shaken & were ready & expected to be led across the river two days after our return to camp. It is now reported that one of our men that is from this Co. was wounded in the late battle & is now in Washington but when men straggle from their Co. in the moment of supposed danger & get wounded in the <u>hand</u> by a <u>chance</u> shot. I have little confidence in the whole especially when the record of the man is not good. It is a little miraculous that so many stragglers are shot in the hand. I prefer they were shot in the head. They are a disgrace to mankind.

There are curious things observed in time of battle. The air seems full of balls & shells. Sometimes shells burst 100 feet high & the whole atmosphere alive with missiles of various kinds. The reports of the guns frightens the birds from the ground but instead of flying away out of danger they fly round & round till it seems as if they court death, yet strange to say I never saw one killed. Whippoorwills are plenty & musical here & although a timid shy bird, on the night of the repulse of the 11th Corps when the very earth trembled with the report of the artillery at every interval in the cannonading you would hear their concert as if nothing unusual was happening. Their song will never sound so sweet to me again. It is associated with too many horrid memories. Gen Griffin, you know is our division commander & is an old artillery officer & a good one. On Monday, the Rebs came out in mass from the wood ½ a mile in front of the point of the line as described on the map sent to Ida. Griffin stood by a brass battery of 12 lb. howitzers double shotted with grape & canister. They were yelling like demons. He stood cool as if nothing was at stake saying to the men, "Hold still boys & let them come! Save your fire!" & so on till they were about 50 or 80 rods then, "Now boys give them Hell!" & O how they fell. It was awful it is said to look at. Although close by I did not see it <u>somehow, everybody had something to do about that time</u>. Each gun would cut a path of 12 or 15 feet right through their ranks, "flesh & blood" could not stand such a fire & they were compelled to break but a man who doubts their courage should see them fight once, I respect them more than I used to for they possess courage if nothing more. If they are beaten soon it will be by an utter failure of supplies & the prisoners I saw looked as well fed as our men & they said that <u>they</u> were comfortably fed that they would say probably whatever the facts might be. We shall surely fetch them in time. But it will take time I think.

One of the men who left us at Antietam for the hospital at Baltimore has just returned. Phillips a good boy of the six who left them at that time. Two are now with us, three discharged, one of them since dead & one remains at Baltimore will never join us is all used up. Our Co. is getting reduced some. 10 are on duty out of the Co. some unfit for duty, 3 in Corps Hospital near us, one at Point Lookout I suppose, one at Baltimore, two wounded somewhere some beside the man just wounded & McBride so you see we are a good deal scattered already. John Giddings who was at home on furlough which has expired, I have not heard from in a long time. Monday morning 6 O'clock I am not feeling quite well for a few days. My stomach & bowels are out of rig but nothing very serious. Col. Rice says we shall move our camp in a day or two to a shady place. There is no green thing about this camp but we have been here so long it seems home like & there it is close to the rail road which is a convenience.

There is a strong feeling of dissatisfaction on the part of those men recruited last summer to fill up the 2 years' regiments. They were promised too that they should be mustered out when the regiments were but the Government now refuses to fulfill the contract. Some have laid down their arms & refuse to do duty & are under arrest on bread & water. I don't know what the result will be but it can't be favorable to the Gov. in its influence. It can ill afford to lose the confidence of the soldiers at this time. The 17th N.G. members of our Brigade & encamped close to us leave for home this morning but a fact that part of our family has served their time out & are going home to friends & social life don't affect us any. O we are soldiers & are not moved by such trifles. You ask in your last if I can stand it through the month of March. Yes, through several of them if necessary. I can stand it as long as the Rebs can I think. The boys are well O. & F. are in good spirits & health. Remember me particular to friends, to Mr.

Miller's & Graham's families especially & don't worry about us, we can stand the storm if it is long. The mail is about to close & I must so good bye, love to the little one & yourself.

Your aff. Husband,

B. Munger

Banks Ford June 3, 1863 Daughter

My Dear Wife & Daughter,

I recd. yours of the 26th, 30th & yours & Ida's of the 28th & June 1st. Also one from N. R. Long & last night one from Gaylord. We are now so far from the outer world that we get little news no dailies but <u>rumors</u> enough it is hard to "sell" us any more with rumors. Our fortifying callouses are finished & O. & myself have just finished a tent for ourselves & I am now writing it. <u>We are alone, thank God</u> & when one family is enlarged I hope to select the subjects we all still miss together. I am feeling more reconciled to this place it is pleasant about here but the particular locality of our camp is very unpleasant an old cornfield, dry & dusty & as we are on a point of land 200 feet above the river. We have wind enough to stir the dust & perhaps in your opinion the fact that we live within easy range of two of the enemy's battalions would not add to its charms but we get <u>used</u> to anything in time.

Monday, we received an order from Gen. Mead that in consequence of the unfavorable report of the brigade inspector of our condition & discipline all leaves, furloughs & <u>privileges</u> withheld from this regiment till future orders. This order was accompanied by one from Col. Rice that daily inspections be held till that the regiment was in condition to insure a favorable report & then another inspection would be ordered. Perhaps our "indignant dignity was not aroused" some & I propose sending up a statement that while cheerfully obey the order, we as to no "privileges", all we ask is our rights. I have not time to tell you all the points in which the order id unfair & untrue but for one. I'll stay here till after the general <u>judgement</u> before I will enter the lists to buy a leave. Our Col. will not resent an insult so long as the general will allow him to keep his wife here. Today the quiet has been broken by two Rebs deserting & swimming to our side & coming to our camp. They are from Alabama. One, a conscript & one a volunteer, both intelligent. I talk with the conscript, he comprehends the principles underlying the struggle & said, "We are fighting for our destination". They think Lee is about to cross the river perhaps at Culpepper & "come round" as he expressed it. You remember I told you a dead Reb lay in the river by the dam. He tried to swim over to us & they shot him it is said. These men say also that one of our 16th Mich, deserted to them yesterday, he says, "He's a powerful fool." The mail is called for & I must close.

Your Husband & Father, B. Munger

Kemper's Ford   June 12, 1863

My Dear Wife & Child,

I wrote L. yesterday & also recd. yours of the 7th fearing that when on the march, I shall not be able to write often. I am now gaining time. Last night we recd. an order from Hooker ordering all superfluous tents, baggage, teams & persons to the rear today, that the command be in readiness to move at the shortest notice. So, we are expecting momentarily an order for motion. Still it is not certain. Two great Generals are playing a great game & it must be amusing to one not personally interested to witness it. Confidence in Hooker's ability is increasing. I am in fair health & I attribute in part to powerful tonics mostly our butter. It is so strong that I have dispensed almost entirely with Quinine. But we ought not complain many of our poor fellows can't even get strong butter. The day is (I was going to write excessively hot but I'll not try to make out that one case is a tough one for I can say in truth I have suffered as much or more at the north with heat.) so I will say the day is warm & dry. We have had no rain of any amount since the 6th of May.

I think it is likely our letters convey an idea of suffering we do not realize. You know it is natural in writing to mention such thing & experiences as differ from those at home & <u>perhaps</u> your imagination may be at fault. In one case, it struck me your fears exaggerated some that was our danger at Banks Ford. That we are in danger I will not deny, so are people at home. The danger is the least or not the greatest of our trials. Again, rumor says Vicksburg is ours. I wish it were so. O. has not left the service nor has he forgotten you, he says but takes as a matter of course that he is to have credit for a part of my letters. I don't know but I may be that guilty of like neglect of Ls family but it is not intentional. Capt. Bourne of whom you have heard me speak & Capt. Nash are sick, chill & fever. We are very busy with our accounts. As now directed it is more work to keep my Co. books than when I was painting & something new added every day. 4 P.M. all quiet. The 3rd Corps has pass up & is not far from us up the river. Cannonading was heard today toward Fred'g.

B. Munger

Aldi, Louden County, Va.   June 20, 1863

My Dear Wife & Daughter,

It is one week tonight since I recd. a mail. I shall probably not have time to give you no detail a history of our marches & halting &c. So, will begin where we yesterday at 2 P.M. we started from the Green Spring & reached this place a distance of 5 miles at about 5. This is the Gap between the Bull Run & Catoctin Mountains where a severe cavalry battle took place on the 17th. (I just left a moment to see 52 prisoners marched passed) We are awaiting orders & expect to move through the Gap into Louden Valley. It is said that the 11th Corps are at Middleburgh & in all probability the next ten days will bring about important results. From the orders & preparations it would seem our commanders expect work & I think hard work. All the men on detached service & daily duty within the regiment are ordered to return to the ranks. I have just learned we may expect a mail today or tomorrow & perhaps I may be able to send this. We are only bivouacked here & have no place to write except to sit on the ground & write on my knee & I am officer of the day & disturbed <u>once</u> <u>in</u> <u>a</u> <u>while</u> but as I may not have an opportunity to write again soon, will write all I can.

As to the future, I need not say much. That this is stern work I am well aware & its dangers I fully appreciate if I do not often mention. But I am here to do duty & not to consult inclinations. I value the interest my friends feel in me but I hope they will not feel or express any desire to deter me from doing what they think is duty but rather encourage if they can. I think I am prepared to meet the worst & hope for the <u>best</u>. <u>Keep</u> <u>a</u> <u>strong</u> <u>heart</u>. Enough of the future. Now for an account of our troubles. I wrote last Saturday I think. At 6 we had an order to move at 7 our supper was not ready & we worked miserable but another order came not to move till dark. It was raining, our tents were down, officers drenched & on a whole it was somewhat gloomy. We moved at dark through thick woods & muddy road. We marched nearly north to Morrisville 7 miles, arrived & bivouacked at 11 with our tents, rained a little but we slept. I reckoned the last 3 miles the road was dry & dusty not having rained. The next morning aroused at 4 but did not move till 12 ½.. Morrisville is a large village containing one dwelling, one old shanty formerly used as a store & one chimney that may have had a house to it someday & perhaps will again & room in anymore houses. (**Note to reader: The last part of this sentence is jumbled & is hard to make any sense of**.)

Sunday at 12 ½ moved northwest passed through Elkton & reached Catlett's on the Orange & Alexandria R.R. at sundown 15 miles we suffered for water some today. Our mules did not come up so we slept without tents or blankets. Monday aroused at 3 ½, moved at 5 ½ along the rail road. This has been the scene of several battles & skirmishes & we saw the remains of a great many cars destroyed on it. This is the hottest day of the season, water scarce & bad. I drank stagnant water from a ditch I would hardly offer to a horse. We marched fast many men fell out & some died but not of our Regt. (& now I remember that I wrote you at Manassas Junction) This to me was the most trying march we have ever made & I think I should have gone to the wall if we had marched another mile. My head felt so strangely it did not seem like my head. We stopped at this place. We stayed through the afternoon & next day & I recovered from the effects of the heat & march.

Tuesday at 10 ½ we were ordered on picket 2 miles & just as the last man reached his post we were ordered back for a march, cooked coffee & were off at 5 ½ toward Centerville. <u>Dust</u>, dust is no name for it. Just imagine a road on which no rain has fallen since the 6th of May (or not enough to lay the dust) passed over by 50,000 men & a train of wagons that would reach from your place to Canandaigua & then consider how close together we march & you have a <u>faint</u> idea of what it is. We did not pass through Centerville as we expected & hoped but left it on our right. Capt. Coleman rode out to see us & several others & it seemed almost like a visit home. If I had the room I would give the names of those I saw. I must confess that the contrast between their condition & ours made me feel sad. They were well dressed & clean life as well as they wish, have their wives & I was told that parties & pick nicks were the order of the day. It's <u>no</u> <u>such</u> <u>life</u> as we see. This day we marched hard it seemed to me unseasonably. It was warm, water scarce & we were crowded like mules, & men dropped out like sheep. Ackley told me he saw 12 officers at one place who had failed & some mounted men failed. Col. Chamberlin of the 20th Maine was so exhausted he will not probably recover.

We started with 39 men & had 13 to stack arms at night. From Centerville went nearly north & camped at or near Gum Spring. All these little places & roads you will see on the map I have mentioned. This day we marched fully 20 miles & something more as you will have observed without any sleep the previous night & I did pity the poor men. They uttered deep curses. About 4 we heard heavy firing to the front & I expected we should have to fight in our exhausted condition but we camped. About 5 near Broad Run had a good bath & felt better. I was the dirtiest man you ever saw & if our Co. had marched into your streets I didn't know as any of you would have had the moral courage to own you knew us. At any rate, I was ashamed to sleep with myself. We stayed there that night. The next day & night marched to this place yesterday after noon the firing I spoke of was at this place, Aldie. It was a cavalry fight & although our troops lost heavily we're victorious. The many little incidents of past week I cannot now relate, perhaps can sometime. I have seen one paper since last Saturday & learned of the raid into Penn. But with what result I do not know. We are expecting marching orders at any time & a fight soon. Orders for cutting down the baggage of officers are very strict. We are now regained to be <u>soldiers</u> in all length & breadth of meaning of the word. The boys are all well & in good fighting trim. Last night it rained hard & has some today. I got more of last night's rain than I wanted but did not take cold. Saw Booth & Sperry at day for the first time since about the first of June. I want to write more but have no room. If we remain will soon.

Your loving Husband & Father, B. Munger

Aldi, Va. June 23, 1863

My dear little Ida,

  I feel today as if I would be glad if "The great Rebellion was over". Not that I am unwilling to do my duty & make all necessary sacrifice. But I am so tired of our restless life. I wish you could see us as we are today. If at home I had had a home in half as mean a place as I now occupy I should not rest until I had better quarters for hire. One great reason of the depravity of soldiers lies in the fact in outward condition they are degraded below the level of brutes. This is perhaps old talk to a little girl but the old part you may give away to mother. What made me mention it is the constant struggle between my pride & self-respect on one side & the inconveniences, filth & depression of our position on the other It requires struggle here to be a man. And I pity from my inmost soul the poor private who has still less than officers to encourage & elevate but enough to depress, seduce & degrade. This is a place that tries men & I am sorry to say many, very many fall.

  Well Darling I will to try to write to <u>you</u> now. You will see on the map that this village lies in the Gap between Bull Run & the Catoctin Mts. & that a road runs from Washington to Winchester though it is a macadamized turnpike & a splendid road. We struck it at Gum Spring. This is a beautiful country as I ever saw & reminds me of the country between Canandaigua & Lima except in buildings but as strange as it may seem the very beauty of the country served to depress me. But you must not understand me as always feeling so but the last 4 weeks have been weeks of intense labor & uncertainty & it is now 10 days since we have had a mail & you will see that's some excuse for depression. Today we got a paper but the news was meager enough. The old residence of James Monroe is in sight & I started to visit it today but was not able to pass the picket. I got within a ¼ of a mile & with a glass could see pretty well. It is built of brick apparently with basement above ground, a colonnade in front enclosed by a rail & balusters. I could see several Union officers & two ladies on the piazza. It is now owned by the Rebel, Major Fairfax who is said to be on Longstreet's staff & occupied by his family. The farm or plantation contains 8,000 acres it is said. One thing that adds much to the beauty & splendor of Virginia residences is the abundance of shade trees around them. The country being old the trees are large & look majestic. Even the houses of the poor are often finely shaded. But the poor are very ignorant men of 40 years not knowing to distance or way to places only a few miles from them.

 A few weeks since I saw a little girl about your size & asked her to come to me. After being told by her mother she came up timidly & I talked with her a few minutes. Told her I had a little girl at home, asked how old she was. That seemed a new idea to her, she looked wondering in my face a moment & her mother told me she was nine. I asked her if she went to school. She seemed a little puzzled at the question & finally said, "Ain't no school." & this girl a fair specimen & is naturally as bright as common children but has not been taught. I have seen one or two ladies of refinement & intelligence. There is about such an assumption of superiority & air of authority not pleasing. Some of these are intensely bitter toward the north that they often seem to forget themselves & make use of epithets that ladies should never utter.

 Our officers perhaps fearing we should get lazy called us up & out on drill at 5 ½ this morning. It is now 7 & I have not yet had my breakfast but it is now ready & I must stop. Well Darling, I have just had my breakfast it was a sumptuous meal. Our table the ground & chairs. I can't describe but as we surround the plate we look like frogs in council. My writing table is also of the best pattern & easily carried. I <u>think</u> I would like to see you this morning. I believe it would cheer my heart. Our whole Corps is here & 4 other Corps in this vicinity & endless numbers of cavalry. Many military men think the great battle of the campaign to be fought soon in in this vicinity. But the plans of the enemy have been so frustrated by our recent engagements that the future movements are uncertain. I am aware that this is a letter of little interest & you may attribute it partly to my dullness & partly to the fact that I know nothing that has been going on in the world for so long a time. I saw Ansell Booth again yesterday. You would not know him. He looks rough like all soldiers but I think he is one of the few who have not suffered in morals in the army. Sperry does not as often visit me but I think him also free from vice. Your aff. Father, B. Munger

Aldi, Va. June 25, 1863

My Dear Wife & Daughter,

 I have written & sent 3 letters from this place. One to you, one to Ida & one to Lyman but I am not sure that either will reach you. But tonight, there will be a regular mail sent out & tomorrow we expect to receive a mail. The army is lying quiet here, that is our Corps & it is the dullest most unpleasant camp we have ever occupied rendered more irksome by an absence of news & all intercourse with the world but we stand it pretty well hoping for better times. Our living is poor we have no vegetables or fruit. Yesterday 53 men were transferred to this Regt. from the 14th & 25th N.G. They are men enlisted to fill up the Regt. Under the proviso that they should be mustered out when the Regt. were but the Govt. refused to fulfill the promises of their agents & they were put into the First Brigade & I suppose they were not very amiable & consequently treated harshly till they are a by word & a tough set of men. None were put into my Co. It rains a little this afternoon & as we are on a red clay soil it is very <u>pleasant</u>. I am not intending to finish this today but I write to keep off the Blues & I hardly succeeded at last. Our orders are so strict that we cannot leave camp. Therefore, see nothing but camp & camp scenery.

I have not recd. my boots, shirts & shall not till we reach some point within the limits of civilization but I can do without them in this place. It does seem to me that if Grant succeeds in taking Vicksburg that the great struggle must soon be over. So far as I know they are not going anywhere & the object of this present move they are quite unsuccessful but perhaps I judge more from what I don't know than from what I do. My thick coat is very rusty & worn & so heavy that it is burdensome. This hot weather I think I shall throw it away soon & wear the other as that is somewhat soiled. This is no place to keep clothes nice & I know not where I can get any more. At present I do not want them.

Yesterday two men in Sykes Division were drummed out of the camp for cowardice. Their heads were shaved close & with "Coward" painted on a board tied to their backs & bareheaded they were marched through the camp to the music of the rouges march & two soldiers with bayonets pointed at their backs till they drew a crowd large enough for an army. There is someone under punishment nearly all the time & tomorrow a man is to be shot there for desertion. The discipline of the army is getting very ridged but the Volunteers are better off than Regulars. Henderson the brother in law of Lt. James has just returned from hospital but brings no news. It is said however that Vicksburg still holds out. There is I think some prospect of a move with us but I am not certain. Prisoners in small numbers are being brought in by our cavalry every day but as they are taken to Headquarters we see nothing of them. Since we arrived here I have 100 or more at different times pass& among them many officers. As a class, they appear as well perhaps as our soldiers. In some of them is a bitter fierce expression we seldom see in our men. But the women (not ladies) are the most bitter so much so they appear coarse. Their first expression usually is, "You can never subdue us."

A squad of Rebs a few days since commanded by a Lt. Col. surrendered to a Union squad commanded by a Sgt. As he approached to take his arms the Col. shot him through saying he would not give up his sword to a Sgt. There is much of that spirit manifested in the inhabitants here. 7 P.M. we have recd. a Baltimore paper & the opinion is expressed that a great battle is soon to be fought probably in Maryland & perhaps at Antietam. It may be only of our Corps the 3rd has just moved to Edward's Ferry. Our cavalry force holds Upperville & are picketing above & below. We have a very large cavalry force in this vicinity& the spirit of the men is good. I learn by the paper that Penn. Is being invaded in earnest& I hope it will wake up all parties that they may put forth such an effort that the enemy may be subdued at once & not prolong this war by keeping just men enough in the field to check & not whip the foe. If the north would make the one hundredth part the sacrifice the people do hear the war would be ended in 30 days. You don't begin to dream of their sacrifices & privations nor of their enthusiasm. It is an expression frequently made by the ladies, "O I wish I was a man." It is dark & rainy & I must stop.

June 26th, 4 O'clock A.M. We are ordered to move, it 7 toward Leesburg. It is raining some. I am not very well, have some diarrhea. June 27th, 11 A.M. We are at the mouth of the Monocacy River in Maryland & we suppose on our wat to Fredericktown, distance 14 miles. We left Aldie yesterday morning at 6 ½ & marched till 9 last in rain & mud, crossed the river at Edward's Ferry on pontoons. Our troops have been passing here since Tuesday night so we must have a large force near here. No mail in two weeks.

Camp near Monocacy Junction June 28th – We arrived here at 6 last night & are to move between now (10 P.M.) & morning. The 126th encamped 1 mile from us. At 4 this P.M. I visited them, found them well but tired, saw Eunice Taylor, Kelly's sister, she will be in Pen Yann before this. There is general dissatisfaction in the army & I must confess I feel sad. To go into such a fight as we have in prospect with almost a certainty of being whipped is not pleasing. I must close for it is late & I must pack. I have commenced a letter to Lyman which I shall finish if I can.

Your Husband,

B. Munger

Ida, you will find the kisses in this sheet for you. Tonight I recd. mail the first in 15 days & only 5 letters, 3 from Mother. We suppose we go to Middletown tonight about 10 miles.

Your aff. Father,

B. Munger

Beverly Ford   Aug. 22, 1863

My dear Wife & Daughter,

I wrote you on the 19th the day of my arrival but have some leisure will begin another. There are great changes since I left in officers in which I have already told you. The promotion of Col. Rice would place the command of the Regt. On Lt. Col. Conner but he is now a member of the Court Martial, so that Capt. Allen is in command & to hear the Col. is relieved from his duties at court. He will command the Brigade & Allen will still command us. Capt. Allen is to me most a stranger. He is a capable officer but not a man of faith whom I have any affinity. This change gives our Reg. an entire different aspect. I have today visited Booth & Sperry, found them well & more cheerful & hopeful than formerly. They think we are going to spend the winter at home. There is no indication of movement in the army. Indeed, it is or seems too hot to move. I wish I had brought a thermometer with me. Two of the nights have been so cold I was unable to sleep much while the days are burning hot. I am aware that our manner of living makes us feel the difference in temperature keenly our little tents hardly keeping out the rays of the sun & so open to admit the chill air of night.

In the morning, the fog is dense & the dew so heavy that it drops from the leaves of the trees as after a rain. I don't experience that depression I did after my visit home last winter & but for the intense heat should (enjoy) myself as well as before. The mail is just in but brings nothing for me. Kelly has recd. one from each mail since my return but O. & myself nothing. an order published today in relation to officer's servants troubles me some as its tendency tends to affect our pay. I will explain when

I understand its working more perfectly. It seems to me the Govt. is not just in dealing with us in this respect & persists in dabbling with my domestic concerns I shall resign.

We are living well on soft bread, (some) potatoes, beef, ham, pork & beans & c. the expense is too great however. We are ¼ mile from the river & 65 from Washington. Last night O. & I took a bath in its sacred waters which greatly refreshed us. I wish you would have Ida's teeth examined & if Uncle Joe thinks best have them cleaned & filled. I have had a long talk with our surgeon on the subject of the treatment of teeth & I can see how I have ended with mine. Darling it will tax your <u>courage</u> some but your father's health depends much on good teeth & your beauty also. Write to me the result. I am to have mine filled even at this late day & is I <u>know</u> you to be <u>brave</u>. I trust if it is thought best you will have a clean set of teeth. There is little transpiring of interest to you or to us here. The men with us are usually well. Ackley is on duty, Johnson, Franciscas & Wert are on the sick list but are able to walk about. Harrington, Strail & O'Neil have been sent to general hospital since I left. We now report only 30 men for duty. One Regt. The 83rd Pa. had 150 conscripts brought to them the night before. I came to camp at 11 O'clock P.M. at 10 next morn, they had out a squad of 20 men looking for those who had deserted during the night & yesterday these men deserted across the river. A few of them will doubtless be shot as an example. Our officers detailed for that service (bringing conscripts) are still absent. We have only 5 captains with us & 1 field officer. It is now 8 P.M. Saturday & is just getting comfortably cool. Our evenings are pleasant very. Last night we had a thunder shower about 10 but as our house don't leak much we let it rain, covered our faces so it could not rain in them & <u>tried</u> to sleep.

The clouds look snowy tonight. If we stay here, you may expect letters frequently unless something new transpires. As for me, you need not have the least anxious thought for I am as happy as a clam & shall be still happier when the weather is cooler. Remember to all friends. I learn Mr. Lock's nephew is still at Corps Head Quarters. I have not yet seen him. O. wishes to be remembered.

Your Aff. Husband & Father, B. Munger

                                                Beverly Ford, Va.   Sept. 3, 1863

Little Wife,

It is 9 P.M. I have been sitting in on Court Martial trial till 4, been on dress parade, eaten supper & have just returned from recitation which makes it a pretty busy day. I don't fancy the business of trying these poor fellows. The severity of the sentences would make you shudder. What would you think of a boys being punished for straggling & disrespectful language to his commanding officer" by forfeiting all pay or pay due from the U.S., be dishonorably dismissed the service, have his head shaved, be drummed out of camp & put to hard labor on the public works for one year. I fear men of naturally course & hard feelings are made more brutal by being put in command of others. To me it is disgusting to hear officers boast how their men will jump when they speak to them. The old officers say this is all necessary to discipline. Perhaps it is but I don't believe it yet. But enough of this. I have not felt very well for a few days but am better now. I have had a foreboding of evil. It seems as if something was the matter at home but I presume it is on account of my health.

We hear nothing more about moving. Day before yesterday we heard firing on our left but have not heard the cause. The Co. is in good condition & health & we are drilling thoroughly & getting ready to put those poor conscripts through. I learn that Capt. Gibbs is transferred to the Invalid Corps. There are changes almost daily in officers but as yet not the least prospect for me. Things now look as if we should winter here & perhaps summer also. Lt. Munger is on picket, went last night & will return Saturday night. It is only a mile & a fine place & light duty it is said. I have never been out & probably shan't for I learned today this court would remain in session as long as we stay here. I have now been here 15 days & have written 12 letters & recd. 2. My friends are <u>thinking</u> of more than usual so that they have no time to write. I have only 4 stamps left. When they are gone, I <u>may</u> stop.

Perhaps by this time you are boarding. I have come to feel that Mr. Miltus people are a part of our family & it seems as if you were going away from home. But it is probably best. I was much pleased with Ida's letter& to hear she had she had got into Miss Gleason's room & above all she was trying to be good. I <u>think</u> she will succeed. My next letter shall be to her. Please send me 50 postage stamps.

God bless & keep you,

B. Munger

Beverly Ford, Va.   Sept. 15, 1863

My Darling Little Girl,

I promised you should have the next letter so here it goes. It is Saturday morning 8 ½ O'clock & although it may <u>seem</u> strange I feel more lonely & sad. Some <u>strong</u> <u>minded</u> people would say that was very foolish in a man of my age & position. Quite likely it is foolish. Still it is true & no easier to bear for being foolish. But I am confessing to you just how I do feel & you "won't tell anybody." We have a pleasant camp here. I told you we were a ½ mile from the river but it is not in sight. We are on the west side of a piece of woodland running ½ mile from north to south. My tent is 10 rods from the woods& I can see no farther east than that. To the north, we can see 2 miles & at that distance the 3rd Corps is encamped & their white tents look pretty in the distance. To the south, we can see about the same distance the space partly covered with camps. But on the west, we can see to the Blue Ridge. On the west side of the river the land rises gradually somewhat like that east side of our lake but not so high or steep & between the top of that & the mountains seem to be a valley as you never saw a mountain chain. I can hardly give you an idea of the appearance. It is not unlike a line of blue clouds you have sometimes seen at sunset lying along the western horizon. They always have a dim blue milky like the atmosphere in an Indian summer afternoon & gives me a melancholy but not unpleasant feeling & always makes me think of dear old friends. The scene would be very pleasant to enjoy with such friends but rather sad to one <u>far</u>, <u>far</u> from home & <u>alone</u>. There are a few I think admire the beauties of fine & wild scenery as much as I but I always want a kindred spirit to <u>help</u> enjoy it. Perhaps I am writing too old a little for a darling little ten year old but need not let anyone see it but <u>particular</u> friends who will make allowances for a dreamy soldier. I am still acting as member of Court Martial. Our Court House is a large piece of canvas stretched over a pole laid on crotches 15 feet high the edges of the cloth reaching within 3 feet of the ground & the ends open. It covers a space 20 feet square, is cool on warm days & cold on cool ones. The weather for a week has been northern weather the last of Sept. This Court House is about a mile north of our camp. I go at 10 & return from 3 to 6. The Court is composed of 9 members & a Judge Advocate. The members are 1 Lt. Col., 5 Capts., & 3 Lieuts. It is dull day business but not as unpleasant for us as for the poor soldiers whom we try. Some of them are bad men no doubt & I fear we shall make them no better. To give you some idea as to the approved method of dealing with men. I will tell you one of the many incidents I have heard related by members. I select members of the court because they are supposed to be as good men as the average at least. A Lt. from a good city of Boston said soon after he took command one of the men saw him in the Co. street taking a chew of tobacco & said too the Lt., "Give me a chew." "Who are you talking to?" said the Lt. "To you." replied the man. The Lt. doubled his fist to sow us how he did and said, "I drew up like this & knocked him clean through his tent out the back side." and added triumphantly, "I never had any more trouble with that fellow." Still this Lt. is courteous to equals & superiors in rank. Rank that is the idea here.

      5 P.M. Well I have been to court & returned. We have been trying a case from our Reg. charged with "Misbehavior in face of the enemy & desertion". If proven against him, he must be sentenced to be shot. He is a boy about 19. He is a fine looking fellow & it makes one sad to think how great his danger is. We have tried I think 8 cases this week & they are coming in much faster than we dispose of them. Since my return to camp I have written 5 letters before this one to you & mother, 1 to Susie & 1 to Lyman & have recd. (2) both from you & mother. I think I shall get my pay sometime. None of the officers & men wounded at Gettysburg have returned to the Reg. yet although the 60 days has expired. As to prospects there are now I think. This portion of the army is entirely quiet although in perfect readiness to move at the shortest notice. I think there is no prospect of getting home this winter & although I sometimes feel sad & so tired of the service. I never feel as if I wanted to get out till peace is finally secured.

      Lt. Munger is still out on picket but will be in tonight I suppose. My duties as member of the Court interfere with study & practice of tactics which I regret still there are opportunities of improvement in other respects which I try to profit by. I will leave this till mail comes in to see if it brings anything for me. We receive a mail every day. It comes in the afternoon from 3 to 6 O'clock & leaves in the morning at 6. We also get daily papers & I have subscribed for the Independent & got my first number Saturday.

      8 P.M. Well little one the mail is just in but brings no letter for me. The Lt. has returned from picket. He recd. a letter from home last night but no mention is made of you. I was much pleased with your letter & I hope you will continue to keep me posted as to your progress & tell me all the news that others forget. Tell me who are coming down to help us fight Rebels & c. The weather is so pleasant that camp life is not so severe as otherwise. The nights however are very cool & as we have not a full supply of blankets. We are not as comfortable as I could desire, only two nights have I slept warm enough. Last night I laid awake several hours with the cold. Lt. is in & with his blankets we shall be warm. You need not need give yourself any trouble about me however I started it well & shall have more blankets soon.

Good night from your aff. Father,

B. Munger

Beverly Sept. 13, 1863

My Dear Wife & Daughter,

I recd. your letter of the 7th on the 10th. Glad to hear you are no worse. Sorry to hear you were no better. I suppose this with you is "The great day of the feast" & Penn Yan abounds with plenty & eloquence of a small dose could be sent to us it would not injure I think. The news is encouraging & the hope & spirits of the army are high. I am still engaged in Court Martial but it does not occupy my time as much as I expected.

Friday, noon we adjourned till Monday & as I am not for duty with the Co. so that I was quite at leisure. I am happy to be able to stroke that milder counsels are prevailing in court. Booth visited us last Friday, was well. Sperry was on duty & could not leave. Yesterday we had a fine shower & another last night. This is the first of any importance since my arrival & is refreshing. We hear nothing from our absent men, Davis & Henderson. Stroup has not yet had his trial, probably will this week. The men are in good health, two only off duty, Herrick & Francisco. I am proud of our Co., think for discipline & cheerful readiness in the discharging of duty it is not excelled. We have spasms here as in other places. Today seems a day for "Orders" I had one before I was up & they have poured in freely since. The only one in which you will feel any interest is one. Informed us that "A reconnaissance in force will be made today in the direction of Culpepper Court House" & that we must hold our commands in readiness to move to their support at a moment's notice & as I write I can hear the heavy "Boom, Boom" of the cannon in that direction & although we are all ready, there is no more excitement than if it was dress parade. My opinion is we shall not be called upon to go, but may if the enemy is in strong force. The booming is less distinct indicating the actions of the enemy. You would be astonished at the little interest manifested in the matter. The only thing unusual to be seen is the guns are stacked in the streets ready for use. I have had a call from Capt. Royce who has just returned from Washington but he brings no news of interest.

The cannonading mostly ceased for a time but just now broke out for a moment very heavy & continues still. I see a writer in Independent thinks Lee will make another raid north. I can hardly believe it but perhaps he may. If he does I think it will be his last raid. We have recd. no conscripts yet. Fred was here one day last week. He is now with Kilpatrick's cavalry at Hartwood's Church, 10 miles from Stoneman's Switch. He is pleased with his position, lives well, gets all the fruit he wants & c.

9 P.M. it rains again, cannonading continues all day in intervals. Our troops are said to have been successful. I recd. your letter of the 6th tonight. I think your letters now arrive

Note to the reader: There appears to be a page missing in this letter.

We have bought two new blankets & the box we sent to Washington has arrived with the two we packed and that we can now laugh at cold nights. This is a dull life. I almost hoped to be called on today to support that reconnaissance just for variety. Although the variety of rifle ball would not be pleasant. We have had "Divine Service" and what an intellectual treat. Tomorrow is general inspection at 9 1/2. Our men are looking finely in their new suits recd. again from Washington. Capt. Bourne has not returned. Kelly recd. a letter from him today. His wound is still awful thinks he will be fine in ten days or so. I forgot to say I recd. the stamps safe & they came just in time. I am sorry to hear Ida is not well, she will soon be better. I hear nothing from Sophia only what I hear through you. Keep me posted as well as you can, also tell me how Lawrence gets along. Remember me to all who inquire after me especially those "sisters". I have come to the conclusion however that friendships don't thrive with 500 miles between the subjects as an evidence that my conclusions have some foundation. I have not recd. a line from any friend but yourself since my arrival. You know it was always my theory to "waste no affection" & think as little of a person as he did of me & I still think I can carry out my theory. It is late and I have spun out this letter too long to interest you perhaps but I feel in a talking mood when it is a pleasure to talk even if you have little to say. As to further movements I am of course ignorant. Tell Fred as soon as I run across an "incident" I will write to him & just tell Susie not feel the least embarrassment. Write what interests her for if she tries to write smart letter I shall get embarrassed & shall never answer it. Goodnight, love & kisses & prayers to & for you & "the little one".

B. Munger

Culpepper Court House Sept. 16, 1863

My Dear Wife & Daughter,

      I feel my last night letter was a little blue for I was not well & things looked shady. We left camp about 7 this morning crossed the river 1 mile above Rappahannock Station on pontoon, struck the rail road at Brandy Station and reached this place at half past one. The day has been warm the men heavily loaded & they tried badly, 4 fell out of our Co. Two of them not well & put into ambulance & the other two are with nor feeling better. I am a little troubled with diarrhea & consequently felt weak but I kept up, have had a good wash, feel better & shall stand it well now. We are aimed toward Gordonsville & it now looks as if we have started for Richmond. There has been cannonading on our left at intervals through the day probably on the Rapidan as you see south of this rail road. By the way this road is in working order. Trains are passing to & from Washington. As usual we are camped out of the village. So at present I cannot tell you anything of the town. The country through which we passed is pleasant, vast & pleasant almost as far as the eye can see & we have passed some fine houses. As I am writing this firing is very heavy but at a great distance. Last night I sent you my old diary by mail. Tell me if you receive it safe. I also sent you a letter but I feared you would be anxious about me so I write this to keep you posted.

      It is now 5 ½ & as yet we have no mail but still hope to receive one. The 2nd Corps in the advance & near Gordonsville it is said & the 1st, 3rd & 12th are also on the move. I think also behind us the cavalry are in advance. I know nothing of the place of this move but hope it will be successful. Several men of the conscripts were sun struck today & of 56 in a Reg. in this Brigade started with us only 2 came into camp with us. Poor fellows, I pity the old men many them almost to death. We passed along the road where that fighting was last Sunday. Dead horses lay along the road as if there had been a "dying time" as our Ontario friend used to say. The whole country shows evidence of war. Old camps & pieces of shells reminds the soldier that he is mortal.

Give Osgood's regards to the prettiest young lady you know. He lies close by me & I asked him who he wishes to be remembered to & that is his answer. The boys are all around & say remember to Mrs. Munger. They are feeling very cheerful. If I do not get a chance to send this tonight I will add to it for the present good bye your aff Husband & Father, B. Munger

Thursday, Sept. 17th, 10 A.M. 3 miles southwest of Culpepper. We are bivouacked in line of battle with two batteries in position which is an indication the enemy is near but I think there will none be formed this side of the river. I am feeling better today. I was unable to send this yesterday & we recd. no mail. It is very foggy so we have not been able to see 50 rods in front. Little is known of the position of our army. 8 P.M. After fooling an hour or two this morning we found out there was no enemy within 5 miles of us. So we camped for an uncertain period. It is a beautiful country so far as prospect is concerned. O these grand old mountains in the distance are magnificent but the blast of slavery is on everything here that can be affected by it. I am quite well tonight & hope to remain so. I have not the least idea how long we are to remain here. Probably not long. Whether we are to move on to Gordonsville I cannot say. If so we shall have a fight probably. I saw Booth & Sperry today. They are well. I hope to be able to send this in the morning. I received a letter from Nancy tonight is well as usual no news from Sophia. Again, good night. As ever, B. Munger

Camp near Culpepper Sept 21, 1863

My Dear Wife & Daughter,

I recd. yours of the 17th yesterday & wrote one to Fred miller by which you will be posted up to last night. This morning our Court convened again in a farmhouse two miles from here belonging to a widow Patten. The house is deserted, most of the furniture has been removed. Many books & old furniture left. The house is old & not unlike old farm houses as the north but in the books, papers & furniture there were evidences of learning & refinement. One of the family had apparently done a wholesale commission business in Culpepper. Lt. Munger went out on picket tonight. The cavalry started for Madison Court House south west about 15 miles & it is rumored we are to move in the morning with 5 day's rations, if so it is probably to follow & support the cavalry. I am not feeling well tonight. I have some cold & diarrhea that marching you know usually causes me.

Capt. Royce leaves tomorrow morning for Philadelphia. I hear he gets a Lt. Colonelcy. There is some party clannish feeling in the Reg. that is not pleasant. Fred was here again tonight, is camped about ½ a mile from us. I conversed sometime with an old slave woman belonging to the Patten estate. She was very intelligent & would cast in the shade many of the whites. She says the younger slaves were all taken with the family but herself & another old woman were left. She thinks slavery a very bad thing. I am quite sleepy & will go to bed & if we do not move in the morning will add more. For the present good night.

Your aff. Husband & Father B.Munger

Today, morning Sept. 22, 7 ½ O'clock. Well we have lived through another night & there is no evidence of motion this morning. It is a cold windy morning like an old fashioned fall & makes me think of former times when I was a boy & had a home & friends. In health I am feeling better this morning & if my diarrhea does not return shall be smart again. Perhaps you may think my letters do not partake enough of enthusiasm & devotion to the cause for which we are fighting. The truth is I feel little. I wish I could feel more but I am not so constituted what I do, I must do from duty. The dull routine of military life with its dangers, privation & hardening influences has few attractions for me. If I had the companionship of some kindred spirits to converse with on subjects pertaining to the war & c it would be a relief. But don't think we are entirely destitute of enjoyment. Yesterday the papers brought news of an engagement at Chattanooga with decisive results. I fear we shall be defeated then but I do hope not. I now see little hope of peace this year even if we are successful it takes a long time to move large bodies & this war has vast machinery. Stroup is to be tried today. I have done all I can for him but it will probably go hard with him but I hope his life may be saved. I think I was the means of saving one poor fellow yesterday.

This I think is Layman's birthday. The thought always thrusts itself upon me as I think of such things. Shall we live to enjoy another anniversary together? We may. Many but as I have often said there is no life which so much impress one with uncertainty as this. When I went to bed last night I did not expect to lie till morning and although I am now ready to go to Court. I am expecting momentarily an order to move. The cavalry & artillery went toward the front yesterday. It is now the general impression that we are to move toward Richmond. 7 P.M. I have been to court. Stroup's case was postponed to enable him to get the testimony of Dr. Fearn who is in New York. We adjourned at 3 ½ & I walked to camp 2 miles without dinner & it makes me about sick. I shall not do it again. We are still expecting orders to move & probably it will be towards Fredericksburg. This is a secret here but by the time you know it, it will be accomplished. I received a pair of letters or rather two pairs, Mrs. Miller's, Susie's & yours & Ida's. You acknowledged the receipt of my letter & diary mailed the 16th & by the time you have received & soon Fred will yet get one by which you will be posted to the present. The papers speak of Rosecrans's fight as indecisive. I fear for the result of it. If we are beaten then it will prolong the war but it seems as if we ought to do something while Lee's army is in fact absent & I think we shall. You ask about Fred rank & pay it is not yet decided when it is. I will inform you. The weather has been cool since the storm & the nights are cold. I have worn my straw hat till today & have now bought a "regulation". The paymaster is said to be with the Brigade. Tell Susie I obeyed her directions & gave her <u>General</u> regard to the boys. They had not heard there was such a Gen. in the army. But I heard a complaint but I fear it would make her vain so I forbear. It is late so goodnight your aff. B. Munger

Camp near Culpepper, Va. Sept. 27, 1863

My Darling Ida,

It is Sunday morning & I believe there is a letter due you but I fear a letter from me today will only sadden you for to confess I feel very sad today much in contrast with the beauty of the morning. It is one of those magnificent autumn days so clear, so bright, so quiet that its very silence is oppressive & makes one realize his own littleness & feel a loneliness & isolation which of late is growing upon me. The longer I live the more painfully am I convinced of the utter heartlessness of the world. But enough of this.

Our camp is laid out on or near the road leading from Culpepper to Michel's Station & a mile or so west of the rail road. There are 4 regiments in our Brigade we face the Rapidan the 20th Main lies next on our right, 16th Mich. next & the 83rd Pa. next. We are in a field with woods in front & rear & a hill or rise of ground on our left but on the right (North West) is beautiful enough to compensate for want of prospect for the other sides. In the distance to the right six or eight miles is the Blue Ridge & it is one of the finest sights or prospects ever seen. As a rule, it is only in the distance that anything in Va. looks well. Nothing bears exception, fields looking green & beautiful in the distance on a close view will be found green with briars & weeds. Houses & their door yard fences that look beautifully white & imposing in the distance are only whitewashed & poorly at that. Everything is for show & sound.

I am not feeling well & will wait a little till feeling better. 7 P.M. I intended to write you a long letter but my head has troubled me so today I have not been able to read or write. For more than a week we have hourly expected to advance & attack the enemy. There is a sort of excitement about such expectation that is somewhat wearing especially to nervous people. Add to that my duties as member of Court & the result is I am not feeling well nothing however that need excite any uneasiness about me. The prospect now is if we are not sent out of the state we shall be comparatively quiet for a time. There has been some talk of sending this Corps to the west or southwest & at one time it was I think decided upon but it is now probably abandoned. But it makes but little difference to us when we go still I prefer to stay here that is in Va. This is a good letter for a little girl but my excuse must be poor health & low spirits. I must give you a description of the fight of the contrabands. This country has not been visited by our troops much so that there were many slaves here. When Kilpatrick crossed the river the other day he took some prisoners, some cattle & some slaves. The latter took teams & wagons in many instances & if the train or columns as we call it had passed through Penn Yan it would have drawn more spectators than all the circuses in the U.S. First the cavalry, they ride in four ranks that is four abreast & the column was two or three miles long. The prisoners (some of them fine looking fellows) next the supply train. This is a train of large wagons twice as large as any you ever saw each drawn by 6 mules or 4 horses then followed the contraband train in their old Virginia wagons. The box is so deep you would just be able to look over the side standing in it & always covered with canvass. Some had 4 horses attached the driver always riding one of the hind ones & driving with one rein. Some had mules & one a pair of horses & a pair of open behind but true to the mule the driver rode the hind near ox: The wagons were filled with negroes of kinds & sizes with their plunder as they call it & the little heads & old heads sticking out over the edges of the box & under the curtain or cover was a most comical sight as you ever saw. The soldiers as they passed joked & laughed at them but they were too happy to mind it. Today a party of 19 passed one old man the rest women & children, some little fellows carried in the arms of their mothers & some in their fear of so many Yankee soldiers hanging to their mother's shirts. All happy in the thought that Mr. Lincoln was going to take care of them.

Fred was here today, is stationed one mile to our right (North West) is pleased with his position. Two months from yesterday you will be <u>ten</u> years old & I propose making you a birthday present in some useful article of clothing or something of that kind which Mother will select. I send it now so that there may be ample time to prepare. I send ten dollars & I want the article purchased to be considered as the present. If we had a home I should suggest a dressing case but as we are situated that would not be best. In my next I shall make mother a present which I want worn, used or dedicated on the 25th of October. I suppose you are aware Orett is promoted to 1st Lt. He is assigned to Co. "G". Capt. Fox who I am sorry to say is not an honor to the service. He is now in arrest for drunkenness while on duty.

One of our Lts. had his pants containing $30 & a watch stolen from his tent last night. We are not living well as present the R. R. is occupied carrying troops.

Your affectionate Father, B. Munger

Near Fairfax Court House, Va. Oct. 15, 1863

My Dear Wife & Daughter,

   It is now Friday morning the 16^t. Just as I had written the first line last night when I was called off by the Col. We have had 6 days & two nights of hard work but are feeling pretty well. We have been in no engagements but have in expectation of one almost constantly. Last Saturday when I last wrote you we left camp at 5 moved to the east near Raccoon Ford & laid down waiting orders. It proved to be a move to support the 1st Corps which had crossed the river at that point for the second instance. We remained till 4 ½ P.M. & returned to our camp, put up our tent & were just ready to put our things in it when an order was received to strike tents & load them onto the wagons. We slept out of doors that night & every night since till the last. We left camp that morning (Sunday) at 8 marched through Culpepper along the rail road. The Rebs followed & engaged our cavalry 8 miles from Culpepper. We were halted & countermarched a mile to the top of a line of hills & formed in order of battle, waited 2 hours for the train to pass, moved back & camped in our old camp at Beverly Ford. Moved at 9 next morning back to the river & laid down as if in expectation of the enemy crossing. Laid till noon, crossed the river, I was then told what was expected of us. The line of hills of which I have spoken should have been held by us but were now held by the enemy. Our Corps was to retake the position. Our Regt. was detailed to turn their left flank. These comparatively small moves that are often not known at home are frequently not the most desperate & destructive we have to encounter. Our task was expected to be of this character. The men felt anxious but determined. Orett usually undemonstrative said as we stood ready to advance, "This business is enough to make young men old." Alluding to the anxiety & tension of mind. As I have remarked to you no one knows who has not tried it how exhausting it is to have mind strained up to "<u>dying pitch</u>" for a week at a time. Well we advanced 4 miles to the position named & <u>found no enemy</u> but we were a tired set of men.

   I was detailed to command our picket force, 50 men. It was dark & in a country full of Rebs & posting the men in the woods at that hour was exacting business. I got some hardtack & coffee about 8 or 9 & laid down but could not sleep. After dozing ½ an hour got up & at 2 ½ got orders to withdraw my pickets & rejoin the Reg. which I did just as they were leaving camp at 3 ½. We moved back to the river & re-crossed at sunrise, marched 2 miles further, had coffee, moved on to Catlett's Station & camped. The objects of the moves you will learn by the papers. We were in line next morning at sunrise & heavy firing was heard to the northwest 6 or 8 miles supposed near Warrenton. This is the anniversary of our joining the Reg. Were up at 3 ½ but did not move far till 9. Our Co. are acting as flanking today. Our duties are to move ½ a mile or so from the column & on the side toward the enemy. Deployed one rod or so apart & keep opposite our Regt. & watch against a surprise. Crossed Broad Run about noon & had coffee. Here the enemy came in sight in the rear & just as we moved off opened on us with their batteries.

They killed a few of our 3rd Division. The 2nd Corps engaged them took their battery & 750 prisoners. The 126th are said to have done well. Tobin's son was killed & David Taylor slightly wounded in the hand. We arrived at Manassas Junction about 4 P.M. & rested or rather a mile beyond (northeast) of the Junction. Here we could see Centerville 4 miles off & our labors most over as the struggle was to reach those defenses before Lee did. The firing in our rear increased & we were ordered to face about & were marched back 4 miles & much of the way on the double quick. When we halted, it was after dark & the flankers were sent out to the left (now our right) to form a line of sentinels 4 paces apart with orders not to speak above a whisper. We remained an hour perhaps & then moved back slowly so as to protect one battery & Brigade. We march till 2 A.M., crossed Bull Run which we had to wade full knee deep which after being up 22 ½ hours & marching most of the time was a bitter pill. We went to bed without supper having eaten 2 hardtack since 5 in the morning, feet & legs to knees wet but we were consoled with the thought Lee was foiled & we had a position we could hold in spite of him. Slept till 7, felt old & before I was on my feet but sitting on my blankets someone took me by the hand from behind & held me asking me what I said. When he let me go I looked up & saw Elmore Wilcox, you may guess I was surprised. I had forgotten he was in that Reg. 126th. Afterword I saw his son, Fred a moment. We moved about 10 toward Centerville expecting to stop there but kept onto this place & halted about 4 P.M. The bugle sounds Strike tents & we must go again.

Good Bye, B. Munger

Camp near Auburn, Va. Oct. 27th, 1863

My Dear Wife & Daughter,

My last was dated the 22nd at New Baltimore & on that day I recd. the last from you. The next day moved camp a half mile or so & put up our large tent. I don't know as I have ever told you the difference with us between bivouac & going into camp. We have one large wagon drawn by 4 mules in which are carried the line officer's baggage. It consists of a valise for each officer, a chest for each mess containing most of our cooking apparatus & a large tent cloth or fly in which we roll our extra blankets & pieces of shelter tents. This is camp furniture we do not use in bivouac. In addition to this the line officers the line officers have two pack mules on which each two carry 3 pieces of shelter tent (that makes a tent with one end opened) & 3 or 4 blankets. These with what we & our cook carry on our backs is all the baggage we have on the march. We frequently lay out our camp without having our camp furniture. Laying out a camp is simply dividing a space into 5 or 10 streets, one for each Co. or Div. & having the tents built in straight rows & at regular intervals. The line officers usually appoint their Co. & the field in the rear. Bivouacking for a night is only lying down <u>anywhere</u> so as you can lie down. I think with that explanation I can go on. The might after writing you I was taken with the most severe diarrhea I have ever had which weakened me very much. It was rainy next day, very cold. We put up or large tent & slept <u>good</u>. The first night rest I have <u>enjoyed</u> since my return. The next day was cheerless, cold, wet, wet, wet! Everything wet. About noon we went to the woods & cut a tree, backed it up & made a good fire in front of our tent & were anticipating enjoining ourselves hugely when about 3 an order came to strike the tents.

It was dark before we left camp but it had stopped raining. We marched, halted till 8 0'clock & bivouacked on very wet ground. We had marched only 5 miles nearly south & through mud &

water. It was a cheerless march & a gloomy bivouac. Not that it is so exceptionally hard but the needlessness of marching us in the night over an unknown road& such roads & their lying in the mud. It does seem sometimes as if they were determined to kill this Corps by unreasonable marching. I heard the Brigade Gen. say that the march from Centerville to Fairfax in the rain of which I told would cost this Division, 200 men. The next day was Sunday & my birthday. I waked up sad & felt so all day. It was cold & windy with the ever present smoke, smoke! About noon we moved a ¼ mile, laid out camp in a mean place & here we still remain. Our camp baggage is not here but the wagon was sent down today so that we got some clean cloths, paper & c.

 Last night we were informed we should probably move before morning but here we are. Heavy firing has been heard to the west of us. Gen. Mead moved his headquarters today from Warrenton to a grove southeast of us about a mile. He with several other generals viewed the position here critically. Today some think with a view of laying out a line of battle here. I don't believe it. It is also said Lee occupies position on this side of the river, his left at Beverly Ford & right at Stafford Court House. I don't believe either. What we are to do I can't say but we are kept revved up, ready for a start at a word.

 Wednesday morning, "I still live." The morning is bright & cold like November weather. I have a good amount of Co. writing to do but can't do it now as all our papers are in the wagons. It is that fact that enables me to write to you. We are doing well for food considering we have no permanent stopping place. We lack variety & get so tired of meat & hard tack. Hard tack & meat, we have had potatoes but once since leaving Culpepper. The mail is in & brings nothing for me. Our baggage is here again so I suppose I must leave this & go to work. I wish in your next you would send me a little black swing silk to mend my coat. I have a moment & am an industrious man, you know. There is a prospect of getting some soft bread today. We have put up our large tent & are now going to make a table for writing & then for work. Things look more like staying a few days. All very quiet. You need not send any butter or any other article by express till I direct as we can get nothing by that means at present. Anything by mail will reach us as usual. My head aches today & "I'm not well myself" so that the world does not look quite as bright as usual. I have no doubt as to our ultimate success but think it will be as soon as most people expect. I get tired & most discouraged at times but in n the whole bare it tolerably well. I recd. list of those exempt from draft reached me yesterday. Some bribery at work your way I think.

 Thursday morning – I had to lay this aside yesterday & all other work & go to bed with head ache. It was not as severe as I sometimes have it but enough. Today I feel languid but much better than yesterday. The mail brings me no letters this morning except business letters. P.M. –We are full of business today & I am not able to do much but shall soon feel better. It is a bright day but cool. Last night was very cold & a severe frost. I dread the coming winter & hope it will be in this place. It is so cheerless far from anywhere. I think we shall stay for a time.

 I just received a compliment. Some officers came along & were "seizing" me. I won't write it finally it would "savor of variety". Shipley is some better, is made Sgt. to date from Aug. 1st. We are making Muster & Pay Rolls, sending Descriptive Lists & c.

 Most of the papers seem to think the campaign for this army is over. If so I shall be disappointed. But I suppose it will take some time to repair the rail road. The Rebs filled the cuts with fallen trees, brush, rails all intertwining with earth& its removal is slow. Tomorrow is one year since we commenced our march from Antietam. These dates are as eras that are stamped on my mind. Remember me to friends. Your aff. Husband & Father, B. Munger

Camp Warrenton Junction, Va. Nov 3rd, 1863

My Dear Wife & Daughter,

I had intended this time to write to Ida for her especial benefit but my Co. writing has kept me busy till this moment (10 P.M.) & is not now quite complete. I should defer writing but we learn tonight that we are to move forward & it is supposed to attack the enemy. I need not say I dread it. Poor patriotism you may think my answer is, "The spirit is willing but the flesh is weak". If I had time I should have much to write but as it is late & we move soon other that's occupy my mind. It is an unexpected move & I can hardly conjecture its nature. I wrote you last from Auburn on the 29th & we moved the next day to this place 5 miles. We are 3 miles north west of the junction on the west side of Warrenton Branch Road. Trains run to Warrenton on this branch but no further west than the Junction. The pontoon train has come up so I suppose we are to cross the Rappahannock again. I received your letters "In a night cap" on the 31st. The cap is just the thing. Please thank Franklin for me & tell her, she shall the best kiss I can give when I come home.

My health has not been quite as good as usual for a week or so but hope when we get to living better I shall feel better. We feel the want of vegetables severely. We have had for our mess of 4 persons 12 potatoes since leaving Fairfax & some of those we gave to a sick man. These are the only green vegetables we have had. Our "Hard Tack" is very wormy & buggy this fall so that we seldom eat a piece but has from 1 to 6 in it. But there is nothing like getting used to it. When I eat them in the dark I swallow strong. We had today some eggs, butter, flour & it was a luxury, eggs at 60 cents per dozen tastes well even if ¼ are bad but enough of this you will think I am complaining when in fact I am only telling why I am not well. I suppose this has been a great day in your state. I hope you have gained a victory. I saw Elmer & Fred, his son Sunday & many Penn Yan boys all well but C. Forshay, he looks poorly. It is 11 & I am cold & must go to <u>bed</u>! Good night & God's choicest blessings. Your Father & Husband, B. Munger

Nov. 4th, 7 P.M., as we did not move I retained this to write to Ida. I think we go in the morning. It is uncertain. We hear New York has gone Union. God grant it. You don't know with what anxiety we look to that state for of what avail is our fighting if not backed up at home. Goodnight again. B.M.

Wednesday Morning Nov. 4, 1863

My Little Darling,

  I wrote a lengthy letter to you & mother late last expecting to move early this morning but we are still here at different times as I have passed along. I have seen & that of many things that I hoped would interest & instruct you but the impressions have worn away to a great degree. I have stopped an hour or so to visit with Fred. This is the first time I have seen him since we were at Culpepper. He is looking well, has had an active time & some hardships but likes his position & duties better than with the Co. He is still with Kilpatrick & has been lying at Catletts. The Gen. left with his forces towards Fredericksburg but did not take his tents & camp equipage. We are probably to follow perhaps tomorrow. I must try to give you some account of Bull Run battlefield. O little girl I am so disturbed by my men coming to see me & talking constantly that I can hardly write. But I will try. We arrived at the scene of our second defeat on Bull Run about 4 P.M. Oct. 19th I was some tired & not well. The appearance of the place disappointed me much. One naturally expects to see very marked differences from such terrible battles as have taken place here. The ground is gently hilly & has like most of this country run to waste since the commencement of this war, is grown over with briars & wild grass which is dead & dying & gives it a look of utter desolation. We camped on a hill ¾ of a mile where our Reg. was engaged in the last battle. By the way, you must keep in mind that "Bull Run" means Bulls Creek & by looking on the map will see it is quite a long stream so that the expression on Bulls Run may mean anywhere on that stream & the two battles that are known by that name were not fought on the same place, but not far apart. This is the place of the 2nd battle.

  On our arrival, I first as usual laid down (on the ground of course) to rest a while but "kept thinking" of the awful scenes that had taken place there. Soon Lt. Col. Connie came along & pointed out the locality & positions of the armies & the place where the 44th lost so terribly on that day. Orett & I went out to cut poles to put up our tents & came across a grave we call it. It was where a poor soldier had been covered with a little dirt which the rain had partly washed off. His skull was entirely bare & as I got down to look at it closely I discovered one hand had never been covered & the flesh & skin had dried to the bone the thumb & first two fingers were perfect except in color. They were dark & looked like sticks. The flesh had dried from the nails so that they appeared like claws. We found many well buried & boards giving name & regiment mostly from Ohio. These were buried by our own men. But when our men are buried by the enemy they are only covered in the slightest manner & the same is true of Rebs buried by us. Some of the officers rode over to that position of the field occupied by our regiment & recognized many of the bodies as those of comrades & relatives some by dress or equipments & some by records on their headboards. ½ a mile before we reached the field we passed a house & near it I saw a grave with a headboard but could not well leave to read it. I learned afterworlds that an officer in our 3rd Division (Penn. Reserves) saw it, and on going to it, found it to be the grave of his brother of whom fate till then he was ignorant. Many remains were found that had never been buried. They had fallen in out of the way places. Dr. Townsend told me where the dead lay thickest. They were put into ravines & gullies where the water washed them out in heavy rains & that piles of bones would accumulate where obstacles lay across the stream. Skulls lie about top of the ground. Men were covered just as they fell. Sometimes face downwards, heads down hill & many things shocking to our feelings but in candor I must say I believe our men to be guilty of equal barbarity.

I would like to spend a day or two on that field but the reflections promoted are sad, sad. The lives so uselessly wasted of competent or loyal commanders. Mistakes in war cost something. By the way, our Division General, Griffin is absent & our Div. is commanded by a Col. whom we have little confidence & are not as anxious to meet Lee as if our Gen. was with us. I must tell you of our other item experience which was an important era in our lives it was nothing less than taking dinner in a house at a table & last if not least with a lady? or a woman & a young woman at that. The day after my birthday, feeling somewhat lonely & got permission to leave the camp & went to the village? of Auburn. It contains but one family named McCormack, brother of the inventor of the reaper. He is 80 years old & has one or more daughters at home. One at least married. Orett was with me & we found 3 Lieutenants of our regiment in the road talking with the old gentleman who is as social as a Yankee. One of the Lts. Asked if he could furnish us with a dinner. He that he could would refer the matter to his daughter who he assured us was a good housewife as any northern woman & could get us a meal with her own hands. The daughter said yes & we were invited into the house or piazza rather & introduced to the lady. She is about 35, middling size, dark complexion & not making a very favorable impression. The father evidently wished it understood that he was a Union man (though he thought slavery a Godly thing) but the daughter could not hide her hate & contempt for the north & perhaps I did not try much to hide mine for the Rebs & all that pertains to them. We were to have dinner at 12 ½ but during the time acting Big. Gen. Chamberlin came & the lady came with a very smooth apology for necessarily delaying our dinner in consequence for true to her southern instincts she measured worth by rank but as I happened to know the officer felt good enough to eat with him & I was in favor of leaving but the Lts. overruled my decision & we stayed, had a dinner of roast beef, boiled ham, fried liver, corn bread, boiled cabbage soup thickened with "Hard Tack" 7 worms & honey. There was variety enough surely to make a good dinner but in the first place the meats were cold, the corn bread was simply corn meal & water baked. The wheat bread I did not take. The honey was good but there is some allowance to be made. I was not in a mood to be pleased & don't you know little one that makes a vast difference with us. The lady had a sick babe & you don't know how I longed to see it, to look at something innocent in this hard, hard, wicked world.

Let me urge you again darling never to do or say a thing you think to be wrong. I always want to think of you as the very personification of innocence & goodness. This will not always be easy for you. You will not always be able to satisfy yourself in being good but don't let this discourage you, "try again". Perhaps I think more on this subject mow for I see so little that is good & pure. I long for a time when I may. If you can find time & not tax your health too much write to me often about yourself but be careful of your health. Lt Mc Cormic returned last night & Orett is relieved from command of Co. K, & reports to Capt. Fox of Co. G, for duty. His Capt. is not a good man. Of course, he will still mess with us. Lt. Kelly tonight recd. a permit from the War Department to go before the examining board at Washington to be examined for a command in a colored regiment. I suppose he will not be able to get it approved by our Gen. at present as a move is in contemplation I have thought quite seriously of making an application for the same kind but am not yet decided. The truth is I am tired of the drudgery of marching. Our coming march will be more severe than usual for our pack mules that I told you about are taken from us & we can have but one blanket & one piece, ¼ of tent carried the rest, we must carry on our backs. So, you see that the Gov. thinks that an officer is worth less than a mule! That is not flattering. It is now supposed that we start tomorrow morning probably towards our old home of last winter. I am feeling better today & am all ready but feel something like Paul, "not knowing the things that shall befall me there". I was much pleased to hear you had so good a home & I think I can trust you to be so good &

discreet that you will make Mrs. Bridgeman little trouble. Your birthday will occur 3 weeks from tomorrow on the same day as our National thanksgiving. I hope it may be a happy one. Mine was so sad I don't want to tell you about it but I am better now, living better (today) and feeling cheerful. Mother did not tell me whether the dressing case was the present or not but I inferred it was. I am ready to hear what yours is when you are ready to announce it. Tell Mrs. Miller, Susie & all to whom I owe letters that I will pay as soon as possible but the need not wait write again. It is more difficult for me to write that for them. I am disturbed so often. I wish Mother would enclose in her next a ribbon neck tie, dark colored. Mr. Beam will tell her what I want. This is a long letter but it does not satisfy me. Much love to all.

Your loving father,

B. Munger

Camp near Warrenton, Va. Nov. 12th, 1863

Dear Brother & family,

    I sent a letter to my wife yesterday but I don't believe you get half the letters we send so I will scatter them along. By the way, you don't claim to have written but once a week & I have written often than that even when we were on the march & it seems to me that there is so little variety here that my letters must be stable but as I have just bought a map of the part of the state over which we have traveled. I can point out almost every rod of the road & perhaps it will interest you some. Of myself, I am tired of writing & have come to the deliberate conclusion that I am a poor good for nothing _____ & am discouraged with trying to make anything of myself.

    Our camp at Antietam was on road from Sharpsburg to Harpers Ferry & opposite the word Shepherdstown where I have made a dot. We left at 8 P.M. Oct 3rd & stopped on the mountain at the next dot. We marched fast & some of the men failed before halting. That was one of the toughest nights I have experienced. I had no blanket except my rubber & it was a cold night but I lived. Next day we passed through the village, crossed the Shenandoah, followed the Potomac for a mile or so but although it is downstream it is up the mountain & steep enough at that. Turned to the right & followed the line made with my pen & halted at dot No.3. That was Friday night. We pitched out tents there & stayed till Sunday morning. I wrote home from that place (I also mailed a letter the day we left Antietam) we were comfortable & lived well here.

    Sunday night about 12 I was aroused & ordered to have my company ready to march at 4 with 3 days' rations. We were hurried off before we were ready. It was a very warm day, the one you speak of as being so pleasant & while I can't say my own physical suffering was greater than I have endured many times that with my anxiety made it a day the like of which I never want to see again. Orders were given to let no man fall out without written leave from me, so I marched in the rear to see to that. The men were loaded heavily & soon began to lag. I carried a gun for one & tried to encourage him. Sometimes I took two guns & stout men with tears running down their cheeks would say, "Captain I can't walk any further." & I would tell them to try to reach such a point & if we did not halt by that time I would give them a pass. At noon, I think none had fallen out but I could plainly see that they could not march so all day. I felt a little tired. We halted about 30 minutes at noon. I ate some Pilot Bread soaked in cold water, sweetened & resumed our march. At 1 ½ were filed off to the left, countermarched a few rods & halted. We were glad of this but could not dream what it meant for this was only our regiment. The Brigade passed on. We stopped perhaps ½ an hour & I slept most of the time & it helped me during the march from 12 to 1 ½. 5 men fell out. One was entirely exhausted that he lay nearly 24 hours on the spot. The road to this point runs between the range of mountains & I have drawn a line with my pen here. We turned to the right & were told we were to go up the mountain to guard a pass. After reaching the base it is 1 ½ miles to the top. I suppose that did not tuck us much, but as my anxiety was over I felt light, for if the men did stop I knew the cold soon would catch up with us. **Note: Possibly missing another page.**

Camp Kelly's Ford, Va. Nov. 16, 1863

My Darling Little One,

I wrote to mother on the 12th from picket line & recd. a letter from you both next day.

That long one from your little pen I was much pleased with & you must do as often as possible especially. Must I have a birth day epistle? I don't mean it must be written on that day necessary but for that day I would defer this till then but everything is so uncertain with me that I dare not wait. It is most 9 P.M. now as I commence & therefor I will not be able to write you a long letter. I saw when on picket last week another little girl of about your age & like the one whom I told you should not know her age. Her name was Georgiana Reese. I think you would have been pleased to see her. I talked with her sometime. Her mother always answering for her & frequently exclaiming, "Georgie wat makes yer ac so ugly? You speak to the Capen". But Georgie could not be induced to speak. When I told her I had a little girl about her age & that I had just recd. a letter from you the mother was all astonished & asked, "Did she write it herself?" I assured her, you & she that you must be an uncommon child. I was sorry for poor Georgie on one account. She has no father. He died when she was only two months old. It cheered me even to talk to such a specimen for it was a child. I guess I must give you the history & incidents of a day & I will select Sunday explaining by telling you the weather has been fine for some time past but Saturday we had thunder shower. We had reveille at 6 and all must be up. Our tent was as wet as water could make it, a puddle of water in front of it & everything soaked in water & very cool. On the whole it was just the most cheerless morning one could well imagine. I forgot to tell you we were camped in a wood & the clouds, woods & smoke from the cook fires made it most as dark as night. About 8 we had breakfast & although our spirits were good we could not but contrast our situation with what it might be of at home. Bad as the weather was I "dressed up" so it would seem like Sunday & at 9 ½ we had our usual Sunday inspection. The men & arms were in good condition but poor Jerome Wheaton was not there you know. He was killed on the 7th at Rappahannock. Before I was through with inspection heavy cannonading commenced to the south west for us & in a few minutes an order came, "Co. Commands will hold their commands in readiness to move at a moment's notice." This we had expected but after two hours the firing ceased & we remained in camp. About this time the clouds broke away & the weather became fine after dinner.

I went down to the Dr.'s tent & was introduced to Capt. Paine the owner of the land we are camped on & living in a large stone house nearby. He is 73 years old & was a Captain in the war of 1812. He don't relish our freedom with his property. At 3 the bugle sounded the "Church Call" & our Chaplain read a Psalm, talked a few moments, made a prayer, dismissed us as the ground is very wet. Now I never get lonesome but I felt that day as if I wanted to go somewhere & I barrowed a field glass & asked Lt. Munger to take a walk. We went toward the river ½ a mile & on an elevation could see a large extent of country & a part of the prospect was that Majestic Blue Ridge. You don't know how I love to look at those mountains. They extend from the north around to the west, one fourth of a circle. In some places there seems to be three rows or ranges of mountains in sight, one behind the other. To the north about 4 miles we could see the fortifications at Rappahannock Station through the glass & men standing on the forts, trains of wagons with white canvass tops were winding off towards the front & in the distance near Brandy Station we could see an enormous camp. The river was about ¼ mile west of us & Kellyville on the west bank ½ a mile south west. As we returned to camp we went toward the house of my friend Capt. Paine, he was in his yard & invited us in. He owns 800 acres here which was appraised before the war at 25 dollars per acre. I think he is a traitor at heart but he does not say so. He wanted me to use my influence to have his property guarded. I fear I shall not try very hard.

We heard tonight that the engagement that we heard today upon the Rapidan resulted in a victory to us but the particulars we have not heard. As we had no fire & I severe cold in my head we went to bed early & I lay a very long time before I could sleep & this ended one day's experience, a specimen of camp life. But it is of late varied often enough by marches incidents. Our food is a little better but not good or plentiful but our appetites perhaps good enough to make that up. The weather is not cold still it is unpleasant campaigning & some severe exposures must be encountered.

The first train of cars crossed the Rappahannock headed for Culpepper today & it is that we shall move in two or three days. I recd. a letter from Nettie tonight. She has taken a school 20 miles from Albion at 4 dollars per week.

Good night & God's blessing & My Love,

B. Munger

Camp Pleasant Nov. 19, 1863

We arrived at this place forenoon, having left the cam from which I last wrote. This morning the name "Pleasant" is my giving for it is the location that is best for a camp of any we have ever camped on. High, dry & somewhat protected from winds. We crossed to the south west side of the Rappahannock for the 6th time this morning & our camp is near where the road from Kelly's Ford to Germania crosses Mountain Run. I have had a severe cold in my head for some days past of the influenza kind so that the Dr. called me sick yesterday but I am much better today & have marched with the Co. & I think on this high, dry ground I shall soon get smart. We know nothing how long we are to stay here. Some think but one day but we are logging up our tents so as to enjoy all the time we do stay. Perhaps you would think it discouraging to fix up & leave so often. It's all in being used to it. Mart our cook worked all day yesterday in logging & fixing his tent & left it this morning a little after sun rise & is now building another as if we were to stay all winter. The 2nd & 3rd Divisions of our Corps have remained on this side of the river since we all camped on Sunday the 8th & now we are now near them. I can hardly believe we are to run much risk to cross the Rapidan. Because I think the position of it would be but little advantage to us or disadvantage to the enemy & it is a position nearly as difficult to take as Fredericksburg &

compel its evacuation it might pay to fight hard here. I shall be obliged to leave to my friend Mead. Friday, A.M. a fine day. Our Reg. is being paid today & I shall send a Draft to L in a few days. I am Brigade officer of the day, the second time I have been on that duty. Last night I recd. yours of the 16th inst. I will answer Ls as soon as I have an opportunity. As to my indebtedness for letters it is very difficult to wright when we are constantly moving as we have been lately. It is said today that we are to move tomorrow. It is useless to speculate as to the nature of the move. I can't tell anything about it. If we cross the river we shall probably have a warm time. Some things look like it. We sick are being sent off, all that are likely to encumber the ambulances, the order reads.

I am much better indeed, about well. Not quite as strong as I was. It is a magnificent day, like our northern Indian summer but it is much like our food we frequently loose half its value by not having the proper accompaniments. We sometimes get butter but we can get no bread, sometimes potatoes & no meat, again meat but no potatoes. So now we have a fine day with few facilities for enjoying it. I don't mean we are not cheerful, <u>we are</u> but it seems a pity to waste such weather on such a country. If possible I will write to Ida or near her birthday. By the way, Gov. Seymour's proclamation is to be published to the N.Y. troops. We may be thankful but where are our "Turkeys"? That is like our potatoes without meat. I have an opportunity to send this by M. H. Squires. So, good bye in haste.

Yours,

B. Munger

Camp near Kelly's Ford, Va. Nov. 22, 1863

My Darling little Daughter,

It is Sunday, 11 A.M. The storm of yesterday has cleared off, bright & warm giving everything a more cheerful look. I had proposed to write you on your birthday but as our stay here is uncertain I thought I would write today & it will I hope will reach you on that day. And what shall I write to my ten year old? Tell her how much I love here & how constantly I think of her? How anxious I feel when I hear she is sick? How glad when she is well. How pleased with a letter from her. How anxious, how inexpressibly anxious that she shall grow up <u>good</u>? I fear I can't tell her this so that she will <u>feel</u> it as I do. Yet it is all true. And let me say for your encouragement darling that so far, I am well pleased with you, if I dare I should say <u>proud</u>. You know "little one" we used to have some real <u>good</u> <u>talks</u> about being <u>good</u>. Your own thoughts "conscience" we call it will guide you. Try to live so that when you are alone & look back upon your <u>acts</u> & <u>thoughts</u> you will be satisfied that you have done right. But don't be discouraged if you don't succeed as well as you desire. "Try, try again" ask God to help you to be good & to forgive you if you are wrong.

The older I grow little girl, the more completely am I concerned that virtue is its own reward. In other words, as men say about other things "It pays to do right" even in this world. Yes, and in the army wicked as that is <u>virtue</u> is <u>respected</u>. But it pays chiefly in the satisfaction to one's own heart. The good opinion of others is valuable if we are conscious we deserve it not otherwise. Did you ever little one receive praise where you that's you did not deserve it? If so did it almost make you feel guilty? <u>I</u> <u>have</u> & it should teach us that the approval of our conscious is of more worth than the opinions of others. Sometimes doubtless you have been blamed where you thought you had done right. If so, how bravely could you bare it because your conscious approved you. Cultivate Darling this little <u>conscious</u> this keen sense of right. This is sometimes what men call "honor". It is true honor. Perhaps this is rather <u>old</u> talk to a "ten year old" but I trust <u>you</u> will understand it all & if I should never see you again you will keep this & read it over sometimes.

   And now I hope that your birth day coming as it does on Thanksgiving Day will be a happy one to you. How I would like to be there I am sorry to tell you that I am not very well & am not doing much duty. Our Surgeon thinks my liver is inactive & he proposes put me through a course of Blue Pills. I am not much sick & hope to be well in a few days/ You & Mother must not worry about me. I thought I ought to state just how I am but you must be calm & patient. I am. My symptoms are headache, some pain in my back, diarrhea & not much appetite, my head troubling most. Day before yesterday I wrote to Mother enclosing a draft for $175 & sent it by H. M. Squires with a request that he call & see you. Ma will please acknowledge if recd. in her next. Yesterday I wrote to Susie Miller. I must stop & take a walk as my head is feeling badly. I wish you would accompany me

   1 O'clock P.M. I have had my walk & feel a little better. I fiend the field on which we are camped is a peninsula made by the curve of the stream (Mountain Run). It is running southeast, meets a range of hills, turns east, runs a a quarter of a mile & a bend in hills or bluffs causing it to turn again to the northwest. It encloses perhaps 50 acres & our camp is about 50 feet higher than the creek the sides of the decent are covered with timber, mostly oak. Rabbits & grey squirrels are plenty & frequently caught. Our dinner is about ready & as I have eaten little today I stop, eat (if I can) & then tell you what we have for dinner. Well I have had dinner little one & been to meeting. I was to tell you of our dinner. In the first place our table for we have a table is made by driving 4 stakes into the ground & put on a top of cracker box boards. Our cloth is a newspaper. But at present we have no seats except the bed answers as a seat for ours. Next, our dishes all of tin consisting of plates & cups only. Now the dinner. First it was a good one, the principle dish was hash of beef boiled yesterday & potatoes. Soft bread, butter, dried apple sauce that is sauce made of dried apples, coffee, sugar & condensed milk. I ate a little hash & had a piece of toasted bread & coffee & if my head did not ache I should feel pretty well. I told you I had been to meeting. Perhaps not like your meeting today. Our house was the woods pulpit & seats the ground. No singing. The chaplain gave us a good talk on the duties of soldiers. It is now about 4 & as usual here at this time of day it is growing cold but still clear & pleasant. It seems to be the general impression that we are to move tomorrow & to apparently to cross the Rapidan with the prospect of an engagement. This is a prospect but not certain. Let it give you no anxiety.

   We have had no papers for the last three days so are behind in regard to news. Now this is <u>all</u> your letter & you may do as you please about letting anyone see it (except Mother of course) it is just for a birthday letter & not public property. May you have a pleasant & happy day & life. Remember me to your little friends & mime, you may keep a few on my account including that baby boy & little Hellen.

Your affectionate soldier father, B. Munger

I thought perhaps you would lack a little money for some trimming. Use it as you please. B.M.

Sunday eve Nov. 22nd, 1863 - 10 ½ O'clock

My Dear wife,

I have been writing to Ida today & will enclose this in hers. I have just recd. yours of the 16th & 19th inst. Inclusion. I can only say a word or two. First, I wish you could throw off your anxiety concerning me in some degree at best. I have often assured you I can stand anything likely to happen to a soldier. I don't complain & while you are only deprived of my society I am deprive of yours & all my acquaintances. I trust also all your material wants are well supplied while mine are not always. Still in the main I am cheerful. That I am sometimes <u>anxious</u> is true but I have learned to hold still & be patient. Perhaps I unconsciously exaggerate in my descriptions. I will amend in that particular. I have written to Ida something about my health. Tonight, I am much better & there is no cause for anxiety that account. Lt. Munger recd. his valise tonight. Cloths rather smart, coat especially. I will add a word in the morn & tell you if we are moving. I recd. the necktie safe. It was not what I described but it's a good one & I have found my lost one safely rolled up in a paper & stowed in my vest pocket. So, I am well provided. Goodnight & it is a beautiful one.

Yours,

B.Munger

Camp near Fredericksburg, Va. Nov. 25, 1863

My Dear Ida,

Tomorrow is your birthday & as everything is so uncertain here I will secure the present hour to write to you. Some of the friends say I am not particular enough. I'll try to correct that fault this time. First, I will acknowledge the receipt of letters on the 21st containing half & yesterday, one in part from yourself. I wrote last on the 22nd. Sunday morning, I was up at 5 and Robert had breakfast most ready & I suppose to be minute. I must tell you what we had for breakfast, first fried pork then we break up pilot bread (the boys wickedly call it <u>hard tack</u>) put on cold water & let it soak overnight. After the meat was fried, pour off the fat & fry the prepared bread then our never omitted coffee & sugar and as you know I am fond of a desert. I have a dry hardtack & sugar when we want anything new we change the order. Now little fellow don't feel sad and think that is all we have to eat. No, we have many pretty good things but it is true that when on the march bread, coffee & sugar are all we can have for a meal for we carry three days' rations & of course it must be light nutritious food.

You see little one I have forgotten Sunday's march already. Well, we ate our meal, packed our goods, struck our tents & carried all to the wagons about a ½ mile, came back & I went to visit the sick. John O'Neil is the sickest with swelled face & fever. I got him into an ambulance. John Mc Laughlin, the next is down with severe cold in his lungs. The Dr. says he must try to walk. Mandeville is down with diarrhea (by the way I am disappointed in him. He makes me more trouble than any other man in the Co.). Just as I had finished with the sick an order came up that we were to be rear guard of the brigade & that today is in the rear of the Corps. 8 ½ the bugle sounds to form in line & an order for Capt. Munger with ½ of his Co. to march over the camp & arrest all stragglers. So away we go with an additional order to hurry. The camp covered about 25 acres & groups of men scattered over it. I took six I think & marched us in and we had one man under arrest from Capt. Kimble's Co. My instructions were to let no man fall back unless he had written permission from the commander of his Co. counter signed by the Dr. All others to prick into the ranks. That means to force them to march even if I had to use the bayonet to make them perhaps that will sound harsh to you darling. It is a hard post, this rear guard especially when we are abandoning the post we leave. Uncle L. will explain that to you & tell you why it won't do to let them fall to the rear when the enemy is following us. Now how do you think your father would feel ordering a squad of men to push a poor, tired soldier with the point of a bayonet? Well, he didn't do it! About ½ a mile from camp I came up to two poor, wonderful looking fellows living beside the road & I spoke cheerfully to them and, "Well boys do you have a pass?" "Yes", they answered. I told them to let me see it. They were genuine & entitled them to a ride in the ambulance. So, I told them they must try to keep up till that train joined ours which would be some distance or they would be left to the tender mercies of the wicked one. Replied, "Capt. if there is anything or anybody more wicked than I have seen for the last 18 months I'd like to stop & see it." I asked, "Have you had it tough my dear fellow?" "O", said he, "it makes all difference who your officers are. They can make it hard or pleasant for us. If you had ordered me up I would not have stirred but I kind of liked your way." And they kept up most of the day. I can't recollect all of the incidents of the day. One however I will tell you. A little after noon we were passing through pine shrubbery & an old grey negro was standing beside the road & apparently, utterly astonished at the number of troops passing called out, "Well I guess you catch um this time massas, but if you don't for God Almighty's sake go home & give um up." It raised a general laugh and all thought it pretty sensible advice for we have men enough to eat them up to give you some idea little one the size of this army.

  I suppose it would take it three days & nights to march past a given point with their wagon trains, artillery & all marching as we do four men abreast. But I have not finished my Sunday yet. There was an immense wagon train before us & toward night another behind us from some other road, but next us in rear was a battery which consists of six cannon & six each drawn by six horses & one caisson drawn by eight horses. Toward night we were hindered by the train & it was getting cold. We halted on a cold hill nearly two hours till we were chilled through. Went on a mile or so into a pine wood & halted in a wet spot a long time, then moved again around ¼ mile & halted in a deep cut in a hill where the pass was just wide enough for a wagon. It was dark, we were cold & our patience was taxed some. After a while I went forward, found a place where my men could climb up the bank, called them & told them they might build fires. That diverted us till we had fires enough to make us comfortable. In about an hour the Adjutant came back to us & called out, "Capt. Munger make your men as comfortable as you can. We shall have to stay here tonight." That was about 8 O. C. Some of them had been to supper, that is had eaten hardtack enough but the officers had not so we selected a place for our fire in a pine grove on the side of a hill, built a fire & had some pork, hard tack & coffee. But not feeling well myself that I would not eat a rich supper so took only hard tack & water as I did for dinner and if you think that was hard I can tell of a worse case. I passed a man & asked the usual question, "Have you a pass?" "Yes Captain, but I have not had a mouth full today & I can't keep up." I asked why he had no food & he said their brigade was out entirely. A fact I had before learned so I gave him a tack & he was as pleased as you would be with a new dress. Now, let me caution you not to get too dark an impression from these incidents in the main we have enough to eat & suffer no more than men do in new countries in the accumulation of property with the exception of a home & family to sympathies with us when the day's toil is done. I say as I have said before, "Let others complain as they may." My physical sufferings don't compare with my mental & even this mostly negative it is not so much what I suffer as what I <u>don't</u> enjoy. So, don't let your lives be saddened by the idea that we are suffering severely though you don't know how we miss your sympathy as expressed in your letters & when I come home I will tell you more about it then. I can't now. It is past 12 O'clock & the boys have long, long been asleep & I will bid you goodnight with an imaginary kiss hoping to be able to add something to this in the morning. **Note: The letter ends here.**

Wednesday morning Nov. 26th

Good morning Darling & happy birthday to you. I am officer of the day today & you must read this with due respect. I will resume mu day's narrative. We were ready to lie down at 10 O'clock. Seven of us had three rubber 7 three woolen blankets. We laid the rubber on the woolen over us. Orett & I lay together, it was a cold night & we built a good fire a little before 12. I got up for the blanket was too narrow on my side, covered Rhets up good, fixed the fire & laid on the ground close to it, then I enjoyed all the pleasures of heat & coal. While one side smarted with heat the other did with cold so I changed often to see which was pleasantest & came to the sage conclusion that the purest happiness is on passing from cold to heat. At 3 I got tired of that & laid down with O. again till five when O. got up. I told him if he always looked out as well for himself, I'd risk him but he complained that I was a very unfair bedfellow & that I took pretty much all the blankets so I was obliged to compromise & call it even but I took cold & paid a severe penalty next day with sick headache. The first severe attack since I left Geneva. Our greatest discomfort now is the ground is cold & we do not of course sleep warm as you do in beds for it is impossible with the means in our reach to keep off the ground so that the cold will not make the lower side smart some. We lay a rubber blanket on the ground & a woolen on it so that the moisture is kept from us pretty well. I sleep very little after three & I lie & think & think & <u>think</u> & what do you suppose it is about. There darling I have given you some <u>particulars</u> of one day of marching day sometime. If I live I will give you a camp day. I would to you write much more but our writing facilities are like our other matters, not of the best.

Your loving father, B. Munger

Rappahannock Station, Va. Dec. 5, 1863

My Dear Wife & Daughter,

I wrote you a line saying we were alive & well day before yesterday & have not had time to write more fully since. Yesterday I rec'd yours of the 23rd & 27th, also Ida's of the 27th. I was glad you had so pleasant a time Thanksgiving & would have enjoyed to have been one of the number. I received also the photograph which I prize more than I can express. (I hope Mary, you will get yours.) I will give you a short sketch of our excursion. On Thursday morning at sunrise we left camp near the point where the road from the Rappahannock southwards crosses Mountain Run. Marched to & crossed the Rapidan 2 miles above Ely's Ford & near the Mouth of Wilderness Run, continuous southward & camped about 8 P.M. on the road from Orange Court House to Fredericksburg where it crosses the Wilderness Run (see Lloyd's Map).

Our Reg. was sent out on picket. It was a very cold night, one of those frosty smarting nights yet we slept without tents & on the ground. That was what little we did sleep. Friday the 27th, moved early. From the time we started on Thursday morning cannonading was heard in front & on our right & frequently we expected a hand in. We moved toward Fredericksburg & till 10today supposed we were going there. We filed to the right, marched a few miles, filed again to the right now southwest& halted near Spotsylvania C.H. Here we expected a fight sum. An artillery fight was in progress & we are moved up as supports. It was on an old cornfield, ground moist & we could have no fires as it would draw the enemy's fire. That is, show them where to fire. We sent mark back to the rear to make coffee & as the ground was wet we laid down rails & slept on them without tents although it looked like storm.

Saturday morning early northwest in a severe rainstorm & at noon halted at a place called Robinson's Tavern near Locust Grove. There we found most of the army & Gen. Mead's Hd. Qr. We stood quietly in the rain most of the afternoon. It stopped toward night. Saw about 75 prisoners. The 3rd & 6th Corps moved off & formed line of battle about a mile or so down the pike. This is the pike from Orange C.H. to Fredericksburg & 20 miles from each. Here we bivouacked for the night & slept good on some pieces of boards.

Sunday, moved at daylight down the pike 2 miles to Mile Run & immediately sent to the front on picket. The Run or creek was the dividing line & impassable except on bridges. The pickets were 500 yards apart, consequently, in rifle range so when they were changed & ours posted were under their fire with all the caution that could be used. 3 of our Reg. were struck, one shot through the right arm near the elbow the other two shot slightly. The 3 right companies (mine being one of them) were held in reserve. At 1 A.M. I relieved the companies most exposed. The night was cold. We laid there Monday & night. Tuesday & night till 3 O'clock. Towards the last there was little feeling. Twice I was shot at while passing along the line but I did not blame the rascals much for they did not know who I was. I suppose I am making this letter too long. Our pickets were silently withdrawn at 3 on Tuesday morning. We were the last & I had to stay as some of the men were said to be missing & I got lost & for once in my life that I should get to Richmond I'll tell you about it sometime. I found our Reg. at the tavern. I spoke of & we marched <u>some</u>. I reckon at 8 we re-crossed the Rapidan at Germania, 12 miles & at noon, bivouacked at Stephensburgh a distance of 22 in about 8 hours.

I will not tell you of our hardships as that is an old story. I will only say we got short of rations & for 60 hours (our mess) had no meat & did our marching & picketing & on pure Hard Tack & Coffee & laid out without tents where water in a running stream froze 3/4 inch thick, still I am well & hardy. The only thing that affects me is sleeping on this cold ground that it gives me severe pain in my bones but I sweat that off the next march. Thursday, we crossed the Rappahannock the 12th time & camped a mile from here. Friday, came to this to guard this fortification & ordered to fix up for a permanent stay. I have little faith in our <u>stay</u> yet we went to work like the Israelites in Egypt with material & have worked till sun down on our tents when an order is recd. to be "ready to move at a moment's". So, we expect to go in the morning. Where I can't guess. Some say toward Washington & some back to meet Lee, who again has crossed the Rapidan they say. Perhaps we shan't move at all. It has ceased to trouble me. It is late, I must stop & if possible will add a word in the morning.

Sunday morning sunrise, no appearance of moving but ain't it cold! Our tent is not half down & we can have no fire & although the morning is clear it looks a <u>little</u> <u>blue</u>. The probability is Lee's movements eased the order recd. last night & perhaps the cold has sent him back. Mail is near ready. Good bye.

Your aff Husband & Father,

B. Munger

Rappahannock Station, Va. Dec. 9th, 1863

My Dear Wife & Daughter,

I write to relieve you of any anxiety you may feel on my account. I am & have been very busy. This is said to be the place we are to winter. At any rate, we are laying out more labor on our tents than usual. Still I have little faith that we shall remain here long & in fact I don't wish to forfeit a desolate spot. We have no tents as of yet to live in & still sleep in our shelters on the ground, hope to get into our tent tonight or tomorrow. Our fireplace is done. I am at present in command of 90 men guarding the rail road to Bealeton. It is hard work. Yesterday I walked 15 miles in passing over the road. We shall be relieved a day after tomorrow. My health is good & I stand or bear the pleasure of soldier life finely. We get very few papers here & know little of what is passing in the world but from what I do see. I have no reason to change my opinion in relation to the length of the war. Would be glad to hope otherwise. I confess I dread the coming winter. We had a foretaste last Sunday. It was much like a Sunday at Stoneman's Switch a year ago. Just think of a day so cold & windy that fire freezes & not even a barn to shelter you from the wind. That tried our grace. We shall soon have our tent done & can laugh at such days. In some respects, there is not as good feeling between officers as formally. There always has been some clannishness here but it doesn't trouble me much. I must leave this as I must go to Bealeton.

10 P.M. I have been to Bealeton & back & my work is done for the day & here I am in my shelter, squatted on the ground like an Indian writing. Orett is asleep beside me & as our mansion is only 5 by 6 feet & "just no high at all" at the edges & our valises & whole wealth of wardrobe are stored here we have little room to spare. We have secured some boards today so that we look forward to a time when we shall have a tent, table & seat. One reason why it is so difficult to write when we are marching daily or

on going into a new camp is the entire absence of everything like furniture. Half of my letters nearly are written with my paper on my lap as I sit on the ground. We are living well now as can be expected & when our tent is done shall be ready to enjoy (!) ourselves. The boys are well, not a sick one in the Co. Rob is looking finely again. He has seen no letter from bro Bush yet & I am just ready to strike his (Bush's) name from my list of "worthies". Ackley is hardy & indeed all the boys. Squires has not yet returned, perhaps he is detained in Washington. Your account of your Thanksgiving most me. I won't say it but I would like to have been there. These Holidays & anniversaries set me thinking. Good night & God Bless.   B. Munger

Rappahannock Station Dec. 11, 1863

My Dear Wife & Daughter,

I wrote you two days since but in such a hurry I could hardly think. Today I have been relieved from duty on the rail road & shall I hope have a little rest which I much need during the three days I was on that duty. I walked over thirty six miles beside my other duties. I am feeling a little blue today probably because I am tired out. One of our Captains (Grannis) left for home this morning on a leave of fifteen days. His mother being sick and today we noticed that two Corps officers from the regiment & one man from each company can go home on recruiting service to report at Elmira. The officers were already designated but I do not know who they are. Probably Capt. Danks & the Adj. I have named Kinner from our company. Lieut. Kelly very much wanted to go but could not get permission. An order was rec'd last night permitting Corps commanders to grant leaves & furloughs. So, the applications will rush in I presume in abundance. I think I shall not be a candidate but the Lieutenants will. I am writing this in Kinner's tent which is comfortable. Ours is not yet done. It is raining & hailing some. & is rather a gloomy day. I have a large amount of company writing to do but need not feel as if I could go about it today & several letters to write not having written any except to you since we left Mountain Run Camp Nov. 26. I must home for several articles of clothing soon & perhaps by Kinner if he goes. I think I shall order another pair of boots immediately. I bought an overcoat yesterday till then I had done all my campaigning without such an article & with their unlined blouse but have stood it well. My dress coat is getting musty but I think I shall make it do till spring. Our board is expensive & I want my dress should be as cheap as consistent.

We bought 40 lb. butter last week for 20 dollars a very fair article. Some of it we resold to the men. In your next please give me a statement of your finances & if at any time you want money call on Layman. I would not get in less as L. has money for anything you may need. I feel entirely at rest in regard to your loading place. I could not have been suited better. Please try to make so easy for them that it will be permanent. As to any anxiety about me, that is unnecessary. I am quite fleshy "hard to kill & shan't die of my own accord". I must tell you one little incident that occurred yesterday. We have forgotten some of the commandments down this way & to build our tents & houses, barns, sheds & c. & use the mate sail. I sent a team & a guard 5 or 6 miles day before yesterday & got a fine lot without accident & reported to the Col. my luck & he sent a team yesterday & 2 of the guard were captured by gorillas. Another guard from the 83rd Pa. were attacked & the aft surgeon taken. Our two men were left with one man with a revolver cocked but when he heard the firing he took their money, one hundred dollars, watch, gun & c. & let them go. It makes the Col. hang his head. We expect lively times with the rascals this winter.

I will soon write to Ida if I get time. Orett is on picket for one day. Squires & 4 others of my company who have been in hospitals returned tonight. It is evening & I am in our own tent with a good fire & I am writing at a table (not much of any) & tonight expect to sleep on a bed (that is blankets spread on boards) I have slept on the ground except one night since Nov. 26th & the ground is frozen 4 to six inches deep so that it is not a good bed. Perhaps I had better describe my tent as it will be our home till spring if we live & stay here. In size, it is 9 x 10 logged up 4 logs high & pretty rough. The roof is of cloth (our fly), the gables boarded, a little fire place built out of brick & mud & a floor of boards, a bunk or bed of boards the long way of our tent (11 feet) wide at one end, (3 ½ feet) & narrow at the other this is for two at one end & one at the other. There so you see our feet will lap some but we must economize. We have just finished our table as yet no seat but the bed. We shall add several improvements but with a bed, table & fireplace we can begin to live. The bed I value highly. I fear sleeping on the ground injured me. Although our tent is not one tenth as good as a northern horse stable. I suppose we feel as "good" over our comforts tonight as some who have houses to live in.

I must write to L. soon. I have asked him several questions which he does not answer & to do some business which I suppose he has forgotten. One thing I wish you would inform me about that is Perry's subscription for an artificial led & how he gets along generally. Please remember me to him. Fred was here yesterday, is in camp at Stephensburgh, is well but has received no pay since leaving the Co. & does not yet know whether he will be Sergeant. I will finish this after the mail comes in.

I have recd. 3 letters from you since the 26th, dates I think Nov. 23rd – 27th & Dec. 3rd. None from L. within my memory. Saturday eve we received no mail yesterday but this morning I recd. yours of the 8th inst. I am glad you are better & Ida also. You refer to my neglect to answer your question in regard to Ida going to school. It was not because I do not feel a deep intent in the subject & I intend to answer every question but that letter was recd. Just before our late advance across the Rapidan. I was obliged to burn my letters having no way of carrying them & the excitement & fatigue of that march made me forget most all I ever knew. You are a better position to judge what is best than I am & I trust you have decided wisely. In relation to our late move I am not at all discouraged of our want of success & think more highly of Mead than ever. That he dared not attack Lee in the position he occupied & if you hear anyone finding fault because he is not willing to fight at a disadvantage invite him come down here. We want just such men. In my next to Ida, I will describe the field & positions as well as I can. You may think it a singular subject for a little girl but I want here informed on the subject for till recent I was entirely too ignorant on that point. I have just received Layman's of the 9th instant. Please thank him for his efforts in my behalf. I will write him soon. I also recd. a letter from Netty and a real hearty good one. She is teaching & thinks doing well. Lieut. Kelly sent up a application for leave of absence today which our Col. approved & Lt. Munger also but the Col. says he must wait till Kelly comes back as the orders allow but two Line officers absent at a time & ours is already home. I think both will be able to go soon. Kelly probably next week & O. in about 3 weeks. On the whole I think unless you are very anxious I had better not come home this winter. It is expensive & the coming back reminds me of the drunkard's description of "a drunk" "It is heaven to get drunk & c" but we will leave the subject for future thought & description.

I think of sending by Kelly for another pair of boots as mine are about "done up". I shall need more shirts before spring but shall do nothing about it at present. We are more comfortably situated than ever before. We have a floor to our tent now a luxury we never before enjoyed & in many respects it exceeds our last winter's quarters. The place is not as pleasant perhaps in winter but for more so in summer. We close to the spot where Wheaton fell & there are very many graves all about us & many evidences of <u>war</u>. The absence of the Captains Allen & Danks will leave me the senior Capt. of the regiment. I have told you I think there were two clans or parties in this regiment. The Chicago of which Col. Couner, Maj. Knox & Capt. Danks are head & Albany party of which Capt. Allen is perhaps as much leader as any one. And like the Jews of old both these unite against the <u>new</u> Companies. That is, they think all the honors probably should be enjoyed by the old 44th. Recently there has been some glaring partialities & there is some bitter feeling but for myself I can do little about either. I don't care "which kills" but would as leave both would. I think I shall be able to hoe my sow. But I suppose Camp quarrels have little matters for you.

       Remember me to all <u>real</u> friends. Yours B. Munger

PS: The body of the Sur, I spoke of has been found pierced with three tally. We will give it to those villains soon.

                                                    Rappahannock Station, Va. Dec 24, 1863

My Dear Wife & Daughter,

       I received yours of the 20th inst. tonight. Orett recd. one from home saying Lt. Kelly had arrived. You have doubtless seen him in this & learned more of what you want to know that I write in ten letters. This makes me think often of what I intended to say to you & especially to Ida. There are a thousand inquiries arise in the mind when hearing or reading of country you never saw & of transaction & things that interest you. In the nature of the case I must fail to give all the information & gratify all the curiosity excited. My suggestion is that you ask such questions & make such inquires as will at least put me on track. I have sent by Kelly a long letter to Ida but at last have to finish it in a hurry. In fact, after the first night I had no time. If there is anything you do not understand ask all about it. George Hobart has had a cousin here a week or so & today he left taking George with him on a furlough ten days. Since Kelly left we have been somewhat exercised on the subject of reenlistment. Order after order has been sent around till finally Gen. Mead sent down an order saying that new Co.'s in old regiments might go home with those regiments & on the same conditions if they would pledge themselves to reenlist at the expiration of their two years' service. That included my Co. & almost to a man & they were ready to make a pledge. All looked bright at 10 A.M. today & as if we should spend a part of the winter at home. But behold another "Special Order". No troops will be permitted to reenlist & go home who have more than <u>one year & three months to serve</u>. An end to our hopes. Some long faces and so on. The result will be very few of the men in the old companies will go. I think I told you Captains Allen & Danks were in our state recruiting for the regiment so that I have been senior Capt. 7 second senior officer present. Yesterday Maj. Knox came after a nice little stay of five months. For a week past, my labors have been light. Monday morning I had one of my A No. 1s headaches & vomited till I was ready to begin the world news. But the next day I went on duty as Field Officer of the day & road 15 miles or so. I am an exception to all rules & am cured by hard work & exposure instead of rest. Tonight, the bugle sounded the Officer's Call & on assembling were informed by the Col. that a raid was expected on this rail road, "Your commands are to sleep with their cloths on & their arms in readiness to fall in at a moment's notice."

You need not be <u>scared,</u> we did not expect to die on their account at present. A little fight would be a good thing to stir us up. But they don't send word when they are coming. We are ready however to give them a Merry Christmas. Maybe you would like to ask if I don't feel lonely about these days! Mary, I want you to distinctly understand that it is beneath the dignity of a soldier to have any feelings and <u>I am a soldier</u>. I think that I wrote in my last that there was some prospect that this Corps would go southwest. I still think that was the intention at that time but given up now. In yours recd. tonight you speak of cloths. I think I will send for nothing at present. Men from my Co. will be going home all winter & I can send at any time. Orett will get a few things & if Kelly or Southerby brings my boots I can get along. You never had a large family of children & perhaps will not be able to sympathize with me in my case. But I can have to remember to have seen my mother in the same dilemma. It is for the Captains to decide who of their Co.s shall go home on furlough & who first & c. Only one can go at a time & each thinks his case is a peculiar one. Most want me to promise that they may go next. Poor fellows, I would let them all go if I could & it was safe. But enough must stay to take care of the Rebs. One poor fellow showed me a letter tonight uncovering trouble enough. Orett was in bed when I commenced this & has long been asleep. I am glad to hear of the return of Mr. Wycoff, Katy's father if it results increased happiness to them. Hope it may.

I suppose while I have been writing here alone & solemn the children & some of them of large growth have been enjoying their Festival. I would like to peer in & just see how it goes. I hope you all may have a happy time. Fred was here this week. He is not yet certain whether he is Sgt. Or not & I urged him to push his claim hard & if he could not succeed alone I would come over & help him. Hobart will probably see you before he returns * I think Kinner will also. If this reaches you before Kelly leaves I wish him to bring me a bottle of Arnold's ink. I am much troubled to get good ink here. It is late. I must close & in the words of the old ballad wish you "A happy Christmas & to all and to all a good night."

Your Husband & Father - B. Munger

PS: The 12 O'clock train has just arrived & no raiders so I think we <u>shan't</u> have the fun of wishing them Merry Christmas tonight.

B. Munger

NOTE: In a small, approximately, 3 ¼ inch by 2 ¼ inch paper wrapper is written the following: "Capt. B. Munger - Retained Copy - Monthly Co. Return for December 1863".

NOTE: There is not a Co. return in this part of the collection for this wrapper.

Elmira, NY Jan. 26, 1864

My Dear Wife,

I am boarding as I expected with Mrs. Mason. 290 Water St. a good place. I have just been assigned to the command of the new barracks in Fassets Ware House. Grey St. I have a Lt., Sgt. & 25 men as guards & shall have about 150 recruits to take care of. As yet I have done nothing about board for you. I have had no time & did not think it best till I was settled in some kind of duty. My present place seems permanent & is much more agreeable than at Barracks No. 3. I am much pleased with the change. I saw E. Whitaker here today he was at the Depot. No Orett reports yet. I am going to hear Madam Anna Bishop sing tonight at Beecher's Church. It's a little lonely here but I get along I hope to be home again soon but not as soon perhaps as Saturday. It is so muddy one can hardly move. There are 4 boarders here, a Lt. & wife an Adjt. & a civilian. I am not acquainted as yet, pleasant enough people. I think maybe I shall like them by & by. Write & direct to Capt, B. Munger – Elmira, NY. Leaving off the Reg. & c. In haste.

Your Husband, B. Munger

Oil City. April 1, 1865

My Dear Little Treasure,

I did not intend writing to you till tomorrow but the boys are playing checkers & I have my choice to look on or write & having finished one letter & the Sprit still prompting I still write. I wrote to mother last night & perhaps you think there is nothing left to write about. Well, I'll tell my experience. On reaching Elmira I went directly to see Henry Morgan & paid him for expense of sending our goods one dollar. I then called on Mrs. Steel, by this time enjoying a severe headache. I soon found it was not Mrs. Steel but my dear Mrs. Badger who wished to see me & that lady & Mrs. Decker were sent for. Their errand was hospital difficulties & could do anything to assist them. They talked a full hour much to the relief of my head (over the left) took a light lunch & went to see Dr. Morse & promised to call again at 5 & take tea. Next called on my old "standby" Maj. Colt & by this time I had to cave & went over to his room & went to bed. It passed off in some degree & I went to the Dr. as agreed redc. my pay. Met Billy Barnes who is as anxious to come & work for me as ever. Mrs. Colt is not at Elmira, went home before the flood.

Thursday morning, left for this city & although I had no adventure was much interested in viewing the effects of the flood along the way. In one place a huge saw log was chained to the middle of a large field & balanced across a stump high & dry like a turtle. In another place a small house was floated half a mile from a little village, turned bottom up & lay upon the roof in a large meadow. Many small out buildings were dropped along in the swamps as if they were lost. I saw a door to a house with an old log run half through one of the panels. Probably it ran through while the house of which it was a part was standing.

At Meadville, the water was three feet deep on the lower floors of the McHenry House where I usually stay. This time I staid all night at Meadville & arrived here at 9 A.M., Friday. Yesterday we bought some blacksmith's tools, provisions & c. & about 300 dollars' worth of rope & today put all on board a steamer & sent to Panther Run. While at the wharf today a young man came up & offered his hand familiarly saying, "How do you do Captain?" I did not know him but on inquiring he proved to be a Reb prisoner who was discharged from Elmira by the name of Searles formerly of Rochester. I well remember him when he told me the circumstances. He has been here some months & is doing a good business, friends are wealthy. He seemed much pleased to meet me. Uncle Lyman is much better today & quite cheerful. It is late & I must say good bye & how I would like a goodnight kiss. Tomorrow I will add a little. God bless my <u>Little</u> <u>One</u>.

Sunday 1 O'clock P.M. – Well my little Pet it is Sunday in Oil City the same as in more favored cities. The morning was beautifully bright & caused one's thoughts back, way back to the almost forgotten past. To absent friends & to you my darling and would (if I were given to sad thoughts) have made me feel sad at my surroundings. The contrast between earth & sky is so great here that one needs to keep his eyes elevated for mud & filth abound as you look earthward. I got up about 8 this morning, dressed for breakfast which we had at 9. Not a quiet home meal but with fifty men of whom I know little & care less. I eat as a <u>duty</u> that must not be neglected. After breakfast, we all went to church (Presbyterian) & heard a sermon which did me but little good. But we took a walk after & scenery was so fine viewed from the hill that it was if not a sermon, a hymn of praise. I have written a long letter & fear said but little, will try to do better next time. Let me hear from you. Be good, cheer Mother& may God bless & keep you all.

Your Loving father, B. Munger

Oil City April 7, 1865

My Dear Wife,

I wrote you Tuesday night expecting to be at Panther Run a week but as I was disappointed in that I staid but two days. I was to take charge of a job to construct a foundation for engine house & derrick for Orett. But the man who had taken the contract could not be bought off so I came back last night & as Geo. Hamlin starts for Penn Yan. I thought I would write to you a line. This is my forth to you & Ida in eight days. As yet I have recd. none from you. I passed you up to Tuesday. Wednesday, we all started for Panther Run carrying about 25 lbs. load each & as I told you my services were not needed at the job I expected to do. I helped measure a pile of lumber & take a derrick to pieces that had been thrown over by the flood. I felt well & the next day was to go to Walnut Bend & Plummer to look at our property there. But in the morning my diarrhea returned worse than ever & I had to give up. I came down on a raft last night. I think I have checked it but am weak. I am not sick enough to excite any apprehension but I feared that you would hear of it & think me worse than I am. L. is down here again today after provisions & c. His health is much improved since I came. O. has gone up the creek this P.M.

L. recd. a letter from Geo. Yesterday. He is expected here this week. He thinks his enterprise a success. He is to be married on the 3rd of May. You may think I am over prompt in writing but you may average them with the once a week letters when I get hard at work. I recd. a letter from Frank the other day by which I learn Emma arrived before I left Penn Yan. I have seen Mrs. Frank Gibbs, she is quite pretty & cheerful as a bird. This is a pleasant place to live especially if one is under the weather so as to be in doors mostly. Lyman recd. Martha's letter written last Sunday I think, last night by which I heard of your health & c. The friend of Maj. Colt don't report & it is just as well for we have no money to share for that enterprise, having use for it all in the new lease on Cherry Run. Barns has sold for 3,000 & talks of buying on the avenue an old & good lot & build. If I omit any point in giving the news & c. point out the omission. A telegram announces that Sheridan has captured Lee & his army. This was all the news we could ask & peace must be near.

Yours, B. Munger

Oil City, Sunday P.M. April 16, 1865

My Dear Wife & Daughter,

  I wrote you last Sunday & posted the letter at Meadsville so presume you have received it. I recd. yours of the 7th also of the 10th. Yesterday was the first I have heard from you since leaving. L. also recd. one from Martha which gives one day's later news * by that I learn you contemplate <u>joining</u> the <u>Wesleyan</u> <u>Church</u>. I hope you will find it pleasant & agreeable. There will at least be one advantage that is conveyance to school. I don't understand all the circumstances that induced the change. Whether Mrs. Bridgman's sickness was all or whatever it was otherwise it was unpleasant & it does not matter if you are more pleasantly situated & pleased with the change. I am satisfied. I am much pleased that Ida seems to be doing so well both in studies & music, hope it will be lasting & that in all that is good, generous & noble she will strive to excel. But your <u>sad</u>, <u>sad</u> look Mary as I saw you from the car window makes me fear you are not enjoining yourself. I would recommend visiting more. Go to Canandaigua, Rochester, Bloomfield & c. it will do you good.

  Lyman is writing & he will tell you all about himself & the boys so I will confine myself to myself. In my last I told you I was to leave for Columbus, O. next day. I left without breakfast & took a lunch at Meadville at 10 A.M. left at noon for Cleveland. Arrived at 7 & left at 10 for Columbus. Rode all night got into C. at 4 A.M. Tuesday as soon as the clerks were in their offices I went to work to get track of our engines, found they had been recd. & sent on to Cleveland. Took the train at 10 A.M. & arrived at Cleveland at 4 P.M. & after a long search found that one engine had been sent on & one remained in the freight house. Staid in Cleveland that night, next morning arrived to have the engine sent on & left for house. At Meadville I learned the one machine had been sent on to Franklin & agreed with the agent to send on the other as soon as it arrived & left for home. Our hurry in this matter was we had contracts with some boatmen who were in Pittsburgh to stop at Franklin & take them to Panther Run & the fear was that the engines would not be ready & the fear proved to be well founded for the boat was there on my arrival & we were not ready so we shall be obliged to hire them to make a trip expressly for them.

  I give you the particulars to give you an idea of our city life. O. & myself go to Franklin tomorrow morning to try it again. We hope to be able to get the other two engines for the new lease on Cherry Run this week. I returned from that trip Wednesday night, found Geo. At office. O. at Franklin & L. at Panther Run. Thursday morning all started for Little Yates & Panther Run. Little Yates <u>won't</u> <u>give down</u>. The proprietors are thinking of drilling a new hole on the same lease. I staid all night at Panther Run & next day went up the river about six miles, bought a lot of lumber & floated it down to the Run. Staid all night & next day with Geo. & O. explored the "Great Cave" which proved a "<u>Humbug</u>". After dinner O. & self got a ride on a raft to this city. Geo. followed on horseback & L. brought up the rear just at night on a raft. We tried the <u>Bachelor</u> of it & cooked our supper at the office (boiled eggs, bread & butter, crackers & coffee) cost 70 cents a saving of at least $1.30 on our supper besides getting a better meal. Today we are following the same plan. So, you see we go economy I wish you would write often.

Lyman will write about the prospects at P. Run & c. He expects to be able to start the pump about Wednesday. If it proves a success, he will visit home. O. will go to Cincinnati with Geo. but not home at present. Business here feels the influence of the flood & depression in finances & speculation is at a standstill. John Cummings is here & I fear is feeling rather <u>blue</u>. It is not a favorable time to come here unless one has money to invest & let it remain till times improve. We are safe from loss I think at all events & hope to make something. The death of Bradley Sheppard is very, very sad. They (his parents) must feel deeply.

The news of the assassination of the President & young Seward seems too devilish to be true. I hardly know how I feel but I fear for the future. If anything was looking to stamp the rebellion with eternal infamy it is supplied in this most damning act. You seem troubled about my health. Don't give yourself any uneasiness. I am doing finely & L. is quite rugged. I hope he will be able to go home soon (by the success of his well).

Your affectionate Husband & Father,

B. Munger

Oil City May 3rd, 1865

My Little Treasure,

I recd. the letter (yours & mothers) yesterday after Uncle Layman left and you can't tell how pleased I was to learn you were trying to be good & succeeding so well. I have been with you so little the last three years & when I am at home there are so many things to occupy time & attention that I don't have the opportunity to talk with you. I could wish and after I leave I think of so many things I wanted to say that I feel almost dissatisfied with myself. One of the things I wanted to talk about was the very thing you wrote big. - Self-culture or self-government- Children who have parents who govern wisely are very fortunate. But how much better it is if children are taught to govern themselves because there are so many times when parents do not know what their children do that if they do right only when told & watched by them, they will be likely to do many wrong things. Civil & parental laws are of little use only as they teach the individual to control himself. What I wish to impress on my Darling is to think deeply what you ought to do in any given thing or case, then do it because you think it right. Not particularly because I think it right but because <u>you </u>do. You will not understand me as advising disobedience to parents. I only want you to accustom yourself to appeal to your own conscious & judgement. I trust you will comprehend all I mean & more still. I have so much confidence in you that I trust you will <u>try</u> to do as your judgement dictates. Do you remember that old couplet?

What conscious dictates too be done

Or warns me not to do

This teach me more than hell to shun

That more than heaven peruse

The other subject on which I wish to write or talk was Sticktoitiveness or tenacity of purpose. That quality of mind which adheres to purpose once formed whatever objects may interpose. Unless circumstances so change as to make it wise to change your purpose. I will not write more about this last subject at present. But will leave it for you to think of. I shall not mail this at present but give you my daily experience. Today I have been waiting the arrival of a boat from Franklin which was to bring me a barrel of lime. The boat was to have been here early this morning. It did arrive at 6 P.M. <u>but did not bring the lime</u>. I have labored since Saturday on that poor bbl. The trouble now it is on a flat boat one mile from Franklin & the water is so shallow the steamer could not get to it. I have not been out of the city today but intend to go to Cherry Run tomorrow. Just about this hour Uncle Lyman will arrive in Penn Yan if he had no hindrances.

April 4th, Well Pet I have walked to Cherry Run & back today & am tired. The day is cloudy & dull. Orett has returned & will leave for Penn Yan in the morning apparently much pleased with the prospect. I think I can do the work for a while. Indeed, I had much rather be busy than idle so that time may hang less heavily. O. says he has enjoyed this visit very much & it seems a pity to keep him while the family are enjoying so much. I send this by Orett so that it will reach you perhaps before my first which I sent by mail. Before this reaches you, you will probably have seen your new cousin & I hope you will love her as I think she is good. I sent you a book by Uncle Layman which I think you will like. May God bless & keep my Darling.

Good bye, your father, B. Munger

Oil City May 7 1865

My Dear Wife & Baby,

It is Sunday in Oil City. I have been to Church & Bible class like a good Christian. The day is cool & cloudy & clear alternately much like autumn. Yesterday it was rainy so we have a new installment of mud. I wrote you on Friday by Orett, therefore have little experience to relate. Friday I was not well & kept close in the office. Saturday I went to Panther Run in the rain. Found things moving finely. The men think the well is producing from six to eight bbls per day. They will not stop it Sunday. Tell Lyman if he is there when this reaches you & if not tell Geo. that I took care of that bank note & paid interest. Also, that nothing definite has been decided about the Hicks well. Hamlin has given notice of an assessment on the Humbolt well which I shall pay tomorrow. I shall go to Cherry Run again tomorrow as I expect they commenced drilling there yesterday. Tell L. not to shorten his visit under the impression that he is needed here. I can do all for the present. I am enjoying myself hugely. Abundance of time to think, I came back from Panther Run about 5 last night not very tired, did my chamber work (You think it should have been done in the morning but you don't know. I am in Oil City & not on earth.). Prepared for a good wash then read till 10 O'clock. Washed & went to bed. This morning put things in apple pie order & after breakfast got ready for church. & at 9 went to Bible class. Since yesterday not a soul has dared to enter the room to disturb me. I forgot to say that I went to the Post Office at 9 last night to get a letter from my wife & <u>did not get</u> it. Therefor I did not sit down & read it.

   I said it was Sunday in Oil City, I meant with <u>good fellows</u> but Oil City is a great city & you must not suppose it is Sunday all over it. For example, we have an institution near our back window (unfortunately we have no other window) called a stable (Not the one that Hercules cleaned. That process was never applied to this one.) In this stable are some rare animals. A goat some dogs & several other animals not belonging to neither of those species, perhaps a cross & much meaner than either. These have no Sunday as we understand it but still it is a <u>special</u> day with them. I think they give evidence of the <u>spirit</u> & I sometimes think they are inspired. I have the full benefit of their meetings as much as if I was an attendant. How can a man be discontented with such privileges? When the steamboats at the wharf don't have any Sunday, they are not that kind of cattle. There are three now at the landing loading & unloading & the pilots fearing the citizens will not know they are on hand below their steam whistles, frequently each striving to make more noise than his neighbor.

   The attractions of the office are so great I can't think of leaving for dinner today. To vary & increase the interest they are now fitting out a lot of horses for a race on the "track", still I can't leave. I am resolved "to hold this position at all hazards". It is evening. I stopped writing, took a walk to Cottage Hill, came back & have had my supper. You are lonely tonight unless you are at Lyman's. I conclude not to attend church but to enjoy my <u>solitude</u> in writing. I have spoken but to one person today except to order something for supper & the like & no has been into the room. You can hardly imagine anything more quiet, but my soldier experience has been of great service to me. I now rather like such isolation. It is much better than uncongenial companions. I expect to be very busy this week. If so, perhaps will not have time to write again this week. I enclose a review of the oil operations for the week. You will see that it is rising. It is most 10 O'clock & as I must maintain good habits I'll stop writing & retire. Please remember to your household & except my goodnight.

Your Husband & Father,

B. Munger

Oil City May 9th, 1865

My DearWife & Daughter,

   I wrote you on Sunday by mail but having an opportunity of sending this by Mr. Geo. Hamlin. Tomorrow will write again. Something that will particularly interest L., I will repeat as this will reach you first without doubt. I was at Panther Run on Saturday & the boys that they were getting from 6 to 8 bbls per day. Everything working nicely. We are not yet drilling at No. 29, want of water is the hindrance. I think we will start on Thursday. Yesterday Fox shipped bill & the bill for one engine was presented by the Express Agent. Bill paid. They bear date Apr. 14th. In the P.M. I recd. a telegram from him saying he would leave last night for this place. I have seen him tonight. He is very mild. I told him we did not want the other engine at that price. We had been subjected to experience by the delay & now we proposed to be as cheap as we could. He replied he would throw off one hundred dollars if we could now buy an engine foe $1,500 & if we took his must have it at that price. He is to see me in the morning. As he left the office he said, "You must have the engine." There Mary, if the forgoing doesn't interest you it will L. & O. & you ay monopolize the remainder. In the first place, you will be pleased to learn that I was pretty sick yesterday. Headache of course. I am bilious somewhat. I kept on the bed most of the day. I am better today & I have been to Cherry Run & will be myself again by tomorrow. I have recd. one letter only from you, may get one tonight.

I am getting along finely & L. need not hurry but make a <u>good</u> visit (perhaps I would like to help a little) I sincerely hope you are all enjoying yourselves. The mail brings me nothing tonight & I have just learned that Hamlin will not leave till tomorrow night therefor I may add something of tomorrow experience. I saw (tell L.) some of those interested in the Hicks well today, but as Hicks is in Pittsburgh nothing can be done.

Wednesday, May 10th - I am not quite well this morning. I have had a dull headache for a few days which with poor appetite makes me feel rather poorly & to confess a little "Blue". It is nothing serious however but think I would tell you fearing Hamlin would say I was sick. & cause you some uneasiness. The day is cloudy & cool & we are still blessed with mud & perhaps our frequent rains are a blessing for where the earth is drying. The stench is intolerable. After seeing Mr. Fox, I shall try to see both Cherry & Panther Runs so as to send the latest intelligence. Shall ride, for I tired out yesterday. Don't get the impression that I am sick. I only feel <u>mean</u> but am confident I am not, you know.

4:30 P.M. Just in from P. R. Wet as a rat. It is still raining like a flood. The P.R. well is increasing in the yield of oil & decreasing in water. Not more than half as much water as when L. left. The boys think from 10 to 15 bbls oil but I think they over rate it. Not yet drilling at C. R. – I bargained with Fox for the other engine at $1,500 & he is to set them up if we wish him to & we pay his expenses but no wages.

In haste. Good bye,

B. Munger

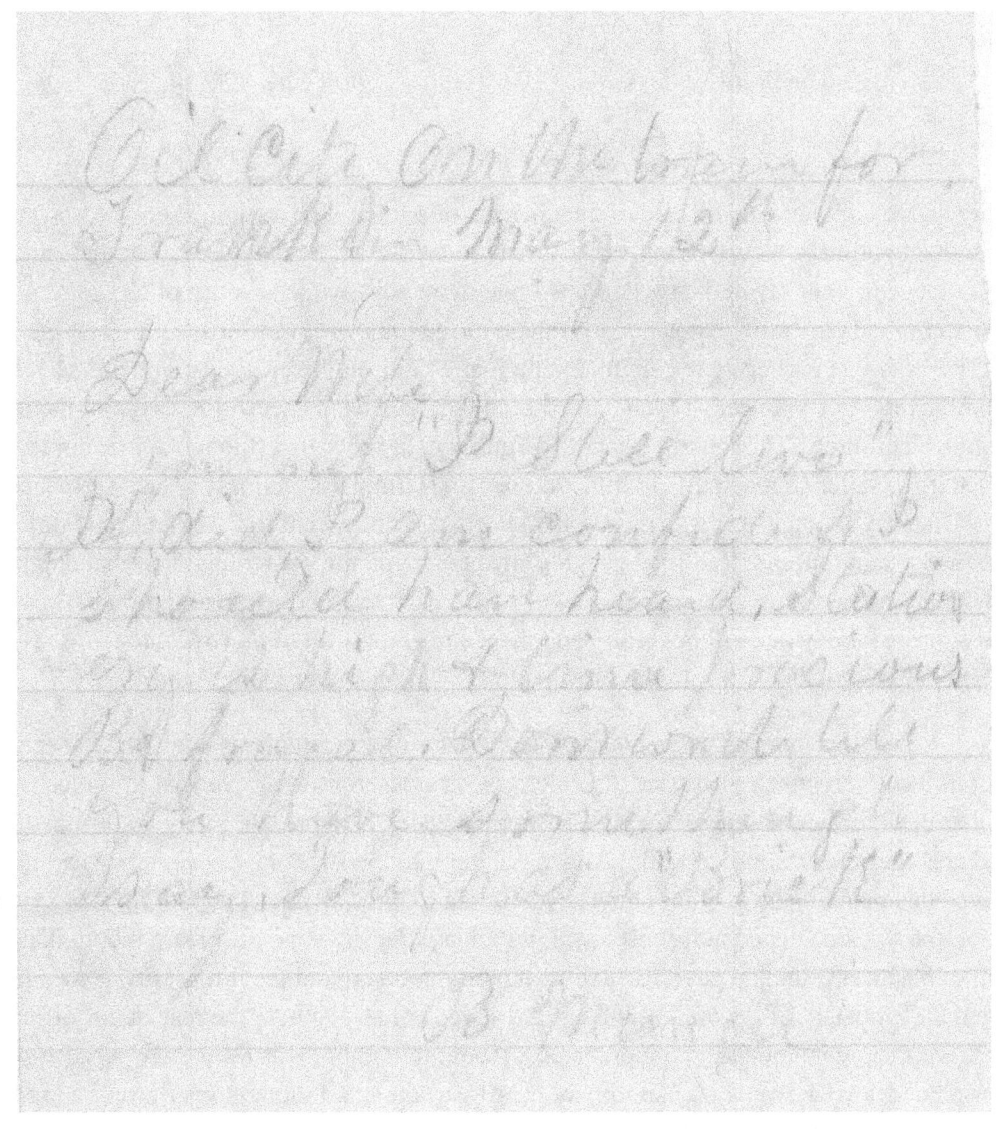

Bennet Munger's letter to his wife dated May 12th, 1865 – Shelly Case collection

Oil City May 14, 1865

My Dear Wife & Daughter,

You are aware I am not an advocate of the doctrine of retaliation except in special cases. It is in accordance with that opinion or theory of mine that I write today. It will be two weeks Tuesday since I heard from you or anyone in your favored city. Perhaps I feel more acutely the absence of all correspondence just now as I am entirely alone a large share of the time with very little to interest me when not at work. Perhaps you purposely refrain intending it as a course of needed discipline. If so I think I can make a favorable report of its success. I have lived & in the main been cheerful & have not the least doubt could continue indefinitely. Though to be candid I think you have written (though a little apt to be negligent) & the letter has failed to reach me. I wrote you last by Hamlin on Wednesday last. (Expect a squib by Sheldon) Thursday it rained & I was mostly in the office. Friday went to Franklin found one of the Fox engines & had it sent to Reno. Rail road freights have gone up fabulously. I paid on that engine $137.85. Saturday Gibbs arrived, will remain but a day or two. I went to Cherry Run after noon. They started the engine & drilled today but will not really commence in earnest till tomorrow (Monday) morning. The engine runs like a clock. From there I went to P. R., found everything right.

The well is yielding about as when I last wrote, perhaps more irregular. Today I have been to Bible class & church. I got very much interested at Bible class in a description of "Special Providences" & the question is left open for next Sunday. Tonight, Bishop Kingsley is to preach. I may go. Friday night a man was robbed near the James House of $500. A man ran out into the street saying someone had fallen into a well & wanted this man to help get him out. They both ran to the well & as the poor dupe stopped to look into the well the rascal knocked him senseless & took his money & was off. I learn the vigilance committee are full of business. I think a good revolver is a pretty good committee. I must give you a little incident that jogged the monetary of my dreams. One night a week or so ago near the rear of our office is a load of ladders & we sleep with the back window raised. About midnight I was awaken by a noise so sudden I could form no idea what was. I was so fully & clearly awake that I thought very fast & as soon as I stirred I heard a low, shrill whistle as I thought for silence. I sprung out of bed caught my revolver & couching near the floor moved out cautiously for battle. I thought in a moment some villains had put one of the ladders up to the window & would be poking their heads over the sill in a moment & I stood ready to send him back double quick. But he did not come. On going to the window, I seemed to be the only man out of place & I felt a little cheap & was debating whether I did really hear a noise when one of the horses in the stable almost under our window kicks a loose board with such force & noise any sleeping man would have been justified in thinking he was attacked by a battery of artillery. The whistling was perhaps done by a poor mouse for as I was going back to bed one tried it again but this time with so poor success I wondered I could have been so fooled. I laid down feeling a little green & slept soundly till morning. Then thinking no one should ever know how nicely I was sold but finally thought it was too good to keep you as you, I believe enjoy my frights.

I think you were sick or dead, I should heard therefore I do not worry about you but trust you are getting along well & I hope happily. Do you need any money? I trust Lyman will attend to any want of yours. It should be pleasing to hear from you often enough to keep posted as to your history & experience. I have had a call this afternoon from a young man from New York. Hathaway, he is a good talker, has seen much of the world & I passed a pleasant hour & he was introduced by Baxter a Penn Yan man. It is tea time & I will close. Will write to my "Little One" during the week if I can to teach this by example my lessons of "Sensuality of Purpose".

Good bye & may God guard & keep you. B. Munger

Oil City May 17, 1865

My Dear Wife & Daughter,

I write in anticipation of being able to send tomorrow by Mr. Bogart. O. arrived this morning quite unexpectedly to me. I was rather looking for L. but not at all for O. There is nothing new to write except daily business. Today we have been to Cherry Run & attended to the delivery of the second engine on that lease. Went to the Hicks' well which is doing well. Frank Gibbs left tonight for home. I shall not be able to write to Ida till Sunday as I go to Panther Run tomorrow. Nettie's address the same as ever, Canandaigua care of t. Benson. You say in your letter, "I send you a communication from Washington" but you do not send it. If it is anything of importance please send it. I will write you more at length & in detail after L's arrival. It is after 10 P.M. & as I fought Bed Bugs last night till after 12 I am somewhat at sleepy. Good night your husband & father,

B. Munger

Oil City May 21st, 1865

My Dear Wife & Daughters,

I recd. your letter by Orett & one dated 17th by mail on Friday, the shortest passage known. Yours was recd. yesterday (Saturday) Lyman, I conclude was not able to leave on Friday. I hope he will soon be better. Not that he is needed here particularly but for his own sake. There is either an unusual scarcity of news or subjects of interest or I am extremely dull. More likely the later. I have a dull headache which does not add to my brilliancy. I write you last on Wednesday I think by Mr. Bogart. Wednesday went to Cherry Run, saw the last engine delivered & the first well drilling. Thursday went to Panther Run. That well is doing finely. Has yielded about 100 bbls of oil. The Hicks well is still increasing. Stowbridge thought it was producing about 12 bbls. Saturday, we went to sell some interests if practicable to raise some money. I must stop & have a nap or a walk as I am too dull to write.

7 P.M. I have had the nap but feel but little brighter. It is a rainy day & since commenced this we have had a violent storm of thunder rain & wind so that our streets are flooded & mud reigns. We have been to church & I to Bible class but the day has hung rather heavily. I feel the want of society. This is enough about myself. I was pleased to learn Ida was doing well in studies & c. How is it about those little duties you used to forget Darling? Can you remember them any better? Did you have a pleasant time at your last Band of Hope? I thought to write you a description of this city but at present my head is too bad.

We have some little <u>domestic</u> troubles such as poor housekeepers are subject to. I allude to fight I had with my bed fellows the other night. We charged on them last Friday & supposed they were entirely routed. They in turn attacked me the next night & although I put 50 to death as it kept me up most of the night. I concluded to retire from the field & now sleep on the floor in peace. We intend to renew the attack. Has David Wagoner paid that note? Do you want money? You have so many things to occupy your attention that many things I want to know you seem to forget. The first & most natural enquiry is, how do you like our new niece & did you have a pleasant time? What disposition has been made of that unoccupied room next to yours? Are Hermans & wife to remain during the summer? (Ida <u>keep</u> an eye to my interests!) Has Bridgeman moved? I wish you & Ida would have your photographs taken without delay & send me several copies. Tell Lyman that Strobridge & Tracy have taken a lease at Pit Hole paying a bonus of $2,500 which they are much pleased with. That locality is all the rage just now. I shall write after L. arrives more about our circumstances & plans perhaps. Orett don't seem to think it is as <u>pleasant here</u> as at home! But he is young & allowance must be made.

Your Husband & Father,

B. Munger

Oil City June 13th, 1865

My Dear Wife,

I wrote you on Sunday & Layman yesterday. But as you will receive this much earlier than those. I will give you a brief sketch of myself. I have not been well since my return. The first two days I kept about. Went to P. R. both days but Saturday I kept in the office & have since. Sunday I went to see a physician. He thought he could throw it off without a settled fever & said if I went home in my present condition the fatigue & excitement would almost surely make me sick & I might calculate on a crown of fever. I have pain in back & head, weakness, bad tong & c. Not much fever. Yesterday I was but today I am not as well. My head is very troublesome. Still the Dr. says I will get along & I think I will. Strowbridge leaves tonight & will hand this to you. Orett or I will write often to keep you advised. Business matters you will find in the other letters when you receive them. O. recd. letters by Hamlin this morning. I have recd. none since my arrival. My head aches too bad to write. You need give yourself no uneasiness about me. As I shall come out right in time. I am not sick in bed but can walk anywhere.

Your Aff. B. Munger

Oil City June 14th, 1865 10 A.M. – I rec'd, yours of the 9th inst. last night.

My Dear wife & Daughter,

I wrote you by Mr. Strobridge yesterday & having another opportunity today will try to do better for I am feeling better. Mr. Denning has been here this morning & will leave for home tonight.

Yesterday I felt very poorly & feared I was to be pretty sick but this morning I am much better & hope to be about soon. What different moods of feelings we poor mortals are subjected to. Without any apparent change in our circumstances our feelings undergo at times a sudden & almost entire revolution. Perhaps I ought to speak only for myself for I mistrust sometimes I am only about half human (As to that other half I would not dare guess.) I was going to make a confession but I believe confessions don't become me. I will only say that I long family, yearn to be at home today in a degree, uncommon for me. As it is useless I may as well "Harden it out".

    To change the subject I will tell you what I did not have for breakfast. I had eaten little yesterday, indeed I have not eaten an ounce of meat since my return & wanted something but did know what. Finally, I told the waiter I would try an egg. He soon brought some fried in grease which made my stomach heave. I told him I wanted the boiled. Could not boil them, they were not fresh, frying was the only way to cook them & have them keep their shape. (More honest than flattering to a poor appetite.) Could he give me some milk? Yes, plenty of milk. Some milk. I had a foolish preference for sweet milk. Had none. The butter was out of the question. So strong as to hold the most powerful man in utter astonishment, so I took some cornbread, dipped it in tea, put on some sugar, eat it, paid half a dollar & felt refreshed. Shall try it again when I am so hungry as to make it necessary. This is one of the "Guides to Health" I expect we see advertised. To add to our comforts an addition has been attached to the rear of our office which discharges its smoke pipe into our window & between our night skirmishing & smoke we are thoroughly stirred up.

    Orett has a severe attack of diarrhea yesterday & last night but is better this morning. If he should be worse he will go home. I wrote to Mr. Sheppard last Friday about tools & have no reply. I find it utterly improbable with our mail facilities to submit questions that arrive to the Co. for decision & await their reply. If I hear nothing I shall purchase the tools here & go to work. We expect Fox or his partner here from Buffalo today & if we are able shall go to P. R. tomorrow. Our "Sixty days" don't shorten any yet. It will be a long sixty I fear ever we are through. It is raining mildly (noon) which is refreshing. Well contrary to my intentions I have been to dinner. Fared better but is a great price for a little food but I "eat to live". We have just heard from the upper lease at C. R. The tools are in the well. The auger stem parted where it should have been welded. There is no end to accidents & hindrances. It is nearly useless to make calculations.

    There is a cheap summer hat worn here by such girls as Ida. I think it is called a Sea Side Hat. It is Chinese in form with but little trimming. It is the most sensible thing I have known the Ladies to tolerate & if they can be bought in your city please supply Ida with one at once & annihilate that little Bob tailed abortion of hers. In form the new hat is much like mine with the rim turned down. I had so little time when at home even to think that many things were left undone that are important. One of them the manner of spending the vacationing. The suggestion that Ida made or heard of studying pleases me much if it would be agreeable to all parties. If not & nothing else offers a system of sewing & needlework or something that will interest as well as instruct. Of course, first of all rest & recreation. I wish she could be with me in my exile for a time at least. I must write to her soon but our tardy mails knock all the poetry out of letter writing.

    I just stopped to take my dose & was reminded it is your favorite Medicine, "Valerian". Mine is compounded with Aqua Ammonia. The one to quiet the other, to stir me up as a model driver whips his horse & then holds him. O! I shall soon be well if not more so. I regret my sheet is so small. It's a pity such a letter must end so. I yield to fate. Yours Affectionately, Love to All who wish it.

B. Munger.

Oil City June 16th, 1865

My Darling Little Treasure,

      It is Friday morning. Orett & Mr. Fox have gone to Panther Run & left me to wait for a man to take some tools & then I am to follow on if I can as they think I can keep up with them. That sounds odd, that your father can't keep up. Well perhaps it is so for I am some weak. I have now been sick one week tomorrow & I assure you it has been a dull week. I wrote to Nettie last night in answer to one from her. She is teaching in Cheshire, Ont. Co. She writes it is a lonely place & she feels sad sometimes. I suppose we poor humans all do at times I expect I shall not be able to finish this now or today but will write as I have opportunity. I want to tell you what Nettie says in her letter & see if you ever experienced such feelings & had such thoughts. She says, "I could bear all my loneliness, all my sad hours & all my little trials if I were only <u>good</u> really <u>good</u>." But my good resolves are all broken & my aspirations never reached.

      Poor, dear Nettie, I know just how to pity her. And I suppose I know just how to pity another <u>Darling</u>. Do I? Well I do pity them both & pity all who are so troubled. Every new position brings with it new trials. So your change of home will not only add to your pleasures & advantages but to your trials & perhaps temptations. You know I have sometimes told you it was misfortunate to be an only child. While to my perceptions very few of the usual results are apparent in your case. Perhaps someone with less affection & equal justice can see in your case what I see in ordinary cases. It will be well my Darling to be on your guard at least to see if <u>you</u> can discover any such effects. Above all Little Pet where you have done a wrong be <u>faithful</u> & <u>truthful</u> in acknowledging your faults. This is not only good cure but good as prevention to the errors. Shun as you shun death the last deviation from <u>truth</u>. Don't understand me as recommending sadness or solemnity. Whatever promotes real cheerfulness & happiness is pleasing to God.

      It is now Sunday, 10 A.M. since commencing this I have been to Panther Run & staid two days. I am much better & there is still room for improvement. As I shall write to Mother today I will give the general news in that so things may be <u>exclusive</u> if you wish it. If I have kept the figures right this is your last school week & consequently will be a busy one. I hope you will fill your own expectations in regard to study & c. & your teachers also. Your music I trust has been resumed & is as agreeable as of old. If we strike a "Hundred barrel well" I'll send for you to come see me in my <u>retreat</u>. As I fear I shall not be able to write much in future. I think of no better way than for you to write more. I suppose I need about two letters to you one having so much less to interest me. Now Little One, I must say Good bye. Be a good girl, O! so good.

Your loving father,

B. Munger

Oil City June 21, 1865

My Dear Wife & Daughter,

I recd. yours of the 15th (I think) at Panther Run yesterday morning & yours & Ida's of the 18th (By way of Meadville) at this place last night. Mr. Hazen of the Union Co. has just arrived to investigate & c. I am writing under difficulties, the office so full. I am better, walked from P.R. after 6 P.M. last night for fixtures & c. We return this A.m. by way of C.R. Mr. Hazen will go with us. Hope to start the Richmond well today & the Uncle Abe this week.

We have the most magnificent supply of water conveyed in wooden troughs from the Run you ever saw. You must not feel anxious about us. We shall get along finely. Tell Lyman not to look at matters through such gloomy "specs". There is surely grounds for strong hope I while it is wise to prepare for the worst it is not wise to assume that the worst will necessarily come to pass. We are doing all that we poor humans can to succeed 7 you might try to be hopeful.

I am glad Mr. Hazen has come. He can do more toward enlightening the Co. than could be done any other way. I am in a great hurry this morning & write because it is the only opportunity probably till Sunday. We have not yet returned the office but are trying to. I hate to give it up but it is best. Be hopeful & cheerful & trust that all will yet be well. Love, a liberal supply to all.

Your Aff. Husband & Father,

B. Munger

Oil City July 2nd, 1865

My Dear Wife,

This has been a week of experiences. I went to Panther Run on Monday morning & staid till yesterday (Saturday) I suppose you have seen Mr. Hazen & learned all he knew of me which was up to Tuesday noon. Monday, we found the tools were too large & would not go into the well & decided to ream it to 5 inches. The first work was to draw the iron pipe & put down wooden. We started the drill on Tuesday & have had the usual amount of accidents & incidents doing the work. The cold water pump would not work. Spent half a day in fixing it. Next the throttle valve was out of rig & would not stop the engine. The consequence was the breaking of a temper screw & a close escape from a broken head. Then a defect in the tools which made it necessary to take them to the city. From Wednesday noon, I worked the drill my regular term of 12 hours per day stopping at midnight. I doubt some whether I shall be able to endure it if it proves too severe I shall give it up. I am not yet strong though pretty well. Our well at P.R. has done little, the engine not working well. We hope it is now in order & that this week will be a more successful one.

If it would not give you the blues I would like you peep at us in our native glory. We come about as near the bone as is possible to get, sleep on straw that is since we were able to but two bundles at one dollar, before that on a board and the board floor. I can't do the subject justice. This is the first week I have spent wholly at the Run but as I have but milk & eat on my own hook when I could not eat at the

Trough. I got along nicely. I think it will take us till about the first of Sept. to finish up the wells & then I hope to make a good visit. Oil has been found only about 5 rods from our Cherry Run wells. The well is said to yield 50 bbls daily. This demonstrates the fact that there is oil on that bluff & increase the probabilities of our success very much. The oil was struck at 620 feet. One of ours is now down 340 so you may hope to hear from us in about 4 weeks. I recd. yours by Pling on Tuesday last. On the 29th I recd. one from you dated the 15th & mailed on the 26th at what place I can't make out but you remark in it that Ione will take it to Meadville. I recd. yours of the 29th last night (a quick trip) and was impressed with the fact that the blues are not confined to Oil City. Indeed, I think you exceed me in the "Ultra Marine" a thing unnecessary. You will be obliged to put up one letter per week while I stay at the Run.

Two years ago, this day I wrote you from the top of a rock near the Gettysburg battlefield thinking perhaps it would be my last (& indeed it came near being). We have not the cause for depression we had at that time. My surroundings that night were as such as I never wish to have repeated. I lay near the Amputating Table you will recollect. O! oildom is better than battlefields & field hospitals & when I reflect I do think it cowardly to complain.

This is a cool, cloudy day we have all been to church. To come to this office, have a good wash & enjoy the comforts of life seem like a little heaven compared with our country life. Pling thinks Jordon is decidedly a hard road to travel & Panther Run not a good place to stop at. Six weeks has a long look to him. Orett will write to his father today, I perhaps will not. I have nothing especially to say. I recd. Ansel Booth's letter & will reply when I can. To say I would love to be home on the coming Forth would be a sinful expression of vain desire. I presume and I am no such man as that.

Pling has had the imprudence to ask me if I would not like to be home today. "Of course", I answered him, as he deserved. The boy shows great want of moral culture he had the brass to say he wanted to see his mother. We'll cure him of all such mention. I suppose there is a family where you board. If so remember me to them. I am seldom reminded of the fact. If I could say a word to cheer & encourage L. would gladly do so but I confess I don't. That he looks as our financial condition with less hopefulness than the facts warranted. I fully believe that we have got to struggle like death to get through is true but I hope to come out sound. If we utterly fail I am inclined to think O. & I had better stay here for a time at least. I know of no place where we can earn as much money without capital as here. We have heard of Hamlin's flowing well? And hope we may be as successful. We will come home about the first of Sept. have a "grand talk". In the mean time, I want so to get strong & I think the world will then look bright to him. I'll finish a letter to Ida if I have time.

Your Affectionate Husband,

B. Munger

Oil City July 4, 1865

My Dear Wife & Daughter,

I am unexpectedly in the city tonight & as Charles Elmendorf will leave in the morning for Penn Yan. I will avail myself the opportunity to write to you. O! the trials of a poor oil digger. If I simply tell you my experience it will sound like complaint. But I am happy to be able to report some progress, the Cherry Run Wells Run is also working & doing finely & the Fox engine at the Uncle Abe well. Panther Run is also working well but the old Richmond engine is not on its good behavior. L. will understand it when I tell him. The throttle valve leaks steam to such an extent that it will run the engine with sufficient force to drill with the valve shut as close as we can shut it. The reason it did not trouble you, is pumping requires so much more power than drilling that the leak had less effect. I expect to get a new value. The danger is great at times & twice I have no one under pay at present. Orett is at work like a lark & we are getting to be No. 1 engineers. Pling is doing pretty well at cooking. I am hardly strong enough yet to work with ease & I am sometimes taxed almost beyond endurance but I hope it will be easier soon. Eb. Smith called this evening, says he called on you yesterday morning but brings <u>no letters, no messages</u>. I was glad to see a man who had so recently been to the house. Has D. Wagner paid that note? If not I wish you would leave it with Esqr. Hoyt for collection. This I suppose has been at least a busy day in Penn Yan. I hope you have enjoyed it. I never want to see another just like it. I took a letter from the office tonight for Orett from Martha. I judge post marked the 20th inst. Love to all. Good night.

Your Husband & Father,

B. Munger

Oil City July 5, 1865

My Dear Wife & Daughter,

I recd. yours of the 2nd tonight & although I wrote you last night by Charles Elmendorf, I will add a word. I have remained in the city all day getting my new valve fitted. It is done & on the boat & will go up in the morning at 7:30. I hope it will work. It cost $25.00. You say it is not good for man to be alone. I have found that to be true but have often wondered how the Lord found it out so quick. But Mary, we must struggle here till we get our money back if that thing is <u>possible</u> or till something better presents itself in some other. My pride & ambition will not allow me to return to Penn Yan a whipped man if human exertion can prevent it. I am not in love with this kind of life I assure you. Mrs. Robbins arrived yesterday. That is tantalizing but "I'm tough".

I am expecting Orett down & have for three hours. It is now 8 O'clock. You say L. is writing. I do not receive it. Perhaps it is in one of Orett's. I go up the river in the morning. I have rested greatly since last night. Am inclined to jaundice continually but am fighting it off. I am rejoiced to hear L. is doing well. I saw Robins today. He told me his wife did not bring a favorable account of him. I felt alarmed & your letter reassures me. I recd. a letter from Abigale tonight. She is full of trouble, is going to leave all & go to Ill. Is trying to persuade Mother to go with her. Abbie will stay at Merrick's. Wishes all letters for her directed to Frank.

Well, Pet you started off with a startling announcement that it is the 2nd of July & the year almost gone. I was astonished! It is indeed the 2nd of July down here but as these Pennsylvania Dutch count time the year is only about half gone. You must live fast in York State, but your tooth affair was clearly a feat & I am heartily glad that you have got rid of it at so <u>small</u> a cost & I confess I am a little proud of your <u>courage</u> I if you can always be made brave at that price you shall never be a cowered while I have money. Ma's ideas of extravagance are perfectly "Foggy".

So, Joseph has a wife eh? Well that's legal & Mother has bought that sensible hat another good thing. I seldom rebel against any fashion as I did against those abominable "Bob & Sinkers". And now with that tooth out & a new hat (Floric one also) I expect great things of you if the year don't slip too quick for you. I will not mail this tonight in hope that Orett will yet be down & I may have something more to write. It is now 9 O'clock.

Thursday morning, 7 O'clock. O. has not come. I leave immodestly on foot for P.R. The morning is fine but warm. The great combined Circus, Menagerie, Caravan, Show & Humbug is entering town with colors flying & I will leave. Shall be down Saturday night. Good morning, much love.

Yours, B. Munger

Oil City Tuesday morning July 11th, 1865

My Dear Wife & Daughter,

As I am unexpectedly in the city I will drop you a word to "Provoke you to good works" and "I've an account of my stewardship". Sunday evening Pling & I walked to P.R. as contemplated we arrived about 9. Burns had a fire in the Fox engine, the boiler of which was leaking badly & as the leak was above the furnace it was difficult to keep a fire. I went to bed if lying down on straw in the engine house is going to bed but could not sleep little as Burns was tinkering the engine & I knew I must get up at 12. When I got up I found that Burns had built a fire for me so I called Nugent & went to work. The reamer sticks badly. The rock being soft, it drives in much as it would into clay, stops our engine & we must jar it loose by hand which is severe work. We had a new hand come on this morning. One of those men with whom nothing is quite right. He knows everything. Our hole is flat not round as it should be. The tools do not turn in the well. The rope only twists. We must have a round reamer or never succeed & c. To all of which I replied, "Do the best you can with the means furnished you since that is all we require of you."

One of the reamers has a fine crack making it unsafe & we are getting it repaired. Walked down last night after 5, making about 20 hours of continuous labor. I was tired, sleepy, some "Blue" & do you believe it, just a little <u>cross</u>. I have got over that feeling better & am most ready to walk back to P.R. & repeat the experience of yesterday. A boat goes up the river daily leaving this city at 8:30 A.M. & by it we send such articles as we have occasion to up or down. My reamer cannot be finished in time to go up this morning so I shall return on foot & have the reamer sent tomorrow.

Orett was at C.R. yesterday. In one of the wells a piece of a center bit is lost but they think there will be no difficulty & little delay in taking it out. O. is much elated with the prospect there. You can't imagine what a convenience this office is. We come down from the river tired, dirty & <u>dilapidated</u> & you do not know how it rests & recruits us to have such a place to go to. I am making an effort to keep it at reduced rent. We had a powerful rain last night & it still looks rainy. I now leave for the modern paradise P.R. I have come to the conclusion when I engineer the reaming of an old well again to save cost to ourselves instead of letting it by the job it will be someday when my benevolence gets the better of my judgement. Good morning.

Much love,

B. Munger

My Dear Wife & Daughter,

I recd. yours of the 9th inst. at Panther Run on the 13th & yours of the 13th last night. I wrote you on last on Tuesday the 11th. I have recd. during the last week letters also Mr. Sheppard, Mr. Richmond's brother (with drafts for $200), Lyman, Abigail & Nettie. Since Tuesday nothing has occurred of special interest. I have come to the full conclusion that reaming an old well is no fool of a job. We get our tools fast that is stuck in the well probably ten times a day which makes the labor severe & progress slow. I continue to run my portion of the time (from midnight to noon) besides being there most of the remainder of the day to assist. I feel today very much worked down though I have performed my labor easier than previously. My part this week has been attending to the drill. I am called at 12 & getting up at that hour is peculiarly agreeable. The nights this week have been very cool which has added to our comforts.

Imagine me at that time of night seated on a stool 6 feet high with one hand hold of the rope & the other on temper screw which moves up & down 40 times per minute turning the rope ¼ round at each vibration & the screw down at the drill penetrates the rock. When the work goes well it takes from one to two hours to drill the length of the screw & I sit there till I fall asleep & would fall from the stool but the support of the rope. If the screw is turned ¼ inch too much the tools stick & everything is brought up standing. Sometimes we can relieve them in 5 minutes & sometimes it takes as many hours. This is the hard work of it. Tools seldom stick in a new well. The cause of sticking is the walls or sides of hole become soft by the action of air & water so that the reamer forced into the hole by the rocks yielding not breaking much as a stake is driven into the ground. We have reamed 80 feet this week and at noon yesterday were down 205 feet. Our well, the Uncle Abe was down 175 so you see they go about as fast as I do & will ultimately beat me. "The Show" is abundant daubing everything & everybody. Crazy Jane is a <u>Hoss</u> of a cook. Excuse the term, I know of no other that will as well express my mind.

This morning is cold, rainy & dreary. I got up at 9 O'clock preferring to lose my breakfast for a good sleep. We have 2 ½ hours to dinner for which I am fully prepared. When I work drilling for the Co. I charge them for my time the same as I pay others in addition to what they pay me for superintending. Is there any wrong in it? Give me your opinion & Lyman's. It will require all we can earn & save to pay our assessments & expenses & a hard rub at that. The prospects at Cherry Run continue as good as ever & perhaps better. Still I am not sanguine & am prepared for the worst. Layman mentioned Hamlin's note & asks if we shall be able to meet it. No, I told young Hamlin when I signed it. There was not the least prospect of our being able to meet it at maturity. I think I will not have time to write to L. today. Show him this. It will give him an idea what we are doing. You ask if you shall send my linen coat.

No, I shall not need it much & you need do nothing about shirts at present. I think I can get along till I can come home if I can get away in September. Which I hope to do for a little while at least. I shall <u>need</u> a full suit then. It is noon & I shall stop till after <u>breakfast</u>.

   3 P.M. I have breakfast & finished another letter. It is raining hard & a walk of 6 miles, a nap of 3 hours & a sitting of 12 hours on my stool are subjects of joyous anticipations. I am not fully rested today & do not feel quite as much like "Stemming the storm" as usually. I can't write to Ida specially today. I hope she is good & happy. I recd. the kisses, all are fresh but to tell the truth I prefer receiving them the <u>other</u> <u>way</u>. Tell little Hattie, hers came safe & good as paper kiss can be & I will pay in genuine when I come. Remember me to Florie also. They ought to be happy though.

   Does L. ever talk with the members of the Union Co.? If he does what is the feeling generally. I rejoice he (L.) is gaining so rapidly, still he must not think of work at present. Have you heard anything about my taxes? Make your financial report &c. My old cloths I brought are just what I now need & my cavalry overcoat I shall take with me tonight for use. These cold nights it will spoil it but better spoil it than me. I regret I did not keep my woolen suites here. This would be good work to finish them in. Remember me to the family & all friends. I hope O. will be able to be home in 4 or 5 weeks as both must not be absent at once. Your Affectionate Husband & Father,

B. Munger

                           Oil City Aug. 2, 1865

My Dear Wife & Daughter,

   I recd. yours of the 30th tonight & though late (10 O'clock) will answer. I recd. a telegram from Mr. Sheppard, Sunday morning & was preparing Monday to execute his orders when L. W. Gage, treasurer of the Co. came & after looking around thought I had better wait till he got home & made a statement to the Co. Consequently, I am not working as hard as usual unless it be in walking. I walked 12 miles Monday, 5 yesterday & 12 again today. We had hoped to test one at least of the wells on Cherry Run this week but I fear we shall not. The tools stuck in the upper well (which is nearest to completion) last Saturday & are still fast. We hope the other to be completed this week. The upper well is very promising & we have strong hopes of a good well but you must be prepared for disappointment for this is the most uncertain business in this uncertain world. But if we fail in oil we are not discouraged it will only take longer to accomplish our object.

   I regret your health is so poor it unfits one for enjoyment. You ask about what time I can come home. I really can't tell. I am more uncertain about it than I was a month ago, but if I can't go by the first of October you may come here if you wish to. I can tell more about it in a week or two. I wrote to Emma Day only a few days since requesting her to visit Penn Yan & trust she will. Well Ida I don't see as you need me at all. I think Mr. Joy devotes himself more than I could if at home. I am really glad he can & will do so much to promote your happiness. I hope you are very good & still growing better. It is very late & I must retire. Love to all. Good night & God's blessings.

B. Munger

Oil City - Aug 4th, 1865

My Little Darling,

It is a long time since I devoted a letter wholly to you. I have been very busy for a month & when I had time sufficient to write felt too tired or too sleepy to do so. I have had "more" leisure this week I think I must visit a little with my Pet. Your vacation is nearly closed I suppose. I hope you have enjoyed it very much & are all rested for a new campaign. Have you followed to your own satisfaction the plan you laid out for yourself at the close of school this strengthening practice your good theory of tenacity of purpose?

Now, you know Darling, I have a good guesser & I guess though you have tried hard you have encountered almost every day something to divert you from your plan of study & c. & in looking back it seems to you that you have alone very little as you intended when school closed. I may be all wrong in my guess. Write & tell me about it & give me your experience & struggles for if you have been good you have had struggles. You will think all to yourself, won't say it to anybody, "I wonder what made Pa guess so? Has anyone been talking to him?" No, but all little girls & boys and what is worse big ones also have had just that sort of experience of they have laid out a plan of good conduct and tried to follow it. In an old school book, I used to read was this passage, "Weak & insolent is man. The purpose of today wore with pain into his plan tomorrow sends away." I guess he meant little girls too.

Mr. Easton has been in & I had to stop & talk with him & I think quite likely some little one will be glad he came & mad a **P** in this letter. Mr. E. seems to think this is a poor country to stay in & is in a hury to get home although he only left home on Monday last. Poor taste his. I suppose Pling will have a great deal of news to tell you for he had an experience here & has seen much that will interest you girls. May be for a time you will not be able to make him eat anything. He is much in love with crazy Jane's cooking. Give him pork that will fetch him to. Well, Mr. Gardener has called & is also going home tonight. I feel I shall get demoralized at this rate. It is 3 O'clock & Pling has not returned only two hours to train time. It thunders & a cloud is visiting which looks like giving us a cooler. It has rained almost every day for six weeks & at times most powerfully.

How I wish I could drop in among you this afternoon & see how you spend your time. I think I could stir you up some. I calculate to visit very fast when I do come so look out. I expect you will be able to play to me so that I shall be astonished. You must sit down some time when you have leisure to think & write me about yourself just as you think we would talk if I was with you. Such letters are most as good as a visit. Tell me all your difficulties in trying to be good. You can't tell how I want to see you sometimes. How anxious I am that you should be a very good girl. I regret that I am compelled to be so much away from you. Do you ever feel as if you wanted a father? Give my love to all the family & there is a great piece in here for you. By the way, the kisses you send though good get so dry I can't hear the smack & I mean to save all mine to give when I come. Be very good.

Your loving father,

B. Munger

Note to the reader: The next letter in this grouping only has a partial date and appears in order after the letter of the 4th of August.

Oil City   August   1865

My Precious Darling,

I rec'd you're your letter with Mother's Wednesday evening. I was glad as always am to receive your letters. My object in writing to & receiving letters from you (besides present pleasure) is to assist you in your efforts to become a <u>noble</u> <u>Christian</u> <u>woman</u>. I take it as granted this is your object. Let me point out to you Darling what seems to me the great <u>lack</u> in the ladies (girls & women are better names) of our country & day & the things I wish you to avoid. It is a want of thought, reflection a want of proper appreciation of the objects of life. In short they are <u>frivolous</u>. This is not true of all but I am sorry to say it is true of too many. Not so much their fault as misfortune. Neither is it a lack of capacity & I think in many cases not for want of real earnest desire to be all they ought to be.

How often I have seen ladies when conversation turned on subjects with which they thought have been familiar appear pained, humiliated that they were unable to take part in it. Perhaps this is rather <u>old</u> <u>talk</u> for my "Little one" but I hardly know how I can make you understand what I wish you to be without pointing out the common errors of others. In your case a want of <u>opportunity</u> to think is your great misfortune. How differently you & I are situated. I am entirely alone three fourths of the time. I suppose you are not one tenth. I visit a great deal with your father. Every person should be alone some portion of each day. I am alone too much it has a tendency to make me unsocial, cold. You are not enough alone the tendency is to <u>frivolity</u>. Why? The mind is occupied for the moment with what you see & hear changing as the scene changes but not impressed with anything. Much like reading a novel you are amused but <u>not</u> <u>instructed</u>.

To make my advice practical let me suggest a plan. Perhaps every day, you see something that interests you & that you do not perfectly understand cultivate the habit of investigating such subjects or things till you comprehend perfectly all about it if it requires a month never mind it. Take a month. My word, for if you are earnest in it, it will be a month well spent. It makes no difference what it is if it contains a principle you do not understand it is worth "thinking out". For example & to give a subject. Why is it that one key of your piano gives a high, shrill tone & another a dull, heavy one? Perhaps you don't see at once & you ask someone. They tell you that the string or wire giving the heavy sounds is much heavier & longer than the other. That is true but if you are a true Yankee you will not be satisfied with that but will seek to know why a large, heavy body makes a duller sound than a small one. You will be obliged to ask many questions. Consult your books on philosophy & discover new facts for many months.

In the case of Aggie, I presume will cheerfully tell you all you wish about the vibrations of strings or wires producing musical sounds &c. if you ask her when she is not too busy. I only give this to give you a idea of what I mean. One can hardly walk a rod without finding a subject for pleasing that and profitable investigation. Ask any one able & willing to tell you & if you do it politely & seek an opportunity where not otherwise occupied most anyone will give you all the information you seek. Uncle

Layman is a natural philosopher & will help you, I have no doubt. If you persevere in your investigations & reasoning's you will ultimately so far as intelligence is concerned be all you can desire. I have little space left for the other subject goodness & will sometime devote another letter to that. I am much pleased to learn you are persevering with your music. I shall hope to be entertained when I come home.

Your loving father,

B. Munger

Oil City Sunday Aug. 6, 1865

My Dear Wife & Daughter,

  I recd. yours by Mr. Robbins last night, previously recd. one by Mr. Sheldon. I wrote you at length by Pling who will tell you all so that I have really nothing to write. The tools remain fast in both Cherry Run wells. I have recd. no message from the Union Co. & shall commence tubing tomorrow morning if I hear nothing from them. The Uncle Abe we intend to tube Monday or Tuesday. If nothing occurs to hinder I think we shall be able to report something definite in relation to Panther Run this week. The closing of the Philpot & Sherman well narrows down our opportunities somewhat. Our work in future will not be hard, nothing but overseeing.

  Hills arrived yesterday at noon, is not favorably impressed, thinks of returning tomorrow or next day. Mr. Looker, Abigail's old boarder came with him to Titusville & is to remain there as agent for a New York City Co. We expect some little trouble with Mr. Burns, he don't like to stop drilling but I think we shall get along without serious difficulty. Philpot & Sherman gave him two hundred and fifty dollars to quit their job. How are you financed? Has Wagner paid? Please answer in your next. Love to all.

Your Affectionate Husband & Father,

B. Munger

Oil City Aug 16, 1865

My Dear Wife & Daughter,

  I have this moment finished reading your Sunday letters. The first from any source I have recd. since Saturday night. As I have written Orett daily since his departure & as you will hear there I will give only an account of this day's proceedings. This morning I started early with a reducer for P.R. Drew tubing which we were obliged to do by hand as the seed bag would not trim. I put on the seed bag to go down 257 feet, reached about 200 feet & the bag stuck & refused to go another foot. We worked on it till night & abandoned the effort & shall draw again & bag to the spot where the bag stuck.

The U. A. is doing as usual, <u>nothing</u>. I left at 6:15 & walked down in an hour & a quarter this securing my supper. I am one tired <u>individual</u>. I assure you. Burns is on the anxious seat but I am very good & kind to him. I paid the Nichols boys today, $60.50. This settles with all but Graham & Miller. The new well nearly opposite us is being tested again today & it unexpectedly yielded some oil & a great flow of water.

There is a well a little below us on the same side of the river over 800 feet deep & will be tested this week. I look with a great deal of interest for the result. This letter is partly for Orett & will be understood by him. Please excuse a short letter tonight for I am very tired & will write at length Sunday. I will explain to Ida that P "paragraph denotes the beginning of a new subject". Do you take?

Yours, B. Munger

"Garden City"

Petroleum Mining and Manufacturing Company,

CAPITAL STOCK $500,000,

DIVIDED INTO 50,000 SHARES OF TEN DOLLARS EACH.

INCORPORATED UNDER THE LAWS OF ILLINOIS.

Principal Office, Room No. 2, Tyler's Block, La Salle St., bet. Lake & South Water.

OFFICERS:

C. J. GILBERT, President. T. P. LAWRENCE, Secretary.
WM. E. ROLLO, Treasurer. J. M. WALKER, Counsel.

DIRECTORS:

C. J. GILBERT.   CHAS. M. CULBERTSON.   J. M. WALKER.
BENJ. F. MURPHY.   WM. F. TUCKER.   E. C. WILDER.
T. P. LAWRENCE.

The property of this Company consists of **Four Hundred and Ninety-two and Sixty-three One-Hundredths Acres** of land in *Lewis County*, Kentucky, being lot number seventeen on J. A. Drake's Subdivision of Oil Lands, and adjacent to the "Daniel Boone," "Simon Kenton," and numerous other tracts, where wells are being sunk with the most flattering prospects for an abundant yield of Oil.

The title is clear and unincumbered, and is transferred to the Company without royalty. By referring to the subjoined Map, and the report by S. W. Ely, Esq., an experienced practical Geologist, who has devoted a great deal of time to the selection and development of oil territory, the geological and superior advantages of this tract will be readily seen.

This tract has been examined by several of the most celebrated oil men of Oil Creek, and it is their unbiased and unsolicited opinion, that it will, upon development, prove as productive as the most favored portions of Oil Creek or Cherry Run, in Venango County.

The Company is composed of business men of this city, *who have purchased the lands for the purpose of developing them*. Every arrangement is being made for a vigorous prosecution of their work.

The Books of the Company are now open, and a limited amount of the Stock only, will be offered for sale to subscribers, at Four (4) Dollars per Share.

The following oil stock documents pertaining to Capt. Munger's speculations are courtesy of Shelly Case, West Chester, Pa.

GEOLOGICAL REPORT:

To the Officers and Members of
   THE "*GARDEN CITY*" *PETROLEUM COMPANY,*
                  Chicago, Illinois.

GENTLEMEN:—Understanding that you have purchased the piece of land in Mr. J. A. DRAKE'S "Oil Tract," in Lewis County, Kentucky, designated as number seventeen, in the recorded plat of the said tract, I comply with a request to give you a description of the same.

The place alluded to contains nearly four hundred and ninety-three acres, on Straight Fork, and the waters of that stream. The tract is in an oblong parallelogram, one hundred and seventy-four by four hundred and fifty-three poles, the shortest diameter being in a north and south direction. The main stream crosses the northwestern portion of the land; and its various branches are so disposed as to create a large amount of boring territory. A glance at the accompanying map will show four of these branches on either side of the main stream. The surface being cut up in so many sections, it follows that the hills between do not attain so great elevation as in those on portions of the great "Tract," of which this piece is near the center. Much of the land has a gently undulating, or nearly level, surface. There is here an extensive swale, bordered by precipitous mountains, and clothed with the finest timber, indigenous to the soil and climate. With these characteristics of your tract, peculiar to it, I proceed to appropriate such portions of my general description of Mr. DRAKE'S land as are here applicable.

Geology.—The geologic layers of this district are based, of course, on the blue limestone formation of the Silurian period, on which our own city is built. Immediately over this, is found the magnesian limestone, (or rather,) calciferous magnesium—for the compound is said to contain sixty per centum of carbonate of magnesia,) which Prof. OWEN says is fifty or sixty feet thick—[Kentucky Geological Report, volume three, article on Lewis County]—and which, dipping southeastwardly, disappears beneath the river bottom at Vanceburg. In some places, however, a marly clay intervenes between the blue and the magnesian limestone. This latter is overlaid by the black *Lingula* shale, which is highly carboniferous—the oils and gases therein contained exuding at a moderate heat, and burning with a bright flame, when ignited. Over this the wall-like slabs and shales are found, which so liken this district to the oil bearing field of Venango County, Pennsylvania. The same beautiful "ripple marks," so common there, the same alternating sandstones and argillaceous slates, which compose the western wall of the great oleaginous valley of Oil Creek, seem transplanted here. In addition, we here observe, in great variety, the petrous remains of those Devonian seaweeds (*fucoids*) which Professor WILLIAMS believes contributed largely to the volume of carboniferous liquid beneath that valley, leaving there, however, no other trace of their pre-existence. Another layer of shale, one hundred and twenty feet thick, overlies these, on which reposes the twelve feet bed of claystone, (resembling *steatite*, and popularly called "soapstone,") from the crevices of which exudes the thick surface oil which discovers itself in the "springs" of the region, and gave rise, some years since, to the conviction that yours were petroleum lands. Over this, is the beautiful "city ledge" layer of freestone, so much used and so highly valued by the builders of Cincinnati. Above this, other beds and layers of shales and sandstones, some of the latter curiously fractured throughout their entire extent, doubtless by some violent tremor or eccentric motion of the earth, are seen out-cropping, and often out-dropping, from the beetling precipices—thus completing the geologic column.

The domolite, or magnesian limestone, which it is fair to infer underlies your entire tract, may be traced in the hills, as one steams up the Ohio, from below Rome, for a distance of about nine miles, to Vanceburg, where, as we have seen, this layer dips beneath the river. Everywhere, along this line, strong marks of erosion or disintegration are visible, and plainly discernable from the boat, as one passes them, displaying irregular seams and caverns in all sorts of fanciful shapes. I am credibly informed, that these are openings into subterranean passages and cavities, which extend hundreds of yards beneath the hills, and have often been penetrated by daring explorers. It has occurred to me that these caves and cells, in the same deposite beneath your lands, furnish receptacles for the repose of oil and gases, as their carbonaceous compound possibly supplies the acid which enters into the formation of petroleum. Salt, saltpeter, potash, and other alkalies, it is now admitted, bear a vital relation to rock oil, to produce which it is no longer deemed necessary to rob the coal beds. The location of your lands bears a comparative relation to the *situs* of the coals and limestones of Greenup and Carter Counties precisely analagous to the relative position of the Oil Creek Valley and the nearest coal, to the southeast of it.

Boring alone can disclose the exact thickness of the oil bearing strata of your lands, as they repose on the demolite aforesaid. From their *congeners* to the westward, it is probable the drill will penetrate the magnesian rock at an average depth of about four hundred and fifty feet from the surface of your lowest valleys.

Oil Signs.—Many of these are inferable from what is said above. A "practical oil man" of my acquaintance quaintly observes, "the best sign of oil is the oil itself." Both of us, and hundreds of others, have witnessed the thick, black, fine surface oil, which exudes from the "soapstone" deposit above described, in several places, on your lands. Salt "licks" and springs are found on the lands, and "gas wells" emitting volumes of inflammable air, both "signs" of the presence of oil, other phenomena being favorable, are seen in various places. It is probable, by the way, that the brines obtainable on your lands, are much stronger than those of the old salt wells immediately back of Vanceburg, inasmuch as the saliferous rocks are several hundred feet deeper in the former than in the latter locality. I shall expect that the borings pursued to the depth of five or six hundred feet, will furnish streams of strong salt water. Wherever stone quarries have been opened, in the vicinity, oil stains and the smell of petroleum are plain to the senses. For years the district has been considered "oil territory," from the number of oil springs, and much of the neighborhood was accordingly "leased," pending the present war. My deductions lead me to prefer your tract as an oil bearing field, to some others, where the surface indications are equally favorable, because it is situate well "into the bowels of the land," farther southeast of the line of outcrop of the lowest layer of the formation than those others, and still not so far as to come in contact with the coal series, or to render the borings liable to prove too deep and expensive.

Within the last six months, great excitement has ensued the examination and development of the Lewis County oil field. The great beds of carbonaceous shale, two hundred and fifty feet thick in the aggregate, which underlie your lands, have been proven to abound with stores of petroleum of the finest quality, and establishments are being erected for distilling the oil from the black and olive layers. Lands have been sold and leased, at high prices, for the purpose of boring, and considerable progress has been made, with flattering prospects of success. On the "Daniel Boone Company" grounds, four miles north of your lands, on Straight Fork, the oil rock was reached at thirty-three feet from the surface, and the indications of a paying yield have rapidly multiplied, as the augur point approaches the base of the shale. In localities where this latter rock shows its entire thickness in the hills, (in the western portions of the field,) a vein of volatile, illuminating oil has been discovered, which undoubtedly exists on the same geological level beneath your lands—for I am forcibly impressed with the belief that petroleum, like salt brines, coals, and other mineral productions, may be found most certainly in the embraces of those rocks in which nature has implanted their producing elements.

In prosecuting your developments, you will meet with great encouragement from the works of your neighbors, whose well directed efforts promise early and complete success. That you will be among the most successful, there is every good reason to believe, and to such end you have my best wishes.

Very respectfully, your obedient servant,

Cincinnati, O., March 1, 1865.

SENECA W. ELY.

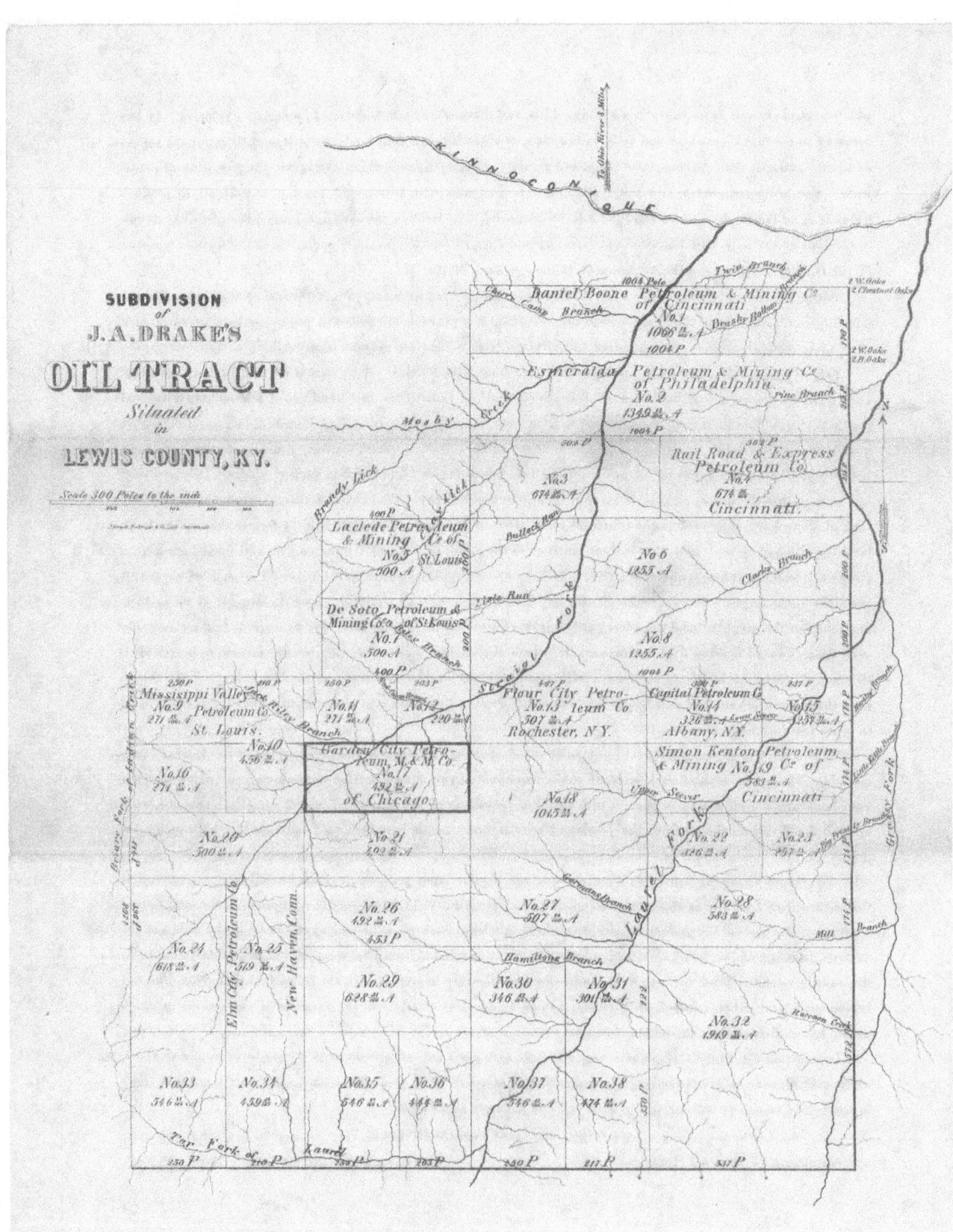

THE LACLEDE PETROLEUM AND MINING COMPANY.

Capital Stock - $200,000.

DIVIDED INTO 4,000 SHARES OF $50,00 EACH.
SUBSCRIPTION PRICE $25,00 PER SHARE.

INCORPORATED UNDER THE LAWS OF OHIO.

DAVID GIBSON, President.   LAFAYETTE DEVENNY, Secretary and Treasurer.

DIRECTORS.

David Gibson, of David Gibson & Co.	Cincinnati.	Ralph Tousey, of Ladue, Tousey & Co.	St. Louis.
Lafayette Devenny, Pres. Queen City Insurance Co.	"	J. W. Donohue, of J. W. Donohue & Co.	Cincinnati.
H. C. Creveling, Supt. St. Louis Transfer Co.	St. Louis.	J. N. Kinney, Gen. Freight Agt. Little Miami R. R.	"

OFFICES.

No. 35 West Third Street, Cincinnati, Ohio, and
Banking House of Ladue, Tousey & Co. Cor. Second & Pine Sts. St. Louis.

This Company was incorporated December 30th, 1864, under the General Corporation Laws of the State of Ohio, and will commence boring for Oil and otherwise developing their land immediately.

Capital $200,000, number of shares 4,000, par value $50 each; *shares are now sold to subscribers at $25.00 each.*

The Company owns, in fee simple five hundred acres of land in Lewis County, Kentucky, 10 miles south of Vanceburg, on the Ohio River, and in the valley of Kinnick-kinnick Creek, a tributary of the Ohio, and is part of the celebrated Oil Tract of J. A. Drake, Esq., recently purchased from him.

This tract is in close proximity to the lands of the celebrated *"Daniel Boone Petroleum and Mining Company,"* which is now engaged in sinking wells upon their property, and has found a fine flow of oil at a depth of 65 feet from the surface, in consequence of which their stock has advanced four fold.

An advantage enjoyed by wells so close to the Ohio River is evident, from the fact that crude oil can be transported to Liverpool England via the Ohio and Mississippi rivers to New Orleans, and thence by ocean; as cheaply as it is now transported from the Pennsylvania Oil Regions via rail road to New York.

The development of oil territory in the Western States will add immensely to the commerce of the Great West, and furnish an article for exportation of incalculable value.

A single well—producing 50 barrels of Lubricating Oil per day—now worth at the wells $20 per barrel—gives an annual income of $300,000 per year—equal to 10 per cent. on a capital of $3,000,000, *or one hundred and fifty per cent. annually on a capital of $200,000.*

The title to the land is clear and without incumbrance, and is conveyed to the Company, in fee simple, and without royalty.

The subjoined report upon this land was made after several thorough examinations, by S. W. ELY, Esq., an experienced and practical Geologist, who has given special attention to the selection and development of Oil Lands.

To DAVID GIBSON, Esq., President of the Laclede Petroleum and Mining Company.

SIR:

Having been requested, as one possessing an intimate knowledge of your lands—their position, topography, geological and oil-bearing features—to give a description thereof, I proceed to do so as briefly as possible.

Said lands consist of five hundred (500) acres, in an oblong body, 200 by 400 poles in extent. They are situate in the north-western portion of the celebrated Oil Tract of J. A. DRAKE, Esq., in Lewis County, Kentucky, ten miles from Vanceburg, the county seat of said county, on the Ohio River. The distance from Cincinnati, by steamboat navigation, is but ninety miles. These lands are in the near neighborhood of the yielding well of the "Daniel Boone Petroleum and Mining Company," and possess the commendatory qualities of that oil-bearing field.

The Lewis County oil district, in which your lands are centrally situate, has rapidly risen in public estimation, and is perhaps, attracting more attention, from capitalists and oil men, than any yielding territory south-west of Venango County, Pa. A complete revolution in prices of and the demand for lands, comprehending a rapid enhancement, are observable there, within the last few weeks; but your tract having been secured before the excitement arose to its present pitch, was selected with great deliberation and judgment. It is hardly necessary to enter into a long argument, in order to prove, geologically, what is now a fact patent to the observation of all who choose to examine, that yours are good oil lands. I take the liberty, however, for the information of strangers, to quote from my former reports on portions of the Drake Tract, such remarks, as are strictly applicable to the tract under consideration, accompanying them with such as especially pertain to this area.

The characteristics of these lands are marked and homogeneous. High broken ridges and deep valleys, characteristic of this portion of the sub-carboniferous region, prevail. In many places "nests" and "broken down" spaces in the hills suggest the probability of strong internal commotion, or important displacement of the deeply concealed rocks. The hills are from 250 to 400 feet in perpendicular height.

The geological layers of the tract are similar to that of Oil Creek, Pa. In this remark particular allusion is made to the free-stone slabs, so profusely impressed with the ripple marks of the "Devonian" sea, and to the intervening shales, most of them carboniferous, which are observable especially on the west side of the Oil Creek valley. Older than the coal measures, these deposits, interspersed with the black *Lingula* shale, seem to afford some solution to the question: What and where is the origin of petroleum? In various places throughout this district oil springs appear, in which exude the fine, black, thick surface oil, bubbling up from the stratum of clay stone which penetrates the valleys of this neighborhood. There is also a salt lick on this tract, well known to the hunters of these regions, being the "out-crop" of the saline deposits of the rocks below. "Gas wells" emitting volumes of inflammable air, are seen in various places, and all these, as is well known, are usual signs of oil.

The lands in question are situate on those mountain streams—Brandy Lick, Clay Lick, and Bullock Run. The last named is a branch of Straight Prong, on which the "Daniel Boone" wells are situate. The first two are the principal branches of the Moseby Creek, on which is situate, (between those two branches,) and within less than half a mile of the northern line of the "Laclede" lands, the famous oil spring which first drew attention to this district as oil territory. All of the above streams afford good oil sites for boring and pumping operations.

The petrolic sandstones, quarried in this region, are found throughout these lands. The lithological characteristics are precisely similar to those of the most famous oil field in the world. Great layers of broken freestone, or *Breccia*, are seen in the hills, and traces of copperas and sulphur, with the red discolorations of the rocks, betray the igneous influences of ages ago. It was impossible, for the close observer, to gainsay the evidences that Nature has stamped upon the rocks and written in the valleys, that this was a most inviting field for operations in developing petroleum. It remains for the enterprising capitalists, who are so eagerly rushing to this new field, to reap the reward of well directed effort.

I should not neglect to state that the whole tract under consideration is clothed with a fine forest of excellent timber, the economic uses of which, in the varied operations of an oil company, need only be alluded to.

Yours Respectfully,

SENECA W. ELY.

Cincinnati, Jan'y 4, 1865.

THE DANIEL BOONE PETROLEUM & MINING COMPANY,

OF CINCINNATI.

CAPITAL STOCK, $300,000,
DIVIDED INTO 30,000 SHARES, OF $10.00 EACH.

INCORPORATED UNDER THE LAWS OF OHIO.

DAVID GIBSON, President.   **A. L. MOWRY**, Treasurer,   **LAFAYETTE DEVENNY**, Secretary.

HAGANS & BROADWELL,   :   :   :   :   Attorneys and Counsellors.

COMMISSIONERS:

DAVID GIBSON, of David Gibson & Co. : Cincinnati.	J. W. DONOHUE, of J. W. Donohue & Co. : Cincinnati.
A. L. MOWRY, President Third National Bank, : Cincinnati.	ALFRED GAITHER, Sup't Adams Express Co. : Cincinnati.
LAFAYETTE DEVENNY, : : : :	: : : : Cincinnati.

Principal Office No. 35 West Third Street, Cincinnati, O.

This Company was incorporated October 31st, 1864, under the General Corporation Laws of the State of Ohio, and will commence boring for Oil and otherwise developing their land, immediately.

Capital $300,000, number of shares 30,000, par value $10 each, *which is sold to subscribers at $5 per share.*

The Company owns, in fee simple, one thousand acres of land in Lewis County, Kentucky, 8 miles south of Vanceburg, on the Ohio River, and in the valley of Kinnick-kinnick Creek, a tributary of the Ohio, and is part of the celebrated Oil Tract of J. A. Drake, Esq., recently purchased from him.

The title to the land is clear and without incumbrance, and is conveyed to the Company, in fee simple, and without royalty.

The subjoined report upon this land was made after several thorough examinations, by S. W. ELY, Esq., an experienced and practical Geologist, who has given special attention to the selection and development of Oil Lands.

To David Gibson, A. L. Mowry, J. W. Donohue, A. Gaither and L. Devenny, Esqrs.

Commissioners, &c.

GENTLEMEN:

In compliance with your request, I proceed to furnish a description of the lands selected for the operations of your Petroleum Company, giving my views of their Oil-bearing and Oil-yielding qualities, &c., &c.

These lands comprise *one thousand acres* in an oblong, compact body, nine hundred and twenty-seven poles from east to west long, and one hundred and seventy-one and one-half, poles broad. The tract is situated in Lewis County, Kentucky, on the south-east side of Kinnick-kinnick Creek, about one mile from that stream, and lying nearly parallel with it, and on two of its principal brances, Straight Prong and Laurel. The affluents of these streams permeate the tract in various directions, dividing the surface into ravines, which generally debouch towards the north, being thus of easy access to the roads along the main creek, and affording a large number of desirable sites for wells, derricks, &c. These lands were chosen with special reference to their convenience, and to the multiplication of wells on the surface occupied.

Their distance from Cincinnati is a little over one hundred miles, nearly all of which is traversed by water navigation. As witnessed by the map, Kinnick-kinnick is one of the largest streams of Northern Kentucky, navigable for Rafts and Keel-boats nearly to these lands, for many months of the year, and easily reducible to constant slack-water navigation, a project entertained by the State when the war broke out. The air-line distance, from the lands to Vanceburg, (the county seat of Lewis County, on the Ohio River,) is, however, but eight miles, while the space is passed over by the present road in twelve miles.

The reasons for choosing these lands, as accepted "Oil Territory," are numerous and weighty. Their position on the western side of the lower carboniferous formation, comprising the vergent slabs and shales, which prevail on Oil Creek, Pennsylvania, stamp them as *geologically right*. It is estimated that the *formation* indicated, has a thickness upon these lands of about 400 feet, before the drill from the surface would penetrate the underlying millstone grit, and enter the upper stratum of the older rocks, filled with cavities for the repose of oil and deposition of gas; surface oil, of fine quality, is obtainable in many places on this tract. Several "springs" exist in the neighborhood and on the lands, from which exude a dark colored rock oil, indicative of the *petrolic* character of the district. Salt water is found, by boring, and carburretted hydrogen gas is observed escaping in many places, from the beds of streams and pools of water, in fact, all the phenomena observable in the most productive oil fields of the country, have been discovered here, proofs multiplying to conviction as the search progressed. It remains for your company to pursue, to profitable development, these promising facts and phenomena. The parallels, topographical, geological, lithological and *oleaginous*, between your locality and those demonstrated to be the best in the country, for the production of rock oil, are certainly so close as to promise the most gratifying results.

The work of developing a Petroleum district, so near the Ohio river, and in the neighborhood of Cincinnati, commends itself as a measure both patriotic and profitable. Besides the most cogent geological arguments above adduced, considerations of climate, convenience and economy commend this new oil field to the enterprise of your Company. Wherever oil fields, holding out so many solid inducements for development, have been improved, the most satisfactory results have been attained.

Although the oil element forms the great inducement for prosecuting your work upon these lands, still they possess many other valuable qualities and commendations. The soil is quite good on the slopes and ridges, and fertile on the bottom lands, which vary from a narrow strip to several hundred yards in breadth. The forest trees consist principally of white, black, red, post and chestnut oak—the last prevailing in quantity—and the poplar, beech, sugar maple, walnut, ash, butter-nut, buckeye, linn and pawpaw, are found in abundance. Tan-bark can be made very profitable; and the stave and hoop material for barrels, so desirable in an oil region, of which the Venango district is entirely destitute, exist here to a great extent. All the grains and grasses common to the climate, can be cultivated on this tract; while it is especially commended by Prof. Owen, and other gentlemen of high scientific and practical attainments, as a choice spot for grape and wine-growing.—[See Owen's Geological Survey of Kentucky, Chapter on Lewis, Greenup and Carter Counties.] The work just alluded to was prepared long before the discovery of Petroleum in large quantities, and thus, of course, does not allude to the subject. So, also, the able and elaborate report of Professor Rodgers, on the Geology of Pennsylvania, published so late as 1856, speaks only of a little Petroleum as existing in the sandstones in the region about Oil Creek [Vol I, page 583]; as I may also state the fact of a like phenomena in the arenaceous slabs of Lewis County. The discovery and development of oil-bearing territory, are of so recent date, that theories on the subject are hardly concreted into certainties. While, upon your chosen field, the "oil signs" are verified by the "oil existence," and the geological equivalents and parallels are all right, I am at a loss to conceive of a single good reason why the oleagenous treasure may not be found there to a great and profitable extent. I have visited the lands four times, and spent a good deal of time in exploring and examining the estate of which they are an important portion. Meantime, I have visited the Oil Creek region, in Pennsylvania, the Bull Creek Wells, in West Virginia, and the country about Marietta. From previous visitations, I am also able to compare the Kinnick-kinnick with the Little Kanawha oil region. These opportunities enable me to say that, the examination of your lands, so far as prosecuted, has disclosed as many commendatory features as either of the other fields naturally possesses.

Very Respectfully, Yours, &c.

S. W. ELY.

CINCINNATI, October 24th, 1864.

OIL TERRITORY.

I have about 20,000 Acres of Land in Lewis county, Kentucky, that is "accepted Oil territory."

The surface indications are more like those of Venango County, Pennsylvania, than any Oil Territory that has been discovered in the country, and promises as abundant a yield.

In order to give capitalists an equal chance to purchase, I propose to receive sealed proposals, based upon cash payments, for any subdivision thereof, remaining unsold up to the 31st day of December next. On that day the bids will be opened, and the awards made to the highest bidder, who will be immediately notified by letter. Payments to be made on the 10th day of January, 1865, when the deeds will be executed. Owing to ill health, and to other business engagements, I have adopted this plan of disposal. I propose it in good faith, and with the full determination of selling, even at much less prices than the same character of Oil Lands are being sold; but if bids are made at prices below the value of the lands before the discovery of oil upon them, I reserve the right to reject them. One thousand dollars per acre has been offered for a portion of this land. Land in the vicinity remaining unsold, is held at from $100 to $1,000 per acre. The first oil discovered in the county, was found on the land now offered. "The Daniel Boone Petroleum Company," of Cincinnati, purchased a portion of this tract, and are now sinking a well with every prospect of success. Other wells are going down in the neighborhood, and nearly all the land in the vicinity has recently been sold or leased to experienced oil men from Western Pennsylvania. Persons wishing to invest in these lands are invited to visit them. From the 1st to the 25th of December, an Agent can be found at the Beverly House, Vanceburg, or on the land, who will render every assistance to enable any one to make a thorough investigation. Boats leave Cincinnati daily for Vanceburg, the county seat of Lewis county, and the landing place of the land. A report on these lands, written by S. W. Ely, Esq., is hereby presented. Mr. Ely is thoroughly acquainted with the whole tract, having visited it six times, and studied its topographical, geological, lithological, oil-bearing and other properties. For years his attention has been given to the geological field in which these lands lie, so that his testimony is presented as of one, who by habit, experience and scientific accomplishments, is qualified to speak with authority.

The title is perfect. For plots, geological reports, blank form of proposals, and further information address, or call in person, at the office of J. A. DRAKE & CO., 53 West Front Street, Cincinnati; A. D. CALDWELL, United States Gazette Building, Third Street, Philadelphia, or to the undersigned, at Room 3, No. 4 Wall Street, New York. Office hours from 10 A. M. to 2 P. M.

J. A. DRAKE.

REPORT

On the Geographical Position, Extent, Topography, Geology and other Characteristics, of J. A. Drake's Oil Lands, Lewis Co., Kentucky.

To J. A. DRAKE, Esq., Cincinnati, O.

DEAR SIR: In compliance with your instructions, I have made a thorough examination of your tract or *district* of land in Lewis County, Ky., and proceed, as briefly as possible, to prepare a description of the same.

1. GEOGRAPHICAL POSITION.—The tract is situate in the southern part of the county of Lewis, nearly adjoining Carter, on Straight Prong and Laurel creeks and their waters—being branches of the Kinickeonic.* Grassy Fork of Laurel and the main stream by that name border the eastern side of the tract, and the Briery branch of Indian creek the western. The northern parallel of 38° 30' passes about midway through the tract.—Several large and permanent streams besides those just mentioned, together with their branches, too numerous to denominate, water the whole district. The northern boundary of the tract is within nine miles of the town of Vanceburg, (on the Ohio river, 90 miles from Cincinnati,) with which place a good road connects within a distance of about thirteen miles. Kinnickeonic is navigable, at times, for rafts and flat-boats nearly up to the lands.

2. EXTENT.—Before your late sale to the "Daniel Boone Petroleum and Mining Company of Cincinnati," of 1000 acres, the entire tract comprised $22467\frac{3}{10}$ths acres, being the extent of $34\frac{200}{640}$ths square miles. As the locations were made at an early day, the patentees secured the lands in regular parallelograms, so that the whole "territory" is symmetrical and compact. I observe, by your map, that you have judiciously divided it into square and oblong pieces, for sale, having due reference to the streams which penetrate and permeate the lands.—Their greatest length, from north to south, is seven miles and twenty-eight rods, and the greatest width, on the southern line, lacks but sixty-six rods of six miles.

3. TOPOGRAPHY.—It might be supposed that a district of country containing nearly $34\frac{1}{2}$ square miles would present a great variety of surface;—but the characteristics of your lands are marked and homogeneous. South of Tar Fork of Laurel, the mountain chain which commences on the Ohio just below Portsmouth, and runs southwestward along the easterly border of Lewis, divides this district from the carboniferous limestone and coal lands of Carter county. North of this range, throughout your tract, the high broken ridges and deep valleys, or gorges, characteristic of this portion of the sub-carboniferous region, prevail. In many places, "nests" and "broken down" spaces in the hills suggest the probability of strong internal commotion, or important displacement, of the deeply concealed rocks. Between the upper waters of Straight Prong and the Tar Fork, an extensive swale, bordered by precipitous mountains, and clothed with the finest timber of all kinds indigenous to the soil and climate, is found. In all parts of the tract, dividing the watersheds of the principal streams, the elevations are from 250 to 400 feet in (perpendicular) height, generally very steep, and displaying escarpments of the upbearing rocks and shales. From the northern to the southern border, as can be seen from the direction of the main creeks, the rise of the surface of the comparatively plane land is considerable—about 20 feet to the mile. The principal inequalities of the entire district are evidently attributable to aqueous denudations operating on the nearly horizontal deposits of sandstones, clays and shales. Apparent anti-clinals are witnessed, but they are probably results of underminings by the streams, and consequent "slips" of large masses of earth and rocks. In the Oil Creek region, I have the testimony of Professor WILLIAMS,† as well as that of my own vision, for saying there is no sensible deviation from the nearly horizontal deposition of the prevailing rocks.

4. GEOLOGY.—The geologic layers of this district are based, of course, on the blue limestone formation of the Silurian period, on which our own city is built. Immediately over this, is found the magnesian limestone, (or rather, calciferous magnesium—for the compound is said to contain 60 per cent. of carbonate of magnesia,) which Prof. OWEN says is 50 or 60 feet thick,‡ and which, dipping south-eastwardly, disappears beneath the river bottom at Vanceburg. In some places, however, a marly clay intervenes between the blue and the magnesian limestone. This latter is overlaid by the black *Lingula* shale, which is highly carboniferous—the oils and gases therein contained exuding at a moderate heat, and burning with a bright flame, when ignited. Over this the wall-like slabs and shales

---

* Kinnick-kinnick, or Tobacco, in the Shawanese tongue.

† See a paper on the subject, in the Cincinnati Commercial of Nov. 24, 1864, by Prof. L. D. Williams, of Alleghany College, Meadville, Penn.

‡ Kentucky Geological Report, Vol. 3, Art. Lewis County.

are found, which so liken this district to the oil-bearing field of Venango county, Pennsylvania. The same beautiful "ripple marks," so common there, the same alternating sandstones and argillaceous slates, which compose the western wall of the great oleaginous valley of Oil Creek, seem transplanted here. In addition, we here observe, in great variety, the petrous remains of those Devonian sea-weeds (*fucoids*) which Professor WILLIAMS believes contributed largely to the volume of carboniferous liquid beneath that valley, leaving there, however, no other trace of their pre-existence. Another layer of shale, 120 feet thick, overlies these, on which reposes the 12-feet bed of clay-stone (resembling *steatite*, and popularly called "soap-stone,") from the crevices of which exudes the thick surface oil which discovers itself in the "springs" of the region, and gave rise, some years since, to the conviction that yours were petroleum lands. Over this, is the beautiful "city ledge" layer of freestone so much used and so highly valued by the builders of Cincinnati. Above this, other beds and layers of shales and sand-stones, some of the latter curiously fractured throughout their entire extent, doubtless by some violent tremor or eccentric motion of the earth, are seen out-cropping, and often out-dropping, from the beetling precipices;—thus completing the geologic column.

The domolite, or magnesian limestone, which it is fair to infer underlies your entire tract, may be traced in the hills, as one steams up the Ohio, from below Rome, for a distance of about nine miles, to Vanceburg, where, as we have seen, this layer dips beneath the river. Everywhere, along this line, strong marks of erosion or disintegration are visible, and plainly discernable from the boat, as one passes them, displaying irregular seams and caverns in all sorts of fanciful shapes. I am credibly informed, that these are openings into subterranean passages and cavities, which extend hundreds of yards beneath the hills and have often been penetrated by daring explorers. It has occurred to me that these caves and cells, in the same deposite beneath your lands, furnish receptacles for the repose of oil and gases, as their carbonaceous compound possibly supplies the acid which enters into the formation of petroleum.* Salt, saltpeter, potash and other alkalies, it is now admitted, bear a vital relation to rock oil, to produce which it is no longer deemed necessary to rob the coal beds. The location of your lands bears a comparative relation to the *situs* of the coals and limestones of Greenup and Carter counties precisely analagous to the relative position of the Oil Creek valley and the nearest coal, to the south-east of it.

Boring alone can disclose the exact thickness of the oil-bearing strata of your lands, as they repose on the domolite aforesaid. From their *congeners* to the westward, it is probable the drill will penetrate the magnesian rock at an average depth of about 450 feet from the surface of your lowest valleys.

5. OIL SIGNS.—Many of these are inferable from what is said above. A "practical oil-man" of my acquaintance quaintly observes, "the best sign of oil is the oil itself." Both of us, and hundreds of others, have witnessed the thick, black, fine surface oil, which exudes from the "soap-stone" deposit above described, in several places, on your lands. Salt "licks" and springs are found on the lands, and "gas wells" emitting volumes of inflammable air, both "signs" of the presence of oil, other phenomena being favorable, are seen in various places. It is probable, by the way, that the brines obtainable on your lands are much stronger than those of the old salt wells immediately back of Vanceburg, inasmuch as the saliferous rocks are several hundred feet deeper in the former than in the latter locality. I shall expect that the borings pursued to the depth of 500 or 600 feet, will furnish streams of strong salt water. Wherever stone quarries have been opened, in the vicinity, oil stains and the smell of petroleum are plain to the senses. For years, the district has been considered "oil territoy," from the number of oil springs, and much of the neighborhood was accordingly "leased," pending the present war. My deductions lead me to prefer your tract as an oil-bearing field, to some others, where the surface indications are equally favorable, because it is situate well "into the bowels of the land," farther south-east of the line of outcrop of the lowest layer of the formation than those others, and still not so far as to come in contact with the coal series, or to render the borings liable to prove too deep and expensive.

In fact, so far as my inquiry and observation have extended—and I have seen all the principal oil fields in the country—I know of no region in which so many oil signs existed, which has not produced richly in proportion to development. Straight Prong, Moseby, Tar Fork, Laurel, and their affluents—if there be any force in surface shows, chemical affinities and geological analogies, with the production of petroleum in view, are as likely soon to become famous in the commercial and monetary world, as are those euphoneous streams, Oil Creek, Pithole, Muskrat, Hemlock, Bull Creek, Horseneck, Federal and Duck Creeks and the Kanawha.

Very truly, yours,

CINCINNATI, *November* 28, 1864.

S. W. ELY.

---

* See Prof. WILLIAMS's article. Mr. JOHN WOLF, a practical well-sinker, on Oil Creek, assured me that the wells, in the lower portion of the Oil Creek Valley, were perforated to the *lime-stone*. What other natural formation of rock is so subject to chemical and aqueous erosion as limestone?

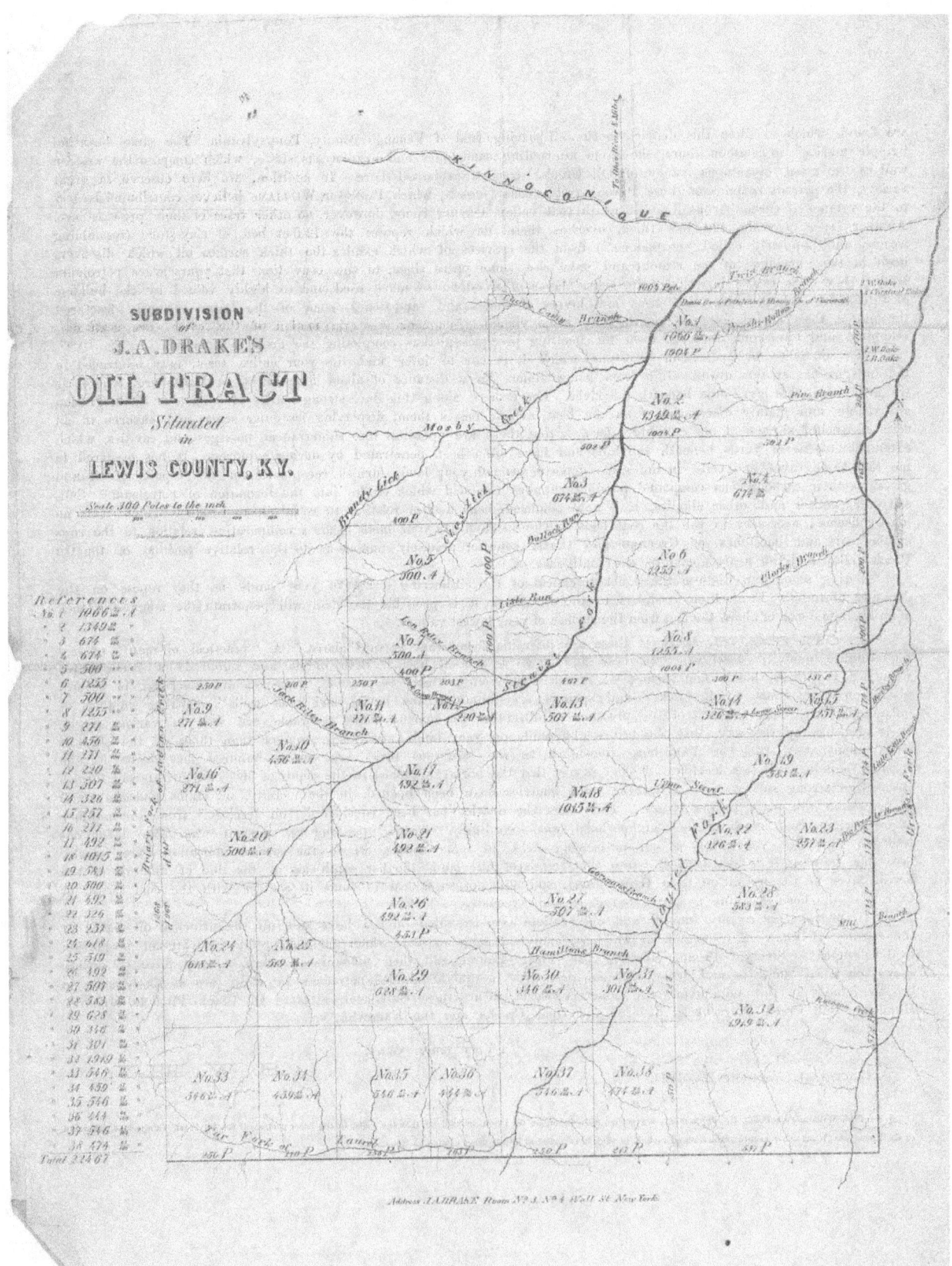

THE DE SOTO PETROLEUM AND MINING COMPANY

OF SAINT LOUIS, MO.

Capital Stock 250,000 Dollars,

DIVIDED INTO TWENTY-FIVE THOUSAND SHARES OF $10 EACH.

SUBSCRIPTION PRICE $5.00 PER SHARE.

INCORPORATED UNDER THE LAWS OF THE STATE OF OHIO.

DAVID GIBSON, President, H. C. CREVLING, Vice Pres't,
E. H. NICHOLS, Sec'y & Treas. B. M. RUNYAN, Banker.

DIRECTORS.

DAVID GIBSON, of David Gibson & Co.	Cincinnati.
H. C. CREVLING, Sup't St. Louis Transfer Company,	St. Louis.
J. W. DONOHUE, of J. W. Donohue & Co.	Cincinnati.
E. H. NICHOLS,	St. Louis.
LAFAYETTE DEVENNY, Pres't Queen City Insurance Company,	Cincinnati.
J. N. KINNEY, Gen'l Freight Agent Little Miami Railroad,	Do.
NATHAN STEVENS, General Agent Union Line,	St. Louis.

PRINCIPAL OFFICES:

49 OLIVE STREET, Union Line Office, - - - - - ST. LOUIS.
35 WEST THIRD STREET, Queen City Insurance Co., - CINCINNATI.

This Company was incorporated February 2d, 1865, under the General Corporation Laws of the State of Ohio, and will commence boring for Oil and otherwise developing their land immediately.

Capital Stock $250,000, number of shares 25,000, par value $10 each; shares are now sold to subscribers at $5 each.

The Company owns, in fee simple, five hundred acres of land in Lewis County, Kentucky, 10 miles south of Vanceburg, on the Ohio River, and in the valley of Kinnick-kinnick Creek, a tributary of the Ohio, and is part of the celebrated Oil Tract of J. A. Drake, Esq., recently purchased from him.

This tract is in close proximity to the lands of the celebrated "Daniel Boone Petroleum and Mining Company," which is now engaged in sinking wells upon their property, and has found a fine flow of oil at a depth of 65 feet from the surface, in consequence of which their stock has advanced four fold.

An advantage enjoyed by wells so close to the Ohio River is evident, from the fact that crude oil can be transported to Liverpool, England, via the Ohio and Mississippi Rivers to New Orleans, and thence by ocean; as cheaply as it is now transported from the Pennsylvania Oil Regions via rail road to New York.

The development of oil territory in the Western States will add immensely to the commerce of the Great West, and furnish an article for exportation of incalculable value.

A single well, producing 50 barrels of Lubricating Oil per day—now worth at the wells $20 per barrel—gives an annual income of $300,000 per year—equal to 10 per cent. on a capital of $3,000,000, *or nearly one hundred and twenty-five per cent. annually on a capital of $250,000.*

The title to the land is clear and without incumbrance, and is conveyed to the Company, in fee simple, and without royalty.

The subjoined report upon this land was made after several thorough examinations, by S. W. ELY, Esq., an experienced and practical Geologist, who has given special attention to the selection and development of Oil Lands.

To DAVID GIBSON, Esq.
President of the De Soto Petroleum and Mining Company.

DEAR SIR:—I have been requested to describe to you the tract of land selected by your Company as an Oil-bearing territory. I beg to state, that I have been over the land several times, and profess to an intimate knowledge of its qualities and indications.

The tract (No. 7 of MR. J. A. DRAKE's sub-division), contains five hundred (500) acres, lying immediately south of and parallel to the lands of the Laclede Petroleum and Mining Company, of St. Louis. Like that, it is situate in the north-western portion of MR. DRAKE's celebrated "Oil Tract," in Lewis County, Kentucky. Vanceburg, the county seat, and an old trading town on the Ohio River, 90 miles, by steamboat navigation, to Cincinnati, is distant from your land, in a direct line, about twelve miles. Communication with that point is at present had by roads running both eastwardly and westwardly from your tract.

There are so many similarities between the characteristics of this tract and those of the "Daniel Boone" and "Laclede" Companies, that I will here appropriate such portions of my description of the lands of the latter as are applicable to yours.

The Lewis County oil district, in which your lands are centrally situate, has rapidly risen in public estimation, and is perhaps, attracting more attention, from capitalists and oil men, than any yielding territory south west of Venango County, Pa. A complete revolution in prices of and the demand for lands, comprehending a rapid enhancement, are observable there, within the last few weeks; but your tract having been secured before the excitement arose to its present pitch, was selected with great deliberation and judgment. It is hardly necessary to enter into a long argument, in order to prove, geologically, what is now a fact patent to the observation of all who choose to examine, that yours are good oil lands. I take the liberty, however, for the information of strangers, to quote from my former reports on portions of the Drake Tract, such remarks as are strictly applicable to the tract under consideration, accompanying them with such as especially pertain to this area.

The characteristics of these lands are marked and homogeneous. High broken ridges and deep valleys, characteristic of this portion of the sub-carboniferous region, prevail. In many places "nests" and "broken down" spaces in the hills suggest the probability of strong internal commotion, or important displacement of the deeply concealed rocks. The hills are from 250 to 400 feet in, perpendicular, height.

The geological layers of the tract are similar to that of Oil Creek, Pa. In this remark particular allusion is made to the free-stone slabs, so profusely impressed with the ripple marks of the "Devonian" sea, and to the intervening shales, most of them carboniferous, which are observable especially on the west side of the Oil Creek valley. Older than the coal measures, these deposits, interspersed with the black *Lingula* shale, seem to afford some solution to the question: What and where is the origin of petroleum? In various places throughout this district oil springs appear, in which exude the fine, black, thick surface oil, bubbling up from the stratum of clay stone which penetrates the valleys of this neighborhood. There is also a salt lick on this tract, well known to the hunters of these regions, being the "out-crop" of the saline deposits of the rocks below. "Gas wells," emitting volumes of inflammable air, are seen in various places, and all these, as is well known, are usual signs of oil.

Your lands are situate on the Len. Riley branch of Straight Fork, on which the Boone Company's wells are situate, about three miles distant. The upper waters of Rock Camp branch drain the south-western portion of the tract, and those of Lisle Run the north-eastern. Between these streams, high broad hills uprise, covered with vast forests of excellent timber, and composed of the shales and freestone rocks peculiar to the formation. The Riley branch crosses the tract, mainly from a north-west to a south-east direction, so as to afford the most favorable development of this oil-producing field, and to give drainage to the greater portion of it. All the above streams are inviting for boring and pumping operations.

The petrolic sandstones, quarried in this region, are found throughout these lands. The lithological characteristics are precisely similar to those of the most famous oil field in the world. Great layers of broken freestone, or *Breccia*, are seen in the hills, and traces of copperas and sulphur, with the red discolorations of the rocks, betray the igneous influences of ages ago. It was impossible for the close observer, to gainsay the evidences that Nature has stamped upon the rocks and written in the valleys, that this was a most inviting field for operations in developing petroleum. It remains for the enterprising capitalists, who are so eagerly rushing to this new field, to reap the reward of well directed effort.

One of the best geologists of the West, Prof. Andrews, of Marietta, has remarked upon the geological identity of the rocks of this region with those of the Cumberland river oil field in the vicinity of Crocus creek. In fact, the analogies between the district of which your lands are a portion and the best petroleum regions in the United States are, to me, so numerous and convincing, that both my reason and judgment point to the development of your lands as a step which cannot fail to be crowned with satisfactory success.

Very Respectfully, Yours, &c.

Cincinnati, O., *January 21, 1865.*

S. W. ELY.

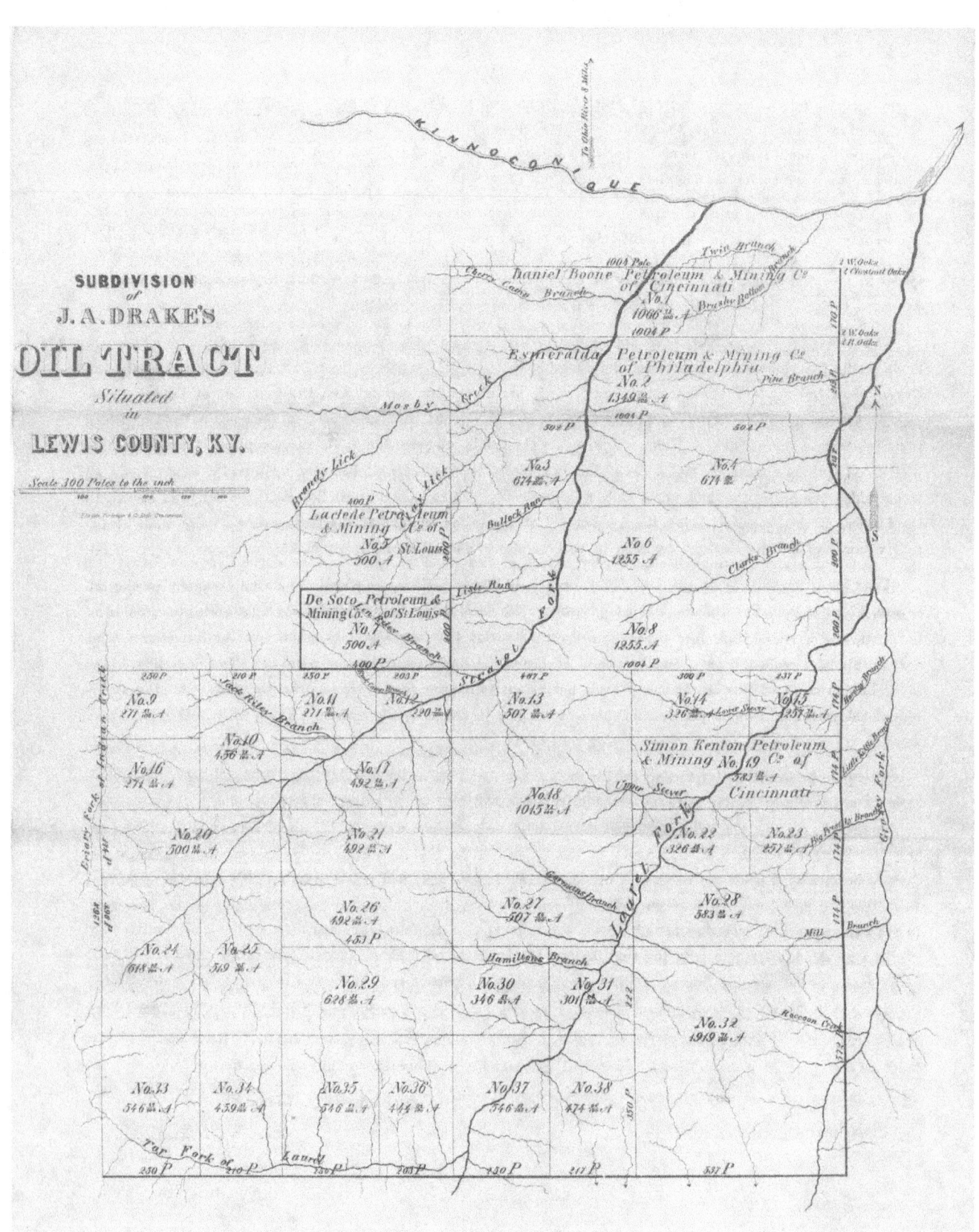

Captain Bennett Munger's spurs, riding crop, leather waist/sword belt remains, including his officer's 1851 belt plate, Casey's tactic books, and his diaries. Photos courtesy of Shelly Case - West Chester, Pa.

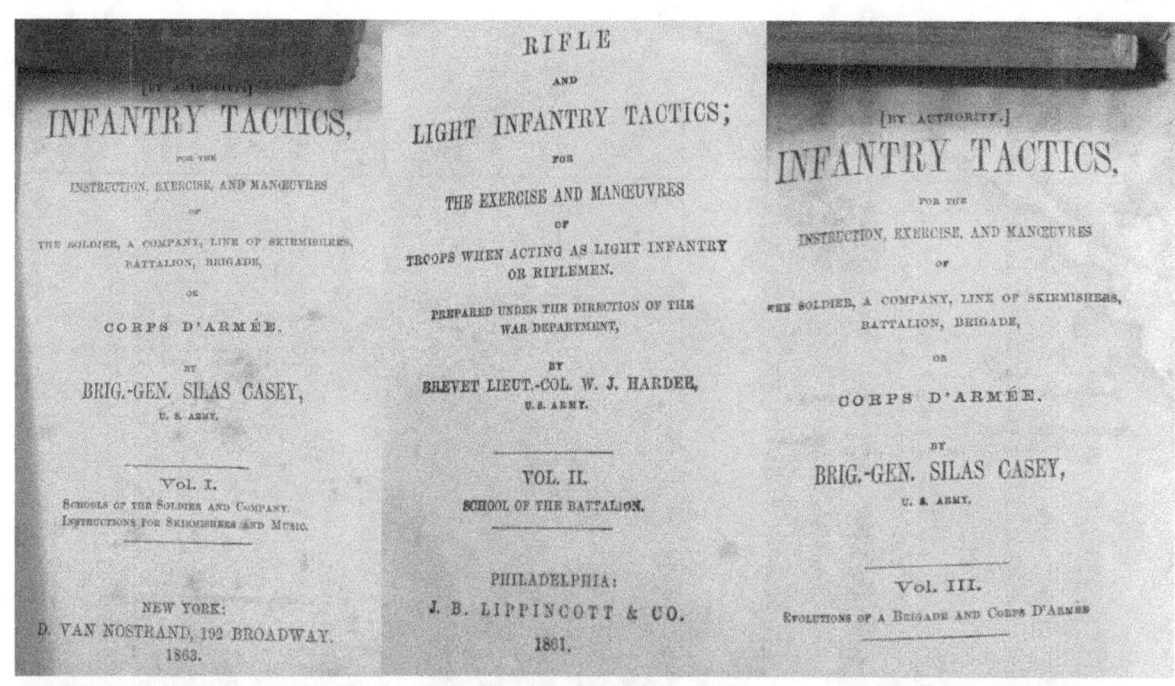

Top picture: Captain Munger's volume #1 & #3 set of Casey's Infantry Tactics & volume #2 of Hardee's Light Infantry Tactics. **Bottom picture**: Captain Munger's small, personal travel trunk/foot locker that he used in the Civil War - Photo courtesy of Shelly Case - West Chester, Pa.

Falmouth, Va. Group in front of post office tent at Army of the Potomac headquarters – Library of Congress

SOLDIER OF COMPASSION

THIS PANORAMIC VIEW OF THE ELMIRA PRISON CAMP WAS PRODUCED IN DECEMBER 1864 BY ELMIRA PHOTOGRAPHERS WILLIAM MOULTON & JOHN LARKIN. THE VIEW OF THE CAMP WAS TAKEN FROM A PLATFORM OVERLOOKING WATER STREET. ELMIRA CONFEDERATE PRISON CAMP WAS BUILT ON 30 ACRES OF THE AREA THAT WAS THE FORMER SITE OF CAMP RATHBUN OR CAMP CHEMUNG. THE TOWERING PLATFORM (IN THE RIGHT-HAND CORNER) WAS BUILT BY THE MEANS BROTHERS WHO CHARGED VISITORS 10-CENTS TO VIEW THE PRISONERS. THIS TOWER WAS SUPPLIED WITH CHAIRS AND BINOCULARS FOR THE SPECTATORS TO WATCH THE PRISONERS GO ABOUT THEIR BUSINESS. IT WAS REPORTED THAT A FAVORITE PAST TIME FOR THE LADIES OF THE AREA WAS TO GO TO THE TOWER TO VIEW THE "DAMNED REBELS". MANY OF THE PRISONERS FOUND THIS OFFENSIVE AS THEY COULD BE SEEN WHILE TAKING CARE OF THEIR PRIVATE BUSINESS AT THE SINKS. IN A NUMBER OF CASES THESE LADIES REPORTED THAT THESE MEN MADE RUDE GESTURES OR EXPOSED THEIR POSTERIORS TO THEM AS A SIGN OF THEIR DISAPPROVAL. PRIVATE RESIDENTS AND BUSINESSES ALONG THE CAMP'S BOUNDARY MADE A CONSIDERABLE PROFIT BY SELLING LEMONADE, CAKE, PEANUTS, CRACKERS, AND BEER TO THESE SPECTATORS. THE OBSERVATION TOWER WAS EVENTUALLY SHUT DOWN BY THE GOVERNMENT AND TAKEN OVER BY FEDERAL AUTHORITIES, THUS ENDING THE INTRUSIVE GAWKING OF PRIVATE CITIZENS. THE TOWER WAS THEN USED AS A GUARD POST FOR OBSERVING THE CAMP.

The Service of Captain Bennett Munger at Elmira Confederate Prison Camp in Elmira, New York is at best based on period returns from the Official Records of the War of the Rebellion and a few firsthand accounts and testimonials provided by Confederate prisoners of war housed there at Elmira. Munger's letters to his commanding officers exemplified the dire need for proper sanitary conditions in the camp, proper nutritional needs, fresh water, proper housing and medical care, as well as proper clothing for the prisoners. Elmira Prison in many respects was even worse than the south's most infamous prison pen, "Andersonville", known throughout the north as the "Hell Hole of the South". The inmates at Elmira coined their own term concerning Elmira, calling it "Hellmira" to describe the inhumane treatment that they received from the United States Prisoner of War Commission headed by General William Hoffman, Commissary General of Prisoners in Washington D.C. One Virginia soldier would write that the compound was, "An excellent summer prison for southern soldiers, but an excellent place for them to find their graves in the winter." Elmira proved to be a black spot on the record of the Union. There were other northern prison camps that had similar issues but Elmira was far worse because many of the deaths of Confederate prisoners of war could have been avoided and thus giving Elmira the infamous title of the "Death Camp of the North".

The camp was in operation from July 6, 1864 to September of 1865. During the camp's fifteen-month operational window over 12,000 prisoners were incarcerated in an old, 30 acre, fenced military camp formerly known as Camp Rathbun. The camp at best was designed for 5,000 to 6,000 prisoners. These men were to be housed in 35, two story, poorly constructed barracks houses that had leaking roofs and poorly constructed clapboard walls that were calked with inadequate plaster putty to fill the gaps between the clapboards. At best these barracks houses could hold 3,000 prisoners without crowding. The initial plan was to house 4,000 in the barracks. The walls of these buildings were not insulated and had gaps between the clapboards that allowed rain, wind and snow into the structures. Official records show that the camp had nearly a 25% mortality rate with 2,963 prisoners dying from a combination of malnutrition, inadequate medical facilities and care, disease from poor sanitary conditions on Foster's Pond (where the sinks and garbage pits were located) and exposure to the cold New York winters that many of the ill-fed and ill-clothed prisoners could not survive. Some of these poor souls froze to death sleeping in the snow or in the "A" tents that were tightly pitched around the compound. Blankets were a luxury in the camp and some of the men were in a state of near nakedness, freezing and starving in the cold, winter air, as they stood in snow up to their ankles during morning roll call. If this was not enough the camp was racked with numerous cases of scurvy followed by an epidemic of diarrhea, then pneumonia and smallpox. Many men had reverted to eating rats that they captured around Fosters Pond to ward off starvation and death.

CONFEDERATE PRISONERS OF WAR LINING UP FOR MORNING INSPECTION AT ELMIRA PRISON CIRCA OCTOBER, 1864 – MOULTON & LARKIN, PHOTOGRAPHERS, 114,116 &118 WATER ST. ELMIRA, N.Y. – PHOTO OF ELMIRA PRISON CAMP PROVIDED BY BILL ACREE OF PIGEON FORGE, TENNESSEE

The low-lying areas of the 30-acre prison site were located along the banks of the Chemung River. These areas were prone to flooding in the rainy season. A number of sick and invalid soldiers who were in these low-lying areas and were too weak to escape the rising water either drowned or came very near drowning. Had it not been for the quick actions of other fellow prisoners, guards and camp officers the situation could have been much worse.

A feeble effort was made to lessen the ever-increasing number of prisoners at Elmira. In late September of 1864 authorities in Washington to ease the problem, issued a directive concerning prisoners that were physically unfit for imprisonment would be exchanged. The order stated that no Confederates would be shipped southward that were "too feeble to endure the journey." The Camp Commander was ordered to "have a careful inspection of the prisoners made by Medical Officers to select those who shall be transferred."

On October 14, five Washington Surgeons examined the 1,200 prisoners who had arrived by train at Baltimore. In the transit five had died en route; scores of others were reported by one of the inspecting physicians as being "unable to bear the journey." The physical state of many of these men, he reported, "was distressing in the extreme, and they should have never been permitted to leave Elmira." By the time the train halted and a steamer had taken the men to the City Point exchange base, forty men were reported dying and another sixty were reported as being "totally unfit for travel." Despite the outcry that this unspeakable deed showed "the grossest indifference on the part of the government" the Officers responsible for the prisoner's transport remained at their posts.

Surgeon C.F.H. Campbell in speaking of the transfer of sick prisoners wrote a frank and highly incensed letter to Col. Hoffman, Commissary General of Prisoners in Washington D.C.: "… these men are debilitated from long sickness to such a degree that it was necessary to carry them in the arms of attendants from the cars to the ambulances, and one man died in the act of being thus transferred. The spectacle was disgraceful to all concerned."

One of the more urgent needs of the prisoners was for proper clothing. The continued pleas for proper clothing brought an immediate reaction from southern families and associates. Col. Hoffman and officials in Washington were apprehensive about issuing the clothing that was sent to the prison and noted that the prisoners could use the clothing in escape attempts to blend in with the local population in their flight back to the Confederacy. Even though Col. Eastman knew the dire need for clothing he withheld issuing the clothing that was sent until he gained permission for distribution of the articles from Col. Hoffman in late August. Due to the fear of possible escapes among the inmates, only gray colored clothing was issued to the men. Large piles of other colored clothing were burned and coats, shirts and trousers deemed saleable were sold to merchants in Elmira for resale. The monetary gains made from the sale of these articles do not seem to have been used to a large degree for the care of the prisoners or for that matter were properly accounted for by the official records.

Officials in Washington also continued to ignore or deny repeated requisitions for badly needed medicines and straw on which the sick could lay on. In effect the pleas from Eastman and other officers at Elmira were being ignored. Col. Hoffman repeatedly turned down requests to complete the ceilings and roofs on the hospital buildings without giving any reason but eventually he did give orders to complete the desired work as soon as possible. Two reasons that were later given for the delay, was the monumental mountain of military paperwork that had backed up coupled with the early winter that had set on three months early in the Camp and had proven to be the coldest winter in nearly fifty years.

Officials in the U.S. Sanitary Commission who had gained access early on into the Camp were soon thwarted along with other benevolent organizations who tried to gain entrance into the camp and were turned down or hindered to such a degree with governmental rules and regulations that it became impossible to gain permission or attend to the sick and dying in the camp. By late December the situation in the camp had grown worse. It was reported that nearly 70 men were lying on the hospital floors due to the lack of beds and straw. The sick wards were reported as being full but another 200 diseased and dying men lay in the regular prisoner quarters because there was no room for them in the sick wards. In excess of one thousand men were reported sick nearly every month in the camp. One federal prison guard wrote, "Prisoners died as sheep with the Rot."

The last prisoner left the camp on September 27, 1865. The camp was then closed; the wooden buildings consisting of barracks, guardhouses and administration buildings were sold at auction and revitalized to be used as private residences or demolished. Some of this wood was salvaged to build homes in 1866. There are a number of these homes that still stand in Elmira to this day. After the war the camp was then converted into farm land. A large portion of the former camp now rests beneath a residential area. Woodlawn Cemetery located nearly two miles from the original prison camp was designated as a National Cemetery in 1877. Today a Confederate monument stands as a silent sentinel over the bivouac of the Confederate dead.

Unfortunately, Captain Munger could do very little by himself to ease the suffering of these men. All that he could do was offered council, help in the process to obtain needed clothing, food, and potable water for the inmates. Munger's official duties were to inspect the camp on a daily basis and report every Sunday morning at headquarters concerning the condition of the prisoners as well as the particulars concerning the camp. Munger had full authority in issuing orders concerning the proper policing of the camp.

Government regulations pertaining to the distribution of clothing continued to be an issue. Continued shipments of inadequate food and medical supplies coupled with the inaction of Col. Hoffman to provide straw for prisoner's bedding, and the repair to the inadequate barracks proved to be the death of many of the inmates. On October 3, 1864, Special Order No. 336 was implemented by Colonel Benjamin Tracy who had taken command of the camp after Col. Seth Eastman retired on September 19, 1864. Eastman had been at odds with General Hoffman concerning a number of aspects relating to the size of the camp, the amount of prisoners that the camp could effectively hold, and the proper care of those prisoners.

Lt. Col. Seth Eastman - Minnesota Historical Society

Col. Benjamin Tracy - Library of Congress

One reason for Eastman's retirement was given as poor health. This may be partly true but tension between Eastman and Hoffman may have played as a factor in Eastman's retirement though no official records state this fact. Hoffman and the administration in Washington won out in the end though and Col. Tracy in compliance to the orders sent down from authorities in Washington, implemented the murderous order. This order cut back food rations that would eventually doom many of these men to the hell of slow starvation. This order also allowed Col. Moore and Major Colt at Elmira to inspect meat rations distributed to the prisoners in the camp. If they did not feel that these meat rations were fit for use they were ordered to dispose of it. At that time beef rations had already been reduced by 20%. After Moore and Colt had rejected the beef, it was conveniently sold to local shops and then sold to the unsuspecting citizens of Elmira who paid uncommonly high prices for the tough, stringy beef. It was true that a drought in the 1863-1864 season had forced many farmers to sell their less than adequate milk cows and beef stock due to the lack of substantial fodder and grain, but it would seem that Government regulations for acceptable beef rations was set very high for men who were in need of food to sustain their existence in relation to citizens who paid a high premium for tough beef to place on their dinner tables.

Captain Munger and several other officers did the best that they could do to ensure that the prisoners were cared for but the inadequate action of the Commissary General of Prisoners and Secretary of War, Edwin M. Stanton proved to hinder any real relief to the inmates at Elmira. Stanton's personal campaign of retaliation against Confederate prisoners of war was no secret to many in the administration and this did not help the situation. The inmates at numerous federal prison camps such as Camp Douglass in Chicago, Illinois and Camp Chase in Columbus, Ohio also told stories of Stanton's deadly edicts. As prisoner of war camps go, Elmira was only in operation for a very limited time, but the official records show that it had the highest death rate, per capita, of any prison camp in the North or in the South. Once again proving, the sad story of lives cut short, the useless loss of life in a land of plenty and man's inhumanity towards his fellow man. Only the milk of human kindness and Christian compassion exemplified by some of the Federal offices at Elmira and other places kept the death rates from being much higher.

One later author/historian noted that due to the drought of 1863-1864 the Elmira area had experienced a less than normal growing season for food crops, thus pushing the prices of vegetables and fruits in the regional markets to higher asking prices. This excuse really does not hold water since nonperishable produce or canned or desiccated produce could have been shipped in or transported in by trains from other areas of the country without any major issues of spoilage. It is true that a large portion of the 730 men who came from Point Lookout had contracted scurvy there, but there was no reason that these cases and subsequent cases could not be dealt with in regards of proper nutrition for each inmate and the assurance that each man got his fair portion without it being stolen by other inmates. The allowance at Elmira for vegetables was two rations of vegetables per week, even though vegetables may have been scarce in the local Elmira markets this was nearly criminal when a national commercial market and a fairly modern industrial rail infrastructure were present and in place for the time period. To expedite this issue Colonel Eastman requested in August of 1864 that the men be allowed to buy vegetables with their own money from the sutler to prisoners as it was felt that the money sent to them from family and friends at home would cover the cost of such necessities. This request was sent to Colonel Hoffman who later permitted the exchange of commerce between the prisoners and the post sutler.

LIBRARY OF CONGRESS

EDWIN M. STANTON 27TH UNITED STATES SECRETARY OF WAR 1862 – 1868

Captain Munger had officially been detailed to Elmira on August 19, 1864 as inspector to examine the camp on a daily basis and make a report every Sunday morning at headquarters concerning the condition of the prisoners in all matters, and the general state of the camp. Captain Munger had power to issue orders in the proper policing of the camp and in this issue, he more or less became a special inside policeman or inspector/detective who investigated all aspects of the camp in the daily operational procedures as well as discovering possible escape attempts perpetrated by the prisoners. In this latter statement one would think that the prisoners would resent Captain Munger but this was not the case. He was always fair with the prisoners and helped them in any way that he could, not contrary to his direct orders as Inspector of the prison.

The following documentation located in the Official Records and the firsthand accounts of several Confederate prisoners of war serve as a testimony to the compassion and sympathy that Captain Bennett Munger exhibited to his fellow man and the care that he took to ease the suffering of other unfortunate souls even if they were numbered among the Confederate enemy. These accounts and testimonials give witness that Captain Bennett Munger and a number of his fellow officers did their duty to their country as well as to their fellow man.

OFFICIAL RECORDS: Series 2, vol 7, Part 1 (Prisoners of War)

WASHINGTON, D. C., May 19, 1864.

Honorable E. M. STANTON, Secretary of War, Washington, D. C.:

SIR: I have the honor to report that there are now about 10,000 prisoners of war at Point Lookout, where 5,000 more may be accommodated. I do not think it would be advisable to assemble a greater number at that point. and to provide for an addition to the number now in our hands which may soon be expected I respectfully suggest that one set of the barracks at Elmira may be appropriated to this purpose. I am informed there are barracks there available which have, by crowding, received 12,000 volunteers. By fencing them in at a cost of about $2,000 they may be relied on to receive 8,000 or possibly 10,000 prisoners. They can be shipped directly from Belle Plain, on steamers already ordered for the purpose, to New York, and thence by railroad to Elmira, which will not make the transportation very expensive.

Fort Delaware can accommodate a few more officers, but no more enlisted men.

I have the honor to be, very respectfully, your obedient servant.

W. HOFFMAN,

Colonel Third Infantry and Commissary-General of Prisoners.

GENERAL WILLIAM HOFFMAN, COMMISSARY GENERAL OF PRISONERS (AT RIGHT) AND STAFF ON STEPS OF OFFICE, F. ST. AT 20TH NW – WASHINGTON, D.C., 1865 (LIBRARY OF CONGRESS)

OFFICE COMMISSARY-GENERAL OF PRISONERS,

Washington, D. C., May 19, 1864.

Lieutenant Colonel S. EASTMAN,

Commanding Draft Rendezvous, Elmira, N. Y.:

COLONEL: You will receive instructions from the Adjutant-General to set apart the barracks on the Chemung River at Elmira as a depot for prisoners of war. The barracks will be inclosed by a suitable fence, and I would respectfully suggest that you construct it after the style found to be most secure at other depots. It should be eleven or twelve feet high, the frame being on the outside, with a walk for sentinels on the outside three or four below the top, thus giving them a good view of all that passes within. There should be ample room between the fence and the buildings, that prisoners may not approach it unseen. Two gates will probably be sufficient, one toward the river. The guard should be outside the inclosure. Please report on the condition of the barracks, the cost of the fence, and any other additions which may be required, and the number of prisoners the place will accommodate. From what I have heard, I judge the number will be 8,000 or 10,000. I am unable to say how soon the barracks will be required, but possibly within ten days. I inclose a circular of regulations for the government of military prisoners.

I am, colonel, very respectfully,

W. HOFFMAN,

Colonel Third Infantry and Commissary-General of Prisoners.

HEADQUARTERS DEPOT FOR PRISONERS OF WAR,

Elmira, N. Y., August 25, 1864.

Colonel W. HOFFMAN,

Commissary-General of Prisoners, Washington, D. C.:

COLONEL: I have the honor to forward the report of the inspector of prison camp at this post for August 21, 1864, with the following remarks: Drainage is being made complete; cook-house and mess-room is too small; the kitchen is being made a little longer; the mess-room will seat from 1,600 to 1,800; another of about the same size should be erected; I will write more fully on that point. There is a sufficient number of medical officers now here to attend to the sick daily, and they are directed to do so. Some of the prisoners have no blankets. Shall everyone have a blanket issued to him? I have written to you in relation to the stagnant water in pond.

Very respectfully, your obedient servant,

S. EASTMAN,

Lieutenant-Colonel, U. S. Army, Commanding.

[Inclosure.]

PRISON CAMP, Elmira, N. Y., August 21, 1864.

Lieutenant T. R. LOUNSBERRY,

Acting Assistant Adjutant-General:

LIEUTENANT: I have the honor to state that I have made the inspection required by Special Orders, Numbers 289, headquarters depot for prisoners of war, dated Elmira, N. Y., August 17, 1864, and submit the following report:

Police of camp, good; police of quarters, good; police of guard-house, good; drainage of camp, progressing, but incomplete; sinks nearly finished on the north side of pond, and good sink south of pond commenced; cook-house and mess-room in good condition, but insufficient in size; hospitals in good condition, but not sufficient for the wants of the camp.

On the 20th instant 226 were reported sick in hospital and a larger number of the quarters. Many of those in quarters are unable to attend sick-call, and in some cases had not been visited by a surgeon in four days. Some are destitute of blankets and proper under clothes, and all without hospital rations; clothing of prisoners deficient, especially in blankets and shirts. The stench arising from the stagnant water in the pond is still very offensive.

B. MUNGER,

Captain, Forty-fourth New York Volunteers, Inspector of Camp.

HEADQUARTERS DEPOT FOR PRISONERS OF WAR,
Elmira, N. Y., August 25, 1864.

Colonel WILLIAM HOFFMAN,

Commissary-General of Prisoners, Washington, D. C.:

COLONEL: I respectfully request some further instructions relating to the issue of clothing to prisoners of war. The friends of the prisoners are sending clothing almost daily for their use, and I have some doubt if it can be issued under Circular, Numbers 4, dated August 10, 1864. They are in need of clothing, and if it be permitted to issue all that is received it will save the Government considerable expense, and I respectfully recommend that it be done. It is difficult to tell whether the clothing came from a friend or a relative. I send with this an application from Noah Walker & Co., of Baltimore, to know if they can send clothing to prisoners when ordered by their friends. Shall I answer in the affirmative?

Very respectfully, your obedient servant,

S. EASTMAN,

Lieutenant-Colonel, U. S. Army, Commanding Depot.

[Inclosure.]

BALTIMORE, August 22, 1864.

COMMANDER OF POST, Elmira, N. Y.:

DEAR SIR: A recent restrictive order in relation to sending goods to prisoners puts us under the necessity of troubling you with an inquiry. We have numerous packages on hand, ordered from us by relatives of prisoners, and we have many orders, as yet unfilled, which we hesitate to act upon. We have been accustomed to furnish only the commonest and most indispensable articles. Applications are handed to us, indorsed, examined by the proper officer at the post. Are we to understand that such indorsement authorizes us to fill the order of the prisoner? We desire to comply in the strictest manner with the requirements of the Government, and any information from you as to our duty will be thankfully received.

Yours, very truly,

NOAH WALKER & CO.

PRISON CAMP, Elmira, N. Y., August 28, 1864.

Lieutenant T. R. LOUNSBERRY:

LIEUTENANT: In obedience to Special Orders, Numbers 289, I have the honor to report the police of this camp good; quarters good, with the exception of wards 24 to 30, inclusive. Ward 32 is overcrowded and the building unfit for quarters; guard-house, good; mess-house, filthy; hospitals, very good. The two wards, Nos. 2 and 4, which were cleaned for patients on Tuesday last are not occupied for want of straw.

Respectfully, yours,

B. MUNGER,

Captain, Forty-fourth New York Volunteers, Inspector of Camp.

[First indorsement.]

HEADQUARTERS DEPOT PRISONERS OF WAR,
Elmira, N. Y., September 5, 1864.

Respectfully forwarded to Colonel William Hoffman, Commissary-General of Prisoners.

S. EASTMAN,

Lieutenant-Colonel, U. S. Army, Commanding.

[Second indorsement.]

OFFICE COMMISSARY-GENERAL OF PRISONERS,

Washington, D. C., September 10, 1864.

Respectfully returned to Colonel S. Eastman, commanding, Elmira, N. Y., and attention invited to instructions which require comments of the commanding officer. Explanations are required why the mess-house is in a filthy condition and why straw has not been provided for the sick. The report is very brief and imperfect.

W. HOFFMAN,

Colonel Third Infantry and Commissary-General of Prisoners.

[Third indorsement.]

The causes of the filthy condition of the mess-house were: First, the building is in such constant use it is difficult to keep it tidy; and, second, there was a temporary neglect on the part of the officers in charge.

B. MUNGER,

Captain, Forty-fourth New York Volunteers, Inspector of Camp.

[Fourth indorsement.]

HEADQUARTERS DEPOT OF PRISONERS,
Elmira, N. Y., September 15, 1864.

Respectfully returned with indorsement of the inspector of prison camp.

Over 9,000 prisoners are fed daily in this mess-room, which leaves but a short time after meals to police it thoroughly. It is swept after every meal and washed as often as possible. Straw cannot be purchased here at this time. Hay will be used in place.

S. EASTMAN,

Lieutenant-Colonel, U. S. Army, Commanding Post.

HEADQUARTERS DEPOT FOR PRISONERS OF WAR,
Elmira, N. Y., August 28, 1864.

Colonel W. HOFFMAN,

Commissary-General of Prisoners, Washington, D. C.:

COLONEL: I have the honor to state that the mess-room and kitchen for prisoners of war at this depot is too small to accommodate 10,000 men. The present mess-room will seat from 1,600 to 1,800, and it requires from two to three hours to feed 10,000. By erecting another mess-room and kitchen to accommodate from 1,000 to 1,200 they can be fed in half that time. A mess-room should also be made for the hospital. The surgeon has applied for it. There is a kitchen attached to the hospital, and will be ready for use as soon as the stoves are put in, which will be done in two or three days. Three wards for the sick have been completed, and a wash-house. Three more wards are being built as fast as lumber can be obtained. When they are all up they will be insufficient for the number of sick now on the sick list.

I have also turned over to the surgeon in charge four barracks for hospital purposes. I would also request to be informed if any arrangement is to be made for winter quarters for prisoners of war, and the troops now guarding them, who are in tents. If so, it should be commenced immediately, owing to the difficulty of obtaining lumber at this point. If temporary barracks are not to be erected I should recommend that Sibley tents be supplied in lieu of the common tent now used.

I am, very respectfully, your obedient servant,

S. EASTMAN,

Lieutenant-Colonel, U. S. Army, Commanding Depot.

PRISON CAMP, Elmira, N. Y., September 25, 1864.

Lieutenant R. J. McKEE, Acting Assistant Adjutant-General:

LIEUTENANT: I have the honor to report that I have made the weekly inspection of this camp in obedience to Special Orders, Numbers 289, and find the police of camp good; police of quarters, good; police of hospital, good; police of guard-house, good; police of kitchen, good; police of mess-rooms. fair. Some clothing is received daily from the friends of prisoners, but there is still great destitution. the weather is cold for the season, and those in tents especially suffer. There are no stoves in quarters or hospital. About 500 are sick in hospital and about 100 in quarters who are fit subjects for, and should receive, hospital treatment. Those sick in quarters are fed on the ordinary prison ration, notwithstanding an order has been issued to treat them as in hospital. During the past week there have been 112 deaths, reaching one day 29. There seems little doubt numbers have died both in quarters and hospital for want of proper food.

Respectfully, yours,

B. MUNGER,

Captain and Inspector of Camp.

[Indorsement.]

HEADQUARTERS DRAFT RENDEZVOUS,
Elmira, N. Y., September 30, 1864.

Respectfully forwarded to the Commissary-General of Prisoners with the following remarks: Drainage of camp is not good. there is a pond of stagnant water in the center, which renders camp unhealthy. This can be remedied by bringing water from the river through the camp. This being done, with more perfect drainage, there is no reason why the camp should not be healthy. Many men are intents without floors or blankets. Barracks should be erected instead of tents. Hospital accommodations insufficient at present. New wards are being built. Hospital mess-rooms to accommodate about 200 patients much needed. Police of hospital good, except sinks; an offensive smell enters the tents from these. I doubt whether, with present mode of construction, this could be prevented. Scurvy prevails to a great extent. Few if any vegetables have been recently issued. Greater efforts should be made to prevent scurvy.

B. F. TRACY,

Colonel 127 th U. S. Colored Troops, Commanding Depot.

PRISON CAMP, Elmira, N. Y., October 16, 1864.

Lieutenant R. J. McKEE, Acting Assistant Adjutant-General:

LIEUTENANT: I have the honor to report that I have made the weekly inspection of camp, in obedience to orders, and find the police of grounds, quarters, &c., good. Drainage as perfect as the situation of camp will allow. During the past week over 1,200 invalid prisoners, 300 of whom were from hospital, were paroled and sent South for exchange. There are now in hospital 588 patients, and receiving medical treatment, 1,021 prisoners. During the four days since the removal of the sick there have been forty-four deaths. The cause of this amount of sickness and death is a matter of deep interest. That the existence of a large body of filthy, stagnant water within the camp has much to do with it can admit of no doubt. Low diet, indifferent clothing, and change of clothing doubtless have some effect. Most of these causes may be removed, and that it be done seems the plainest duty of humanity.

Very respectfully, your obedient servant,

B. MUNGER,

Captain, Forty-fourth New York State Vols., Inspector of Prison Camp.

[First indorsement.]

HEADQUARTERS DEPOT PRISONERS OF WAR, Elmira, N. Y., October 20, 1864.

Respectfully submitted to Colonel William Hoffman, Commissary-General of Prisoners, Washington, D.C.

I desire to call the attention of the Commissary-General of Prisoners to the large number of sick in this camp. A little over a week since over 1,200 sick prisoners were sent South from this camp. This I supposed would so relieve our hospitals that our accommodations would be ample, but I find they are still insufficient. The mortality in this camp is so great as to justify, as it seems to me, the most rigid investigation as to its cause. If the rate of mortality for the last two months should continue for a year you can easily calculate the number of prisoners there would be left here for exchange. I have, therefore, the honor to request that a thorough investigation be made into all the probable causes of disease in this camp, including the sufficiency of the present diet and clothing to maintain the standard of health in this climate the effects of the pool of stagnant water in the center of the camp, and the competency and efficiency of the medical officers on duty here. It seems to me that such an investigation, conducted by competent men, would do much to discover the cause and remedy the evil.

B. F. TRACY,
Colonel 127th U. S. Colored Troops, Commanding Depot.

[Second indorsement.]

OFFICE COMMISSARY-GENERAL OF PRISONERS, Washington, D. C., October 26, 1864.

Respectfully submitted to the Secretary of War, with the recommendation that a medical inspector be ordered to investigate the causes of the unusual sickness among the prisoners of war at Elmira.

W. HOFFMAN,

Colonel Third Infantry and Commissary-General of Prisoners.

PRISON CAMP, Elmira, N. Y., October 23, 1864.

Lieutenant R. J. MCKEE, Acting Assistant Adjutant-General:

LIEUTENANT: In obedience to orders I have made weekly inspection of camp and have the honor to report its police as good as the condition of the grounds (muddy) will allow. There is nothing special to report except perhaps a want of conveniences for doing the washing for the hospitals. The work is done by a detailed of nine men. The number of pieces washed daily is about 600. This work is all done in one kettle in the open air and with only as head of eight by twelve feet for the men. At least three kettles are needed and building that will protect them from storms.

Yours, respectfully,

B. MUNGER,

Captain and Inspector of Camp.

[Indorsement.]

HEADQUARTERS DEPOT OF PRISONERS OF WAR,
Elmira, N. Y., October 24, 1864.

Respectfully submitted to Colonel William Hoffman, Commissary-General of Prisoners, Washington, D.C.

The report relative to the want of conveniences for washing at hospital is correct. A laundry is required, also an addition to the hospital kitchen, and a new mess-room to accommodate about 200 patients, who are able to walk to their meals. The hospital wards will be very cold this winter and should be coiled, as it is too late and they are too full of patients to be plastered.

B. F. TRACY,

Colonel 127th U. S. Colored Troops, Commanding Depot.

PRISON CAMP, Elmira, N. Y., October 30, 1864.

Lieutenant R. J. McKEE, Acting Assistant Adjutant-General:

LIEUTENANT: I have the honor to state made the weekly inspection of camp in obedience to orders, and report the police of quarters, hospitals, cook and mess rooms good. A severe rain-storm has prevailed during the week, making the camp muddy and raising the water in the pond so that crossing to that part of camp beyond it was prevented for one day. The number of deaths this week is but 40; sick in hospital, 637. The case of smallpox brought from Fort Morgan has nearly recovered and no new cases have occured. Another supply of clothing is needed, as the weather is becoming cooled and many are still poorly clad.

Respectfully, yours,

B. MUNGER,

Captain and Inspector of Camp.

[Indorsement.]

HEADQUARTERS DEPOT PRISONERS OF WAR,
Elmira, N. Y., November 2, 1864.

Respectfully submitted to Colonel William Hoffman, Commissary-General of Prisoners, Washington, D. C., with the following comments: In addition to making the camp muddy and raising the water in the river, from the effects of the heavy rain, it disclosed the poor condition of the roofs of the oldest barracks.

I have directed the quartermaster at the post to issue sufficient lumber to repair them, the work to be performed by the prisoners. I am fearful that the heavy rains of the spring and fall will cause some considerable trouble at camp, for the ground between the mess-houses and the river is considerably lower than the remaining portion and is at almost every hard rain overflowed. The new barracks are being erected on the high ground. In relation to the ditch ordered dug and pipe laid, see my letter dated this date.

B. F. TRACY,

Colonel 127th U. S. Colored Troops, Commanding Depot.

PRISONERS' HOSPITAL, SURGEON'S OFFICE,

Elmira, N. Y., November 1, 1864.

Brigadier General J. K, BARNES, Surgeon-General U. S. Army:

I have the honor to forward the monthly report of sick and wounded at prisoners' hospital, Elmira, N. Y., for the month of October. The ratio of disease and deaths has been fearfully and unprecedentedly large and requires an explanation from me to free the medical department from censure. Since August, the date of my assignment to this station, there have been 2,011 patients admitted to the hospital, 775 deaths out of a mean strength of 8,347 prisoners of war, or 24 per cent. admitted and 9 per cent. died. Have averaged daily 451 in hospital and 601 in quarters, an aggregate of 1,052 per day, sick. At this rate the entire command will be admitted to hospital in less than a year and 36 per cent. die. the prison pen is one-quarter of a mile square, containing forty acres, located in the valley of the Chemung River. The soil is a gravel deposit sloping at two-thirds of its distance from the front toward the river to a stagnant pond of water 12 by 580 yards, between which and the river is a low sandy bottom subject to overflow when the river is high. This pond received the contents of the sinks and garbage of the camp until it became so offensive that vaults were dug on the banks of the pond for sinks and the whole left a festering mass of corruption, impregnating the entire atmosphere of the camp with its pestilential odors, night and day.

On my arrival the subject of drainage, sinks, enlargement of the hospitals, providing a kitchen, mess-hall, laundry, dead-house, offices, and store-rooms were all considered and their importance impressed upon the commanding officer. On the 13th to August commenced making written reports of the following dates: August 13, August 23, August 26, September 3, 5, 16, October 5, 9, and October 17, calling attention to the pond, vaults, and their deadly poison, the existence of scurvy to an alarming extent (reporting 2,000 scorbutic cases at one time); recommended fresh vegetables daily to the scurvy patients and an increase in the capacity of the hospital; pointed out the necessity of a kitchen, laundry, mess-room, and dead-house, and presented plans from the same; called attention to improvements in cooking and method of serving the rations; great delay in filling my requisitions for the hospital; the sickness and suffering occasioned thereby; a more general observation of the sanitary laws governing human beings herded in crowded camps and the inevitable consequences following neglect. How does the matter stand today? The pond remains green with putrescence, filling the air with its messengers of disease and death, the vaults give out their sickly odors, and the hospitals are crowded with victims for the grave. A single ration of vegetables was given for a while and discontinued. Three rations in five of onions and potatoes were allowed from the 1st of October for a fortnight and discontinued. The men are hurried in to their rations of bread, beans, meat, and soup, to half gulp it down on the spot or to carry it hastily away to their quarters in old rusty canteens and improvised dirty dippers and measures.

Hospital wards with the addition of three barracks, buildings poorly adapted for hospital purposes, are insufficient to accommodate the sick. Kitchen half large enough. Washing and drying done in the open air at a time when we have not been able to dry our clothes for a month. Nurses, full-diet patients, &c., eat in the wards, kitchen, or wherever they can. Post-mortem performed in a little tent exposed to the gaze of the camp and an office 12 by 20 feet, in which are crowded together drugs and druggists, stewards and clerks, doctors and dressings, commissary clerks and hospital supplies, in a state of confusion worst confounded.

While Lieutenant-Colonel Eastmen, of the Regular Army, was in command I reported directly to him, and was able by direct communication to expedite business, personally explain the wants of the hospital department, and to a limited extent act as medical adviser of the medical interests of the prisoners. Since Colonel Tracy, of the U. S. colored troops, has been in command all direct communication has been cut off, and I am ordered by him to report to a junior military officer in camp, who has merely a forwarding power. So far as garrison duties are concerned, I do not object to reporting to a junior military officer in camp, who has merely a forwarding power. So far as garrison duties are concerned, I do not object to reporting to a junior military office in camp, who has merely a forwarding power. So far as garrison duties are concerned, I do not object to reporting to a junior military officer, but in the administrative duties of a large hospital department the surgeon in charge must have direct communication with the commander, who is the only authorized executive officer. My provision returns, my bill of purchases, my requisitions for hospital fixtures and medical supplies, must all be forwarded to him, subject to his approval or disapproval, without any medical representations to advise or guide in the exercise of opinions and actions based upon common sense alone. Common sense is a very good thing, but does not work in physic. to illustrate: The requisition for medicine sent October 7 through the intermediate channel for approval was never heard from; the second was delayed two or three days; my provision returns or often forty-eight hours getting back to me, and applications for straw and fixtures for hospital are frequently made some three or four weeks before I need the articles. My application for straw, put in October 21, for beds, is not filled yet, and the patients are compelled to lie on the floor. My application for caldron, stovepipe, and cover for washing purposes, put in on the 5th and 16th of September, was finally filled October 28. I was ordered to feed patients in quarters, and yet my requisition for cooking utensils came back disapproved. When the sick were sent from here for exchange I received no official information, nor wass advised in reference to the matter. I was informed by a captain of the examining board, in the original examination, not to send those who were unable to travel. I was totally ignorant whether the journey would exceed two or three days, only as I judged from the number of days' rations required, viz, two; although the day for forwarding prisoners' returns was the day before the prisoners started, October 11, and mine went in promptly. I did not receive my supplies, and the patients were sent off without coffee or sugar. The train started without reporting to the medical officer, and before the nurses were assigned, blankets distributed, and many had been fed after a fast of more than twelve hours. I was ordered to appoint a given number of nurses and doctors, and my application for an increased number received no attention. A camp inspector is appointed who takes the liberty of entering my wards at all times, instructs my ward-masters and nurses, finds fault to them of my management, and quizzes them in regard to the medical officers. Medical officers have complained that he changes the beds of the patients, corrects and changes their diet, directs the washing of my wards without regard to my rules, orders pneumonia patients with blisters on their sides bathed, &c. I have entered a written protest without avail. I cannot be held responsible for a large medical department of over 1,000 patients without power, authority, or influence. Our post is without a medical representative, and as senior medical officer of this post the whole administrate duties should be entrusted to my care, when it would be hoped that the interest of the sick would be consulted.

Respectfully, your obedient servant,

E. F. SANGER,

Surgeon, U. S. Volunteers, in Charge

OFFICIAL RECORDS: Series 2, vol 7, Part 1 (Prisoners of War)

CORRESPONDENCE, ETC. -UNION AND CONFEDERATE.

MEDICAL DIRECTOR'S OFFICE, DEPT. OF THE EAST,

Numbers 125 Bleecker Street, N. Y., November 5, 1864.

Brigadier General J. K. BARNES,

Surgeon-General U. S. Army, Washington, D. C.:

SIR: The accompanying report of Surgeon Sanger, U. S. Volunteers, in charge of the prisoners' hospital at Elmira, N. Y., is respectfully transmitted to the Surgeon-General with the following remarks: In September, Surgeon Sloan, U. S. Army, acting medical inspector for this office, was sent to Elmira to make a general inspection and report upon the condition of affairs at that post. the difficulties under which he labored from the impossibility of obtaining what he deemed necessary for the proper administration of the medical department were represented by doctor Sanger. Surgeon Sloan informed him that there was but one effectual way of remedying the evils complained of, viz, a reference of all his wants in proper from for the approval of the medical director and the action of the general commanding the department. Immediately upon the return of Surgeon Sloan from his tour of inspection the following communication was sent to Surgeon Sanger:

MEDICAL DIRECTOR'S OFFICE, DEPARTMENT OF THE EAST,

New York, September 24, 1864.

* * *

You are instructed to prepare the necessary requisitions for such alterations, repairs, and improvements as you may require at the prisoners' hospital, for my approval and the action of the general commanding the department, and with special reference to the water-closets, dispensary offices, and the additional store-rooms. I will urge everything essential to a good and proper administration of your department. * * *

From the date of that letter to that of the accompanying report no complaints have been made by Surgeon Sanger, nor were any requisitions ever received from him as above instructed, except the usual requisition for medical supplies. He did not avail himself of the means suggested to discontinue his apparently futile attempts with the local authorities and to appeal through me to the commanding general, which, as in other cases, would have been successful.

Very respectfully, your obedient servant,

C. McDOUGALL,

Surg., U. S. Army, and Medical Director of the Dept. of the East.

HDQRS. PRISON CAMP, Elmira, N. Y., December 4, 1864.

Colonel B. F. TRACY, Commanding Depot Prisoners of War:

SIR: I have the honor to submit the following inspection report of the condition of the prisoners of war at this station for the week ending December 4, 1864:

Conduct-good. Cleanliness-good as practicable with the limited supply of clothing. Clothing-insufficient for this climate. Bedding- many destitute of blankets. State of quarters-fair. State of mess-houses-good. State of kitchen-good. Food, quality of-good, with the exception noted in remarks. Food, quantity of-legal ration. Water-good and abundant. Sinks-sufficient and in fair condition. Police of grounds, good. Drainage-good. Police of hospital-excellent. Attendance of sick-good. Hospital diet-good. General health of prisoners-fair. Vigilance of guard-good.

Remarks and suggestions. - A portion of the beef is very lean. Cows milked through the season and too poor for a respectable farmer to winter, are slaughtered and the beef issued to prisoners. I caused a quarter to be weighed, then boiled and the parts weighted. The quarter weighed 92 pounds before cooked; the meat, carefully taken off the bone, weighed 45 1/2 pounds; the bones, 19 pounds; tallow, 4 pounds. This was a forequarter and one of the poorest. They are very nearly of the same quality. About one-half of the flour used this week has been of very poor quality. One thousand six hundred and sixty-six are entirely destitute of blankets, or have blankets nearly worthless.

Very respectfully, your obedient servant,

B. MUNGER,

Captain, Forty-fourth New York Volunteers, Inspecting Officer.

[Indorsement.]

The invoice of a large among of clothing and 4,000 blankets has just been received and the articles will be issued immediately upon their arrival.

Respectfully referred to the Commissary-General of Prisoners.

B. F. TRACY,

Colonel 127th U. S. Colored Troops, Commanding Depot.

U. S. MILITARY CAMP

OFFICIAL RECORDS: Series 2, vol 8, Part 1 (Prisoners of War)

HDQRS. TENTH REGIMENT VETERAN RESERVE CORPS,
Camp Fry, Washington, D. C., January 10, 1865.

Major BLAGDEN,

Assistant to Commissary-General of Prisoners, Washington, D. C.:

MAJOR: I have the honor to inclose herewith an extract from a letter written by John Brusnan, a rebel prisoner at Elmira, N. Y., to a sister of his residing near Baltimore, Md. Some time ago his friends represented to me that he (Brusnan) was loyal to the Union; that it was want of forethought placed him in the rebel ranks, and after being sometime in the rebel service he repented his rashness, and on two occasions attempted to desert to the Union side. On this representation (which I have no doubt his friends believed to be true), and he being also a relative of mine, I wrote twice to the Commissary-General of Prisoners to effect his release, if possible, by the first of the new year, providing he would take the oath of allegiance. At present I am glad that he is not released; and further, I most respectfully request that no action will be taken on the letters which I have written in his behalf. Whether he has or has not taken the oath of allegiance it does not make much difference, as it is evident from the inclosed extract he is an incorrigible and an ungrateful rebel. In my humble opinion he deserves (instead of the rations he now complains of) to be kept on bread and water during his remaining term of confinement.

I am, very respectfully, your obedient servant,

P. E. O'CONNOR,

Lieutenant and Adjutant Tenth Veteran Reserve Corps.

P. S.--I call your attention to the fact that letters pass from the prison to outsiders without going through the proper channel.

P. E. O'C.

[Indorsement.]

OFFICE COMMISSARY-GENERAL OF PRISONERS,

Washington, D. C., January 11, 1865.

Respectfully referred to Colonel B. F. Tracy, commanding Depot Prisoners of War, Elmira, N. Y., for his information. These papers to be returned.

By order of Brigadier General H. W. Wessells, Inspector and Commissary-General of Prisoners:

W. T. HARTZ,

Captain and Assistant Adjutant-General.

[Inclosure.]

PRISONERS' CAMP, Elmira, N. Y., December 30, 1864.

MY DEAR SISTER: I take this opportunity of writing you a letter (which the Yankees will not see). I wrote you a few days ago acknowledging the receipt of the money. I will give you some idea of my situation. I would never have written to you for money, but I am almost starved to death. I only get two meals a day, breakfast and supper. For breakfast I get one-third of a pound of bread and a small piece of meat; for supper the same quantity of bread and not any meat, but a small plate of warm water called soup. I would never take that oath if I was not starved to do it. You know that without my telling you. When I came here this prison contained 10,000 prisoners, and they have all died except about 5,000. They are now dying at the rate of twenty-five a day. You know this is no place for me.

       Your affectionate brother,   JOHN BRUSNAN.

OFFICE COMMISSARY-GENERAL OF PRISONERS,

Washington, D. C., January 19, 1865.

Colonel B. F. TRACY,

Commanding Depot Prisoners of War, Elmira, N. Y.:

COLONEL: Your letter of the 5th instant, requesting that the balance of the requisition for clothing made by you on the 1st ultimo may be forwarded to Elmira, has been received. The requisitions were held awaiting your reply to letter of the 12th ultimo from this office, which explained the necessity of strict economy in the issue of clothing to rebel prisoners at the present time, and requested that you would report your views on the necessity of such issue at Elmira, N. Y. No reply to this letter has been received, and the requisitions are still in this office. The clothing received by you was sent to Elmira by mistake, and was no part of that required for by you. It was reported as issued before the error was discovered. As the cotton from the South referred to in my letter of the 12th ultimo is daily expected, you will please make immediately requisition for such clothing as may be absolutely necessary within the next three or four weeks, after which time it is hoped clothing from the rebel authorities may be ready for issue.

Very respectfully, your obedient servant,

H. W. WESSELLS,

Brigadier General, U. S. Vols., Inspector and Com. General of Prisoners.

RICHMOND, February 15, 1865.

Lieutenant Colonel JOHN E. MULFORD, Assistant Agent of Exchange:

SIR: I understand from returned prisoners that Private Edwin Harris, Seventh Louisiana, now a prisoner at Point Lookout, was in close confinement for some time at that place. Will you not deliver him under our agreement?

Respectfully, your obedient servant,

RO. OULD,

Agent of Exchange.

BALTIMORE, MD., February 15, 1865.

Surg. J. SIMPSON, U. S. Army,

Medical Director, Baltimore, Md.:

SURGEON: I have the honor to report that in compliance with your instructions I examined the rebel prisoners who arrived this date from Elmira, N. Y., and found nineteen of the number unable to proceed farther on their journey. They were sent to hospital-eighteen to West's Buildings and one, a case of smallpox, to the Marine Hospital. Three died en route from Elmira to this city in consequence of chronic diarrhea. Their bodies were sent to National Hospital for burial. The deaths of these men soon after leaving hospital and the condition of the men retained here would suggest that there was not a proper medical inspection made of these troops before leaving camp.

I am, sir, very respectfully, your obedient servant,

HENRY PALMER,

Surg., U. S. Vols., Actg. Medical Inspector, Eighth Army Corps.

[First indorsement.]

MEDICAL DEPARTMENT, EIGHTH ARMY CORPS,

Baltimore, February 18, 1865.

Respectfully forwarded to the Commissary-General of Prisoners.

The inspection made by Surgeon Palmer was by my order (a copy of which is inclosed), and was suggested by the report of the commanding officer of the department that he had a large number of prisoners who were unable to travel. The surgeon in charge of the West Hospital has been instructed to take up on his rolls the names of the men admitted to hospital and state the circumstances under which they were received. Proper care does not appear to have been exercised by the medical officer at Elmira in the examination of the prisoners for transfer, for it is not possible that so short a journey could have brought about the condition in which these sick were found on their arrival at this point.

J. SIMPSON,

Surgeon, U. S. Army, Medical Director.

[Inclosure.]

MEDICAL DIRECTOR'S OFFICE,

MIDDLE DEPARTMENT, EIGHTH ARMY CORPS,

Baltimore, Md., February 15, 1865.

Surg. HENRY PALMER, U. S. Volunteers:

SIR: You will proceed to Bolton Station to superintend the removal of eighty rebel prisoners reported by the officer in charge as just having arrived from Elmira, N. Y., and said to be unable to travel.

BALTIMORE, MD., February 15, 1865.

Surg. J. SIMPSON, U. S. Army,

Medical Director, Baltimore, Md.:

SURGEON: I have the honor to report that in compliance with your instructions I examined the rebel prisoners who arrived this date from Elmira, N. Y., and found nineteen of the number unable to proceed farther on their journey. They were sent to hospital-eighteen to West's Buildings and one, a case of smallpox, to the Marine Hospital. Three died en route from Elmira to this city in consequence of chronic diarrhea. Their bodies were sent to National Hospital for burial. The deaths of these men soon after leaving hospital and the condition of the men retained here would suggest that there was not a proper medical inspection made of these troops before leaving camp.

I am, sir, very respectfully, your obedient servant,

HENRY PALMER,

Surg., U. S. Vols., Actg. Medical Inspector, Eighth Army Corps.

[First indorsement.]

MEDICAL DEPARTMENT, EIGHTH ARMY CORPS,

Baltimore, February 18, 1865.

Respectfully forwarded to the Commissary-General of Prisoners.

The inspection made by Surgeon Palmer was by my order (a copy of which is inclosed), and was suggested by the report of the commanding officer of the department that he had a large number of prisoners who were unable to travel. The surgeon in charge of the West Hospital has been instructed to take up on his rolls the names of the men admitted to hospital and state the circumstances under which they were received. Proper care does not appear to have been exercised by the medical officer at Elmira in the examination of the prisoners for transfer, for it is not possible that so short a journey could have brought about the condition in which these sick were found on their arrival at this point.

J. SIMPSON,

Surgeon, U. S. Army, Medical Director.

[Inclosure.]

MEDICAL DIRECTOR'S OFFICE,

MIDDLE DEPARTMENT, EIGHTH ARMY CORPS,

Baltimore, Md., February 15, 1865.

Surg. HENRY PALMER, U. S. Volunteers:

SIR: You will proceed to Bolton Station to superintend the removal of eighty rebel prisoners reported by the officer in charge as just having arrived from Elmira, N. Y., and said to be unable to travel.

OFFICIAL RECORDS: Series 2, vol 8, Part 1 (Prisoners of War)

OFFICE COMMISSARY-GENERAL OF PRISONERS,

Washington, D. C., January 19, 1865.

Colonel B. F. TRACY,

Commanding Depot Prisoners of War, Elmira, N. Y.:

COLONEL: Your letter of the 5th instant, requesting that the balance of the requisition for clothing made by you on the 1st ultimo may be forwarded to Elmira, has been received. The requisitions were held awaiting your reply to letter of the 12th ultimo from this office, which explained the necessity of strict economy in the issue of clothing to rebel prisoners at the present time, and requested that you would report your views on the necessity of such issue at Elmira, N. Y. No reply to this letter has been received, and the requisitions are still in this office. The clothing received by you was sent to Elmira by mistake, and was no part of that required for by you. It was reported as issued before the error was discovered. As the cotton from the South referred to in my letter of the 12th ultimo is daily expected, you will please make immediately requisition for such clothing as may be absolutely necessary within the next three or four weeks, after which time it is hoped clothing from the rebel authorities may be ready for issue.

Very respectfully, your obedient servant,

H. W. WESSELLS,

Brigadier General, U. S. Vols., Inspector and Com. General of Prisoners.

OFFICIAL RECORDS: Series 2, vol 8, Part 1 (Prisoners of War)

You will make a careful examination of these men, and such of them as are, in your opinion, too ill to accomplish the journey to City Point you will send to the West Buildings Hospital, and make a full report to this office.

Very respectfully, your obedient servant,

J. SIMPSON,

Surgeon, U. S. Army, Medical Director.

[Second indorsement.]

OFFICE COMMISSARY-GENERAL OF PRISONERS,

Washington, D. C., February 20, 1865.

Respectfully referred to Colonel B. F. Tracy for report.

The instructions from this office directing that invalids who were well enough to bear the journey should be forwarded does not appear to have been obeyed.

By order of Bvt. Brigadier General W. Hoffman, Commissary-General of Prisoners:

W. T. HARTZ,

Captain and Assistant Adjutant-General.

[Third indorsement.]

HEADQUARTERS DEPOT PRISONERS OF WAR,
Elmira, N. Y., February 25, 1865.

Respectfully returned to the Commissary-General of Prisoners with the following extracts from the report of Lieutenant-Colonel Trotter, in charge of the detachment, as to transportation:

The train left Elmira at 5 p. m. February 13 and reached Baltimore, via Northern Central Railroad, at 10 a. m. February 15, after many delays. During the night of February 14 neither water nor lights were provided for any car upon the train, as required by the terms of the contract, and three of the prisoners died from the continued exposure. The train consisted of seventeen cars, with only one brakeman for the entire number, to which ten or more cattle cars were added when the train left Williamsport. * * * I would beg leave to call attention to the indifference of the officials of the Northern Central Railroad, who paid not the least attention to repeated applications for lights for the cars, which I was finally compelled to purchase myself. Neither did they supply any water or fuel after the train left Elmira. * * *

The surgeon was strictly charged to send no one unable to endure the journey. It requires a pretty strong man, however, to endure a railroad journey of forty-one hours during such weather as prevailed at the time this party of prisoners was forwarded.

B. F. TRACY,

Colonel 127th U. S. Colored Troops, Commanding Depot.

OFFICIAL RECORDS: Series 2, vol 8, Part 1 (Prisoners of War)

PRISONERS OF WAR AND STATE, ETC.

HEADQUARTERS DEPOT PRISONERS OF WAR,
Elmira, N. Y., January 5, 1865.

Brigadier General H. W. WESSELLS,

Commissary-General of Prisoner, Washington, D. C.:

GENERAL: I have the honor to state that I forwarded from these headquarters December 1, 1864, a requisition for clothing for issue to prisoners of war. About December 7 we received a quantity of clothing, partly filling the requisition, which was issued to prisoners. December 12 we received a communication from Brigadier-General Beall, agent for rebel authorities, addressed to prisoners of war at this depot, notifying them of an arrangement between the United States Government and rebel authorities, by which each was to supply its own prisoners with necessary supplies on their arrival. This request was complied with and report forwarded through General Paine December 17. December 14 we received a communication from your office advising us of the fact that, by a mutual agreement between the United States Government and rebel authorities, a large amount of cotton had been shipped for New York to be sold, the proceeds to be applied to the purchase of clothing for prisoners of war, and that in view of this fact it was not deemed advisable to provide any more clothing for prisoners than was absolutely demanded by the ordinary dictates of humanity. December 18 we received a communication from your office directing that, in pursuance of the arrangement between the United States and rebel authorities, commanding officers of military prisons will afford every necessary and proper facility for the purpose upon the request of Brigadier-General Paine. We have heard nothing further in relation to the subject since. A number of prisoners will soon be destitute of trousers and other articles of clothing. There are still due upon requisition of December 1 1,000 jackets, 2,500 shirts, 3,000 pair trousers, 8,000 drawers, 4,000 boots, 7,000 socks, 1,500 caps, and I would respectfully request that these amounts of jackets, trousers, shirts, bootees, socks, caps, and 4,000 pair of drawers be furnished immediately for issue to prisoners, unless the Department is advised that supplies will be speedily forwarded by the rebel authorities.

I am, general, very respectfully, your obedient servant,

B. F. TRACY,

Colonel 127th U. S. Colored Troops, Commanding Depot.

[First indorsement.]

OFFICE COMMISSARY-GENERAL OF PRISONERS,

Washington, D. C., January 7, 1865.

respectfully referred to the Quartermaster-General and attention invited to the statement of commanding officer of the prison camp at Elmira, N. Y. The delay in the arrival of rebel cotton renders it necessary to issue clothing to prisoners of war in our hands during the inclemency of winter.

H. W. WESSELLS,

Brigadier General, U. S. Vols., Inspector and Com. General of Prisoners.

[Second indorsement.]

QUARTERMASTER-GENERAL'S OFFICE,

January 14, 1865.

Respectfully returned to Brigadier-General Wessells with information that the requisition referred to within was not received at this office, office for such articles as in his opinion should be sent to the prisoners of war at Elmira.

By order of Quartermaster-General:

ALEX. J. PERRY,

Colonel, Quartermaster's Department.

OFFICE COMMISSARY-GENERAL OF PRISONERS,

Washington, D. C., January 5, 1865.

Colonel B. F. TRACY,

Commanding Depot Prisoners of War, Elmira, N. Y.:

COLONEL: I am directed by the Commissary-General of Prisoners to acknowledge the receipt of your inspection report for the week ending December 25, 1864, and to inform you that if cases of smallpox continue to multiply you are authorized, after consultation with the proper medical authorities, to put up temporary buildings for the isolation of that class of patients. Place it within the inclosure, if practicable, but if circumstances require it to be established outside it should be suitably guarded.

Very respectfully, your obedient servant,

W. T. HARTZ,

Captain and Assistant Adjutant-General.

Courtesy Chemung County Historical Society, Elmira, New York

This war time sketch was made by W. Newman. Newnan was a Confederate prisoner of war at Elmira. This sketch was made on September 10th, 1864 and in the distance the guard/observation tower can be seen beyond the prison wall and a small guardhouse can be seen perched on the prison wall overlooking the compound.

CONFEDERATE TESTIMONIALS

The following testimonials concerning Captain Bennett L. Munger were taken from the writings of several Confederate prisoners of war housed there at Elmira.

Testimonial of Washington B. Traweek a member in Captain J.T. Montgomery's company of the "Jeff Davis" Artillery, attached to the Army of Northern Virginia

In the personal recollections of Washington B. Traweek who was a member in Captain J.T. Montgomery's company of the "Jeff Davis" Artillery, attached to the the Army of Northern Virginia, we have an interesting account dealing with Captain Munger and how Traweek outsmarted the Federal command at Elmira to make good his escape. On May 12, 1864 Traweek was captured at the Battle of Spotsylvania in Virginia when his artillery position was overrun by charging Federal forces. Traweek and other captured prisoners were quickly shuffled off and loaded aboard trains heading toward northern prison pens. He was first sent to the Federal prison at Point Lookout, Maryland but was soon transferred to Elmira, New York around July 1, 1863. After the war Traweek wrote of his exciting and dangerous escape from Elmira prison camp, *Escaping Elmira*. The story details the tunneling operations that were being implemented and undertaken by Confederate soldiers in the hopes of escaping the prison. The following is an excerpt dealing with Captain Munger from that memoir:

Traweek notes, "… After notifying our associates in my tent the next morning, we prepared ourselves and went down in front of hospital No. 1. About twilight we saw a man pass and go under hospital No. 1. It proved to be James W. Crawford (of the 6th Virginia Cavalry and later a member of the tunneling organization). The prison authorities threw a guard around the hospitals, 17 in number, and captured Crawford, took him out and court-martialed him, sentenced him to a dungeon during his imprisonment.

Afterwards our tunnel was also discovered and we went back to work at our first tunnel. Putegnat and I worked in the back of the tunnel, the others carrying the dirt off. About four o'clock in the afternoon I became tired, and came out to the mouth of the tunnel and changed my clothes by turning them wrong side out. About this time five Yankee guards, with bayonets and guns, asked if my name was Traweek. I said it was and they said Major (Henry V. Colt commanding the camp) Colt wanted to see me at his headquarters. I became very uneasy and asked if there was a letter for me. One of the Yankees winked at the other and replied that the major would explain that to me, come on, and I was marched down to Major Colt's headquarters.

After we arrived Colt greeted me by saying, "Good morning, my young tunneler, they tell me you are engaged in tunneling." I replied that I didn't know what a tunnel was.

He replied by stating, "We have a way here of making you know what a tunnel is."

At this time the members of my tent not knowing where I had gone, made inquiry, and Maull and one or two of others came to where I was at headquarters and stood around to ascertain what I was carried there for. In the meantime, Major Colt ordered me to a sweatbox. I was placed in it and the crank turned on me, and had my breath squeezed out. They claimed to have kept me there three quarters of a minute, but it seemed to me to be three hours and a half.

After I got my breath Major Colt said, "Now you have to state where you are tunneling and who was with you." I still told him I didn't know, and he ordered me back to the sweatbox and carried me through the same process.

After the second time...I saw it was my death anyway, and pointed my finger at Colt I told him I would see him in hell as far as a blue bird could fly in a year before I would tell him and that I would rather he would kill me; that he and his comrades were too damn cowardly to do it. He ordered his guards to come around, which they did, and I told him that no brave soldier would treat a man as he had me, with my hands behind my back.

At this time, Fox Maull pushed me two or three times and showed me his pocket knife in his sleeve. At about the same instant a man came up, who was afterward known to me as Captain (Bennett) Munger, the officer of the day, and said, "Major Colt, I know this boy, and if you will turn him over to me, he will tell me all about this tunneling, etc." Major Colt replied: "All right Captain, but he is a sassy son of a bitch and ought to be shot."

Following the headquarters episode, Captain Munger took me to the front of the Federal tents, and said to me, "Wash, they have you, and you might as well tell it all." I said to him: "Who are you?" He responded by saying, "I am Captain Munger, the officer of the day here, and I heard you lie to Colt about the tunnel, saying that you didn't know what a tunnel is, and I know that you do know what a tunnel is, because you went to school to me. You remember I taught school, at Summerfield, near Selma, Alabama, before this war began, ...and what I have said to you, Wash, is for your own good."

I said, "Thank you Captain Munger, I know who you are, and I thank you for your kind intercession, but do not know what tunnel you are talking about."

He said, "You know, Wash, that you are engaged in tunneling under hospital No. 2," and pulled out a list of names who were engaged in that effort. I then acknowledged to tunneling under No. 2, then realizing that he had not discovered the one under the tent. He said, "You should have told Colt this," and I said: "This was not a tunnel but a ditch."

After confessing that I had been a participant, the captain marched me back to Major Colt's headquarters, and told Colt that I had acknowledged, and showed him the list of tunnelers. Major Colt asked me who was engaged in this tunneling with me, and I replied that it was done at night, and I could not tell who they were, except that I knew I was there myself. Then he ordered Captain Munger to take me before the court, which was composed of several Federal officers, who, after making some inquiries, sentenced me to the dungeon, which was in an old military barracks.

Munger carried me, and on reaching it, some twenty or thirty yards off, Captain Munger ordered the diamond holes to the cells opened so that I might see faces of the prisoners, as he had agreed to allow me to go in with some of the other prisoners. As I went down the line I asked each man what he was in there for. Some said for stealing rations, others for fighting, and asked me what I was in for. I told them for tunneling, and a man from the extreme end calling, "I am a tunneler on No. 1, come in with me." I told him I would take a look at him, and if his face looked all right I would go in with him. The cell door was opened, and I was placed in with him. Captain Munger then ordered all the diamond holes closed. He left my hole open, and in talking with me said they were going to have a general inspection and break up all the tunneling. He further stated that he would be off the next day, but would see me the day following.

In the meantime, no one in my tent knew what I was imprisoned for, but suspected it. After getting the information from Munger that there was going to be an inspection, about dark they sent my rations to be by Scruggs, one of my tent mates. He handed it to me through the hole. It consisted of soup and light bread. I took a piece of candle out of my pocket, that I had used in tunneling and lighted it, and took a memorandum out of my pocket and wrote on it that Captain Munger informed me that an inspection would be made the next day to ascertain who was tunneling, and to close down the tunnel. I folded this up, and put it down in the bottom of the soup, crumbled my bread in it and handed it back to the guard, explaining that I was sick and wished either Scruggs or Maull to have my rations, that I knew they were hearty eaters and would want it. The guard gave Scruggs the rations, who soon found the note and delivered it to Maull. They immediately proceeded to close down work on the tunnel.

The next morning, when my ration came in, I received a note from Maull saying that everything had been closed down. I ate about half of the soup and sent Maull another note, saying that I would let him know the next day how everything went.

The next day, when Captain Munger came in, he stated to me that they had gotten them corralled at last, and that they had found 28 tunnels. I asked him how No. 2, my tent, had come out, and he replied that they had been complemented on being kept so clean. I then wrote Maull a note that he could proceed with the work.

They went on with it for about a week. By this time, Crawford became very inquisitive, wanting to know what I was writing so much about. In holding the candle for me he had seen the work tunnel, and told me he knew we were tunneling somewhere, and wanted to know about it. I told him I would let him know in due time.

About this time Maull wrote me that he was making fine progress with the tunnel, and it would be only a few days before it would be completed. I then wrote Maull of Crawford's suspicions, and explained that I could not make my escape without his assistance, and wanted to know if I could swear him into the organization individually. He replied that it would be all right, and knowing that I could not swear Crawford in without a Bible, I asked Captain Munger if he could get me one. He said: "My God, boy, what use have you for a Bible there, where you can't see your hands before your face, and particularly after giving Major Colt the cussing you gave him." I replied that if he was in my fix he would be glad to have a Bible to put his head to sleep on. He said "Well, as there is no harm in the Bible, I will step out and try to get you one." He brought in a small gilt-edged Bible. I then swore Crawford in, and made him a member of the tunnel organization.

After examining the cell overhead, I found two rods with taps on the ends, and in order to get the taps off I had to have a file. I notified Maull of this, and he went out to where the prisoners were making rings of buttons and bones, and sat around awhile, and slipped one of the files and sent this to me in a loaf of bread, at the same time telling the guard that inasmuch as I had divided my rations with him when I was sick, he would divide his with me now that he was sick.

About that time a downpour of rain fell, which was in our favor. I got astride Crawford's neck and filed off the taps. About eleven o'clock I got one of the rods loose, and filed on until four o'clock, when I finished the other rod. After taking the rods loose, I raised the trap door and went into the upper story. On that floor, there were glass windows through which I could see the tunnelers at work on the tunnel. Maull also looked and saw me, and I notified him that I was ready, and he replied that he was also ready.

As this was Captain Munger's day on duty, I told Crawford that I would make one more effort through him to get out. I told Captain Munger to see Major Colt and tell that I thought he had punished me enough for what he would have done under similar circumstances. Captain Munger took the message to Major Colt, and about a half hour after returned saying that he would take us to Major Colt's headquarters. I insisted on Crawford's talking to Colt when we arrived there as I thought Colt would be prejudiced against me for the way I had spoken to him before sent to the dungeon. Crawford refused and I had to talk to Colt myself.

I commenced by apologizing to him, as what I said was in the heat of passion, and told him I thought I out to be released as I did not consider myself any more dangerous than the other 45,000 men in prison, not even having a pocket knife. He studied awhile and finally agreed to release us, but wanted to give advice. I told him if ever a man needed advice, I needed it then, and would appreciate any advice he could give me. He began by saying, "My lad, you were too hasty. If you had been more cautious and taken more time, you would have made your escape. Next time, don't be so hasty and you may get out." I told him that at that time I felt too despondent to undertake tunneling again, that I had enough of it. I thanked him for the advice and bid him good-bye, and went to my tent. We had been confined three weeks in the dungeon before being released.

On reaching the tent and making a careful inspection of the tunnel, I discovered that a bend had been made in it. We went to work and corrected this. That part of the tunnel already dug, which could not be used for depositing the newly dug dirt resulting from further work to complete the tunnel. This relieved us from having to carry the dirt so far, in small quantities, to conceal it. In two nights after I got out of the dungeon, our tunnel was ready to be opened outside the wall.

A question arose as to who should go out first. I volunteered to go out first, with J.W. Crawford, my cellmate in the dungeon, and J.F. Maull agreed to go next. As I broke the dirt on the outside the sentinel called, "Half past three o'clock and all is well." As I crawled out and stepped into the streets of Elmira, Crawford followed immediately.

Before leaving the prison, we had all agreed to meet at a church in the city, whose steeple we had seen from the prison, and there it separates into pairs. But as it was almost daylight, Crawford and I did not wait long. We waded across the river and went into the mountains...."

Washington B. Traweek would make it back to the Confederate lines at Winchester, Virginia after being guided by several of Mosby's men. He then made his way back to Greenville Alabama and lived a peaceful life, eventually retiring in his old age to the home for Confederate Soldiers and Sailors at Biloxi, Mississippi, "Beauvoir." For all of the remainder of his life, Washington B. Traweek always spoke kindly of Captain Munger and noted that he was a fine man and a good soldier who had much sympathy and compassion for the suffering of the poor Confederate soldiers at Elmira. Washington B. Traweek died at "Beauvoir" in 1923, he was the last remaining member of the Elmira tunneling association.

Testimonial of Pvt. Walter Addison, Company A, Breathed's Battery of Stewart's Horse Artillery

From the "Recollections of a Confederate Soldier" by Walter Addison in the Southern Historical Collection of the University of North Carolina Library, Chapel Hill we have the following, partial account presented by Walter Addison who was a private in Company A, Breathed's Battery of Stewart's Horse Artillery commanded by Captain Preston P. Johnson of Baltimore, MD. Walter Addison had been taken prisoner in the summer of 1864 at the time of the Wilderness Campaign, and was sent to Point Lookout and then transferred to Elmira with other Confederate Prisoners of War. The following is his account of the transfer from Point Lookout and the deplorable conditions at Elmira that he witnessed and then his voyage home where he was exchanged at City Point and then moved on to Richmond:

"From Point Lookout, and various other Northern prisons there were about Ten thousand prisoners transferred to Elmira, N.Y. in the summer of 1864, the writer being amongst the number. The first installment from Point Lookout was dispatched by sea via New York City in the month of July upon a miserable old Government transport only fitted to carry cattle. About twelve hundred men were crowded upon this old tub between decks with only the hatches open, and there they remained crowded together like sheep for many days, only allowing one or two at a time on the main deck for a few minutes, when they were ordered into their horrible quarters below. The sight of these holds was sickening in the extreme, and the condition and sufferings of the prisoners therein confined was indeed horrible, and a large number of the men being already sick when placed on board their wretched condition upon the voyage can be imagined better than described. After reaching the harbor of New York we were released from the ship until the following day, and upon clearing the vessel the sight presented can never be forgotten. Think of their journey by sea, several hundred miles, crowded together as we were, with so many sick in the sweltering heat of July. It was on a par with the condition of the Yankee slave ships with a cargo of human souls purchased with a cargo of Boston rum. Our rations consisted of fat pork ad a loaf of bread.

No beds, nor straw to lie upon, only a blanket spread beneath us on the filth covered hard boards only comparable with hog or cattle pen. Never upon the whole voyage was there any attempt made to sweep or clean the floors. There was scarcely an inch of space where there could be a step between the crowded mass of human freight. The insufficient ventilation of the ships holds rendered the stench and the foul air unbearable, and many deaths were the result. The writer owes the preservation of his own life to the kindness of one of the prisoners (now residing in San Francisco) who was fortunate enough to enjoy a little more freedom than the rest, and who managed to smuggle me a small lump of ice, and a swallow of tea when I was lying jammed in amongst the rest of the hold and sick almost to death. Some were already dead when the ship reached New York, and I feel certain that many died afterward from the affects f that horrible voyage. The continuation of the trip afterward to Elmira was attended with less suffering.

When showing the prisoners on the ship at Point Lookout they were supplied with their rations for the voyage, consisting of a piece of very fat mess pork and a loaf of bread, and it can be imagined what was the condition of things between decks when rolling on the billows of the deep, and hardly one escaped the effects of his first experience at sea. It reminded me of only one other scene I witnessed when passengers upon a ship at sea, which was converging at market nearly two thousand huge densely crowded together upon deck, the animals having been fed upon raw potatoes just before starting. The sea affects them as it does a human being. Those swine were accommodated better than we, they being upon the upper decks in the fresh air, whilst we were between decks almost poisoned by the foul air, which was intensely polluted by human excrement.

The return trip to Richmond from Elmira was no more comfortable than the one described. We were marched from the prison to the depot in Elmira through about two feet of snow -- the weather intensely cold -- in February 1865. Upon reaching the depot wet and cold we were crowded into cattle cars wherein was a little dirty straw scattered over the floor, and not a particle of fire. Thus, we were transferred to Baltimore in nearly forty-eight hours, including two whole nights. At Baltimore, we were marched a long distance through a blinding sleet and snow storm to the steamboat upon the wharf from noon till night, when we were placed upon a dilapidated government cattle transport and landed at City Point below Richmond. A violent storm of wind, sleet, and snow raged the entire night of our passage down the bay, and unprotected as we were upon the hurricane deck with only a blanket the night was a hard one. Many of the sick of which there were a large number were placed below decks in the stalls formerly for cattle, and but slightly protected from the weather, and but little more comfortable than there on the hurricane deck. There can be no doubt that it was the grossest indifference on the part of the Government in thus permitting sick prisoners to be conveyed in such an inhuman and cruel manner. I do not believe that in any instance during the war when Northern prisoners suffered as much, if as, it was for lack of provisions and the refusal on the part of the North to exchange prisoners, it seeming their intention to let the latter die rather than refrain from their endeavor to eat out the substance of the South.

The conduct of many of the physicians in charge of the hospitals herein named deserves especial notice, and the strongest condemnation. If they had been dumb brutes, instead of human beings as they were supposed to be, they could not have exhibited greater brutality. I was ward master in one of the hospital barracks at Elmira, which contained from eighty-five to ninety patients crowded, as they sometimes were two or three in a bunk. The physician, a doctor Van Ness made his visits once and sometimes twice every twenty-four hours. For the many different diseases incidental to such places, nearly every patient received opium pills. That being the favorite prescription no matter what the nature of the disease. On one occasion, three persons so being treated were visible shaking, the surgeon-in-chief, a Dr. Sanger, was called in. He directed Dr. Van Ness to write four or five drops of Fowler's solution of arsenic. He wrote forty-five and the patients in a very short time breathed their last breath. No investigation ensued. No reprimand. Dr. Van Ness continued in his position. Hundreds of our prisoners died. I can truthfully say not twenty percent of those in the hospital left it alive. This is no exaggeration of what I believe was a terrible crime growing out of, to put it mildly, the deplorable ignorance of the medical men in charge, if not willful murder.

They had our poor helpless soldiers at their mercy. Often have I heard them, when gathered together in the dispensary discussing their experiences of the day, exult over the numbers of the Rebs they had put through, i.e. killed' and expressing their desire to, in this way, get rid of the whole number of the Confederates there, thus avoiding an exchange. All in authority at Elmira seemed to be of this opinion.

Who that was confined at Andersonville can recall a single instance where there was a greater outrage than at Elmira, where thousands of prisoners were confined in small tents until early winter in such a dreadfully severe climate as that of northern New York where is situated Elmira. I have known persons to be frost bitten, and when some of them provided for themselves little mud chimneys to their tents, gathering chips and other small fuel, the Yankee officers would send a guard to ruthlessly destroy them and Major Beall, who was then in command, would go to the rounds himself, in the middle of the night and deprive them of the extra blankets which were their own personal property, leaving the soldier to freeze to death. No coffee, no tea, no vegetables but a few beans to make tasteless watery soup consisting of the liquid in which the pork had been boiled. After many months, the old soldier barracks -- barns -- were used as hospitals. Hundreds were wedged in, and crowded together like packed sardines. Two and frequently three in a bunk. They had no opportunity to cleanse themselves of vermin there first found, therefore who can wonder at the fearful numbers of deaths, arising from ignorant medical supervision, and total lack of proper ventilation. Of the false statements of the humanity then boasted by the Yankee, the bored will get a truthful statement. Humanity equal to that shown at the time they burned, so termed witches. The Northern people, not descended from Yankees, will when the whole truth is known, believe the palm of humanity belonged to the South, and will see through the intentional falsehoods of a prejudiced press.

There is no doubt in my mind as to the intention of our enemies to rid themselves of as many of our prisoners as was possible, no matter what the means to which they resorted. Witness in various instances when contagious diseases were introduced into crowded prisons. I recollect, in one instance at Elmira hundreds of deaths were the result of smallpox introduced by patients from Blackwell's Island, New York. Up to that time not a case of the disease had been known there. In a few days, it manifested itself in one of the new importations. Instead of being isolated, he was placed immediately adjoining one of the wards used as a hospital, and there remained for days. Other cases rapidly developed, and soon broke out in a virulent form. Tents were then placed inside the stockade where hundreds were confined, and immediately upon their convalescence were again distributed amongst the well prisoners, even occupying the same beds, thus spreading the disease to an appalling degree. No comfortable buildings were provided for the wretched victims, even when the temperature fell twenty degrees below zero. Very few smallpox patients survived. When discharging smallpox cases, they were led to a pump, and there stripped and washed in the coldest weather, and then assigned new quarters for a brief time, when they were returned to the hospital to meet their deaths. Their sufferings were laughed at. Considering their ill usage, premeditated torture, insufficient food, and the prevailing lack of any show of humanity it seems a miracle that one again reached his home. I repeatedly heard it said by Federal officers that the mortality at Elmira far exceeded that at Andersonville. I will say in justice to two officers, Captains Whiton and Munger that they did what they could to alleviate the sufferings of the prisoners, but were almost powerless to render the aid they deserved."

Testimonial of Sergeant Joe M. Womack a member of Wade Hampton's Cavalry Legion

Sergeant Joe M. Womack a member of Wade Hampton's Cavalry Legion had been captured in Virginia and sent to Elmira on August 1, 1864 and eventually made his escape to freedom on October 26, 1864 after being incarcerated there for only three months. Womack had posed as a guard and simply walked out of the prison after giving the guard and the officer on duty a bogus pass. In a letter written to his friend Sergeant Melvin Mott Conklin who was a Federal guard assigned to Barracks No. 3, many years after the war, Womack noted: "The memory of Major H. V. Colt and dear old Captain Munger, and their kindly and parental solicitude about the boys under their care, has always been to me a tender spot, and years ago, I had occasion to write that the Lord would reward them both with a high seat in heaven…." Womack reached Richmond, Va. on December 14, 1864 and reported to Judah P. Benjamin, Secretary of War, ready for duty.

An interesting point of fact in this story concerns Sergeant Melvin Mott Conklin formally a member of Company A, 151st New York Volunteers. In August of 1862 Conklin was serving as a private in this unit and served at the front until July of 1863 when he and a number of other men were detailed for recruiting duty and sent to Elmira. While at Elmira he was assigned to Barracks No. 3, where he worked in the Adjutant's office and acted as Sergeant Major in the Adjutant's absence. Conklin's duties encompassed administrative duties ranging from paperwork to taking care of duties within the camp's grounds and boundaries, but he was not responsible for any of the guard duty performed at the camp. Sergeant Conklin was also given the duty as commissary with two prisoners doing the cooking for the mess. Interestingly enough, Conklin had another secret calling in the grand scheme of Camp operations. Conklin was a secret policeman or prison detective directly commissioned by none other than, Captain Bennett L. Munger. Conklin's duties involved, ferreting out tunneling and escape plots perpetrated by the prisoners to gain their liberty. Conklin proved to be an able master of disguise and on many occasions perpetrated the ruse of being a Confederate prisoner of war to get next to any devilry that might be going on in the camp. He was an expert at gaining information on tunneling operations and all but one of the tunnels was discovered on his watch as a special investigator for Captain Munger. Conklin left camp and was sent back to the front on February 23rd, 1865. He was mustered out with his regiment on June 26th, 1865. Several years after the war he came back to settle in Elmira and became one of the town's most respected and prominent citizens, becoming Postmaster and a member of the local G.A.R Post. Through his efforts, the Post helped mark the boundaries of the camp and set up monuments in 1900. Through Conklin's efforts much of the prison's history was preserved.

Note: The following letter from the Shelly Case collection is a written testimonial of commendation by Sgt. Leroy Summerfield Edwards of Company E, 12th Virginia Infantry who was a prisoner of war at Elmira, N.Y. that was given to Captain Bennett Munger as a letter of introduction & a testimonial of Munger's kindness. The letter was to be presented to Edwards' friends, family & associates in Virginia & the Kanawha Valley in West Virginia when the Captain visited West Virginia in early 1865 to speculate in land & natural resources. This letter was addressed to Rev. John Ellis Edwards, a prominent clergy member of the Methodist Episcopal Church in Richmond, Va. and Leroy S. Edwards' father.:

Elmira Prison Camp, NY. Jan. 15, 1865

Capt. B. Munger, while connected with this prison in an official capacity, ever manifested the liveliest interest in the well-being of the Prisoners of War in his charge. Courteous, attentive to their complaints, alleviating as he was able their sufferings & active in adding to their comforts, he is entitled to the regard of all true men & especially of the friends of the Prisoners of War, - in who's behalf his labors were so earnestly directed – does his generosity demand the highest consideration. Personally, the Captain has been particularly attentive, doing much to make my condition pleasant. I shall ever remember him with liveliest gratitude, and pray that should any misfortune befall him, & my friends be enabled in any way to assist, that they will not permit his past kindness to me go unrequited. Should this word come to my father, he will recognize the sincerity.

L. S. Edwards

Co. E, 12th Va. Inf.

Sgt. Leroy Summerfield Edwards

Post war photograph courtsy of the McGraw-Page Library at Randolph-Macon College, Ashland, Va.

Leroy Summerfield Edwards: Born in 1839, he was the son of Reverend John Ellis Edwards & Elizabeth Agnes Clark Edwards of Richmond, Va. He attended Randolph-Macon College from 1857 – 1859 & graduated with an A.B in 1859 and received an A.M. in 1866. In 1861 when war was declared he was teaching at Petersburg Female College. He made haste & enlisted as a private in Company E, 12th Virginia Infantry. He was wounded in the arm September 4, 1862 at Crampton's Gap, Md. & promoted to Sgt. in 1863. He was engaged at the Seven Days Battles & wounded severely at Smith Mountain. Edwards participated in the fights at Sharpsburg & the Wilderness. He was captured by Federals on May 8, 1864 when en route to Spotsylvania Courthouse. He was sent to Point Lookout, Md. As a P.O.W. from May to Aug. 1864 & then transferred to Elmira, NY. & remained there from August, 1864 until he was paroled & exchanged in February, 1865, returning to Richmond by March, where he participated in the evacuation of the Capitol in April, with Lee's forces and fell back to surrender in the fields at Appomattox Court House with the rest of the Army of Northern Virginia where he was paroled.

During his lifetime Edwards accomplished a great deal to benefit the lives of others around him. He became home agent for the Piedmont & Arlington Life Insurance Co. in Richmond; president of the YMCA in Richmond; secretary for the Association of the Virginia Division of the Army of Northern Virginia; and a teacher/professor/principle in several schools including Petersburg Female College. He died in 1901 & is buried at the Hollywood Cemetery in Richmond, Virginia.

THE CLOSING STORY OF CAPT. BENNETT L. MUNGER

Major Henry V. Colt was in direct command of Elmira Prison under Lt. Col. Seth Eastman and later under Col. Benjamin Tracy, by all reports he was a fair and decent man who was liked by most of the Union and Confederate soldiers alike. He was noted as being a personable man with a jovial disposition who liked cigars and who tried to deal fairly but firmly with the prisoners housed at Elmira. He was also the brother of the famous, Samuel Colt of Colt Firearms fame.

In a deposition given by Henry V. Colt on March 29, 1887 at Genesee, New York before J.M. Clancey, a Special Examiner of the Pension Office concerning the case of Captain Bennett L Munger, we have the following, "…I was Major in the 104th New York Volunteer Infantry. I knew the Captain; he was Captain of one of the Companies of the 44th New York Volunteers. He was on duty with me. I had charge of the camp at Elmira. He was inspector. I cannot tell what month it was Oct. or Nov. of 1864. We stood together inside the camp near my office, the guard a relief of the inside guard, was standing around a fire nearly behind us and a pistol was accidently discharged by one of the guard, taking effect or the ball striking the back of Capt. Munger just below the shoulder blade. He was taken to his quarters and treated for his wound. He was treated by some of the surgeons on duty at the prison camp. I cannot tell the name of the surgeon that treated him there were quite a number of them there. He did some duty after that but always complained of the effects of the wound."

MAJOR HENRY V. COLT – Chemung County Historical Society

The facts of the actual story relate that in October of 1864, a rusty revolver was discovered stuck in the mud by one of the Confederate prisoners who then turned the revolver over to one of the guards on duty. The guard on reporting the incident was told to dispose of the weapon. While standing around a fire several of the guards were inspecting the weapon and trying to get the cylinder free so that it would revolve when the gun discharged with the bullet striking Captain Munger in the back. The surgeons made repeated efforts to extract the ball but did not succeed in retrieving the ball which was lodged near

Captain Munger's lung. An investigation into the incident proved that the incident was an unfortunate accident and not a deliberate act. This wounding and the previous wounding at Gettysburg were attributed to Captain Munger's failing health and his eventual death in 1877.

After the war, Captain Munger worked on his farm as a farmer and also served as justice of the peace of Canandaigua, New York on numerous occasions. He was a highly-respected citizen and many residents of his town attested that he had a sterling character. At his funeral in 1877 many citizens also attested that he was a good soldier, good man, honest and upright and faithful to all of his obligations of citizenship and in every relation in life. Strangely enough, just a few days prior to his death, Captain Munger's brother, Lyman came from his home in the West to visit his brother and the family. Bennett L. Munger died October 27, 1877 from pneumonia and complications caused by the old war wounds that he had received at Gettysburg and at Elmira. Bennett L. Munger was 60 years old at the time of his death.

Captain Bennett L. Munger is buried in section 13, lot 26 of the West Avenue Cemetery at Canandaigua, Ontario County, New York

Photographs courtesy of Gail Wiechmann - Wood Library Canandaigua, New York

THE UNUSUAL STORY OF CAPTAIN BENNETT MUNGER'S PERSONAL EFFECTS RECOVERED IN THE 21ST CENTURY

In the summer of 1972 I was ten years old and my parents loaded up my brother, Brent and myself in the family station wagon and headed for Gettysburg, Pennsylvania for vacation. At that time, I had no idea of the lasting impression that this trip and subsequent trips to Gettysburg would make on my psyche as well as on my life in general. As my family drove the winding roads that snaked over the battlefield we eventually passed Devil's Den and then came to a stop at Little Round Top. As we walked along the ridge we looked at the monuments and then entered the impressive monument of the 44th New York Infantry. As we stepped into the foyer of the monument we were greeted with a number of large bronze tablets listing all of the names of the men from the 44th who were either killed or wounded on that spot, on July 2, 1863. Before climbing the narrow stairway to the observation deck of the monument I decided to read all of the names of these men. One name in particular made an impression on me for some reason, and that was the name of Captain Bennett L. Munger of Company C, who was one of the officers wounded during the defense of Little Round Top. I thought. "What an unusual name." Years later I would return to the site and read the tablets again and note the name of Captain Munger. Little did I realize that on these repeated trips to Gettysburg and my continued pilgrimage to the 44th New York monument would one day beckon me to the letters and diaries of Captain Munger.

In the summer of 2009, I was contacted by local Civil War re-enactor and historian, John Haddox of St. Marys, West Virginia. John explained that he knew a gentleman in Marietta, Ohio who wanted to sell a group of Civil War letters and a diary. I took the contact information and set up a meeting with Shawn Darra, a local Marietta jeweler. Shawn explained that he had taken a job cleaning out a local Marietta businessman's business and rental property on Green Street after the 1989 visit of Hurricane Hugo to the valley. The deal included that Shawn could keep anything that he found from the cleanout. As Shawn cleaned up the mess left by flooding and the storm he came across a plastic shopping bag containing Civil War letters from a New York soldier. Shawn related that he had also found old magazines and periodicals which he later sold, but for some reason he did not part with the letters. As I looked over the letters and the diary it did not instantly occur to me that these were the letters of Captain Munger, but something kept telling me that I should make an offer on the material. I was too wrapped up in the moment of actually discovering such a large cache of Civil War letters, but the question was, would they be of use in my research since I was actually looking for letters from West Virginia and Ohio soldiers? As Shawn and I talked we came to an agreement on his asking price for the letters and diary. I knew that I had broken one of my own cardinal rules of buying letters that did not deal with my particular line of interest. I felt a bit apprehensive, but something kept telling me that I had made the proper decision. Upon arriving home I spent about a half an hour researching the letters and then it hit me like a ton of bricks! These were the letters of Captain Bennett Munger from the 44th New York Infantry of Little Round Top and part of the famous 3rd Brigade, 1st Division, 5th Army Corps! I could not believe my luck and quickly started reading over the letters and the diary. While at Shawn's house I had only looked at two of the letters superficially and glanced at one of the entries in the diary that dealt with weather conditions for the day. Not really a good thing to do, but my time was limited and we both wanted to cut a deal that was acceptable to both of us. After reading about ten of the letters I realized that these were important enough for future publication and I soon started the task of transcribing the letters and the diary. Unfortunately, none of us were able to figure out how Captain Munger's letters got so far away from Pen Yan, New York to end up in Marietta, Ohio but for me it was a stroke of luck if not the fulfillment of destiny and everything coming full circle, or at least I thought that.

The next year, my girlfriend and I attended the Mansfield Civil War show held at the Richland County fairgrounds on May 1st and 2nd, 2010. I had no idea that I was about to have a very unusual and strange situation take place. As I made my rounds through the building looking for artifacts, letters, weapons and possible items related to the 44th New York Infantry to add to my collection, I noticed a man sitting at one of the tables and for some reason I had the impression that I should go over and speak with him for some reason, but I let that feeling pass and I continued on my hunt through the various buildings scattered throughout the fairgrounds for the items that piqued my interest. It is not uncommon to go through the numerous buildings several times to look at all of the artifacts several times. Each time that I came back to the building that had this man in it I was almost compelled to go speak with him, but as before I shook off the urge and continued on my quest looking for items dealing with the 44th New York Infantry and possibly Captain Bennett Munger. At the end of the first day I had bought several books and a number of dug artifacts and a nice CS 12Lb cannonball dug at Petersburg, Virginia but not a single item belonging to the 44th New York Infantry. I thought to myself, "Maybe tomorrow I will have better luck."

The next day at the show I started the process all over again and I passed this man several times just as I had done before on the first day without stopping to talk to him. The day wore on and eventually it was time to go. I was about ready to leave when I told my girlfriend, Donna who had come to the show with me that I was being strongly compelled to go over and talk to this man. I explained that I did not know why but I had to talk to him before we left for home. Donna and I made our way through the crowd to the table where the man was seated and I said. "I had seen you several times before while going through the show and I felt like I needed to talk to you." The man said, "That is strange, because I had seen you and felt the same thing." I then introduced myself and he in turn introduced himself saying, "I am Bill Acree it is nice to meet you". I then said, "Do you have anything on the 44th New York infantry?" The expression on Bill's face then looked as if he was transfixed, and looking straight ahead as if in a trance with his eyes fixed on an object far in the distance said almost in a staggered cadence, "Captain Bennett Munger, Company C, 44th New York Infantry" I was in a state of near disbelief and reported, "I have his letters and diary." To which Bill reported, "I have his picture and his sword." Both of us were now in a state of near disbelief. It has often been said that at times in our lives we are guided by some higher power when searching for insight, truth or meaning. I cannot help but think that this was one of those times. Bill and I went on to exchange contact information and the next year at the 2011 show he brought his pictures of Elmira Prison and Captain Munger along with Captain Munger's sword. My girlfriend, Donna brought her camera and took a number of pictures of the relics that now appear in this publication. I asked Bill in 2010 to send me an account of how he found the photos and the sword of Captain Munger. The following is his account:

Bennett Munger Sword and Photo - 44th New York Infantry – Letter dated July 1, 2010

Brian: Sorry for the delay in answering your request, but have been busy with family matters (mother's estate). Here is the story you requested:

Several years ago, I acquired an image (CDV) of Capt. Bennett Munger, 44th NYI from a Civil war dealer at one of the shows that I attended. The research that was with the photo appeared to be good, so I bought it. Research showed that he (Munger) was wounded at Gettysburg on Little Round Top, and due to the severity of his wounds, was assigned as a Prison Inspector at Elmira Prisoner of War Camp, and in October of 1864 he was shot in the back by accidental discharge of an old revolver found by a Confederate prisoner while he and another officer were inspecting a line of prisoners (shot by a guard examining the revolver who was behind him at the time). The bullet was never recovered and had lodged under his right lung, which caused him trouble the rest of his life (subsequently died of Pneumonia and general deterioration caused by the old wound several years later).

In 2007 at the Marietta, Georgia CW Show, I had just begun looking at items when at about the sixth table, I saw a foot officer's sword in a scabbard missing the lower third and drag part. I also noticed a presentation on the throat of the scabbard. The sword was in average condition, so I picked it up to look at it, and read the presentation on the throat of the scabbard. I couldn't believe it when I read "Presented to Capt. Bennett Munger, 44th New York by his men". As the price was acceptable, I certainly bought the sword. Several months later, an image of Elmira Prison which showed the tents and lines of prisoners being inspected was offered on Ebay for sale. I was the winning bidder, and received the image in the mail a few weeks later. The image was in average condition, but when I turned it over; I found a tax stamp on the reverse which was cancelled with the date of Oct. 1864 (the same month Capt. Munger was shot at Elmira). All are now a part of the Munger collection (sword, image of Munger, and image of Elmira).

Let me know if you need more information. Good luck on your book.
Bill

Civil War dealer and historian, Bill Acree of Pigeon Forge, Tennessee with the sword of Captain Bennett L. Munger at the May, 2011 Mansfield, Ohio Civil War Show.

Photograph by Donna L. Setler - New Port, Ohio

This early war photograph of Captain Bennett L. Munger of Company C, 44th New York Volunteer Infantry was taken by photographer, J. H. Abbott, No. 480 Broadway, Albany, N.Y. – Photo Courtesy of Bill Acree, Pigeon Forge, Tennessee

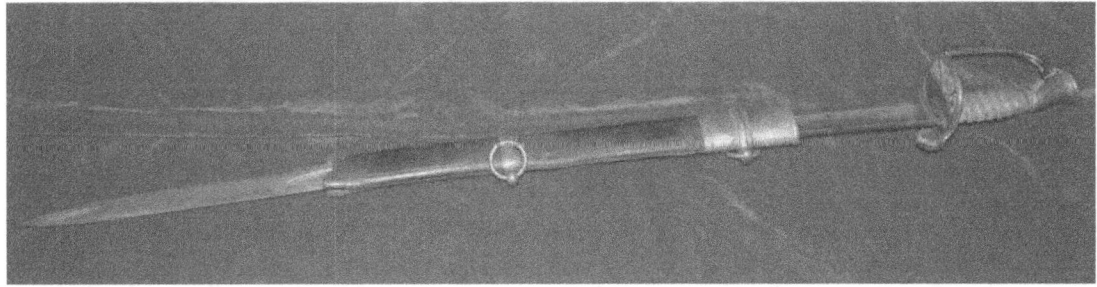

Photographs by Donna L. Setler – New Port, Ohio

Presentation Infantry sword and scabbard belonging to Captain Bennett L. Munger, 44th New York State Volunteer Infantry - Note that the lower half of the scabbard and drag are missing from the scabbard.

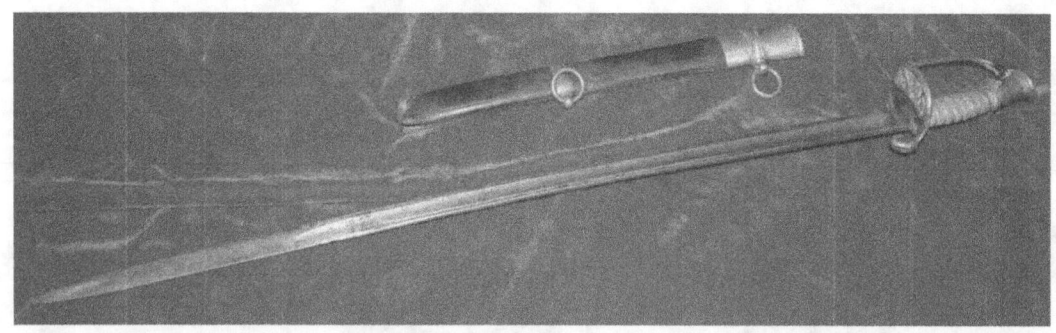

Top photograph – The remaining scabbard section of Captain Munger's infantry officer's sword

Bottom Photograph – The brass throat of Captain Munger's sword scabbard with the inscription, "Presented To Captain Bennett Munger 44th New York By His Men"

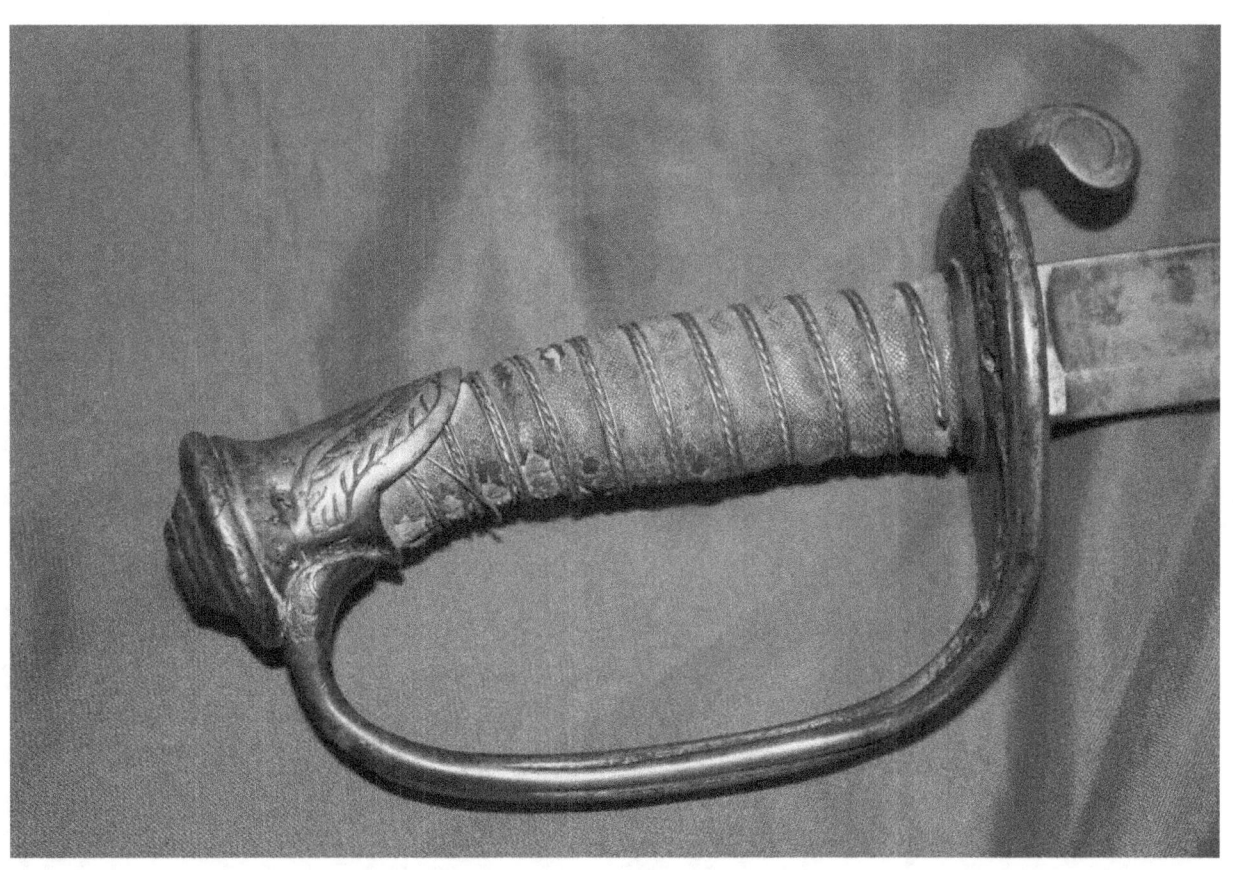

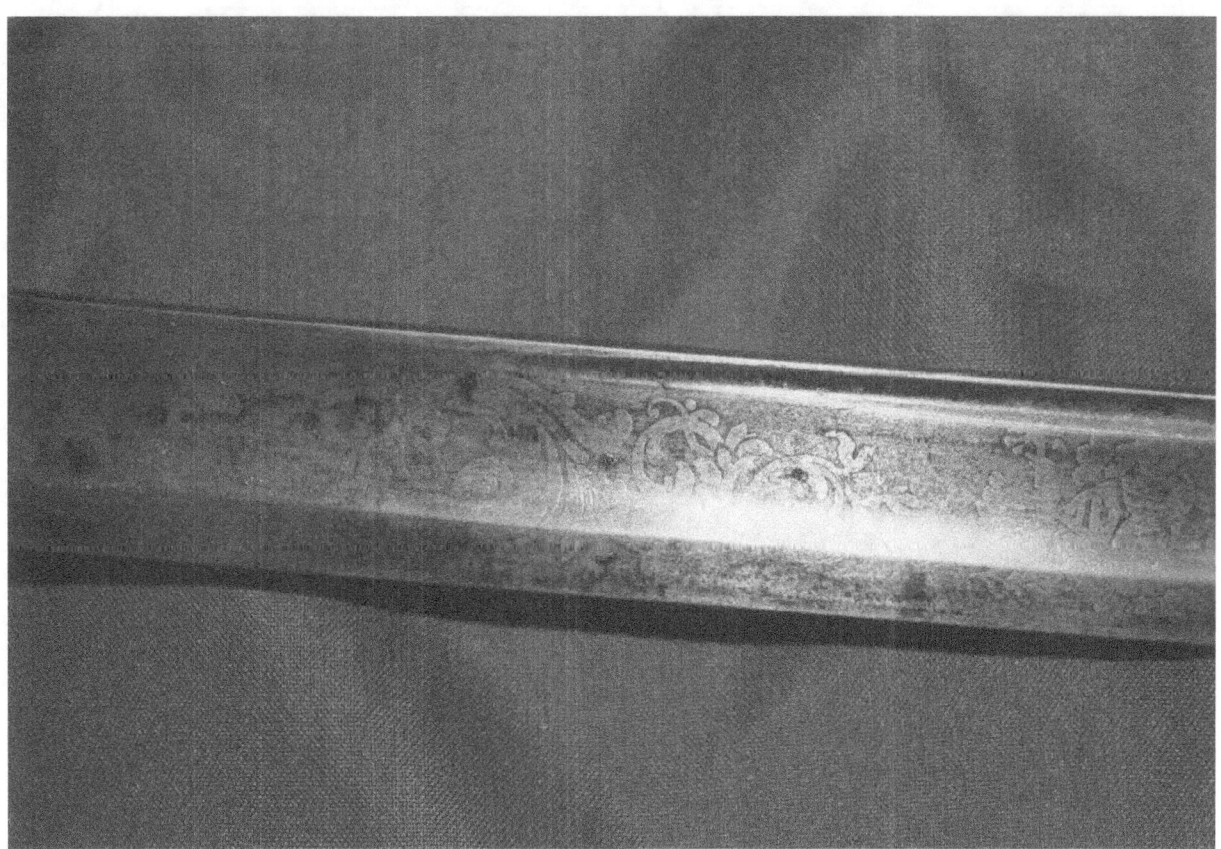

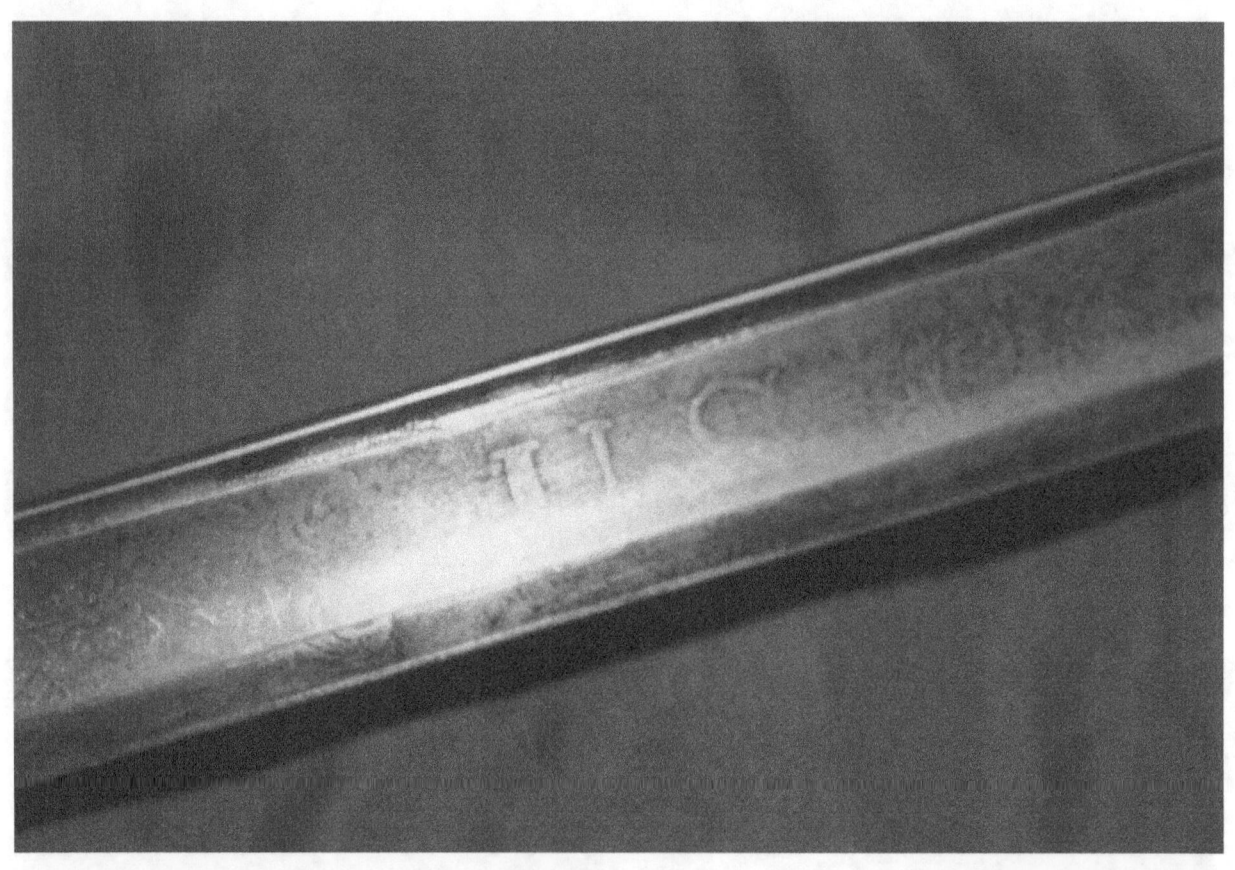

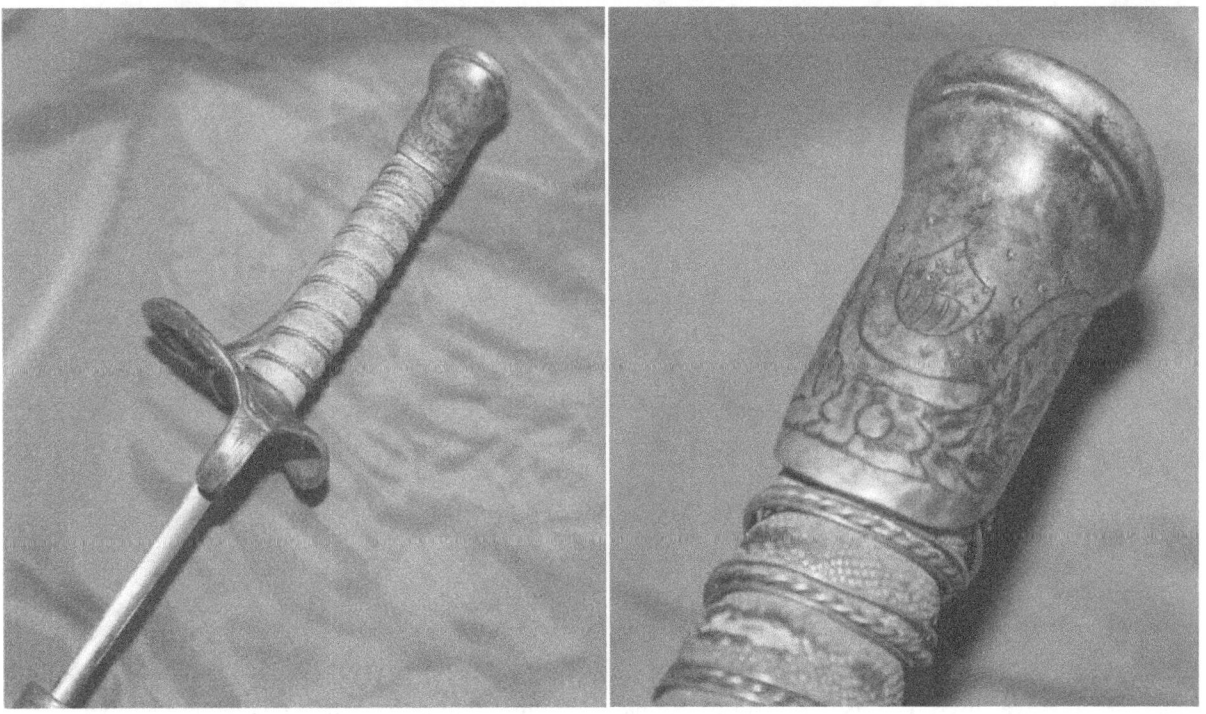

DOCUMENTS PERTAINING TO CAPTAIN MUNGER'S SERVICE

The following documents were recovered in a large, white envelope titled, "Request form for Straw BKS (Barracks) No. 1". The following forms deal with acquisitions, orders and mustering out information pertaining to Captain Bennett L. Munger's service in the 44th New York Infantry and his service as Inspector of Elmira Prison Camp in Elmira, New York.

This collection also contains several documents from Captain Munger's nephew, Orett Munger dealing with ordinance returns for regimental equipment. There are also a number of loan and promissory documents from other soldiers who either owed money or asked Captain Munger to be a retainer for their money. These documents though few in number give a unique insight into the daily business, duties and affairs that Captain Munger dealt with on a daily basis while stationed at Elmira.

A number of these documents also come from the massive Munger document collection owned by his great, great granddaughter, Shelly Case of West Chester, Pennsylvania.

When scanning these documents, it became necessary to resize several of them so that they would fit the page format. Aside from these minor alterations these documents were scanned from the originals that were part of Captain Munger's personal papers.

It should also be noted that the photograph of Elmira Prison belonging to Bill Acree of Pigeon Forge, Tennessee that was used for this publication also has a revenue stamp that was canceled in October, the same month that Captain Munger was wounded.

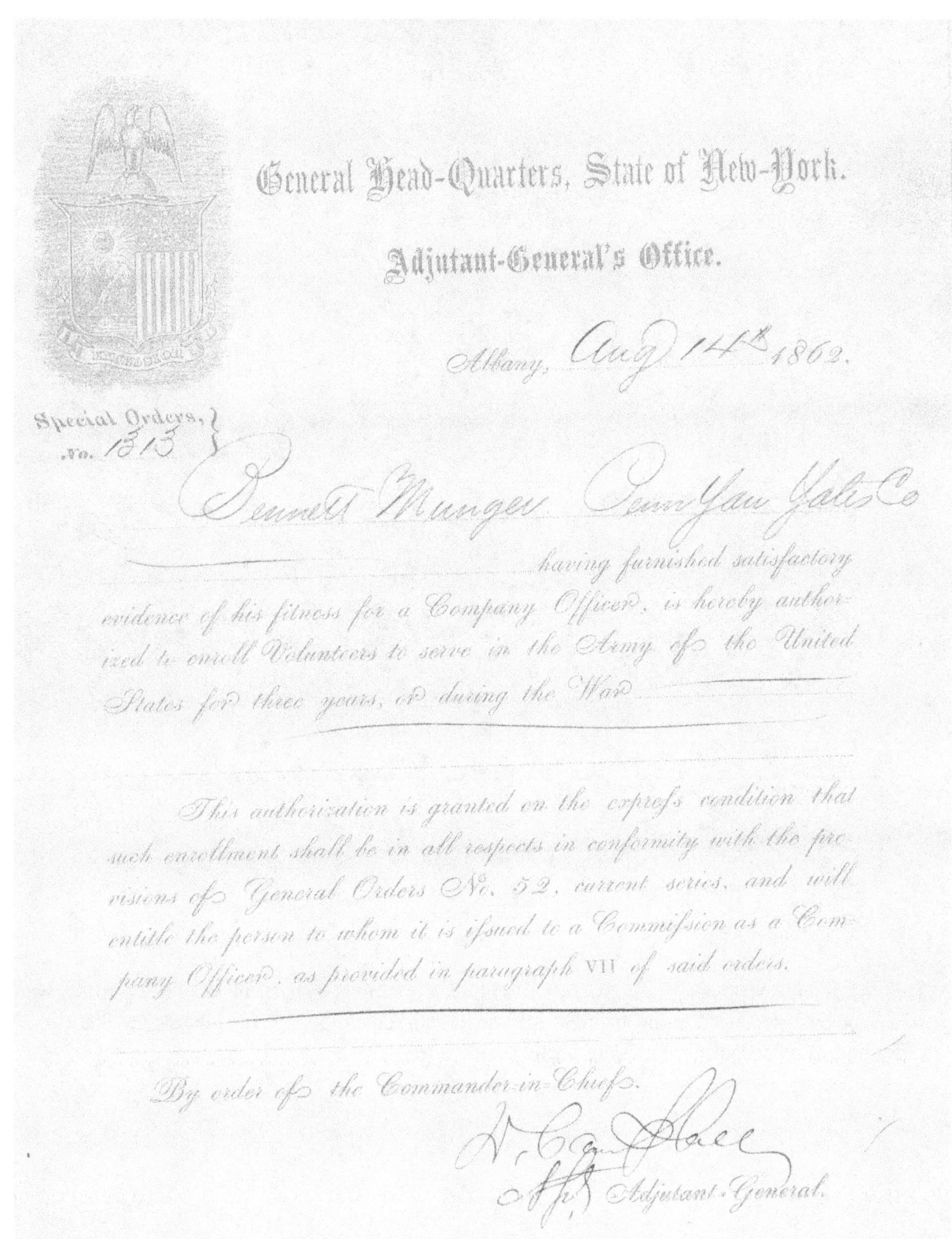

Capt. Munger's August, 1862 certification to enroll a company of volunteers into the U.S. Army. Courtesy Shelly Case.

This "Abstract of Materials" for Company C, 44th New York Infantry shows that 650 ball cartriges were consumed by Company C, during the fight at Little Round Top on July 2nd, 1863 during the Battle of Gettysburg. This document courtesy of Shelly Case.

Head-Quarters, Middle Department,

8th Army Corps.

Baltimore, Md., July 7th, 1863.

Special Orders,
No. 182

Capt Bennet Munger 44th N.Y. Vol. wounded in the late battle at Gettysburgh, having procured a Surgeon's certificate of his disability, is, in accordance with instructions from the Secretary of War, allowed to proceed to his home at Pen Yan. Immediately on his arrival there he will report to the Adjutant General at Washington, D. C.

By command of Major General Schenck,

N. L. Jeffries
Assistant Adjutant General.

This July 7th, 1863 "Surgeon's Certificate of Disability" was issued to Capt. Munger for his wounding at Gettysburg, Pa. on July 2nd, 1863. This document courtesy Shelly Case.

Medical Director's Office, Middle Department, 8th Army Corps,

Baltimore, Md., July 7 1863.

Capt. Bennett Munger 44th N.Y. Vols. wounded in the late battle near Gettysburgh having applied for a certificate of disability, I hereby certify that I have carefully examined said Officer, and find him unfit for duty in consequence of said wounds G.S.W. Groin and further I believe said officer will not be fit for duty in a less period than Ten days.

Z. E. Bliss
Surgeon U. S. Vols.
In charge of Invalid Officers.

Capt. Munger's Certificate of Disability. Courtesy of Shelly Case.

I do hereby certify that I have carefully examined Capt Bennett Munger of the 44th Regiment of New York Volunteers who was wounded in the late battle near Gettysburgh Pa, and find him still unfit for duty in consequence of said wound being a gunshot wound in the lower part of the left side of the abdomen near the groin, and that in my opinion and belief said officer will not be fit for duty in a less period than two weeks from the 17th of July inst

Penn Yan N.Y. July 28. 1863.

H. P. Sartwell M.D.

State of New York
County of Yates } ss: Sworn to and Subscribed before me this 28th day of July 1863; and I hereby certify that the above named Dr Sartwell is well known to me as a Physician and Surgeon now and for many years in actual practice, and that he is reputable in his profession.

In Testimony whereof I have hereunto set my hand and affixed my notarial seal at Penn Yan in said County.

Sam'l H Booth Notary Public
In & for Yates Co N.Y.

Certificate of medical examination for Capt. Munger. Courtesy of Shelly Case.

Members of the court-martial commission that Capt. Munger was on in August of 1863.

> Members of Gen. Court Martial. convened by Gen. Order No 37. Hd.Qrs. 1st Div. 5 Corps. Aug 27th 1863.
>
> Lieut. Col. Wm A Throop 1st Mich Vol.
> Capt. Wm C Beck 62d Penna "
> " J. F. McGunnigle 9th Mass "
> " L. L. Crocker 118 Penna "
> " B. Munger 44; N York "
> " Jo. F. Land 20" Maine "
> 1st Lieut Wm Kydd 16th Mich "
> " " Robert Smith 22d Mass "
> " " James E March, 32d " "
> Capt. C. Allen 44; N York Vols.
> Judge Advocate.
>
> Sept. 8th 1863.

Courtesy of Shelly Case

Court-martial proceedings against Private Jacob Stroup of Co. C, 44th New York Infantry. Courtesy Shelly Case.

Charge & Specification
Against Private Jacob Stroup of Co. C. 44th Reg N.Y.S.V.

Charge Desertion

Specification
In this that he the said Jacob Stroup a private in Co. C. 44th Reg. N.Y.S.V. did on or about the 29 day of June 1863 at or near Frederick City, Md. desert from his Co and Reg and did remain absent until delivered up as a prisoner in citizens dress and without arms or equipments at Camp near Beverly Ford Va. on or about 29th of Aug 1863

B. Munger Capt Co. C. 44th N.Y.S.V.

> Rappahannock Station Va. Dec 31 1863
>
> I Certify on honor that on the 7 day of November 1863 at Rappahannock Station the Stores enumerated below were lost under the following circumstances. Ninety men of our Reg had been detailed to act as Skirmishers when the charge was made on the enemies fortifications, the skirmishers advanced with a portion of the 6th Corps. Jerome Wheaton a private in my Co was killed on that charge & his gun & equipments were taken by other parties probably officers of the 6th Corps
>
> 1 Springfield rifled musket Cal .58
> 1 Cartridge box & plate
> 1 " " belt & plate
> 1 Waist belt & plate
> 1 Cap pouch & cone pick
> 1 Gun Sling
> 1 Bayonet Scabbard
> 1 Screw driver & cone wrench
>
> Bennett Munger Capt
> Comd Co. L 121th N.Y. Vols

Capt. Munger's documentation of Pvt. Jerome Wheaton's death. Courtesy Shelly Case.

"Copy"

Head Qrs 44th NY Vols
January 20th 1864

Special Orders
No 11.

In compliance with S.O. No. 9. Hd. Qrs. Army of the Potomac January 11th 1864 the following named Officers of this command will proceed to Elmira N.Y. and report for duty to the commandant of the draft rendezvous at that place.

x   x   x

Capt. B Munger 44th N.Y. Vols.

By Command of Lieut Col Conner
Comm'dg Regt,
Geo. B. Herendeen
Adjutant.

Capt. Munger's orders to report to Elmira Prison. Courtesy of Shelly Case.

> Head Quarters Depot for Drafted Men
> Elmira N.Y. January 22nd 1864
>
> Special Orders   "Extract"
> No 84   x   x   x
>
> The following named Officers having Reported at these Hd. Qrs., are assigned to duty at Barracks No 3, and will report to Majr Ramsey without delay.
>
> Capt. B Munger 44th N.Y. Vols
>   x   x   x
>
> By Order of Lt Col S. Eastman
> C. S. Blake
> Lt & A. Assistant adjt Genl.

Capt. Munger's orders to report to Barracks No. 3 – Courtesy of Shelly Case.

TREASURY DEPARTMENT,
SECOND AUDITOR'S OFFICE,
Feb. 9th, 1864.

Sir:

Your return of Arms &c appertaining to Compy. C. 44th New York Vol for the following quarter 4th of 1862.

has been received, examined, and found correct. except.

Voucher for (26) Muskets &c turned over to Qr Master required

Lieut E. B. James
Co. C 44th N.Y. Vol

Respectfully,
Your obedient servant,

E. B. French
Second Auditor.

No. 27.

LIST OF ~~QUARTERMASTER'S STORES~~ Camp & Garrison Equipage, &c., Transferred by Lt Col E C Brooks 64 N Y Vols Quartermaster No 1 U.S. Army, to Capt B Munger 44 N Y Vols Quartermaster U. S. Army, at Elmira New York, on the 28th day of March, 1864.

NUMBER OR QUANTITY.		ARTICLES.	COST WHEN NEW.		CONDITION WHEN DELIVERED.	REMARKS.
			Dolls.	Cts.		
24	Twenty four	Camp Kettles			New	
41	Forty one	Mess Pans			"	
10	Ten	Spades			"	
5	Five	Axes			"	
5	Five	Ax helves			"	
5	Five	Pic Axes			"	
5	Five	Pic ax helves			"	

I CERTIFY that I have this day Transferred to Capt M Munger 44 N Y Vol Quartermaster U. S. Vol Army, at Elmira New York, the articles specified in the foregoing list.

E C Brooks Lt Col 64 N Y Vols
Quartermaster.

No. 36.

REQUISITION for STRAW, for ~~Company~~ Volunteer Recruits, ~~Regiment~~ of _____, commanded by Capt B Munger, for the month of April, 1864.

STATION.	Non-commissioned officers, musicians, and privates.	Laundresses.	Servants.	Total drawn for.	Monthly allowance to each. Pounds.	Total allowance. Pounds.	REMARKS.
Barracks No 1 Elmira N.Y.	964	—	—	964	12	11568	
Total	964	—	—	964	12	11568	

I CERTIFY, on honor, that the above requisition is correct and just; and that straw has not been drawn for any part of the time above charged.

_____ Commanding Company.

RECEIVED, at _____ the _____ of _____, 186 , of _____ Quartermaster U. S. Army, _____ pounds of straw, in full of the above requisition.

(SIGNED DUPLICATES.)

_____ Commanding Company.

Alexandria Va. April 9th 1864

Capt. Bennett Munger
    In A/c with Lieut. O. L. Munger Dr.

To 1/3 of Servant for two months & Nine days		13.65
" 1/2 " " 15 days (during Lt. Kelly's leave)		4.13
" Paid Aggie per his order		5.00
" " Westcott for Washing		1.65
		$23.43

Cr

By Paid for Servant for Three months		49.50
" Soldier's Ticket from Troy to Baltimore		4.60
		$54.10
Balance due the Captain		$30.67

Lieut Kelly has paid me for his part of the servant during those three months, so I have credited the whole amount to you and charged you with your own share of the expense.

                         O. L. Munger

Alexandria Va. April 28th 1864

Capt. B. Munger

Dear Uncle

I enclose papers for your Ordnance return for January and February 1864, which require your signature. Lieut. Kelly will receipt for all the articles for which you are responsible, if you will agree to receipt to him, when you return to the regiment, for the same discrepancies. I have had a careful inventory taken of all the Ordnance Property in the company and find a great discrepancy between what is really on hand and what you are responsible for. Lieut. Kelly receipts for 3 Bay. Sheaths – 1 Cap Pouch – 4 Cart. Boxes – 22 C. Box Belts – 34 C. Box. Belt Plates – 4 Waist Belts – 5 Waist Belt Plates – 11 Screw drivers – 1 Ball Screw – 20 Tompions and 2 Bayonets more than are on hand in the company. On the other hand there are in the company – 3 Muskets – 3 Cart. Box Plates and 7 Wormers – more than he receipts for. If you will sign and return the enclosed papers, as soon as possible, I can probably get them off my hands before we move. Nothing exciting here.

Lone and John came to Washington Saturday night and staid till Wednesday morning. I visited them in Washington Sunday and Monday. Tuesday they visited me in camp and Returned with them in the evening and attended the Presidents levee in Washington. Had a splendid time. John got his National bank through all right. It is now 11 O'clock P.m. and I must close. I have written you one or two letters lately, to which I have received no answer. Did Kelly pay you for the clothing he had drawn. I am well. Love to Aunt Mary and Eda. Write soon.

Your Aff. Nephew
Orpett E. Munger

No. 27.

LIST OF QUARTERMASTER'S STORES, &c., Furnished by P. Clauzen Capt 46th N.Y. Quartermaster U. S. Army, to B. Munger Capt Comdg Bks No 1, Quartermaster U. S. Army, at Elmira N.Y., on the 3rd day of May, 1864.

NUMBER OR QUANTITY.	ARTICLES.	COST WHEN NEW.		CONDITION WHEN DELIVERED.	REMARKS.
		Dolls.	Cts.		
1	Writing Desk				
1	Oil Can (one gallon)				
2	Pine Tables				
2	" Benches				
2	Lamps				

I certify that I have this day turned over to B Munger Capt Comdg Bks No 1 Quartermaster U. S. Army, at Elmira N.Y. the articles specified in the foregoing list.

P. Clauzen
Capt 46th N.Y. Vols, Quartermaster.

Head-Quarters Depot for Drafted Men,
ELMIRA, N. Y., May 14 1864.

SPECIAL ORDERS,
No.

Capth Cattrell V.R.C. has delivered to me $6.20 of the Money taken from James Scott alias John McKeon to reimburse M.T.D. officers for money paid to said Scott as a recruit for the 15th Engineers

A. Strood
Capt & Bvt

By Order of Lt. Col. S. Eastman.

Assistant Adjutant General.

Head-Quarters Depot for Drafted Men,
ELMIRA, N. Y., June 21st 1864.

SPECIAL ORDERS,
No. 342.

I. Major Geo. H. Clarke 98th N.Y. Vols. is hereby relieved from duty as Receiving Officer, and also from Command of Drafted Men & Substitutes, at this Rendezvous. The duties heretofore performed by Major Clarke will hereafter be performed by Capt. B. Munger, 44th N.Y. Vols.

Major Clarke will turn over to Capt. Munger all books and papers in his possession as Receiving Officer, or as Commanding Officer of Drafted Men and Substitutes; and also all orders pertaining to his duties as the same.

By Order of Lt. Col. S. Eastman.

D.R. Lounsbury
Lieut. & A. Assistant Adjutant General.

To
Capt. Munger
44th N.Y. Vols

Capt. Munger to take over as Receiving Officer. Courtesy of Shelly Case

Hd. 2nd Barracks No. 3.
Elmira N.Y. June 22nd 1864

Received from Major Geo. H. Clark 98th N.Y. Vols the books belonging to Receiving Office and Depot for Drafted Men and Substitutes Barracks No. 3. named in the following list.

one (1) Record book of Recruits received
one (1) Infantry Record Book of recruits
one (1) Cavalry   ~   ~   ~
one (1) Artillery   ~   ~   ~
one (1) Record Book of Drafted Men and Substitutes
one (1) Order Book
Two (2) Index   ~

B. Munger
Capt 114 N.Y. Vols
Comdg Drafted Men & Substitutes
Barracks No. 3.

Mans House Bks No 3
Elmira N.Y., June 22nd 1864

Received from Capt. B. Munger
One Hundred and forty five dollar

$145
George Wilbur

Head-Quarters Depot for Drafted Men,
ELMIRA, N. Y., *July 2nd* 1864

SPECIAL ORDERS.
No. 25...

The following named Officers are detailed for duty with prisoners of war, and will report to Major H. V. Colt. Comdg. Bks No 3. for duty without delay.

Capt. B. Munger 4th N.Y. Vols.

By Order of Brigadier General Quinby.

T. R. Lounsbury,
Assistant Adjutant General.

Capt Munger
his
C. O. Bks no 3.

Capt. Munger's orders for detail to duty at Elmira Prison, NY. July 2nd, 1864. Courtesy Shelly Case.

No. 27.

Camp & Garrison Equipage

LIST OF QUARTERMASTER'S STORES, &c., transferred by Capt Munger A.Q.M, Quartermaster U.S. Army, to Capt Cottrell 16th Reg't V.R.C. Quartermaster U. S. Army, at Elmira N.Y., on the 2nd day of July, 1864.

NUMBER OR QUANTITY.		ARTICLES.	COST WHEN NEW.		CONDITION WHEN DELIVERED.	REMARKS.
			Dolls.	Cts.		
1	One	Writing Desk				
1	One	Oil Can (1 gal)				
2	Two	Pine Tables				
2	Two	" Benches				
2	Two	Lamps				

I CERTIFY that I have this day transferred to Capt Cottrell 16 V.R.C. Quartermaster U. S. Army, at Elmira N.Y., the articles specified in the foregoing list.

B. Munger
Capt & A.Q.M. Quartermaster.

> HeadQuarters Prisoners Camp.
> Elmira, N.Y., July 28, 1864.
>
> Special Orders }
> No. 24, } Extract:
>
> × × ×
>
> 2. Captain B. Munger, 44. N.Y. Vols. is hereby relieved from the command of Wards 27 & 28, and is appointed Inspector of this Camp.
>
> By order of Major H. V. Colt.
> R. J. McCoy
> Lt. & Act. Adj't.

Capt. Munger's official appointment as inspector of Elmira Prison. Courtesy of Shelly Case.

Head-Quarters Depot for Drafted Men,

ELMIRA, N. Y., August 9th 1864.

SPECIAL ORDERS,
No. 282

Leave of absence for six (6) days is granted to the following named officer.

Captain B Munger — 44th N.Y. Vol

By Order of Lt. Col. S. Eastman.

T. B. Lounsbury
Ex-a. Assistant Adjutant General.

PROPERTY RETURNS DIVISION.
(DELINQUENT SECTION—FORM II.)

Ordnance Office,

WAR DEPARTMENT.

Washington, D. C. *Sept 14th* 1864.

Captain B Munger
Co "C" 44th N.Y. 2 Infy

Sir:

The Quarterly Return of Ordnance Stores, for which you are accountable, pertaining to *Co C 44th N.Y. Vols* for the *1, 2, 3, 4th* quarter *s*, 186*2*, ha*s* not yet been received at this Office, although you were notified to this effect on the _____ 186_.

Your attention is now called to paragraphs 1, 9, and 18 of "Instructions for making Returns of Ordnance Stores," approved by the Secretary of War February 10, 1863, and to the fact that you have this day been reported to the Adjutant General of the Army as a delinquent for the quarter named above; with the recommendation that measures may be taken to stop your pay, until the required Returns have been rendered by you, examined in this Office, and adjusted by the Second Auditor of the Treasury.

Respectfully,
Your obedient servant,
By order of the Chief of Ordnance:

Crouly
Lieut ~~Captain~~ of Ordnance,
Assistant to Chief of Ordnance.

(B. 8 7. 64. 10.)

Washington D.C. Oct. 16th

Captain

I have the honor to send you enclosed a copy of Special Orders No. 275 Extract 2. Hd. Qrs. Army of the Potomac dated October 11th 1864 authorizing your muster out of the service

Respectfully
Your Obt. Servt.
B. K. Wood Jr.

Capt. B. Munger

Head Qrs Prison Camp
Elmira N.Y. Decr: 10. 1864

Special Order }
No. 127 } (Extract.)

In compliance with instructions received from War Dept. A.G.O. Washington D.C. Decr: 9. 1864. Capt. B. Munger 44th N.Y. Vols, is hereby relieved from duty in Prison Camp. He will be furnished with Muster out Rolls by the Com'dg Officer of Prison Camp.

By Command of
Lt. Col. S. Moore.
H. V. Mott
Capt. & Acty Adjt

Head-Quarters, Fifth Army Corps,
OFFICE, COMMISSARY OF MUSTERS.

December 17, 1864

To
Capt B. Munger
Late 24. N.Y. Vols.

Capt.

I am directed by the Adjutant Genl to forward you your Muster-out rolls and discharge. Your rolls I think were made out by Capt Work and if so have been lost by me and I have not the necessary data to make them out correctly. but enclosed I send you five rolls the blanks of which you will please fill out also your discharge. two of the rolls you will please return to me

Very respectfully
Your Obt Svt
W Frenley
Capt 17 Inf
C M.

A CLOSING WORD TO THE READER

It may be of some interest to the reader that my family also has stories of my great, great, great grandfather, Private Isaac Fortner of Company D, 14th West Virginia Infantry who was captured by members of the 17th Virginia Cavalry after the battle of Cloyd's Mountain, Virginia on May 9, 1864. Fortner had straggled due to exhaustion after the main engagement and was captured. He was then sent south with a number of other Union prisoners and wound up finally being sent to Andersonville Prison. The prison had been in operation since February of that year and was enlarged in June from 16.5 acres to 26.5 acres. There is no need to describe the horrific scenes that took place there and the extreme suffering that brave Union soldiers endured while imprisoned in the "Hellhole of the South" or the loss of 13,000 lives during the operation of the camp. As for Isaac, he was liberated with the rest of the Andersonville survivors after the fall of Atlanta in the autumn of 1864 and Sherman's march to the sea. Isaac Fortner had suffered greatly while in Andersonville. Prolonged exposure, poor food and water and the camp diarrhea brought the 28-year-old Fortner to such a poor condition of health that he was never able to work again and lived the remainder of his life greatly afflicted and seldom able to walk. His wife, Nancy (Matheny) Fortner had to care for him until he passed away thirty years later from complications suffered at Andersonville. (He is buried at Bethel Baptist Church grave yard in Lubeck, West Virginia.) I felt that the reader should know this story in part, in case there were those who pointed the finger of accusation at me for reporting the poor conditions at Elmira and not at Andersonville.

With that said, I will close with one last story concerning a strange coincidence dealing with Isaac Fortner that took place here in Wood County, West Virginia when the James Cooper home (formally used as a Confederate post office and a location used to smuggle sorely needed medical supplies south) at Mineral Wells, was being dismantled around 1999. I had stopped at the site to gather information on the property to locate the possible site of a Yankee camp that was located nearby. I started talking with the crew that was dismantling the structure and the foreman stated that the structure predated the Civil War by several decades. As I shared some stories with this man I asked him where he hailed from as I noticed a rich southern accent that was even more pronounced than a Virginian accent. He told me that he had come from Georgia and that his great, great grandfather had been a young man at the time of the Civil War. He had been too young to serve in active combat but was made a prisoner of war guard at Andersonville. The man and I quickly deduced the months that each of our respective relatives were there and found that the dates overlapped nearly perfectly with his relative coming only a short time before to act as a guard along the wall of the prison. As we exchanged our stories we both talked about how sad the whole affair was for Americans and how it changed America forever in so many ways for the good as well as the bad. Before parting I said to the man, "Would it be possible for the grandson of a former Union prisoner of war to shake hands with the grandson of a former Confederate prisoner of war guard to thank you for your kindness in sharing your stories?" The man looked me straight in the eye and extended his hand and said, "Only in America can the sons and descendants of such men grasp each other's hands in the eternal bonds of fidelity and friendship without the animosity of the past." With these good words said we parted as friends and honored our heritage as we saw fit.

ELLSWORTH'S AVENGERS!
AIR: Annie Lisle. -- By A. L. HUDSON.

Down where the patriot army,
Near Potomac's side,
Guards the glorious cause of Freedom,
Gallant Ellsworth died.
Brave was the noble Chieftain,
At his country's call,
Hastened to the field of battle,
And was first to fall!
Chorus : Strike, Freemen, for the Union,
Sheath your swords no more,
While remains in arms a traitor.
On Columbia's shore!
Entering the traitor city,
With his soldiers true,
Leading up the Zouave columns,
Fixed became his view:
See: that rebel flag is floating
O'er yon building tall,
Spoke he, while his dark eye glistened:
Boys, that flag must fall! Chorus.
Quickly, from its proud position,
That base flag was torn,
Trampled 'neath the feet of Freemen,
Circling Ellsworth's form.
See him bear it down the landing,
Past the Traitor's door:
Hear him groan: Oh! God! they've shot him!
Ellsworth is no more! Chorus.
First to fall, thou youthful martyr!
Hapless was thy fate!
Hastened we, as thy avengers,
From thy native State;
Speed we on, from town and city,
Not for wealth or fame;
But because we love the Union,
And our Ellsworth's name! Chorus.
Traitor's hands shall never sunder
That for which you died!
Hear the oath our lips now utter,
Those out Nation's pride:
By our hopes of you, bright Heaven!
By the Land we love!
By the God who reigns above us!
We'll avenge thy blood!.. Chorus.
H. De MARSAN, Publisher,
54 Chatham Street, New-York.

ABOUT THE AUTHOR

BRIAN STUART KESTERSON: The son of William Kenneth Kesterson and Betty Lou (Roush) Kesterson was born September 1, 1961 at Parkersburg, West Virginia and has lived at Lubeck, West Virginia since 1965. He graduated from Parkersburg South High School in 1980 and received an Associate of Arts degree from Ohio Valley College in 1988. He received his Bachelor of Arts from Marietta College in 1990, and received a teaching certification from Ohio Valley College in 2003. He completed his Master's Degree in Education at Ohio Valley University in 2012. He has served in numerous historical organizations and has been on the lecture circuit since 1988, having presented programs to historical organizations in West Virginia, Virginia, Ohio, Maryland and Pennsylvania. He has been a guest speaker at the West Virginia Department of Culture and History at the Capitol Complex in Charleston, West Virginia and has also spoken to the history department of West Virginia University at Parkersburg on numerous occasions. Mr. Kesterson has been employed by the Wood County Board of Education as a history teacher at Parkersburg High School since 2014. He also spearheaded, and oversaw the Parkersburg High School Centennial Historical Marker Committee from 2016-2017.

On March 17, 2005, he was presented with the *West Virginia History Hero Award* at Charleston, West Virginia for outstanding work and significant contributions to the preservation and promotion of West Virginia history. He was honored by the Captain James S. A. Crawford Chapter of the United Daughters of the Confederacy and the Virginia Division of the United Daughters of the Confederacy at Staunton, Virginia, on May 27, 2007 with the *Jefferson Davis Historical Gold Medal Award*, for his research, writing, and the preservation of Southern history and culture through his living history programs. On February 11, 2011 Ohio Valley University presented him with the *OVU Alumni Association Medal of Merit Award in Literature*.

Kesterson was one of the individuals who pushed for the preservation of one of Parkersburg's most significant Civil War era sites, Fort Boreman. He was subsequently appointed as a member of the Fort Boreman Parks Commission on March 3, 2003, with a second appointment accepted on February 1, 2007 and his most recent appointment accepted on December 27, 2010.

He is the author and editor of his 1993 book, <u>The Last Survivor, The Memoirs of George William Watson, A Horse Soldier in the 12th Virginia Cavalry</u>; his 2005 award winning work, <u>Campaigning with the 17th Virginia Cavalry, Night Hawks at Monocacy</u>; and his 2007 book, <u>Dear Sir… Dear Miss…, The Letters of Granville B. Mann Company A, 30th Battalion Virginia Sharpshooters & Miss Lucinda Maria Virginia (Chandler) Mann</u>. He also co-wrote an article, which appeared in the Men and Material section of the July 2004 issue of America's Civil War Magazine entitled, "The 'Nighthawk Rangers' of the 17th Virginia Cavalry lost their banner after the Battle of Monocacy". Kesterson is also the 2009 author of Arcadia Publishing's *Images of America* history series title; "<u>West Virginia National Guard 1898 – 1919</u>". This book in the series; is a pictorial history with over two hundred original photographs spanning the time periods from the Spanish-American War to the start of World War One. In 2013 Kesterson published, <u>Incidents of Morgan's Raid, With an Account of Stovepipe Johnson's Retreat Through West Virginia</u>, detailing the escape route of Colonel Adam Rankin "Stovepipe" Johnson and over three hundred of John Hunt Morgan's cavalry after their defeat at the ill-fated battle of Buffington Island.

Kesterson appeared in the (2000) movie production of the "Patriot" starring Mel Gibson, as a special abilities re-enactor for the Revolutionary War time period. Kesterson also appeared in the award winning, 2003, Ohio Bicentennial, PBS documentary, "Opening the Door West", detailing the early settlement of the Northwest Territory and the Indian Wars time period of the 1790's. He also appeared (2004) as a guest speaker for a documentary on West Virginia PBS television detailing the Battle of Droop Mountain, and has also participated in Civil War documentaries for the History Channel. In 2012, Kesterson appeared as a guest speaker for the Travel Channel's "The Dead Files" dealing with the history of Quincy Hill and Parkersburg, West Virginia during the Civil War and post-Civil War time periods. Kesterson also appeared as a guest speaker for the 2012-2013, documentary, "The Issue is Upon Us: Civil War in the Mid-Ohio Valley" produced by the Walkabout Company, the Stonewall Group, and the Greater Parkersburg Convention & Visitors Bureau. He was also a contributor to the 2013-2014 documentary "*Burning Springs*" detailing the oil and gas industry in West Virginia and the Confederate military operations against the Burning Springs oil fields in Wirt County, West Virginia during the Civil War era, produced for West Virginia PBS television by Motion Masters Studios.

Kesterson is also a member of the 6th Ohio Volunteer Cavalry. He and this reenactment unit have been actively engaged in their critically acclaimed living history, boot camp programs for the school children of West Virginia and Ohio since 1990. In 2006 the unit was honored with a requested to present mounted cavalry demonstrations and living history programs for the cadets at the West Point Military Academy in New York. In May of 2007 the unit was again honored and requested to perform mounted cavalry demonstrations for the National Park Service at Gettysburg, Pennsylvania. The unit has also appeared in numerous motion picture productions and documentaries as dismounted skirmishers and mounted cavalry extras. Kesterson has also served as chief musician/bugler for the general staff of the (USV) United States Volunteer Infantry for the sesquicentennial era of the Civil War.

This photograph was taken during the 150th Antietam reenactment that was held from September 14-16, 2012. Part of the General Staff of the 2nd Division U.S.V., proceed to the battle field. Sgt. Brian S. Kesterson is at the far right mounted on Midnight. Below: members of the 2nd Div. U.S.V. General Staff

Photographs by Donna L. Setler – New Port, Ohio

BIBLIOGRAPHY & RESEARCH

Primary Sources

Addison, Walter, *Recollections of a Confederate Soldier,* in the Southern Historical Collection of the University of North Carolina Library, Chapel Hill; San Francisco: Sept. 30, 1889.

Hoffman, Michael A. II, *Union War Crimes Against Confederate Prisoners In NY.,*

Revisionist History, No. 25 - Extract www.hoffman-info.com : 11-29-2.

Holmes, Clayton Wood, *The Elmira Prison Camp: A History of the Military Prison at Elmira, N.Y.,* New York: G. P. Putnam's Sons, The Knickerbocker Press, 1912.

Horigan, Michael, *Elmira, Death Camp of the North*, Mechanicsburg, Pa: Stackpole Books, 2002.

Johnson, Robert Underwood & Clough Buel, Clarence (editors); *Battles and Leaders of the Civil War* (4 Volumes), *Union and Confederate Officers*, The Easton Press, Norwalk, Connecticut: The Easton Press, 2002.

Langland, James (editor), *The Chicago Daily News Almanac and Year Book for 1919* (pg. 205, Commander Orett L. Munger), Volume 35, Chicago: The Chicago Daily News, 1918.

McIntosh, W. H., *History of Ontario Co., New York, with Illustrations Descriptive of its Scenery, Palatial Residences, Public Buildings, Fine Blocks, and Important Manufactories, from Original Sketches by Artists of the Highest Ability*, New York: W. H. McIntosh, 1876.

Meade, George Gordon, *The Life and Letters of George Gordon Meade, Major-General United States Army*, Vol. 1. New York: Charles Scribner's Sons, 1913.

Miller, Francis Trevelyn & Lanier, Robert Sampson (editors), *The Photographic History of the Civil War* (10 Volumes), NY: Review of Reviews, 1911.

Nash, Eugene Arus, *A History of the Forty-fourth Regiment, New York Volunteer Infantry, in the Civil War, 1861-1865, (The Adjutant's Story)*, Chicago: R. R. Donnelley & Sons Company, 1911.

United States, War Department, *The War of the Rebellion: A Compilation of the Official Records of the Union and Confederate Armies,* 70 volumes in 4 series. Washington, D.C.: United States Government Printing Office, 1880-1901.

OFFICIAL RECORDS: Series 2, vol 7, Part 1 (Prisoners of War)

OFFICIAL RECORDS: Series 2, vol 8, Part 1 (Prisoners of War)

News Papers

Harper's Weekly May 2, 1863.

Harper's Weekly - January 2, 1864 - THE ARMY OF THE POTOMAC AT MINE RUN - GENERAL WARREN'S TROOPS ATTACKING - SKETCHED BY A. R. WAUD

Harper's Weekly- January 2, 1864 - FEDERAL SOLDIERS CROSSING AT GERMANIA FORD

Harper's Weekly 28 May 1864 – COLONEL JAMES CLAY RICE

Leslie's Illustrated Newspaper, January 11, 1862

Ontario County Messenger (NY) - Marriages and Deaths from the "*Ontario County Messenger*" Canandaigua, Ontario County, New York

Penn Yan Democrat (NY)

Yates County Chronicle (NY)

Yates County, New York Court Records

Yates County, NY 1860 Census

Yates County, NY Innkeepers' Recognizances, for the years 1823-1830 and 1855-1865 - Yates County Courthouse, Pen Yan, New York

Yates County, NY Marriage, Birth & Death Records – Yates County Courthouse, Pen Yan, New York

Research Resources

Booth Library at the Chemung County Historical Society, Elmira, New York
McGraw-Page Library at Randolph-Macon College, Ashland, Va.

Minnesota Historical Society, St. Paul, Minnesota

New York State Archives - New York State Education Department - Cultural Education Center Albany, NY.

New York State Military Museum and Veterans Research Center, NYS Division of Military and Naval Affairs, Saratoga Springs, NY.

Penn Yan Public Library, Penn Yan, New York

U.S. National Archives and Records Administration – Military Service Records - Washington, D.C.

U.S. National Archives/Library of Congress – Prints and Photographs Division - Washington, D.C.

Photographs - Mathew Brady collection - Library of Congress Prints and Photographs Division
Photographs - Timothy H. O'Sullivan - Library of Congress Prints and Photographs Division

U.S. National Park Service – U.S. Department of the Interior – Military Service Records - Washington, D.C.

Wood Library, Canandaigua, New York

www.ingramcontent.com/pod-product-compliance
Lightning Source LLC
Chambersburg PA
CBHW081414230426

43668CB00016B/2233